Author

ics.

Introduction to Psycholinguistics

Introduction to Psycholinguistics

Insup Taylor
York University

HOLT, RINEHART AND WINSTON
New York Chicago San Francisco Atlanta
Dallas Montreal Toronto London Sydney

Credits for figures and tables

Fig. 1–3: From Premack, D., "Language in chimpanzee" in *Science*. Copyright 1971 by the American Association for Advancement of Science. Reprinted by permission of the author and the American Association for the Advancement of Science.

Fig. 2–5 a, b.: From Liberman, A. M., Mattingly, I. G., and Turvey, M. T. (1972), "Language codes and memory codes" in A. W. Melton and E. Martin (Eds.), *Coding processes in human memory*. Reproduced by permission of Hemisphere Publishing Corporation, Washington, D.C.

Fig. 2–6 and Fig. 2–9: From Liberman, A. M. (1957), "Some results of research on speech perception" in the *Journal of the Acoustical Society of America*. By permission of the author and the American Institute of Physics, New York.

Fig. 2–10: Lieberman, P. (1965), "On the acoustic basis of the perception of intonation by linguists" in *Word*. By permission of the Linguistic Circle of New York.

Tab. 3–1: O'Neill, B. (1972), "Defineability as an index of word meaning" in *Journal of Psycholinguistic Research*. By permission of Plenum Publishing Corp., New York.

Tab. 5–1: Denes, P. B. (1963), "On the statistics of spoken English" in the *Journal of the Acoustical Society of America*. By permission of the author and the American Institute of Physics.

Tab. 5–2: A part from Poole, I. (1934), "Genetic development of articulation of consonant sounds in speech" in *Elementary English Review*.

Tab. 5–4: From *Thought on the Japanese Language*. © 1967 by Susume Ono and others. By permission of Yomiuri Shinbun, Japan.

Fig. 5–4: Modified from Howes, D., "An approach to the quantitative analysis of word blindness" in J. Money (Ed.), *Reading Disability*. Copyright 1961 by the Johns Hopkins University Press; and from Carroll, J. B., *Language and thought*. © 1964 by Prentice-Hall, Inc., Englewood Cliffs, N.J. By permission of both publishers.

Tab. 5–6 and Fig. 5–5: Zipf, G. K. (1949), *Human behavior and the principle of least effort*. By permission of Addison-Wesley Publishing Co., Mass.

Fig. 5–9: Modified from Miller, G. A., Heise, G. A., and Lichten, W., "Intelligibility of speech as a function of the context of the test materials" in *Journal of Experimental Psychology*. Copyright (1951) by the American Psychological Association, and from Carroll, J. B., *Language and thought*. © 1964 by Prentice-Hall, Inc., N.J. By permission of the senior author, APA, and Prentice-Hall.

Fig. 5–7: Miller, G., *Language and communication*. Copyright 1951 by McGraw-Hill Book Co., New York. By permission of the publisher.

Library of Congress Cataloging in Publication Data

Taylor, Insup.
   Introduction to psycholinguistics.

   Bibliography: p. 396
   Includes index.
   1. Languages—Psychology. I. Title.
P37.T3   401'.9   75-11627
ISBN 0-03-012981-8

To Martin, Mia, and Ian.

Preface

This book is about languages and users of language. There are many kinds of unspoken "language," such as the dance language of the bees, African drum languages, and "body language," but this book is concerned mainly with human language using spoken words, and with forms of language derived from speech.

Language is studied from a formal viewpoint by linguists and from a functional one by psychologists. Linguists describe language: they establish and define units of language, and search for rules and principles that determine how sounds are grouped into words, and words into sentences. Psychologists, on the other hand, try to describe the behavior of people: speaking is one of the important things people do, and psychologists study how people learn and use language.

The methods of linguists and of psychologists are different. Linguists tend to accept a body of natural language as given, and try to fit rules to it. Psychologists are more likely to experiment, to put people in positions where they must use language in particular ways, and see what the people do in these specially contrived circumstances.

Psycholinguistics is the technical term for a relatively new field of enquiry that weds the aims and techniques of psychology and of linguistics. As an independent topic, it has been recognized for only a couple of decades, and seems to be growing in popularity among university students. This book introduces psycholinguistics to university students from all disciplines.

I would like to emphasize the fact that this book is not limited to the question of whether or not a particular linguistic theory is a model of speech. This question is only a part, though an important part, of the book. I plan to explore many varied topics related to language and language users: how we produce and comprehend sentences; how we acquire our first and subsequent languages; how speech and language disorders develop; what roles speech and language play in our understanding of the world, and other questions. It is premature at this stage to discuss such varied topics in a single rigid theoretical framework. Rather, within each chapter I try to present observational and experimental data on an important issue, with the idea that in this manner a coherent over-all theme will develop.

The book is expository rather than polemic. Usually an experiment spawns a number of subsequent experiments based on various flaws or ambiguities in the original one, and one issue spawns a multitude of theories that can dramatically contradict each other. These controversies are often ignored in the text, so that a coherent theme, based on a reasonable position, may be developed in each chapter. The student who wishes to go into the arguments in more detail is referred to further reading material.

The book is self-contained; it can be read by itself without reference to other books. I explain new concepts or technical terms when they first appear. For diligent readers, there are references that can lead them to any depth in many topics. Visual, pictorial presentations always help to clarify points—so there are plenty of tables and figures.

This book is comprised of eleven chapters and an Epilogue. Each chapter deals with a separate major topic in psycholinguistics and has its own short introduction and a summary with conclusions at the end. The eleven chapters are grouped into three sections, the first (Chapters 1–5) dealing with the nature of language; the second (6–9) with the acquisition and use of language; and the third (10–11) with abnormalities of language and speech.

In the first section, Chapter 1 can be described as an appetizer that exposes readers to various aspects of languages. Chapter 2 is on linguistic units, especially speech sounds. Many of the linguistic terms used in the book are introduced in this chapter. Chapter 3 on "word" is an overflow of Chapter 2: there are so many things to be said about "word" that the topic requires a separate chapter. Chapter 4 deals with grammars, especially with syntactic component of grammars. It also deals with cognitive processes of comprehending and producing sentences. Chapter 5 is on the statistical structure of language, which profoundly influences our speech behavior.

In the second section, Chapter 6 is on language acquisition. Modern explanations of language acquisition tend to be closely tied with modern linguistic theories, hence this sequence. This topic is covered in a few other chapters, namely Chapters 7, 8, and 10, from slightly different angles.

Chapter 7 is on bilingualism. It deals with problems of learning two languages, as well as bilingual information processing. Chapter 8 deals with how our speech and language influence the way children and adults understand the world. This chapter involves diverse languages, as does the preceding chapter. Many of the topics covered in Chapters 1, 7, and 8 are often considered under the heading of "sociolinguistics" in other books. Chapter 9 asks whether phonetic symbolism exists universally; it also involves speakers of diverse languages.

The third section includes two chapters on abnormal language and speech behavior. Chapter 10 deals with deafness and voice disorder briefly, and with two "psychological" speech disorders—articulation disorder and stuttering—in depth. The last chapter is on aphasia. Unlike other speech disorders, aphasia is a result of brain damage, hence reveals brain mechanisms of speech and language. Since I start this book by comparing human language with animal communication (Chapter 1), I end the book by discussing the neurological basis of human speech and language. Animals seem to lack this neurological basis.

In writing this book, I have immensely profited from frequent, and often heated, discussions I have had with Dr. Martin Taylor of the Defence and Civil Institute of Environmental Medicine, Toronto. As a psychologist working outside psycholinguistics, he has inspired me to look at things from fresh viewpoints.

Dr. Brian Templeton of York University, also not a psycholinguist, read the entire manuscript and made many helpful comments.

In addition, the following colleagues in Toronto gave their time to read my chapters and talk to me on the topics of their special interest: Dr. Margarete Wolfram at York University on Piaget's developmental stages; Dr. Henri Barik, Ontario Institute of Studies in Education, on bilingualism and phonetic symbolism; Dr. Maureen Dennis, the Hospital for Sick Children, on brain mechanisms of speech.

I also wish to thank anonymous critics whose praise gave me encouragement and whose criticisms taught me how to write.

Everybody who has read my manuscript could not help but correct mistakes in my English writing, if nothing else at least to insert or eliminate "the" and "a," whose usage I have yet to learn.

Toronto   *I. T.*
October 1975

Contents

1

Language: An Informal Look

HUMAN VERSUS ANIMAL LANGUAGE

What is human language? It is hard to define human language in a few sentences that are satisfactory and comprehensible to everyone. For one thing, there are many ways of looking at human language. In fact, each chapter of this book gives us a slightly different way of looking at it. A complete understanding of what human language is may emerge only at the end of the book.

Instead of following the normal custom of defining human language in a few sentences at the outset, let us proceed to examine some of its characteristics. We shall examine below the facts that human language uses basically mouth-to-ear communication; it accepts arbitrary relations between words and events; it has levels of construction; it is an open system; it is acquired; and so on.

Oral-auditory language

Human language evolved as a mouth-to-ear communication system. Why? Oral-auditory language has a number of advantages over other human communication systems, such as written language or the sign language of the deaf. Writing needs tools, but oral speech and sign language are always available, since they are produced by the unaided human body. Sign language can be used only between people who can see one another, but oral speech can fill the entire space around the speaker. No line-of-sight connection between speaker and hearer is necessary for speech, since the signals can travel around corners and are not usually interrupted by obstacles. Possibly for such reasons, monkeys in dense forest tend to communicate vocally, whereas monkeys that have a more open habitat often use visual modes of communication (Altmann, 1967). Oral-auditory language can be used day and night. One can speak while doing other things, and speaking requires little energy. Lastly, oral speech is very flexible, as the vocal system has evolved. We can produce many different sounds by using different parts of the speech organs in various manners, and these sounds can be combined in countless ways, all easily discriminated by a trained ear.

One of the shortcomings of direct mouth-to-ear communication is that it has a quite short range. Conversations are rarely continued at distances over 50 feet, although under extreme conditions much larger distances can be covered by shouting. Modern electronic technology has expanded the useful distance of voice communication almost without limit. Even without such technology for long-distance talking, the Indians of Mazateco, Mexico, and the islanders of Madeira developed whistle languages, and the Congolese in Africa invented drum languages. Whistle and drum languages are both based on the speech of their users. Drum language (Carrington, 1971) can carry as far as five to six miles in optimal conditions, and whistle language (Cowan, 1964), over a hill or a valley, again about five miles.

Oral-auditory language is evanescent; speech signals are gone as soon as they are uttered. Humans have developed various writing systems to compensate for this shortcoming. Written language, like whistle language, is secondary to oral language—writing is based upon spoken language. Alphabets more or less represent one sound with one letter. The English letter *t* represents the sound [t],[1] as does the Korean letter ㅌ . Unfortunately, the ideal correspondence of one speech sound to one letter is often not realized in practice. Compare *few*, *sew*, and *so*. A syllabary is a quite different way of writing sound patterns, in which each entire syllable has its own symbol. The Japanese letter マ represents the syllable [ma], and ミ represents [mi]. A third type of writing is ideography, in which one character represents one concept. The Chinese character 日 represents "sun," and 月 "moon." Together, 明 means "bright." Written language is not as universally human as is oral language—no human community is known to be without oral language, but even today there are many living languages that do not have corresponding written forms.

The main concern of this book is oral-auditory language.

---

[1] Square brackets [ ] are used to denote speech sounds.

How is human language different from animal communication?

The unique nature of human language becomes clearer when we compare it with animal communication systems. Animals communicate vocally and otherwise to signal danger, sources of food, mating needs, the availability of shelter, and so forth. Such animal communication systems are closely tied with the survival of an individual animal and of the species. My coverage of animal communication will be confined to that of nonhuman primates, because they are the animals closest to us in the evolutionary scale, and that of foraging honey bees, because their nonvocal communication system has been well studied and seems to have been decoded. Although porpoises and whales may well have developed language systems of their own, we do not know much about them, and they will be ignored here. The following discussion of primate communication is based on Altmann (1967), and that of bee communication on Wenner (1964).

How much do primates rely on the oral-auditory channel of communication? Terrestrial or semiarboreal primates usually rely more upon visual communication than on any other channel. Species of primates that live in dense forests commonly use loud vocalizations in long-range communication. For example, howlers that live in the dense rain forests of Central and South America have spectacular howls that proclaim their territories. Such a howl, one of the loudest sounds in the animal kingdom, can be heard for miles. Rhesus monkeys, most of which live in crowded urban areas in northern India, have a vocal repertoire of at least seven calls but these calls account for only 3 percent of their social messages. Even if we consider, in addition, cases in which calls are combined with some nonacoustical component to form a compound signal, only 5 percent of the social messages consist of vocalization.

In human language, signals and words symbolize or "stand for" events in the real world. The word "dog" stands for a particular type of animal. Alarm calls and food calls of nonhuman primates are often symbolic. Baboons, for example, have a loud, two-phased bark that is given in a situation of danger, such as the appearance of a leopard. They have been observed to bark for more than an hour after an unsuccessful attack by an adult male leopard. The calls were given after the baboons had left the water-hole basin in which the attack had taken place and had circled through the trees to the opposite side of the water hole, from which the leopard, if still present, was no longer visible. Such barking serves to alert the baboons of every group in the area to the danger.

Bees communicate with a "dance language." When a foraging bee finds a source of food, it flies back to its hive and conveys to its fellows the distance and direction of the source. In order to do so it performs on the vertical surface of the comb a waggling "dance" in which the bee usually traces a figure 8 as shown in Fig. 1–1.

The direction of the nectar, relative to the sun, is communicated by the orientation of the "straight run" of the dance relative to the vertical. The interior of most hives is dark, but the bees follow the dance by means of their antennae, which touch the dancer's body. Distance is communicated by the type of dance, which may be round or figure 8, and by the frequency of the abdomen's lateral movement during the straight run. During the straight run the bee also produces a sound that signals the distance to the nectar.

The relation between a word and what it stands for is arbitrary in human language. If the relation were not arbitrary, we would be able to understand the words of other languages. The word "dog" stands for the animal dog, but there is nothing in the word itself that reflects the characteristics of the animal. If we called the animal in question "woof" we would be imitating the barking of a dog, and the word in this case would be less arbitrary than the word "dog." Because the relations between words and what they stand for are arbitrary, entirely different arrangements of sounds can stand for the same animal in different languages—"Hund" (German), "chien" (French), "goou" (Chinese), "inu" (Japanese), "gae" (Korean), and so on. The predator warnings of baboons are as arbitrary as human words: there is no obvious resemblance between the contours of the call and the contours of a leopard. The bees' round dance for a short distance and figure 8 for a larger distance are also arbitrary signals.

Primates' calls become louder and more frequent as the danger becomes more imminent; bees increase their waggles and their sound production during the straight run portion of the dance with an increase in the distance

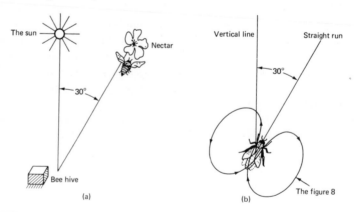

FIGURE 1–1   (a) The direction of nectar relative to the sun and a beehive. (b) The direction of the nectar is communicated by a foraging bee with its figure-8 dance. (Adapted from K. v. Frisch, 1959.)

between the hive and the nectar. Here, then, the animals' signals reflect certain properties of the events they stand for.

This correlation between the magnitude of signals and the magnitude of what they stand for is not commonly found in human language, in the sense that we say "big dog" or "many dogs" rather than "dogdogdog." There are some exceptions to the rule. In Japanese, "I" is "ware" while "we" is "wareware." Korean "mallang" (soft) becomes "mallangmallang" for very soft. Chinese "len" (man) becomes "lenlen" for "every man." A hybrid language called "pidgin" spoken by natives in Africa and Oceania often uses repeated words to indicate "more," "longer," or "often." "Drunkdrunk" means continuously drunk, and "sheepysheep" means many sheep. In English we may say "a large dog," stressing and prolonging the [a:] in "large" to emphasize the size of the dog. So also can we say "SOFT-soft" in advertising.

Humans can talk about all sorts of things that are "once upon a time," "far away and long ago," "in the world of Never-Never Land," and so on. By combining the arbitrary symbols in arbitrary ways, whole worlds of discourse are opened. Speech is about ideas, not preprogrammed possibilities. A worker bee can indicate the presence of nectar in directions and at distances that are new to its experience and to that of all the other workers in the hive and still be understood. Yet this is a limited sort of freedom. The bee's dance and sound communicate only about the presently available food source and hive sites, and perhaps a few other items that are closely tied with the survival of the hive. Bee communication is then a closed, preprogrammed, and stereotyped system.

In human language we have several levels of construction. Without construction we have no communication. A small set of meaningless sounds is used to build words, which are in turn combined in varied ways to produce meaningful utterances. Morse code is similar to oral speech in this respect: the Morse operator uses a very small number of individual elements, two lengths of pulse and about three lengths of pause. But an infinite variety of messages can be transmitted by rearranging these elementary message units. Primates may do a very limited amount of such combining of elementary messages. If a vocalization signifying aggression or annoyance is given by a less dominant monkey and combined with a strong submissive gesture, the submissive gesture outweighs the aggressive in the perception of the receiver. But this is not really the same kind of combination we use in making sensible utterances out of meaningless sounds.

All human languages are acquired. Humans have to be at least exposed to a particular language over some length of time, preferably when very young, before they can acquire that language. The so-called "wolf" or "attic" children who grow up without human contact do not have language. Animal communication seems to have a lot of instinctive and reflexive components. Bees reared in isolation from adults can dance. However, there is some evidence of a learned component even in the bee dance. Inexperienced bees find a prospective site of food by using odor cues in the environment, and not distance and direction information obtained from the dance maneuvers of successful bees. Such odors are left by regular visitors to a food site, and are attractive to bees from the same hive.

The availability of different types of communication is limited among animals. So far, we have no evidence that animals naturally use negations or questions, although in at least one case of a chimpanzee trained by humans the ability was there. Animal communication seems to consist mainly of directives, commands, and expressions of emotion. Communication is one-way rather than being a conversation. Porpoises and whales may prove to be exceptions to this rule, but we do not yet know enough about them to be sure.

In conclusion, the communications of primates and bees have some very rudimentary features of human language. Therefore, some people may think there is a continuity between animal and human communication systems. However, the features animals share with humans are so limited and rudimentary that animal communication has to be considered as qualitatively different from human language.

Can we teach human language to animals?

It has seemed reasonable to start our effort of teaching human language to animals (and it is a great effort!) with those animals that are closest to humans in their anatomical and cognitive capacities. Chimpanzees have been selected as obvious candidates.

Viki—speech sounds   Hayes's (1951) chimpanzee Viki had learned to make only a few words that grossly approximated English words, "mama," "papa," or "cup," in six years of intensive training.

Washoe—gestures   The Gardners (1969, 1971) bypassed the articulatory problems of the chimpanzee, and taught a gesture language to their Washoe, starting before she was one year old. By the time Washoe was about four, she had been taught to make reliably more than 80 signs. In 1972, at age seven, she had a vocabulary of 175 words. All signs were arbitrary to some degree: she learned the concept of "open"—open a specific door, open a drawer, open a book, and so on. In the early stages she did not learn to ask questions such as "What do you want?" or to make negatives. To produce "sentences" she used various orderings of signs indiscriminately without basic grammatical relations. For example, "me," "you," and "tickle" occurred in all possible orders without reference to situations. But in a later stage she could produce "Roger Washoe tickle."

Sarah—plastic symbols   Premack (1970, 1971) achieved an even greater success in teaching his six-year-old female chimpanzee Sarah a working vocabulary of more than 120 words. "Words" were symbols cut out of plastic and mounted on metal bases. A blue triangle, for example, meant an apple, and a red square a banana. Sarah not only could comprehend the meaning of these words but also could dip into her glossary to answer questions and build original sentences of her own. For example, using symbols for "Mary" or "Sarah"; "apple" or "banana"; "give" or "take," she could produce either "Mary give apple (to) Sarah" or "Sarah take banana (from) Mary." Figure 1–2 shows some examples of the sequences of symbols used by Sarah to communicate with her experimenter.

At a later stage of training, Sarah could respond even to a complex sentence that included the relation "if–then" and negative particles, as in "If Sarah take apple then Mary give Sarah chocolate," and "If Sarah take banana then Mary no give Sarah chocolate." Sarah's words then "stood for" arbitrary or symbolized objects, and her words were used to build organized sentences in a creative way. While Sarah's achievement was considerable, and, as the designer of her language, Premack's achievement was even more considerable, we must remember that Sarah's achievement was the result of two years' intense training. Compare Sarah with human children who master the basics of language naturally, without intense and specific training. One can always say that perhaps language training procedures with chim-

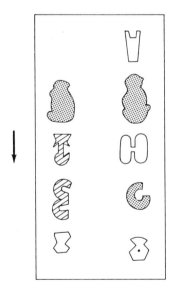

FIGURE 1–2   Sarah's plastic symbols used for communicating with her teacher. The symbols vary in size, shape, color, and texture. Sentences are written on the vertical. The two sentences are: (right) "No Sarah take honey-cracker" and (left) "Sarah take jam-bread." (From Premack, 1971.)

panzees were not intensive, prolonged, and suitable enough to provide better evidence of language learning, but Premack seemed to have reached the limit of Sarah's patience when he had to stop. Also, we do not know the optimal age for chimpanzees to learn human language. In humans there seems to be an optimal period—between age two and the early teens—when languages are learned easily and well.

Lana—computer-controlled   Recently, Rumbaugh, Gill, and Glaserfeld (1973) have reported good results with a 2½-year-old chimpanzee, Lana. After six months of computer-controlled language training, Lana proficiently read projected word-characters that constituted the beginnings of sentences and, in accordance with their meanings and serial order, either finished the sentences for reward or rejected them. For example, a valid sentence beginning was "Please machine give" to which Lana could add, at her option, "juice," "M & M," or the correctly ordered sequence "piece," "of," and "banana." But she would reject a sentence presented with the invalid beginning "Give machine."

In conclusion, chimpanzees can learn human language to some degree, the amount of achievement depending often on the trainer's resourcefulness. The best results so far have been with nonacoustic communications using plastic symbols or word characters. The content of the best chimpanzee communication is fairly sophisticated though concrete, but still is far short of human achievement. When a chimpanzee communicates to its trainer, "Why do you bother teaching me human language when I don't feel or think like a human?" we might be able to say that it is close to the human level of sophistication.

LANGUAGES OF THE WORLD

Let us once more turn to human languages, and see how many languages there are in the world, and what they look like.

. . . we know of no people that is not possessed of a fully developed language. The lowliest South African Bushman speaks in the forms of a rich symbolic system that is in essence perfectly comparable to the speech of the cultivated Frenchman.

This is a quotation from the noted American linguist Sapir (1921, p. 22). We may ignore groups such as Trappist monks, who choose not to speak. A survey by Kieckers (1931) listed almost 3,000 living languages. If we count only the languages used by over one million speakers, the number is reduced to 140. Such figures must be highly arbitrary. National boundaries do not always define language boundaries: Switzerland has three, and Belgium and Canada two official languages. English is spoken in many parts of the world, in many nations. Nor is mutual intelligibility always a reliable criterion for defining language boundaries: many dialects that are mutually unintelligible are included as "Chinese" or as "English," while Danish, Norwegian, and Swedish, which are mutually intelligible, are counted as three languages. Here, political rather than linguistic considerations seem to prevail.

The many world languages can be grouped into language families according to their historical linguistic relations. By far the most intensely studied family is the Indo-European Language Family, which includes languages used by about half of the world population and covers most of the territory of Europe, India, America, and a part of Asia Minor. Figure 1–3 shows the relationships among many members of the Indo-European Language Family. Within this family, there are subfamilies such as Indian, Germanic and Italic. We can trace the development of modern English from its

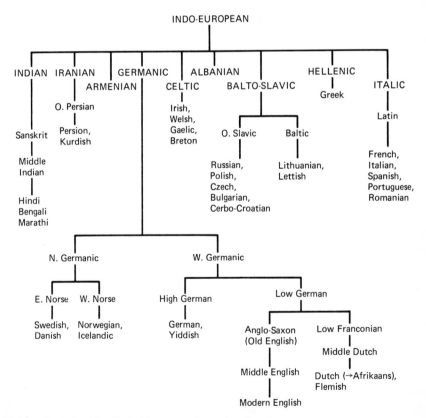

FIGURE 1–3   The Indo-European language family.

ancestors in Figure 1–3. In most Indo-European languages, the numerals from one to ten and the words for close family relationships, as well as a number of other fundamental words, are recognizable as coming from the same roots.

TABLE 1–1   The Word "Three" in Some Indo-European Languages, Grouped by Subfamilies

"three"	Languages
three	English
thrjá	Icelandic
drie	Dutch
drei	German
tre	Swedish
	Danish
	Norwegian
tres	Latin
tre	Italian
três	Spanish
tres	Portuguese
trois	French
tri	Romanian
tri	Russian
	Bulgarian
trzy	Polish
tris	Lithuanian
trayas	Sanskrit
tri	Irish
tre	Albanian

We see in Table 1–1 that words for "3" in many Indo-European languages are similar. Note that all these words start with one of the three dental consonants [t, d, th], followed by [r]. According to Hogben (1964), we can usually decipher the speech and writings of an unfamiliar Indo-European language with a few instructions on the coherent ways in which patterns of sound and meaning change between different territories.

There are many other language families in the world, most not as well studied as the Indo-European Family. In this book I will be taking examples from Chinese, Japanese, and Korean, because these languages are sufficiently different among themselves as well as from Indo-European languages, and because I am familiar with them. Chinese belongs to the Sino-Tibetan Family, which includes a few other Asian languages such as Burmese, Tibetan, and Thai. Chinese alone has about 700 million speakers, the largest number of speakers of any one language in the world. Korean, and possibly Japanese, may be members of the Ural-Altaic Language Family, which extends across northern Asia from the Pacific to the Urals, and has extensive outcrops in Europe, of which the best known are Finnish, Hungarian, and Turkish. The Ural-Altaic Language Family is less cohesive than the other two families, and linguistic similarities among its members are less obvious.

Now we shall survey briefly some of the linguistic differences and similarities among these three language families and their members. The survey has to be sketchy and informal at this point, as we have not yet studied the technical terms of linguistics. An awareness of language differences and similarities at the beginning will help readers with the rest of the book. In particular, the questions that readers can keep in mind in reading further are:

1. Can we envisage a single universal grammar for all human languages, with minor variations to take care of the obvious differences among languages?
2. Can we have a single model that explains how we acquire and use languages, applicable to all human languages?
3. Do different languages influence speakers to think differently?
4. What kind of language similarities and differences should learners of foreign language be aware of?

Language differences

Differences among language families and family members are extensive and obvious, and usually make different languages mutually unintelligible. Such differences inspired Whorf (Carroll, 1956) to propose the "linguistic relativity" hypothesis: that speakers of different languages have different ways of thinking, and that the different languages influence the way their users think. Differences among languages can be found in all levels of language—in the systems of sounds, words, sentences, and even linguistic expressions.

Sound systems The numbers and kinds of speech sounds and the ways they are combined differ in languages. The number of speech sounds adopted as potentially meaningful in a language can range approximately from 10 to 70. An example of a language with a small number of speech sounds is

Hawaiian, which has 11 or 12 sounds, Abkhaz, spoken in the Caucasas, has 70 sounds. English, with nearly 40 speech sounds, stands between the extremes. Some sounds occur in most languages, others in very few. The German and Scottish [kh], as in do*ch* and lo*ch*, or the click sounds of African Bushman-Hottentot, are foreign to speakers of English and many other languages. English [th] as in *th*ing is very rarely found in other languages. On the other hand, some speech sounds such as [i, a, u] and [m, p, t] occur almost universally and are similar in most languages. Some sounds, even when they are expressed with the same symbol, are not pronounced in the same way in different languages: compare French [t] and English [t]— the tip of the tongue touches the back of the upper teeth for the French [t], while it touches the ridge of the upper gum above the upper teeth for the English [t].

Languages differ still more widely in their methods of combining speech sounds. Some of the characteristics of the Ural-Altaic Language Family are: (a) No consonant clusters, such as *str*ike, occur at the beginning of words. (b) No [r] or [l] occur at the beginning of words, except in loan words. (c) They show "vowel harmony"—vowels are distinguished between male [a, o, I, u], and female [e, ö, i, ü], and these two types do not both occur in one word. Examples from eighth-century Japanese are: "kumo," cloud, male vowels only; "sönö," garden, female vowels only. Vowel harmony seems to be breaking down in modern Japanese and Korean, though apparently not in Turkish. (d) Words may be polysyllabic—they can consist of more than one syllable as in "ha-ra-ki-ri" and the syllables do not have independent meanings. (e) In Japanese, but not in other members of Ural-Altaic, every syllable ends in a vowel or [ng]. The English word "steel" becomes "su-ti-ru" when transcribed into Japanese (Japanese has no [l]).

The Indo-European Family is different from Ural-Altaic in all the features enumerated above except that words may still be polysyllabic. This family has one feature that is not found in the Ural-Altaic Family, namely *ablaut*, a consistent internal vowel change in grammatically related words, as in English s*i*ng, s*a*ng, and s*u*ng.

The Sino-Tibetan Family differs from Indo-European and Ural-Altaic in two ways: although compound words of more than one syllable are possible and frequent, almost all syllables have meanings, and can be used as words. For example, "brother" is "shiongti," and "shiong" alone is "elder brother" while "ti" alone means "younger brother." If "mai" (buy) and "mai" (sell) are joined, what compound word should emerge? "Business," of course. Chinese lacks many of the sounds of Western languages, and words generally end in vowels or in [n] or [ng]. There are a few hundred syllables in Chinese (compared to over a thousand in English), and each syllable can be a word. This means that many words will share the same sound patterns as the above "mai" (buy) and "mai" (sell). "Fu" means "husband, rich, prefecture, axe, to sit cross-legged, putrid, happiness, to bind, snake scales, wild duck" and over 80 other meanings (Wieger, 1965). The use of tone or pitch variations (of which four are used in Mandarin Chinese) becomes essential in differentiating meanings of words otherwise similarly pronounced. A hackneyed anecdote in linguistic circles is that in one Burmese dialect, "ma" pronounced in five different tones spells out the whole sentence: "Help the horse; a mad dog comes!"

Vowel-to-consonant ratios can vary in different languages. Hawaiian has about an equal number of vowels and consonants, while Abkhaz has only two vowels and 68 consonants. Vowels and consonants alternate in words of many languages, but alternation patterns can be different. In Japanese no consonant clusters are permitted anywhere in a word. On the other hand, a whole sentence can be formed with consonants in Czech, as in: "Strč prst skrz krk," "Stick a finger through the throat!" (Here [r] might be functioning like a vowel. See Chapter 2 for discussion of consonants and vowels.)

When a word has more than one syllable, one of the syllables usually is stressed more than the others in Indo-European languages. Stress patterns vary in different languages. The accent may be "free" as in English or Russian, in the sense that the syllable on which it falls is not generally determined by simple rules. There is some tendency in the Germanic languages, including English, for stress to be on the initial syllable. Of the Slavic languages, Czech and Polish have a "fixed" accent—Czech stresses the initial, and Polish regularly stresses the next to last syllable.

Languages like Japanese and Korean do not use stress patterns, either for signaling different aspects of meaning of the same words or for rhythmic effects. Naturally, different intonation patterns may accompany different types of statement, states of emotion, or dialects. In these two languages the musical effect of poetry cannot be achieved by means of stress patterns. Their poetry is based on the number of syllables in a line, or the sound structures of the syllables. For example, a terse Japanese verse style called *haiku* derives its poetic effect from its rich imagery of the content of the verse contrasted with its rigid syllabic structure. There are only 17 syllables in the haiku; the first and third lines contain five, the second line seven syllables. The following is a famous one, by a seventeenth-century master, Basho (1644–1694), together with my translation.

Shizukasaya   Such quiet!
Iwani shimikomu   A cicada's cry
Semino koe.   Penetrates the rocks.

A four-syllable word like "O-ki-na-wa" is pronounced with equal stress on each syllable by the Japanese, but as "O-ki-ná-wa" by an English speaker, with primary stress on the third syllable. An English speaker, in pronouncing a foreign word, cannot help but impose English stress patterns. In learning a foreign language, learning the correct intonation patterns is important if we want to sound like fluent speakers of that language. The comedians Danny Kaye and Victor Borge imitate foreign intonation patterns so expertly that they sound as if they are speaking the various foreign languages even when they talk gibberish!

We often get the impression that unfamiliar languages are spoken fast. Is this a real effect or is it due simply to unfamiliarity? One reason for such an impression may be that we do not know the boundaries of the linguistic units, such as words or sentences. Another reason may be that we do not notice short pauses contained in the normal speech of unfamiliar languages. In our native language, speech filled with many pauses is perceived as spoken slowly. What are the relative speaking speeds of different languages? This is admittedly a very difficult question to answer because speech units are not exactly comparable in different languages. One investigator (source unknown) shows that the speaking rates in words per minute of various languages are: French, 350; Japanese, 310; German, 250; English, 220; and South Seas, 50 (reflecting perhaps the slow pace of life there?) In another study, Osser and Peng (1964) did not find a difference in speaking rate between Japanese and English speakers of similar verbal ability. They compared the rates of the two languages in terms of phonemes, or speech sounds. Syllables or phonemes (which will be explained at length in the next chapter) may be more appropriate units than words with which to compare the relative speaking rates of different languages.

Variation of word forms   One characteristic of the Indo-European Language Family is that it has many complex inflections. Some examples of inflections are: The forms of nouns, pronouns, and sometimes adjectives and articles vary according to gender (masculine, feminine, and neuter—as in "he, she, it"); number (singular, dual, and plural—as in "he," "they"); case (nominative, genitive, and so on—as in "he," "his"). Verbs vary according to person and number (as in "he goes," "they go") and tense ("he goes," "he went"). The only invariant parts of speech are prepositions (in, to . . .), and adverbs (always, never . . .). Language learners find memorization of all these inflections, especially French verb conjugations, to be one of the most onerous aspects of learning the Indo-European languages. In desperation, one asks: Do languages really require all these inflections?

The answer to this question is "no," if we look at the Sino-Tibetan Language Family, which lacks inflections. With the help of the content of words, the word order in sentences, a handful of particles, and extralinguistic, situational contexts, Chinese speakers can get by perfectly well without inflections. Chinese needs a small number of particles that serve specific functions, such as indicating completion of action, plural number, or genitive case. For example, "woo" (I) does not change its form to indicate the function of "me" or "my." But a particle "de" can be attached after "woo" to make it function as "my," as in "woode shu" (my book).

The Ural-Altaic Language Family is between the Indo-European and the Sino-Tibetan Families in its degree of inflection. Many Ural-Altaic languages have *post*positions instead of prepositions. The postpositions are used after nouns (as, water-*wa*), and vary to indicate different functions of nouns in a sentence. In the above example, "water" is a subject of a sentence, while for "water-*o*," "water" would be an object in Japanese. Verbs and copulas ("is") conjugate for tense, voice (active vs. passive), or levels of politeness in Japanese and Korean. There is no gender or number difference for nouns in Japanese, Korean, or Chinese. Speakers of these languages have to use additional or different words if they want to indicate gender or number specifically.

Sentence structure   The importance of word order in a sentence depends on the degree of inflection in the language, as well as on the availability of either post- or pre-positions. If words inflect heavily according to their functions in a sentence, then word order can be flexible. Thus the Latin sentences, "Petrus videt Paulum" and "Petrus Paulum videt" means the same, as -*um* and -*us* endings of nouns designate the actor and the recipient of action in these two sentences regardless of word order. In Japanese and Korean, too, because of postpositions that signal the subject and the object of a sentence, one can be flexible in word order to a certain degree: "Peter-*wa* Paul-*o* miru" or "Paul-o Peter-wa miru" in Japanese both mean "Peter sees Paul." In Chinese, which does not have inflections or postpositions, the word order (and perhaps the semantic content of words) is about the only means by which the function of words in a sentence is clearly designated. "Goou yeau len," "Dog bites man," is different from "Len yeau goou" in Chinese. English, which is less inflected than Latin, also has to resort to word order to distinguish the above two sentences.

The basic structure of English is subject-predicate, where the subject is often an actor, and the predicate its action, as in "A man weeps." According to Chao (1968), the subject-predicate in Chinese is often a topic-comment relation rather than an actor-action relation. Actor and action can apply as a particular case of topic and comment. A typical sentence might be "(As for) wine, (do you) drink (or) not drink?" The words in parentheses are added in English. The answer might be "Wine not drink, tobacco smoke." To paraphrase: "As for wine, I don't drink it, but I do smoke tobacco." Thus, Chinese does not require the dummy actors so common in English, as in "*It* rains." The actor as the subject of a sentence is often omitted in two-person conversation in Japanese, Korean, and Chinese. The above question and answer serve as Chinese examples. From Japanese "Wakaru-*ka?*" meaning "(Do you) know?" can be answered "Wakaru," "(Yes, I) know." The actor of the sentence is obvious from the conversational context, and communication does not suffer from the lack of subject-actor in the above sentences. If, however, the actor is not clear from the context, or if it has to be emphasized, it may be explicitly named. Incidentally, note that a statement can be changed into an interrogative sentence by merely adding a question particle, -*ka*. Korean and Chinese use the same device.

Variations in cultural expressions using words   The enumeration of cultural variations of expressions can be inexhaustible. Here we will look at only one interesting case that rounds off our discussion on differences among world languages.

Some languages, such as Japanese, Korean, and Javanese, have honorifics (polite manners of speech), which are quite foreign to speakers of Indo-European languages. German, French, and many other Indo-European languages have two different forms of addressing "you"—"du" (informal) or "Sie" (formal) in German, "tu" or "vous" in French. In Chinese, a specific word (or words) is also used to show respect to the listener, or even to the listener's brother: "lingshion" means "excellent older brother" as opposed to "shiong" alone, "elder brother."

In Japanese honorifics are so pervasive that the choice of vocabulary, as well as the conjugation of every verb and copula, is affected. In fact, not a single sentence can be uttered without indicating the level of politeness. There are different levels of politeness, from plain to polite, and to super-polite, depending on the relationship between the speaker and the listener—sex, occupation, age, status, of both the speaker and the listener, are all considered. In Japanese, languages of female and male are readily distinguishable. Sex and status are compounded in the speech between husbands and wives—husbands speak to their wives in the same manner as they would speak to their inferiors, while wives speak to their husbands in the same manner as to their superiors. The emperors have their own formal style of speech to which no one else is entitled. For example, only an emperor can use "chin" referring to himself. Lesser mortals can choose from over ten different words referring to "I"—"boku" (male, informal); "watashi" (female, informal); "ware" (male, addressing an inferior person); and so on. Then there is the deferential prefix "o-" which, when prefixed on a noun, glorifies the object thus honored as well as the person addressed, as in "*o*-benjo" (honorable toilet). Verbs can be thus honored too—"osuwari," "please sit down." The speaker who uses "o-" profusely is considered refined.

Dialects

Regional variations of one language are dialects, which also involve differences in speech sounds, intonation, vocabulary, and syntax (the grammatical way words are put together in a sentence). However, differences among dialects of one language are supposed to be smaller than those that exist between two languages. Speakers of one dialect usually understand speakers of other dialects of the same language, but not always. Whether two dialects are mutually intelligible may be determined by the geographical distance that separates them. Two dialects in adjoining regions are usually intelligible to speakers of each, while dialects separated by great distances can be mutually unintelligible. One can observe such a relation clearly by traveling through the vast territory of China.

Differences among dialects are usually greatest in the speech sounds, next in vocabulary, and then in syntax. For example, it is how one pronounces constantly used vowels that may distinguish English dialects like Liverpudlian, Brummagem, or Cockney,[2] and fix a gulf between their speakers and some of the great prizes of life in England. This social pattern derived in part from the distinctive speech of courtiers who tried to emulate the speech of the German king of England, George II. Those who did not learn their affected manner of speech were obviously not of court, and belonged to the lower orders.

In Great Britain one of the many dialects rose to prominence over the others and became, in course of time, modern Standard English, or the "Queen's English." Standard English is a bastard dialect not native to any particular region of England, though close to many dialects of south central England. It presumably arose through the interaction of social leaders from various regions and the court. In general, a standard language is the prestigious dialect used by the leaders of the society, taught at schools, and spoken by announcers on national TV and radio. It is often, but not always, the language of the capital or central city. For example, a variety of Parisian French is Standard French. A standard language serves as a link between speakers of different dialects.

In spite of Oscar Wilde's witty remark: "We have really everything in common with America nowadays except, of course, language," differences between British English and American English are minor, not usually enough to hamper communication. There are sound differences such as "can't" being pronounced as in "cat" in the USA and Canada, and "father" in Britain. In vocabulary, there are a few discrepancies, such as "fall" in America and "autumn" in Britain; in idioms (in Britain) "spend a penny/

---

[2] The dialects of Liverpool, Birmingham, and London, respectively.

powder one's nose" (in USA), "standing for office/running for election," and "(wake up) knock up/knock up (make a girl pregnant)." There are hardly any syntactic differences to speak of.

What about dialects within the USA? Thanks to the mobility of the population, both physical and social, dialects involving substantial differences in sounds, words, and syntax have not developed in the USA. We may recognize Southern "drawl," but understand it just as easily as Standard English (SE: American version). Some areas where people have not had much contact with distant regions and have not moved for generations have developed or kept idiosyncratic dialects, which may be the way that their ancestors talked. Mountain people in Appalachia often speak an archaic English hard for other Americans to understand.

Black English (BE)

One dialect in the USA that differs substantially from SE is Black English. For three centuries, BE has been the language of most black people in the USA—80 percent of black people, according to Dillard (1972). Lately, a number of linguists (for example, Dillard) have come to believe that the dialect originated with the slaves themselves. The early slave traders practised language mixing, so that the slaves could be more easily controlled. This forced the slaves to find a common tongue, which turned out to be the Portuguese Pidgin. A pidgin is a hybrid language that mixes two languages— usually, parts of the vocabulary of some European language are incorporated into the sound system and syntax of an indigenous language of Africa, Asia, or Oceania. It serves as a *lingua franca*, a common language used by people whose native tongues are mutually unintelligible. Many black slaves learned the Portuguese Pidgin in the slave "factories" on the west coast of Africa. The restricted contact of most of them with their masters precluded their learning the standard language.

Here is a brief sketch of BE (based on Dillard, 1972). BE syntax tends to simplify or regularize some of the SE syntactic features.

Tense unmarked[3] in ". . . he go yesterday";
Irregular verb regularized in "felled, frozed";
Third person singular verb unmarked in "he run";
Preposition omitted in "put the cat out the house";
Pronoun inappropriate and "is" (the copula) missing in "he a nice little girl";
Double negatives in "Dat ain' no cup" for "That is not a cup";

[3] The grammatical device of marking tense of a verb is not used. If tense is marked, "he go" will be "he went."

Relative pronouns missing in "Ray sister she got a new doll baby";
"Ray sister go to school at Adams she got a new doll baby"; "Ray
sister seven year old go to school at Adams. . . ."

In the above, possessive and plural are not marked (Ray's sister; seven
years old).

There is a syntactic rule that permits
    He be sick all the time.
    He sick right now.
but not
    *He sick all the time.[4]
    *He be sick right now.

The auxiliary "to be" implies continuation or habitual action, whereas
its omission indicates a temporary state. This may be expressed in a more
roundabout way in SE. Another example might be: "You makin' sense, but
you don't be makin' sense," meaning something like "You've blundered into
making an intelligent statement for once" or "That's a bright remark—but
it's not the usual thing for you."

Vocabulary differences are not large. BE has "savvy" (to understand)
which can be traceable to Portuguese "saber"; BE uses "heap" in the sense
of "very, very much"; BE has "fancy talk" as in "If my memorandum
[memory] am correct. . . ."

In pronunciation, [th] may be pronounced as [d] (that = dat), and
as [f] (bath = baff). BE also has a characteristic intonation pattern that is
distinct from SE.

In spite of all these differences, BE is intelligible to speakers of SE,
perhaps because the vocabulary is largely in common between BE and SE.
Vocabulary similarities play an important role in determining whether two
languages or dialects are mutually intelligible. See how well you can understand the following sample of BE. This sample is from one of the experimental reading books, *Ollie*, prepared by Stewart at the Education Study
Center in Washington.

Ollie big sister, she name La Verne.
La Verne grow up now, and she ain't scared of nobody.
But that don't mean she don't never be scared.
The other day when she in the house, La Verne she start to screaming and
hollering. Didn't nobody know what was the matter.
Everybody been thinking that she be hurt. . . .

---

[4] An asterisk in front of a speech segment means that the segment is ungrammatical.

The idea here is that black children in the ghetto might more easily learn how to read first in BE, and then transfer to SE later. Whether this is a good strategy is a moot point, but at least it may help make black children bilingual in BE and SE.

BE can occasionally cause misunderstandings. For example, a young field hand brought into the kitchen was instructed to *heat* a dish of "hopping John." Instructions in the youth's own dialect should have been to *hot* the dish; striving to obey orders, the youth ate the dish.

We have made a broad, if superficial, survey of languages of the world and some dialects of the English language. The differences among languages, especially unrelated ones, in speech sounds, vocabulary, and syntax are impressive and make them mutually unintelligible.

Language similarities

We now remind ourselves that we started this chapter by considering many features that all human languages have in common, and that make human languages stand out from the rest of animal communication. We once again attend to similarities of languages.

Human languages require anatomical equipment for sound production and cognitive capacities for the use of rules. Having reached the same evolutionary stage, all humans, regardless of differences in race and culture, possess these two basic biological requirements, enabling all of them to have languages that are similar in fundamental aspects.

In what fundamental aspects are languages similar? We consider here only those similarities that we have not discussed so far in this chapter. Human languages all seem to strive toward maximum communication with least effort. In general, we avoid sounds or sound arrangements that are too complex to articulate or to discriminate by ear. Words that are used frequently tend to be short. Objects or events that are important in a culture tend to be coded economically in a single word. Although in principle sentences could be made structurally as complex as we like, we tend to prefer them less complex. We process speech in medium-sized units—units too big may strain our memory span, and units too small may be inefficient or wasteful of processing time and effort.

The usage of language by all humans is similar. In person-to-person communication, one has to refer to the same environment and affairs of life— space reference (here, there); human relations (father, mother); time reference (today, tomorrow); numbers (one, many); and so on. One has to make statements, negations, questions, commands, and exclamations. Thus in all languages we expect to find some means of expressing these fundamental matters, although the particular means employed will be varied.

Languages seem to be different also in precisely how they express the above matters.

Because this chapter is meant as an "appetizer," I have tried to cover a little bit of many topics in an informal and superficial way. In the course of this book, we shall have the chance to talk about many of the topics mentioned here in more detail. But our future discussions of language and language users have to be more formal, and will use technical terms and rely heavily on experimental data.

SUMMARY AND CONCLUSIONS

In several features human language contrasts with the communication systems of primates and bees. Humans use primarily the mouth-to-ear channel, and accept arbitrary relations between words and their referents. Human language has levels of construction and varied types of communication. Finally, it is acquired.

Although the communication systems of primates and bees have some very rudimentary features of human language, they are qualitatively different from human language. Even our efforts to teach either oral or sign language to so advanced a species as chimpanzees have met with only limited success so far.

There are numerous languages and language families in the world. Three language families—the Indo-European Family, the Sino-Tibetan Family, and the Ural-Altaic Family—were chosen for closer examination. We examined how some of the languages from these families—English, Chinese, Japanese, and Korean—differ in their linguistic systems and in cultural-linguistic expressions.

The sound systems of languages differ in the number and types of sounds they utilize. Their word systems differ not only in the ways sounds are combined to form words, but also in the degrees and types of word inflections. Their syntactic structures differ in the importance of word order and in the linguistic means by which different sentence types are formed.

Dialects are regional variations of one language, and they too involve differences in linguistic systems, particularly in the speech sound system. Black English in the USA shows some syntactic differences from Standard English.

Even though world languages are different in many obvious features, they share some fundamental characteristics in goals and usages.

The chapter ends with the promise that the topics mentioned here will be covered in detail and in a technical manner in the course of the book.

2

Linguistic Units
and Speech Behavior

So far we have managed to talk about languages informally, without using many technical terms. In order that we may later talk more clearly about the psychology of speech behavior, we must now learn a little about language itself, and about how language can be described. First, we must learn about linguistic units, which include speech sounds, phonemes, syllables, morphemes, words, phrases, and sentences. Figure 2–1 shows some linguistic units and their interrelationships.

We deal with the simpler and smaller units in Chapters 2 and 3, leaving phrases and sentences for Chapter 4, where they are discussed along with syntactic rules.

SPEECH SOUNDS

The basic building-blocks of spoken language are speech sounds. They form the smallest or the lowest units of language. Speech sounds, by international linguistic convention, are written inside square brackets, thus: [p]. The International Phonetic Alphabet (IPA) has symbols for most of the speech sounds commonly found in many languages, although, as we have seen for the French and English [t], the subtle details of a sound may differ from language to language.

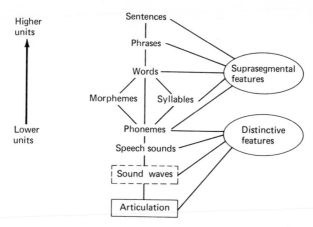

FIGURE 2–1   Linguistic units and their interrelationships. Unmarked words are the units, and the circled words are characteristics possessed by some of the units. For example, distinctive features are relevant to phonemes, speech sounds (or phonetic segments), sound waves, and articulation.

TABLE 2–1   International Phonetic Alphabet (IPA)

IPA	Key words	IPA	Key words
æ	f*a*t	k	
e	d*a*te	l	
a	c*a*r	m	
ɛ	t*e*n	n	
i	m*ee*t	p	
ɪ	*i*s	r	*r*aw
o	g*o*	s	
ɔ	h*a*ll	t	
u	t*oo*l	v	
ʊ	b*oo*k	w	*w*e
ʌ	*u*p	y	*y*es
ə	*a*go	z	*z*ip
:	lengthen any vowel, as in [a:] in "large."	tʃ	*ch*urch
b		ŋ	si*ng*
d		ʃ	*sh*ip
f		θ	*th*ink
g	*g*o	ð	*th*is
h		ʒ	a*z*ure
dʒ	*j*ump	ʔ	a throat sound produced by infants. Not in spoken English.

Let us examine speech sounds from three viewpoints: articulation, acoustics, and auditory perception.

Articulation

Articulation refers to how speech sounds are produced by the human articulatory organs.

Vocalizing and human articulatory organs   What does take place in vocalizing?

As we get ready to talk, air is drawn into the chest, which is momentarily poised in a slightly inflated position. As speech begins, the abdominal muscles contract slightly in advance of the first syllable. The contraction forces the viscera against the floor of the chest cavity and provides a firm support for the action of the chest muscles. Muscles between the ribs then contract in quick strokes that force air upward through the vocal organs during each syllable. The abdominal muscles continue to contract in a slow controlled movement, and as a breath phrase ends, the large muscles of inspiration quickly inflate the lungs for the next phrase (Miller, 1951, p. 12).

The pulsations of breath characterizing syllabic rhythm are controlled not primarily by the lungs but by closure in other parts of the speech organs, such as the lips or the tongue contacting parts of the oral cavity. These articulatory organs are shown in Figure 2–2. The fundamental voicing sound of speech is made by the vibration of the vocal folds, which are not "cords," as they are commonly called, but a pair of substantial fibrous lips. When relaxed, the vocal folds leave a V-shaped opening called the glottis (Fig. 2–2). The vocal folds are inside the larynx, a "voice box," immediately behind the Adam's apple. The larynx in turn sits at the top of the windpipe.

In making a noise, the following sequence of events occurs: the vocal folds come together and close the glottis. Pressure builds up below the blockage of the closed vocal folds. When the pressure has built up sufficiently, the vocal folds are forced apart briefly, and a puff of air escapes. The folds then close again until the pressure once more builds up to force them apart. Pitch and volume are varied by changing the tension on the vocal folds and the force of the passing stream of air during voicing. The successive puffs of air can each carry a great deal of energy, which is mostly transformed into auditory energy in speech. Whispered speech, which does not carry far, is produced with a steady air stream, uninterrupted by closure of the vocal folds.

The human articulatory organs serve functions other than speaking. They are also used for breathing and eating. Some evidence suggests that the human mouth is not optimal for eating and breathing, but that it is for speaking (P. Lieberman, 1968). The position of the epiglottis (see Fig. 2–2) is lower in humans than in primates; this sometimes leads to difficulties in swallowing (note it when it happens to you next time). But the low position of the epiglottis allows us to conduct the glottis-produced sounds through the oral cavity; in other primates, the sounds are directed through the nasal cavity.

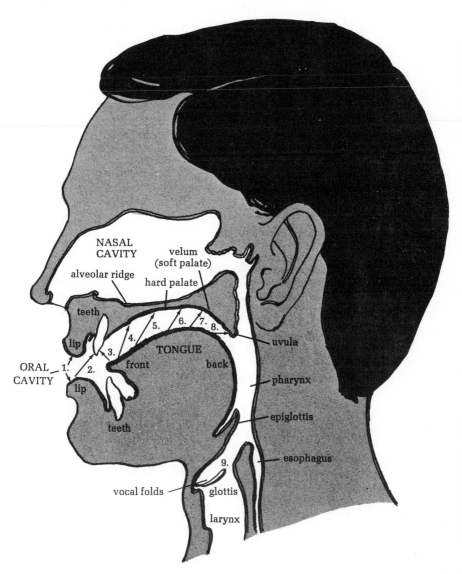

FIGURE 2–2   Human articulatory organs and areas in the oral cavity (numbered 1 to 9) of consonant production. (From Fromkin and Rodman, 1974.)

In his book *Biological Foundations of Language*, Lenneberg (1967) cites various characteristics of the human face that have a decisive influence upon speech-sound production. Here let us examine only a few of the most prominent characteristics mentioned by Lenneberg. For example, the human's small mouth and highly mobile, powerful lips allow very rapid building up of air pressure, followed by the sudden release employed in the labial stops [p, b]. These speech sounds are among the earliest produced by a child when it tries to utter meaningful words. The human lacks the enlarged canine teeth that are so prominent in males of most other primate forms. Owing to the relative evenness in height and width of all teeth in the human, the denture forms an unbroken palisade around the oral cavity. This structural peculiarity is essential for the production of sibilant (hissing) sounds such as [f, v, s, ʃ, θ].

The human vocal apparatus is in several aspects simpler and more streamlined than that of great apes. We have only one set of functional vocal folds, as opposed to two sets in primates; the vocal folds are mounted in the air tunnel in such a way that when drawn together they can produce sound much more easily on expiration instead of allowing both inspiratory and expiratory voicing.

In addition to such organs as the tongue, lips, and vocal folds, the cavities of the mouth, throat, and nose are involved in speech production: they act as resonators so that sound energy at certain frequencies is selectively emphasized. The sizes and shapes of these cavities determine their resonant frequencies. Of the three cavities, the nasal cavity is the least important as a resonator. Its shape is relatively fixed, and the only change we can make in it is to open or close the passage between the nose and the throat by moving the "door," the velum (the soft back part of the roof of the mouth: see Fig. 2–2). If you pinch your nose tightly, or have a severe cold, you can still utter all the English sounds without difficulty, except the three nasal sounds [m, n, ŋ]. English-speakers with a lazy velum leave this door to the nasal cavity hanging open most of the time, and so have an unpleasant nasal resonance in all their sounds. On the other hand, the mouth and the throat are capable of large variations in size and shape, and together comprise a double resonator, whose changes shape all our speech sounds.

Classification of speech sounds   From the point of view of articulation, we may divide speech sounds into vowels and consonants. To articulate vowels, we leave the vocal tract comparatively unobstructed. All vowels (except whispers) are voiced, which means that the vocal folds vibrate to produce vowels. The different acoustic qualities arise from different resonances, as the mouth and the throat are molded into different shapes and sizes by movements of the tongue and the lips. We can describe the vowel articulation in terms of lip position (rounded-unrounded), tongue height (high, middle, low), and tongue advancement (front, central, back).

The sounds of vowels are less stable than those of consonants. Across different dialects, the pronunciations of the vowels change while the consonants remain unchanged. To take examples from English, contrast American "can't" [kænt] and [keint], which rhyme with "ant" and "paint," to British [ka:nt] in which the [a:] is the same as the [a] in "part"; "love" [lɔ:v] in southern USA and [lʌv] in the rest of the USA. Australian English sounds different from American or Standard British English mainly because the Australians pronounce vowels differently: Australian "trine" for "train." Within England, regional accents such as a Liverpudlian, Brummagen, or Cockney "accent" identify a person who is probably not acceptable in "society." John Deane Potter (quoted in Critchley, 1970, p. 241) says:

Britain has created a mandarin class. And the entrance to it is guarded by the most craftily concealed traps in the world. They consist of five little sounds—the vowels of the English language. It is how you pronounce these tiny, constantly used sounds which may fix a gulf between you and some of the great prizes of life.

In contrast to the relatively free air flow that characterizes vowel production, we produce consonants by making a particular obstruction to the flow of air through the oral cavity. Each consonant can be described in terms of the position and manner of the obstruction. The position of articulation refers to the place of the obstruction and the organs that participate in creating it (see Fig. 2–2). The position may be more precisely determined than is the set of resonances that characterize a vowel, and this may well account for the stability and consistency of consonants as compared to vowels.

The positions of articulation distinguish consonants such as:

1. *Bilabial* [p, b]—both lips in area 1 in Figure 2–2.
2. *Labiodental* [f, v]—lower lip and upper teeth in area 2.
3. *Dental* [θ, ð]—tip of tongue and back part of upper teeth in area 3.
4. *Alveolar* [t, d]—tip or middle of tongue and alveolar ridge in area 4.
5. *Alveo-palatal* [ʃ, dʒ]—tip or middle of tongue and the section of the hard palate in area 5.
6. *Palatal* (not used in English)—middle of tongue and the hard palate in area 6.
7. *Velar* [k, g]—root of tongue and velum in area 7.
8. *Uvular* (not used in English).
9. *Glottal* [h]—edges of the vocal folds in the space between vocal folds and the glottis.

We can distinguish types of consonants in another way: by their manner of articulation, instead of by their place of articulation.

1. *Plosive sounds or stops* [p, t, k]—the vocal tract is closed completely, with the lips for [p] and with the tongue for [t], allowing air pressure to build

up behind the closure, which is then abruptly opened. The sharp sound produced when the air is released is often followed by a fricative sound or aspiration.

2. *Fricatives* [s, ʃ, f, v, z, ʒ, ð, θ]—the vocal tract is partly closed at some point and air is forced through the constriction at a velocity high enough to produce turbulence.

3. *Nasals* [n, m, ŋ]—complete closure of the oral cavity is accompanied by an outflow of air through the nasal cavity.

4. *Laterals* [l]—there is complete closure in the center of oral cavity accompanied by a restricted outflow of air on its sides.

5. *Affricates* [tʃ]—complete closure is released into partial closure.

Consonants of most of the above types may be voiced or voiceless; the vocal folds vibrate in [b] and [v] but not in [p] and [f].

Table 2–2 shows English consonants classified by the position and manner of articulation.

TABLE 2–2   English   Consonants[a]   Classified   by   Position   and   Manner   of Articulation

Position = Point of Articulation and Articulator Manner	Bilabial	Labio-dental	Dental	Alveolar	Alveo-palatal	Velar	Glottal
Stops	vl p vd b			t d		k g	
Affricates	vl vd				tʃ dʒ		
Fricatives	vl vd	f v	θ ð	s z	ʃ ʒ		h
Lateral	vd			l			
Nasals	vd m			n		ŋ	
Semivowels[b]	vd w			r	y		

[a] There is a slight disagreement among linguists on the number and types of English consonants.

[b] Semivowels are articulated like vowels but function like consonants. For example, /w/ is articulated like /u/ but is used in the position normally occupied by a consonant, as in "wet."

Acoustics of speech sounds

Acoustics is the study of physical sound waves. Any vibrating body sets the surrounding air molecules in motion, producing a sound wave. Speech organs, too, vibrate and resonate, setting up complex wave forms. Figure 2–3 shows a single complete cycle that represents the successive compression and expansion of the air as the sound wave moves along in time. The two main characteristics of such a wave are its *frequency* and its amplitude. Frequency is related to pitch, while amplitude is related to loudness of sounds we hear. Frequency refers to number of vibrations per second, or the number of times per second that the whole wave is repeated. Frequency is expressed in cycles per second (cps) or Hertz (Hz). The current practice is to use Hz because cps can stand for other events and hence is ambiguous. The range of frequency we can hear is about 20–20,000 Hz. A vibrating body produces not only a fundamental frequency but also a whole series of harmonics. The fundamental frequency is the peculiar frequency of the entire vibrating body. The fundamental frequencies of speech are determined by the rates at which the vocal folds open and close, and are usually in the region of 125 Hz for men and a slightly higher frequency for women.

Spectrograms   Through a sound spectrograph, the acoustic patterns of speech can be converted into visual ones so that they can be studied at leisure. A spectrograph contains a bank of filters, each of which selects a narrow band of frequencies in the audio spectrum. The spectrograph determines the energy of continuous speech in several frequency bands by means of such filters. The moving paper is blackened according to the relative intensity of the energy in the different frequency bands. The output of the spectrograph is a spectrogram, such as the one shown in Figure 2–4.

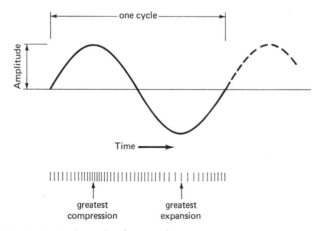

FIGURE 2–3   A single cycle of a sound wave.

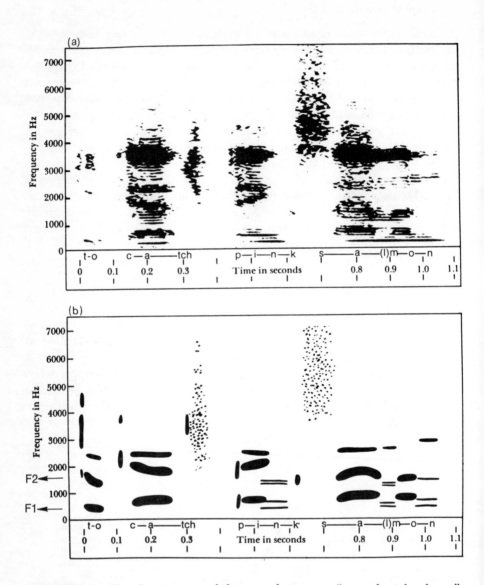

FIGURE 2–4 *Top:* Spectrogram of the natural utterance "to catch pink salmon."
Bottom: Playback spectrographic pattern for this utterance. The darkened regions
in both spectrograms represent concentrations of acoustic energy. (From Liberman et al., 1972b.)

The darkened regions in spectrograms indicate concentrations of energy in certain frequency bands. When the air puffs pass through the resonating cavities of the throat and mouth, the cavities respond at some frequencies more than at others. Usually there are two or three resonance peaks for vowels—two or three frequencies have strong acoustic responses with more energy than other frequencies. These peaks in the energy distribution are called *formants*. Different vowels are characterized by having their formants at different frequencies; but the two lowest formants, called Formant 1 (F1) and Formant 2 (F2), are the most important in identifying the vowels.

The spectrogram in Figure 2–4a shows that consonants have less of the darkened regions, indicating that they have less acoustic energy than do vowels. In general, voicing vastly increases the acoustic energy; all vowels are voiced, while some consonants are voiced and some are not. In one measurement of conversation the average power of vowels ranged from 9 [æ] to 47 [ɔ] microwatts, while some consonants were too weak to be measured. An ordinary 100-watt electric light bulb uses 100 million microwatts. The consonant with the greatest power was [ʃ] (an unvoiced consonant), with 1.8 microwatts (Sacia and Beck, 1926). Thus "show" has more power than "theme" and is intrinsically more audible.

Spectrograms are useful not only for studying the physical characteristics of speech sounds but also for other purposes. There have been some rather unsuccessful efforts to teach deaf people to "read" the speech on spectrograms. The spectrograms are not finely differentiated enough to reflect all the rich variations of actual speech sounds. Perhaps, also, the spectrogram obscures essential features of speech. On the other hand, even an early computer program designed for visual pattern recognition was able to identify spoken digits from spectrograms (Uhr and Vossler, 1961).

Because spectrograms reflect the idiosyncratic characteristics of the speaker's voice, as well as the words, spectrograms have sometimes been used for identification in courts of law. Scientists' researches into voice identification through visual inspection of spectrograms show that identification is quite reliable. Tosi and his five associates (1972) conducted a two-year experiment on voice identification. From a homogeneous population of 25,000 males speaking general American English, 250 were selected as subjects. Twenty-nine trained (but nonprofessional) examiners performed a total of 34,996 experimental trials of identification. The examiners made a forced decision (identification or elimination) in each trial, taking an average 15 minutes.

The researchers' conclusion was that a trained examiner's expected errors of false identifications would be approximately 6 percent, and the expected errors of false elimination would be approximately 13 percent. A professional examiner, who is aware of the serious consequences of the test performance and takes longer than 15 minutes, may perform identification with even smaller error rates.

However, other scientists (such as Hollien, 1974) advocate additional research before using spectrograms in the legal community.

Auditory perception

Auditory perception refers to the hearing of sounds by listeners: which acoustic cues are important in our perception of different consonants? Much important work on speech perception has been carried out at Haskins Laboratories in New Haven, Connecticut, notably by A. M. Liberman and his associates. One of their research instruments is a *pattern playback*. They paint their own spectrograms, using a highly simplified form that omits many of the constant accompaniments of speech. Examples of simplified, hand-painted spectrograms are shown in Figure 2–4b. The investigators introduce a wide range of experimental changes in the spectrographic pattern. Then they convert the spectrograms into sounds using the pattern playback. They can now find out which of these changes in the spectrographic pattern are important for auditory perception and which are not.

Transitions   Using the pattern playback, the investigators were able to isolate some of the acoustic cues important in the perception of individual consonants of American English. For example, variations in direction and extent of second- and third-formant *transitions* are cues for the perception of various consonants according to place of production, while comparable variations of the first formant are cues for manners. Transitions are frequency glides produced as the vocal cavity shifts from one place of articulation to another. In Figure 2–4b, the rapid movements of formants through a range of frequencies at the left of each pattern are transitions. For each consonant there are characteristic frequency positions, or loci, at which the formant transitions begin, or to which they may be assumed to point. Note the second-formant transitions of the spectrographic patterns in Figure 2–5, all of which record [d] before different vowels. All of these transitions seem to be pointing to a starting point in the vicinity of 1,800 Hz.

However, transitions are not the only cues for consonant perception. The frequency position of the burst enables listeners to distinguish among

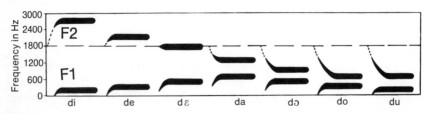

FIGURE 2–5 Spectographic patterns of /d/ before different vowels. (From Liberman, 1957.)

voiceless stops [p, t, k] (Liberman, Delattre, and Cooper, 1952). According to Cole and Scott (1974), invariant features, based mainly on the frequency domain, provide information about some individual consonants. The fricatives [s, z, ʃ, ʒ] and affricates [tʃ, dʒ] are characterized by noisy energy or friction at specific frequency. The amplitude of the noise distinguishes [f, θ] from [s, z], while the frequency of the noise distinguishes [s, z] from [ʃ, ʒ]. These consonants can be distinguished even when the same vowel [a] follows them, lacking transition cues.

As we have seen, there are relations among articulation, acoustic characteristics, and auditory perception of speech sounds. However, the relation is not one-to-one. For example, small differences in articulation sometimes cause very large differences at the acoustic level, and the converse is also true. Further, not all acoustic variations are reflected in our auditory perception. When articulation and the sound wave go their separate ways, which way does the perception go? According to Liberman, perception always goes with articulation. That is, we perceive speech sounds not strictly by the way they sound but by the way we articulate them.

The perception of a speech sound is also influenced by its sound context. An artificial sound consisting of a short burst in the region of 1,440 Hz is heard either as [p] or [k] depending on whether [i], [a], or [u] follows it. The burst with [i] or [u] is heard as [p], and the burst with [a] as [k] (Liberman et al., 1952).

Liberman (1957) proposed the "motor theory of speech perception" to explain relations among acoustic characteristics, articulation, and perception of speech sounds. Before we talk about the motor theory, however, we have to learn about phonemes, the speech sounds that are "potentially meaningful" in a given language.

In sum, we produce various types of speech sounds by involving different articulatory organs in varied manners. Two main classes of sounds are consonants and vowels: the vocal tract is obstructed in some manner to produce consonants while it is unobstructed in vowel production. Speech sounds have such acoustic characteristics as frequency, amplitude, and formant, which we can study using spectrographs. Such acoustic cues as transitions influence our speech-sound perception. However, perception does not entirely reflect acoustic characteristics.

PHONEME

Definition

People produce a very large variety of sounds. Actually, there is no natural limit to the divisibility of the range of speech sounds that can be produced. If a very large variety of sounds were used meaningfully in some language, it would tax the listener's ability to discriminate and the speaker's ability to articulate precisely. Thus, each language divides the available range of sounds into classes. Each class of sounds represents a phoneme. The internationally agreed linguistic symbol for a phoneme is a pair of oblique lines enclosing a speech sound, thus: /p/.

The phoneme is a class of similar sounds all of which speakers of a given language choose to regard as the same. For example, /k/ in English is pronounced slightly differently in varied phonetic environments: the initial [k] in /kin/ has a puff of breath after it, while [k] after /s/ as in skin does not. Try to pronounce both types of /k/ with the back of your hand close to your mouth and feel the difference. In many languages, these two sounds of /k/ would be classified as separate phonemes. Sanskrit "kala" with the puffless [k] means "indistinct"; "kʰala" with a puff means "threshing floor." In English both types of [k] are classed as one phoneme /k/—if you pronounce [kʰ] in kin without a puff, it does not change the meaning of "kin" but it may sound odd. The difference between [k] and [kʰ] is always a *phonetic* difference, in whatever language it occurs. We can hear it in English and we can hear it in Sanskrit. But in Sanskrit /k/ and /kʰ/ are *phonemically* as well as phonetically distinct.

The crucial criterion for deciding whether a particular pair of sounds belong to the same phoneme or not in a given language is not whether they sound different, but whether substitution of one for the other changes the meaning of a word in that language. A phoneme change is the smallest change that can convert one word into another. By this criterion, even pitch or tone variation is phonemic in some languages, such as Chinese, because in these languages pitch variation distinguishes meanings of words otherwise pronounced alike. "Ma" can mean four different things depending on its tones: mā (level tone); má (rising tone); mǎ (falling and then rising); mà (falling tone).

How do we determine which sounds are phonemes in a given language? We find *minimal pairs*—word pairs that have different meanings thanks to a difference in only one phoneme. The following three pairs of English words are minimal pairs:

*l*ot; *r*ot
*l*ot; *l*et
*l*o*t*; *l*o*g*

In the first pair, the difference in the initial consonants [l] and [r] changes the meaning. Thus, /l/ and /r/ are separate phonemes. Likewise, in the second pair, the middle vowels /ɔ/ and /ɛ/, and in the third pair, the final consonants /t/ and /g/, are phonemes. In Japanese [l] and [r] are not two phonemes, because in any pair such as "malu" and "maru" the difference between [l] and [r] does not change the meaning of the word "maru." The phoneme /l/ does not exist in Japanese, and if a foreigner mispronounces [r] as [l], it is merely taken as a strange sort of /r/.

Motor theory of phoneme perception

Although each phoneme includes a range of sounds, our perception of consonants is usually categorical: we tend to hear only which phoneme is spoken, and not the variations in sound. For example, we normally hear only /k/, and not the distinction between [kʰ] and [k]. How and why we perceive phonemes in categories is an important but difficult question to answer. The motor theory of phoneme perception is an early attempt to answer this question. According to Liberman, categorical perception occurs because listeners covertly evoke idealized articulations for possible interpretations of the sounds. The discretely different types of sensory feedback from covert articulations control the overt identification and discrimination. In Liberman's motor theory, the sequence of events in speech perception is not as in Figure 2–6a, but rather as in Figure 2–6b.

Evidence   In support of the motor theory, Liberman and colleagues (1957) demonstrated that acoustically continuous stimuli were perceived in distinct and discontinuous phonemic categories. The stimuli were simplified, synthetic speech signals that varied in 14 small, acoustically equal steps through a range sufficient to produce three stops: /b/, /d/, and /g/. The stimuli were presented to subjects singly and in random order. The subjects did not hear steplike acoustic changes, but heard essentially a quantal jump from one perceptual category to another. That is, the subjects' perception turned the 14 continuous stimuli into three sharply discontinuous categories of /b/, /d/, and /g/. These categories also show up when one of those three sounds must be discriminated from one another: if the two sounds belong to different phoneme categories, discrimination is easy, but if they are in the same phonemic category, it is difficult. To put it in another way,

(a)   (b)

FIGURE 2–6   The sequence of events in speech perception—(a) or (b)? (a) Vocal response (R_V) forms an acoustic stimulus (S_A), which leads to discrimination response (R_D). (b) In the motor theory of speech perception, S_A leads to subvocal response ($R_{V'}$), which in turn leads to proprioceptive feedback (S_P). S_P elicits R_D. (After Liberman, 1957.)

discrimination is better near the phoneme boundaries than it is in the middle of the phoneme categories. Such categorical perception does not occur with vowel stimuli.

In another experiment, Liberman showed that diverse acoustic stimuli were heard as similar sounds, apparently because they were articulated in similar ways. [Gi], [ga], and [gu] form a continuous series from the point of view of articulation and perception, but are not acoustically neighbors. There is an abrupt change in acoustic stimuli when /g/ is followed by /i/ or /e/ as compared to /u/, as shown in Figure 2–7. Earlier in this chapter we saw an example in which the same acoustic stimulus, a 1,440 Hz burst, was heard as [k] or as [p] depending on the articulatory responses associated with the vowels that followed.

There is even some evidence that the auditory hallucinations of schizophrenics may have a motor component. Both Gould (1949) and McGuigan (1966) were able to amplify subvocal activity in patients who were actively hearing "voices"; the investigators found a close correlation between what the patients actually said and what they heard the voices say.

The motor theory in its extreme form says that we overtly mimic incoming speech sounds and then respond to the sensory stimuli produced by our own articulatory movements. To be more subtle, Liberman (1957) assumes that ". . . the process is somehow short-circuited—that is, that the reference to articulatory movements and their sensory consequences must somehow occur in the brain without getting out into the periphery" (p. 57). In a more recent version, the theory says that ". . . the listener uses inconstant sound as a basis for finding his way back to the articulatory gestures that produced it and thence, as it were, to the speaker's intent" (Liberman et al., 1972a, p. 41).

Counterevidence   Lane (1965) documented a body of evidence against the motor theory. He showed that categorical perception occurs in auditory perceptions of vowels and of entirely nonlinguistic stimuli such as complex tones, and in the visual perception of sectors of circles and patches of colors.

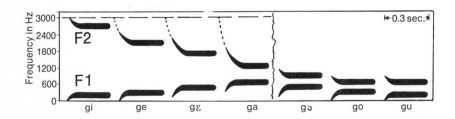

FIGURE 2–7   The spectrographic patterns that produce /g/ before various vowels (the dashed lines are extrapolations to the /g/ loci. Note a break between [ga] and [gɔ]). (From Liberman, 1957.)

For vowels the mediating articulations that are continuous and not categorical provide continuous sensory returns. Thus, organisms seem to learn to make sharp discriminations at the boundaries of any categories, whether they are speech sounds or not. If this is so, the concept that articulation mediates the auditory perception of consonants becomes superfluous. The categories mirror the articulation patterns because the speaker's articulation patterns define what categories are useful.

Further evidence against the motor theory is provided by cases in which activity of the articulatory organs is prevented for various reasons, yet speech perception is normal. Speech remains comprehensible even to one whose laryngeal muscles are removed or anesthetized; it can be understood even by persons who never speak, like an *anarthric* (one who cannot articulate) whom Lenneberg (1962) described. The patient could not articulate speech sounds because of congenital neurological defects, but learned to understand language.

We may become able to distinguish the phonemes of a foreign language before mastering their production, just as children often can discriminate the phonemes of adults before they use them. The age at which infants can make rudimentary discrimination of a few phonemes is shown to be as early as 4 months (Eimas et al., 1971; Trehub and Rabinovitch, 1972). Brown and Berko (1960) report on a young child who could hear a phonemic contrast such as that between /s/ and /ʃ/ before he could produce it. The investigators asked the child: "That's your fis?" "No, my fis," replied the child. "That's your fish?" to which the child now answered, "Yes, my fis."

Taking motor activity into the brain (Liberman, 1957), the usual sanctuary for retreating psychological theories, does not seem to save the motor theory; motor activity that has never existed in the first place, as would be the case in young children and anarthrics, cannot retreat to the brain.

Speech-sound processor   Recently, Liberman's motor theory has been further modified in a paper by Studdert-Kennedy, Liberman, Harris, and Cooper (1970).

> We . . . are willing to . . . entertain the hypothesis that categorical perception reflects some structurally determined process, adapted to the complex code that links the sounds to the phonetic message they convey. The basic difference between stops and steady-state vowels is that stops are encoded in a more complex way and, therefore, are more in need of a special speech sound processor. Categorized perception is only one consequence of the operation of the speech-sound processor (pp. 247–248).

What is the speech-sound processor and why do we need it? The physical characteristics of speech sounds are notoriously indefinite. For one thing, formant transitions carry important cues for perception of most consonants, but the transitions are often influenced by following vowels, and are difficult to specify and track physically. How do we then consistently identify consonants? According to Studdert-Kennedy and co-workers, we need a processor specialized for decoding the acoustic signal. The processor receives the signal and restructures the acoustic information so that meaningful phonetic messages can be extracted.

The output of the processor might be a cleaned–up description of the signal resembling the simplified synthetic spectrogram of Figure 2–4b. In short, the speech-sound processor decodes and converts the acoustic signal to a phonetic message by restructuring information. Such a special decoding device is available to us as part of our species-specific capacity for language.

Recent research on speech sound discrimination by animals questions whether perception of phoneme categories is a uniquely human ability. Kuhl and J. D. Miller (1975; in press) asked whether a chinchilla, a mammal with auditory capabilities fairly similar to man's, could correctly discriminate between the members of a large number of pairs of syllables on the basis of voicing contrast.

The acoustic properties that distinguish between voiced and voiceless plosives or stops is a timing difference, termed voice-onset time (VOT), between the onset of the plosive burst and the onset of voicing. VOT is measured in milliseconds (msec), and ranges from positive (voicing comes after the burst = voiceless phonemic category) through zero (voicing begins simultaneously with the burst = voiced phonemic category) to negative (voicing leads = prevoiced phonemic category).

Kuhl and Miller trained chinchillas to discriminate between synthetic speech sounds having VOT values of 0 (voiced sounds) or 80 msec (un-- voiced sounds). When the chinchillas could discriminate the members of a pair almost perfectly, a test was run to see how they would react to sounds having VOTs between 0 and 80 msec. When English speakers identify these synthetic speech sounds, perception changes abruptly from voiced to voiceless at VOT values which depend on the syllable. For example, the transition occurs at VOT = +22 msec for [ba–pa], at +35 msec for [da–ta], and at +41 msec for [ga–ka].

The chinchillas reacted like English speakers. For example, in the pair [da–ta], for VOT values below +33.5 msec they responded as if the voiced member [da] were presented, and for larger VOT values they reacted as if the voiceless member [ta] were presented. Note that +33.5 msec is extremely close to the +35 msec at which English speakers change their perception from the voiced [da] to voiceless [ta]. Similarly for the other syllables, the transition VOT closely matched that for the English speakers.

The researchers point out that while these findings do not rule out the possibility that human listeners process these speech sounds in a highly specialized way, they do demonstrate that uniquely human processing is not essential, at least for these particular tasks. The finding seems to indicate that the speech-sound oppositions used in real speech have evolved because they are highly distinctive to the auditory system.

Infants 1 to 4 months old discriminate between synthetic stimuli that fall on different sides of the English [b–p] phonetic boundary whether they are reared in an English-speaking environment where the boundary is phonemically relevant (Eimas et al., 1971), or in a Kikuyu-speaking environment where it is not (Streeter, 1974). However, Streeter and Landauer (1975) showed that the ability to discriminate [b–p] improved for Kikuyu exposed to English training over the years of school age. Trehub (1974) also showed that infants from unilingual English-speaking homes discriminated between [za] and [řa], [ř] being used by Czech speakers. English-speaking adults failed to differentiate the same Czech contrasts.

The findings seem to indicate that infants are born with an auditory system that can and does discriminate many speech sounds, but exposure to a particular phonemic system has some influence on development of phoneme perception; discrimination of relevant phonemes will further develop while discrimination of irrelevant speech sounds will atrophy.

How does categorical perception of relevant phonemes develop? Although we hear continuous ranges of similar consonants, we must be hearing consonants in the middle of their allowed range, namely target consonants, oftener than more deviant consonants. Thus, merely from frequency of exposure, we learn to recognize the target consonant better than any other similar sound, and to assimilate any consonant sounds into one or another possible target consonant. A similar effect occurs with out-of-tune singing, when the correct tune can be heard if it is known. A similar mechanism of perception should apply to vowel perception, as well as to nonlinguistic stimuli such as patches of colors where common targets exist. Vowel targets are usually less clear than consonant targets, hence show less sharp categorical discrimination. The five Japanese vowels are more stable (invariant across dialects) and are perceived as clearer targets than are English vowels. Perhaps this is why Japanese vowels are more likely to be processed by the left hemisphere than English vowels are (Tsunoda, 1973).

The proponents of the speech–sound processor, Studdert–Kennedy and colleagues, do not deny that experience may affect the speech processor, or even be a necessary condition for its proper operation. But they emphasize that phonetic perception cannot be explained by discrimination learning alone.

The phoneme in speech behavior

The phoneme is a linguistic unit. In studying linguistics, we segment speech hierarchically into different linguistic units—phonetic segments, phonemes, syllables, morphemes, words, phrases, and sentences. In processing speech, do we segment a speech stream in these units? Is the linguistic hierarchy reflected in perceptual representation? If so, is it done always from bottom to top, or smaller to larger, units? In other words, do we recognize phonetic segments first, then phonemic ones, then syllables, and so on? These questions are not easy to answer, as we see below.

Savin and Bever (1970) used monitoring techniques to study these questions. Subjects responded as soon as they heard a target in a sequence of nonsense syllables. The target was a complete syllable (such as bæb, sæb) or a phoneme from that syllable—the initial consonant for some subjects (for example, /b/ or /s/), and the middle vowel for other subjects (for example, /æ/). Subjects responded more slowly to the phoneme targets than to the syllable targets. The authors concluded that the phoneme identification may be subsequent to the perception of larger sound-based units, namely syllables. Syllables may be perceptually "real" units—that is, subjects hear them directly—while phonemes are not directly perceived but are inferred.

Foss and Swinney (1973), using the same monitoring technique, found that within subjects the order of reaction times (RTs), from longest to shortest, was phoneme, syllable, and two-syllable words. Thus they ask: Is the honor of being the perceptual unit reserved for the word?

McNeill and Lindig (1973) point out that the monitoring techniques used by the above authors do not answer the question of what are "the" perceptual units of speech. McNeill and Lindig showed that the minimum reaction time in such experiments occurs whenever the linguistic levels of the target and the search list are the same. For example, if phonemes are given in a search list and subjects have to detect a phoneme target, RTs will be short; but if subjects have to detect a syllable target in the same phoneme list, there is a mismatch and RTs will be longer.

Further, upward or downward searches showed no systematic difference, at least for syllables or words, in their data. In an upward search, the target is on a linguistic level lower than the search list, as in a search for phonemes in syllable lists. The experiment of Savin and Bever (1970) was such an upward search. In a downward search, the target is on a level higher than the list. An example is the search for one of the phonemes of a syllable target in a list of phonemes. The fact that the downward search increased RT at least as much as the upward search does seem decisive evidence that such monitoring techniques cannot reveal "the" perceptual units for speech. The RT was shorter in their data for lower linguistic levels. They interpret this finding to mean that RT is shorter when the stimulus is shorter and hence less complex than a higher unit.

McNeill and Lindig argue that "What is 'perceptually real' is what one pays attention to. In normal language use, the focus of attention . . . is the meaning of the utterance. Subordinate levels become the focus of attention only under special circumstances" (p. 430).

Let us now examine some features of our ordinary speech behavior that lead to the conclusion that phonemes are important in real life. (1) The first evidence of the use of the phoneme as a unit is the existence of alphabetic writing systems. In an alphabet, one letter in principle represents one phoneme: The letter *t* often represents the phoneme /t/. (2) In alliteration, the initial phoneme is repeated in successive words, as in "I *d*are say you'll *d*ig the *D*ancing *D*onkey—*d*elightfully *d*esigned for *d*iscerning *d*evotees of *d*rama." (3) In a spoonerism,[1] the initial phonemes of some words get mixed up, as in the classic "our queer old dean" for "our dear old queen" (Victoria). (4) Historical changes in language can be described very simply in terms of phonemes and only clumsily and arbitrarily without them. For example, English /f/ ("father," "foot") often corresponds to Latin /p/ ("pater," "pes"). English /θ/ in "three," "thank," "think," "through," and "thin" corresponds to German /d/ in "drei," "dank," "denken," "durch," and "dünn." (5) Numerous regularities in every modern language can be stated satisfactorily only by referring to phonemic features. For example, in English plural formation, the phoneme at the end of a noun determines whether /s/, /z/, /iz/, or none of these is used. The rule here is that a word that ends in a voiceless consonant takes on /s/, as in "cats"; a word that ends in a vowel or voiced consonant takes on /z/ as in "boys" or "dogs"; a word that ends in /s/, /z/, or /ʃ/ takes on /iz/ as in "roses," "masses," "wishes."

A variety of slips of the tongue observed by Fromkin (1973)—particularly in sounds such as /tʃ/ in "church" and /dʒ/ in "judge"—is revealing. Each of these two sounds is a cluster of two consonants on the phonetic level, but each is a phoneme. When these sounds are involved in speech errors they always move as a single unit, as in "chee cane" instead of "key chain" and "sack's jute" instead of "Jack's suit." Other consonant clusters such as /sp/ and /gl/ are made of two phonemes, and can be split up in errors as in "speech production" becoming "peach seduction."

In conclusion, we might say that phonemes are linguistic units and are indispensable in describing languages adequately. Ordinary speakers are not too familiar with the term phoneme or with its function as a unit, perhaps because phonemes are seldom used in isolation, as syllables or words are sometimes. Nevertheless, phonemes are used as units in our ordinary speech. For one thing, we hear diverse speech sounds in phoneme categories. If a foreigner speaking English produces a speech sound that is slightly divergent from our regular one, we tend to hear the regular one (for example,

---

[1] Named after Rev. W. A. Spooner (1844–1930) of Oxford, who was very prone to invert chunks of his speech—"It is kistummary to cuss the bride."

French [t] is heard as English /t/). But if he produces a grossly divergent sound (as, /t/ for /θ/), our attention may be called to it.

We have seen that phonemic units are used in alphabets, alliteration, and so on. We shall see more examples of phoneme perception in the discussion of distinctive features that follows. We shall also compare phonemes with syllables as perceptual units when we discuss syllables later in this chapter. We may then be in a position to develop a model of speech perception.

Distinctive features of phonemes

Definition   So far we have assumed that the phonemes of a language are not susceptible to further analysis. According to a recent trend in linguistics, spearheaded by Jakobson, Fant, and Halle (1963), phonemes may be further analyzed into distinctive features. A phoneme is characterized as a bundle of attributes, or distinctive features, such as voiced–voiceless; nasal–nonnasal. A feature is usually either present (+) or not present (−) in a particular phoneme. The bases of such distinctive features were originally articulatory and acoustic, but later (as in Chomsky and Halle, 1968) have been considered to be purely articulatory. One phoneme is distinguished from another by virtue of a difference in at least one feature. For example, the feature that differentiates /b/ and /p/ is the voicing of the former as contrasted to the voiceless quality of the latter; the two share all other features, such as being bilabial stop consonants.

Jakobson et al. distinguished about 20 features that occur in binary opposition. With these we can describe all the speech sounds of the world, although different languages may require different selections of these 20 features. For example, in Chinese the opposition of aspirated–nonaspirated is a distinctive feature, while the voiced–voiceless opposition is almost lacking. The same speech sound may realize different combinations of distinctive features in different languages. Which features distinguish one phoneme from all others in the language depends entirely on what language is being spoken.

Table 2–3 is a simplified distinctive-feature representation of 19 English consonants. Each phoneme is classified in a binary fashion on each feature. Individual sounds as well as classes of sounds can be uniquely defined with this system. Note that each phoneme has its own unique pattern of pluses and minuses. One can talk about distances between phonemes in terms of how many such binary oppositions separate them.

Distinctive features in speech perception   Does a distinctive feature exist as a singular feature in speech, or is it merely an abstract entity invented by linguists? In the speech errors of normal people, a single feature

TABLE 2–3   Distinctive Features of 19 English Consonants

	p	b	f	v	m	t	d	θ	ð	n	s	z	tʃ	dʒ	ʃ	ʒ	k	g	ŋ
Consonantal	+	+	+	+	+	+	+	+	+	+	+	+	+	+	+	+	+	+	+
diffuse ≒ Anterior	+	+	+	+	+	+	+	+	+	+	+	+	−	−	−	−	−	−	−
grave ≒ Coronal	−	−	−	−	−	−	+	+	+	+	+	+	+	+	+	+	−	−	−
Voice	−	+	−	+	+	−	+	−	+	+	−	+	−	+	−	+	−	+	+
Continuant	−	−	+	+	−	−	−	+	+	−	+	+	−	−	+	+	−	−	−
Nasal	−	−	−	−	+	−	−	−	−	+	−	−	−	−	−	−	−	−	+
Strident	−	−	+	+	−	−	−	−	−	−	+	+	+	+	+	+	−	−	−

Articulatory Characteristics of Features

Anterior–nonanterior: Anterior sounds are produced with an obstruction located in front of the palato-alveolar region of the mouth; nonanterior sounds are produced without such an obstruction. The palato-alveolar region is that where the ordinary /ʃ/ is produced.

Diffuse: Articulation in the front part of the mouth, from the alveolar ridge forward. "Diffuse" formerly characterized both the distinction between high/nonhigh vowels and that between anterior/nonanterior consonants. As a result, the articulatory and acoustical characterization of the feature became quite complex and rather implausible. Hence, "diffuse" and "grave" are no longer used, but they are included in Table 2–3 because some experiments described in the book used this terminology. "Diffuse" is similar to "anterior."

Coronal–noncoronal: Coronal sounds are produced with the blade of the tongue raised from its neutral position; noncoronal sounds are produced with the blade of the tongue in the neutral position.

Grave: Point of articulation in the very front (the lips) or the very back (velum) of the mouth. "Grave" is similar to "coronal."

Voice: Periodic vibration of the vocal folds during articulation.

Continuant: An uninterrupted expiration of the air stream through the oral cavity.

Nasal: Articulation characterized by release of the air stream, wholly or partly, through the nasal cavity.

Strident: Articulation characterized by relatively great noisiness resulting from forcing the air stream through a complex impediment. (Based partly on Chomsky and Halle, 1968.)

can be disordered, in the same way that phonemes are disordered in spoonerisms, while all other features remain as intended: "clear blue sky" was transposed to "glear plue sky." There was a voicing switch: the voiceless velar /k/ became a voiced /g/ and the voiced labial /b/ became a voiceless /p/ (Fromkin, 1973).

Experiments by Halwes (1969) and by Studdert-Kennedy and Shankweiler (1970) show that listeners sometimes extract one feature from the input to one ear, and another feature from the other, and combine them to hear a segment that was not presented to either ear. Thus, given [ba] to the left ear and [ka] to the right, listeners who make errors will far more often report [pa] (place feature from the left ear, voicing from the right) or [ga] (place feature from the right ear, voicing from the left) than [da] or [ta], which have features not present in either input.

Next, we see that distinctive features index the perceptual distances among phonemes. In Table 2–3, /p/ and /k/ share all features except one, namely, diffuse. Between /p/ and /g/, on the other hand, diffuse and one additional feature, voicing, separate the two phonemes. Greenberg and Jenkins (1964) asked the following questions: (1) Would listeners judge /p/ and /g/ (two feature differences) to be more distant from each other than /p/ and /k/ (one feature difference)? (2) Among those that are one feature apart, are pairs agreeing in manner (such as /p/ and /k/) rated closer than those that agree in position of articulation (such as /p/ and /b/)? (3) Is the greater articulatory distance between the labial–velar (front–back) position as against labial–alveolar (front–middle) or alveolar–velar (middle–back) position reflected in perception?

To answer these questions, the experimenters asked five subjects to listen to a tape-recorded set of 30 sound pairs such as [pa]:[ba] or [ga]:[pa]. As usual when consonants are used as test material, a vowel, in this case /a/, is added to each consonant to make it sound more natural. Subjects assigned numbers to their judgments of psychological distance.

The answers to the above three questions were all "yes." If the consonants were voiced, they appeared similar, and the other features had little effect. For unvoiced consonants, however, differences in the other features caused relatively large perceived differences. Hence, the distances among /b,d,g/, all voiced, were small compared with /p,t,k/, all voiceless.

The distinctive features turned out to be excellent predictors of listeners' confusion patterns as well. Consonants are important for intelligibility of speech, but are notoriously confusable. Miller and Nicely (1955) compared 16 important consonants in English. The consonants were spoken in a consonant–vowel context, the vowel being again /a/, creating nonsense syllables such as [ga] and [ka]. Listeners were asked to identify these syllables against a background of various amount of noise. Experimenters often introduce noise in speech-perception tasks to increase the error rate to a measurable level, because the patterns of errors often reveal important and interesting data. The experimenters found that consonants articulated in the same manner, but at different positions of articulation, were confusable. For example, /p/, a voiceless stop, was most likely to be confused with two other voiceless stops, /k/ or /t/; /p/ was not confused with another bilabial /b/. Consonant /n/ and /m/, which differ from each other in only one feature—place of articulation—were more often mistaken for one another than pairs like /n/ and /b/, which differ on two features—place and nasality. Consonants with still more differences were easier to distinguish. Roughly speaking, the 16 consonants reduced to 5 groups: /ptk/,

/bdg/, /fθsʃ/, /vŏzʒ/, and /mn/. Few confusions occurred between groups, and most of the confusions occurred within the groups.

These results tie in with the findings from the preceding experiment on psychological distances among consonants. The listeners judged consonants with only one feature difference to be closer in psychological distance, and these consonants were more confusable auditorily than the consonants with two feature differences. Perceptually, manner emerges as a more important factor than the position of articulation. There is a form of articulatory disorder (see Chapter 10) in which one consonant articulated in the back of the mouth, such as /k/, is likely to be replaced by another sound, such as /t/, that is produced in the same manner but at the middle or front of the mouth. According to Miller and Nicely, English texts prepared by substituting /ptk/ with /t/; /fθsʃ/ with /s/; /bdg/ with /d/; /vŏzʒ/ with /z/; and /mn/ with /n/ were intelligible over a high-quality communication system, although they sounded as though the talker had a speech defect. A ventriloquist who has to talk without moving his lips uses a similar system of articulatory substitution, sometimes so skillfully as to escape detection even by a trained acoustician.

Distinctive features thus seem useful concepts in describing speech behavior. We shall see further evidence of their usefulness when we discuss sound acquisition by children in Chapters 6 and 10. However, as Postal (1968) notes, speech perception and production involve considerations such as timing factors and coarticulation effects, which are not specified in distinctive-feature models.

Suprasegmental phonemes

Other kinds of phoneme recognized by linguists are suprasegmentals—they do not exist as inherent characteristics of any particular sound but are superimposed on consonants and vowels (segmentals) without affecting their inherent qualities. Suprasegmentals are secondary phonemes in English, serving to distinguish subtle differences in meaning or to mark phrase boundaries. They may be variations in pitch or stress, or slight breaks in the speech flow. The most widely accepted English intonation system is that of Trager and Smith (1951), which distinguishes four pitch levels, four stress levels, three terminal junctures, and one internal juncture.

Pitch and junctures Pitch is assumed to be correlated with frequency of vocal-fold vibration. However, pitch differences are perceptible in voiceless sounds, in spite of the absence of vocal-fold vibration of a fundamental frequency component. Pitch variations in tone language change the meanings of homophones, which are words with the same sounds but with different meanings. "Die" and "dye" or Chinese "mai" (buy) and "mai" (sell) are homophones. In English, pitch levels may signal slightly different meaning aspects of one word as they range from the lowest level, 1, to the highest level, 4. Compare the meaning of "mother" and "Macaulay" in the following pairs of sentences (adapted from Hockett, 1958):

²"What are we having for ³dinner | ¹ ¹Mother ¹↑ " (cannibal)

²"What are we having for ³dinner | ¹ ²Mother ²↑ " (ordinary query)

²"What are you ³reading | ¹ ¹Macaulay ¹↑ " (Macaulay is reading)

²"What are you ³reading ↓ ¹ ¹Macaulay ² ²↑ " ("Macaulay" is being read)

The three terminal junctures are: sustained pitch (|), a falling pitch (↓), and a rising pitch (↑). These three junctures provide acoustic cues that tell a listener where phrases or sentences begin or end. For example, a falling pitch signals the end of a statement; a rising pitch, the end of a question; and a sustained pitch, the end of a phase signalling that the sentence is not completed yet. An internal juncture (+) signals that two words are combined, as in "night + rate" or "Nye + trait." There is a sharp transition within such two-word combinations at the places indicated with (+). Without a juncture, there is a muddy transition as in "nitrate."

"Wait till evening and make your call at the night rate."
"That type of syndrome is called, after its discoverer, the Nye trait."
"It contains a lot of sodium nitrate."

Stress   Stress refers to the relative degree of perceived intensity with which a syllable is pronounced. Spectrograph analysis shows that stress may be carried by pitch, duration, and intensity. Even a pause can be stressed. The four Trager-Smith stress levels are: primary (′); secondary (ˆ); tertiary (ˋ); and weak (˘). A primary stress may occur on any English word. Secondary stress may occur when a stress that in an isolated word would be primary is reduced somewhat because of the presence of another primary stress in a compound or a phonemic phrase.

What makes stress phonemic in a language is not the strength with which the air is expelled from the lungs, but the existence of contrasts in the position of the intensity. Stress is phonemic if its position is not automatic, but makes a difference in meaning. Hungarian has quite strong intensity on the initial syllable of each word, but by the very fact of its being automatic, this intensity is not phonemically significant. In English, on the other hand, stress levels sometimes distinguish certain word classes from each other, as in "pérmit" or "óbject" (nouns) vs. "permít" or "objéct" (verbs). Stress patterns also can distinguish subtle meaning differences in homophones, as in "a sáfe job" (burglary) vs. "a safe jób" (a job with security). Carroll (1964) has observed an interesting function of stress in its "honorific" use in indicating that something is well-known, famous. For example, for an ordinary person the stress might be Clárk Gáble. But make him a movie star, and you have Clàrk Gáble.

The same word can signal a slightly different meaning in a sentence according to the stress patterns. Compare. "Did yóu get the book?", "Did you gét the book?", and "Did you get the bóok?" In constructing artificial speech, workers at the Bell Telephone Laboratories have found that we need far more than four stress levels to make computer speech sound natural.

Some linguists think that English, unlike some other languages, is characterized by what has been called stress-timed rhythm (Hockett, 1958). This means that it takes about the same length of time to get from one primary-stressed syllable to the next, in speaking at a given over-all tempo, whether there are no syllables between primary stresses or many. If there are none, we slow down our rate of speech slightly; if there are many, we squeeze them in fast. To diagram this, we shall use long vertical lines like the bar-lines of music before each successive primary stress, ('). The typical timing of examples can be shown as follows:

| The | wínd | bléw ùp | the stréet ↓ |
| The | wínd blèw | úp | the stréet ↓ | (Hockett, 1958, p. 53) |

This type of timing is the rhythmic basis of English verse. An iamb, for example, is a metrical foot of two syllables, the first unstressed, and the other stressed, in English verse.

Tŏ stríve, | tŏ séek, | tŏ fínd | ănd nót | tŏ yíeld

Perception of suprasegmentals We have already noted that the acoustic basis of the perception of suprasegmentals is complex. According to P. Lieberman (1965), there is not much objective, acoustic basis for their perception even by linguists. Lieberman asked two linguists familiar with the Trager-Smith system to listen to acoustic stimuli and mark suprasegmentals. To prepare the stimuli, Lieberman eliminated the words of the test sentences (such as "They have bought a new car") and reproduced the sentences as modulations of the fixed vowel /aː/, retaining the timing, the fundamental frequency, and the amplitude contours of the sentences. Figure 2–8 shows what the test sentences look like as fundamental frequency contours.

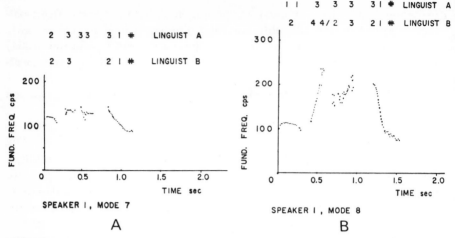

FIGURE 2–8   Two fundamental frequency contours demonstrating that the pitch levels (ranging from 1 to 4) of the Trager-Smith phonetic notation often have no direct acoustic basis. The symbol (#) marks the end of a breath group. (From Lieberman, 1965.)

Breath group   Note in the figure that the final portion of fundamental frequency contour B (from 0.6 sec to the end of the stimulus) bears the same Trager-Smith transcription as the entire contour A, though the fundamental frequencies of the two contours are markedly different. The linguists apparently responded to the suprasegmental breath groups rather than to pitch levels. A breath group is the portion of an utterance between pauses for taking breath. Short sentences (a few seconds' duration) are usually uttered in a single breath group. A normal breath group is characterized by a fundamental frequency that has an initial rise, remains steady over most of the interval, and falls in the last few tenths of a second.

Further, each linguist changed 50 percent of his assessments of the pitch levels and junctures as compared to his transcription of the complete sentence, in which, of course, he heard the words of the message. As for stress, when a linguist heard the complete speech signal he was able to transcribe four degrees of stress. However, when he heard the wordless acoustic contours only, he was unable to transcribe acoustically more than two degrees of stress—stressed or unstressed. In other words, although pitch levels and terminals were supposed to provide acoustic cues about where phrases began or ended, in fact the linguists inferred them from the words of the sentences and their knowledge of the language.

On the other hand, very young children respond to the intonation patterns of an utterance before they can understand its individual words. Perhaps they respond to very gross features such as the rising juncture of a question or the falling juncture of a statement, or the stressed, high-pitch utterance of an "angry" tone. They may rush to you when you invite them with gentle "come," but burst into crying in response to an angry "come." In production, too, a two-year-old child can ask a question using only one or two words, chiefly by the means of a rising juncture. Even dogs seem able to respond to intonation patterns, regardless of the words used.

SYLLABLE

The syllable is based on sound rather than on meaning. It is above the phoneme and below the word in the hierarchy of linguistic units. Loosely, a syllable is defined as a unit that contains one and only one vowel or diphthong (a diphthong = two vowels that merge as in "*coil*"). The most common syllable structures are consonant–vowel (CV) and consonant–vowel–consonant (CVC). The morpheme (to be discussed below) occupies a similar level in the hierarchy, but is a unit of meaning. Sometimes a word is of one syllable and one morpheme, as is "cat." "Cats," on the other hand, has one syllable, but two morphemes—"cat" + /s/. "Potato" has three syllables but one morpheme. Syllables, especially nonsense syllables such as [gɔg] or [ka], which are not morphemes in English, are used often in psycholinguistic and verbal learning experiments, because they allow good control over the characteristics of test material.

We have seen that all experiments investigating perception of consonants (such as Greenberg and Jenkins; Miller and Nicely) had to present the consonants along with a vowel, usually /a/, to produce syllables such as /ka/. Thus, these studies were in fact using syllables as units. When investigators vary consonants while holding the vowel constant, any difference in perception of these syllables may be attributed to consonant differences, although the syllable may be the unit directly perceived and the phoneme difference may be inferred from it. Individual phonemes are often influenced by surrounding phonemes, but a syllable is relatively invariant, and includes the information contained in consonant–vowel transitions that determines much of what we perceive. For example, in a V_1CV_2 utterance ("era," "ago"), information concerning the place of production of the consonant is provided in part by the directions of the formant transitions from V_1 to C and from C to V_2; manner of articulation and voicing may be signaled by the rate of change of these formant transitions, as well as by the properties of the signal in the central portion of the utterance. Thus, data that contribute to an identification of the consonant may extend over an interval from the middle of V_1 to the middle of V_2 (Öhman, 1966).

A model for speech perception

There are a number of models of speech perception (as in Neisser, 1967; Stevens and House, 1970). We have already discussed one, namely the motor theory. All these models, although they may differ in detail, assume an active listener. The listener uses his knowledge about linguistic units and rules. Further, some models incorporate a close tie between the processes of speech production and perception.

In many models the first stage of perception is peripheral analysis, during which incoming acoustic stimuli are subjected to rough, perhaps passive, preliminary phonetic processing. According to Stevens and House (1970), through peripheral processing the acoustic (speech) signal yields auditory patterns that may be described as strings of attributes.

In some cases, the auditory patterns provide a direct indication of the features— the acoustic attribute bears a one-to-one relation to the linguistic feature. For example, the presence of a stop consonant is signaled by an interval of low acoustic energy followed by a rapid rise in the intensity; a voiced sound is characterized by periodicities in the signal. In other cases, however, particularly when the sound indicates the place of articulation for a consonant, there is no invariant acoustic attribute to identify the phonetic feature. The acoustic attribute that provides cues for the feature depends upon the context of other features (p. 51).

Since a number of such attributes characterize each phoneme, several attributes must be processed in parallel. Humans seem to develop early a speech processor for much of the peripheral analysis of speech.

Are linguistic units identified at the next stage? If so, what are the perceptual units? We have seen that each linguistic unit—phoneme, syllable, word, and so on—is potentially useful as a perceptual unit. However, under normal circumstances the speech stream is not likely to be perceived phoneme by phoneme. Auditory perception of each phoneme is too much influenced by phonetic and semantic contexts. Phonetically, a syllable is a more stable unit than a phoneme. But a syllable is not a meaning-based unit, and the whole object of speech perception is to get semantic content. Thus, after the peripheral analysis, the received syllables may have to be stored in memory until enough of them have been heard to form a syntactic unit, such as a phrase, which usually has some relatively coherent meaning. Heard speech, if it consists of sentences, may often be processed phrase by phrase.

In the process of identifying speech segments and grouping them into appropriate processing units, the listener may constantly hypothesize what he must have heard, and predict what he will be hearing. Prediction is possible because he has considerable knowledge about linguistic units and rules, as well as the meaning of the speech and its relation to real events. This final stage of speech processing will be discussed further in Chapters 4 and 5.

If a model incorporates a close tie between speech production and perception, it may also postulate another stage. The listener makes a hypothesis concerning the message intended by the talker, and then proceeds to generate this message internally, using the same internal generative rules and the same framework of linguistic units that would be invoked if he were to operate as a talker rather than as a listener. Halle and Stevens (1959) used the term "analysis by synthesis" to describe such a process.

Analysis-by-synthesis models have been strongly supported for general perception, especially by Neisser (1967), but they seem scarcely credible for understanding speech. The models must predict that a listener is able to understand only what he could produce. Yet we know that children can understand phonemes and sentences that are far more complex than those they can freely produce. Further, in learning foreign languages, it is possible to develop skills selectively either in reception (reading or listening) or in expression (writing and speaking). These observations seem incompatible with analysis-by-synthesis models of speech perception.

MORPHEME AND WORD

Morpheme

The morpheme is a linguistic unit between the phoneme and the word, and is the minimal unit of grammatical analysis. It may be a word or a part of a word. How to identify a morpheme can be best explained by examples. In the word "un-friend-ly," *un, friend,* and *ly* are each a morpheme. To find out whether a speech segment is a morpheme or not, ask: (1) Does the portion recur with a similar meaning in various utterances? *Un-* can recur in words like "unfit," "unusual"; *-ly* in words like "manly," "lovely"; *friend* in words like "friendless." (2) Can the form be broken into smaller meaningful pieces? "Friendly" can be broken into two morphemes, *friend* and *ly,* but neither *friend* nor *ly* can be further broken into smaller pieces without losing its meaning. The morpheme is a meaning-based unit, as opposed to the syllable, which is a sound-based unit.

If a morpheme can stand alone, as can "friend," it is a free morpheme; otherwise it is a bound morpheme. *Un-, -ly,* and plural morphemes *-s* or *-es* are bound morphemes, as they exist only bound to free morphemes.

Bound morphemes are not favorite speech units in psycholinguistic experiments, perhaps because they are not familiar to ordinary people as units. Morphology, the use of inflectional endings such as *-s* in books, Jim's, or eats, is of interest to psycholinguistics, and is discussed in Chapters 6 (in children) and 11 (in aphasics). Free morphemes are more usually considered as words, and are used extensively in psycholinguistic experiments.

Word

Definition The word as a linguistic unit is above the morpheme and below the phrase or the sentence. Linguists seem to have a hard time defining "word" in a way that satisfies everyone. One well-known definition of "word" runs as follows: "A word may be defined as the union of particular meaning with a particular complex of sounds, capable of a particular grammatical employment." An entire phrase, "the new book," satisfies the above definition. Then add, "the smallest segment of utterances that fulfills the three conditions" to the definition. A bound morpheme, *un-*, can satisfy the new expanded definition. The problem can be solved by adding "a minimum free form" to the already complicated definition.

Lyons (1968) resolves the linguists' difficulty in defining words with the following observation: one of the characteristics of the word is that it tends to be internally stable (in terms of the order of the compound morphemes; for example, "boy-s" but not *"s-boy"), but positionally mobile (permutable with other words in the same sentence; note the position of "boy-s" in the following three sentences).

The-*boy*-*s*-walked-ed-slow-ly-up-the-hill.
2nd
Slow-ly-the-*boy*-*s*-walk-ed-up-the-hill.
3rd
Up-the-hill-slow-ly-walk-ed-the-*boy*-*s*.
7th

Under all permutations certain pairs (such as "boy-s" or "walk-ed") or triples of morphemes will behave as "blocks," always occurring not only together, but also in the same order relative to one another. This same binding effect determines what portion of our visual world we choose to call "objects."

Whatever the linguistic definition of "word" may be, speakers of a language are usually aware of a word as a unit, and use it so. They can pause between words, if required, and can count the number of words in a sentence. In Czech, each word is stressed on the first syllable. In some writing systems, such as English, writers leave spaces between words. In Chinese writing, one character is usually a word.

In English, a word can consist of from one morpheme ("cat") to about four ("un-gentle-man-ly"). A rare six-morpheme English word is "anti-dis-establish-ment-arian-ism." Word overshadows morpheme as a unit in psycholinguistic experiments, since words as units of speech are relatively independent, familiar, and unambiguous to ordinary speakers.

Word classes Words have been classified into parts of speech at least since ancient Greek days. The eight classic parts are: noun, pronoun, adjective, verb, adverb, preposition, article, and conjunction. This traditional division into eight parts of speech has proved unsatisfactory for a number of reasons. (1) Inconsistencies exist in criteria of classification. (2) The number of parts, eight, is not completely agreed upon. (3) Although this classification is roughly suitable for describing many Indo-European languages, it is not easily adapted for some other languages, such as Hopi, an Amerindian language spoken in the southwestern United States. We shall discuss the first inadequacy in some detail, since it is important in the general study of language. Fries (1952) points out that ordinarily a noun is defined as the "name of a person, place, or thing," but "blue," the name of a color, in "blue tie" is classified as an adjective. An adjective is a word that modifies a noun or a pronoun. Then, "boy's" in "the boy's hat" or "his" in "his hat" should be adjectives, but they are not so classified. A pronoun is a word used instead of a noun. Which of the following words are pronouns?

"John and James
"The undersigned
"The Chinese
"Two
"These   } brought their letters of recommendation."
"They
  .
  .
  .

We have seen that the basis of the definition of some classes is lexical meaning; function in the sentence for others; and formal characteristics for still others (as in "It is fun/funny"). Fries proposes that words should be classified according to one set of criteria that can be consistently applied, namely the positions that words occupy in sentences. First of all, instead of the traditional names, Fries suggests the use of neutral numbers and letters like Class 1, 2, 3, and 4, and Group A, B, and so on. The words that occupy the underlined positions in the following two sentences belong to Class 1.

Frame A: "(The) food(s) was/were good."
Frame B: "The clerk remembered the tax."

The words that fit into the underlined positions in Frames C, D, and E belong to Classes 1, 2, 3, and 4, as indicated.

Frame C: "(The) good man is sweet lately."
              3   1   2   3   4
Frame D: "(The) man remembered (the) lady fondly."
                1   2   3   4
Frame E: "(The) man went down rapidly."
                1   2   4   4

All the words that do not belong to Classes 1, 2, 3, and 4 belong to Groups A to O. Group A, for example, includes any word that occupies the underlined position in the sentence: "The food was good." "John's," "my," "that," "some," and so on should belong to this group. Other words in Groups B to O include such words as "not," "very," "but," "oh," "yes," "although," "at," and "can." Sometimes the position in the sentence is not an adequate criterion, and formal contrast has to be used, as in: "This is fun" and "This is funny."
                                                                    3   4

The merit of Fries's proposal is now widely recognized, but few psycholinguists or ordinary speakers use his classification system. That is to say, few people will call "man" a "Class 1 word" instead of the usual "noun." Fries uses numbers and letters for designating different word classes so that we do not get misled by traditional descriptive names. But we seem to be lost without the descriptive names, which give us useful and, most of the time, correct information about the class of a word. The traditional eight parts of speech have usually been adequate in talking about Indo-European languages. If we make some modifications, we may use the traditional classification in talking about some non-Indo-European languages as well. For example, in talking about Japanese or Korean, we may have to add a new part of speech, namely postposition, and drop articles and prepositions. Furthermore, not even Fries's system has one consistent criterion for classifying words; he uses position of word in a sentence for most of the words, but sometimes uses formal characteristics of words.

Classifying words according to the positions they occupy in sentences is not always satisfactory. Fries classifies "John's" in "John's food was good" as a Group A word, considering it same as "the." But "the" belongs to a closed system (that is, we have only two articles, "the" and "a/an"), whereas proper names like "John" belong to an open system; we can go on forever inventing new names. Fries divides pronouns into two subgroups. One group fits into the position occupied by his Class 1 words, as in "Food (it, he) is good." Another subgroup of pronouns belongs to Group A words because they can occupy the same position as that occupied by "the," as in

"*The* (*my, his, its*) food is good." Both subgroups of pronouns belong to closed systems, and consequently both share many characteristics of other function words discussed below.

Content and function words   Words of Classes 1, 2, 3, and 4 (they are, if I may sneakily replace them with traditional names, nouns, verbs, adjectives, and adverbs, respectively) are content words. They have semantic content, and make reference to the world of experience. The number of content words is vast, making up the bulk of our vocabulary. This is an open class—new words are continually being added, and old words continually dropping out through disuse. Think of lately added words—"hippy," "megadeath," "countdown," and so on. But nobody notices and mourns the words that have recently dropped out, such as "burke," "gree," "smutch."

Function words include all those words that do not belong to the four content-word classes. Their traditional names would be: preposition, article, conjunction, and pronoun. Function words do not have specific semantic contents, but mark grammatical relations among content words in a sentence. Function words form a closed system—there is a small, fixed number of function words in English, and no new pronoun, preposition, conjunction, or article has been adopted into English in at least the last 100 years.

The dichotomy between content and function words is frequently used in experiments by psycholinguists. Content and function words influence speech behavior in different ways. For example, the 10 most frequently used spoken English words are "I, he, it, you, the, a, to, of, and, in." In Fries's system, the first four pronouns should be Class 1 words and belong to content words, because they occur in the slots where nouns would occur in a sentence. I prefer to consider them as function words, because their characteristics are similar to other function words. Note that the 10 words are all very short, and many of them start with vowels. In German, too, the most frequently used words are such function words.

Another characteristic of function words, perhaps derived from the above characteristics, is that they carry little information, and can be omitted in speech without affecting the main message. We deliberately omit function words to save money when we compose a telegram: "Car disabled; lost wallet; send money Amex Paris" omits "my, has, been, and, I, have, my, to, me, at, the, in," all function words. Children just beginning to acquire syntax often omit function words to produce so-called "telegraphic speech." An example is "baby high chair," a typical two-year-old's utterance which could mean "*The* baby *is in the* high chair." A certain type of aphasic (people who have a speech disorder due to brain damage; see Chapter 11) omits function words. So do foreigners with limited skill in English.

Because of its familiarity, because of its importance in understanding speech behavior in general, and because of its interesting and complex nature, the topic of "word" has generated a large number of experiments in psycholinguistics and in verbal learning, and merits another chapter to itself.

SUMMARY AND CONCLUSIONS

Speech sounds form the smallest units of language. To study their articulation, we examined speech organs and their functions. Consonants involve obstruction of the vocal tract, while vowels do not. Consonants are further differentiated in terms of the position and manner of the obstruction.

We can study some of the acoustic properties of speech sounds by the use of spectrograms, which show the energy distributions in different frequency bands as a function of time. The frequency regions with most energy are called formants. The relative positions of the lowest two formant peaks serve as acoustic cues for differentiating vowels, and the patterns of formant transition differentiate some consonants.

The phoneme designates a class of similar speech sounds that speakers of a given language regard as if they were the same. Liberman's motor theory says that articulation mediates between acoustic stimuli and their auditory perception; this is why we perceive consonants categorically even though each consonant, acoustically, includes a range of similar sounds. There is evidence for and against the motor theory, but the evidence against it seems to be more convincing on balance. Liberman and associates subsequently modified the motor theory. They now hypothesize that categorical perception of consonants is one result of the operation of a species-specific speech processor. The speech-sound processor decodes physically indeterminant acoustic stimuli—consonants—into a phonetic message.

English has about 38 phonemes—24 consonants and 14 vowels. We use the phoneme as a unit in alphabets, in alliterations, and so on. There is a controversy as to whether phonemes are perceived subsequent to syllables, and syllables in turn subsequent to words.

Phonemes of any language can be analyzed into a handful of distinctive features, such as voiced–voiceless, based on articulatory features. A distinctive feature seems to be a singular entity perceptually. The number of binary feature oppositions separating phonemes is a useful index of perceptual distances among consonants.

English has suprasegmental phonemes such as pitch, stress, and juncture. They are secondary phonemes in English; they signal subtle differences in meaning and emotional tones, and mark constituent boundaries. The objective acoustic bases for suprasegmentals are complex.

A syllable is a sound-based unit, and usually consists of a consonant and a vowel.

A simple speech perception model has been proposed to account for how a listener extracts meaning out of the speech stream. He perceives features, identifies speech segments, and groups them into appropriate processing units, using his linguistic and extralinguistic knowledge.

A morpheme is the smallest unit with meaning.

Above syllable and morpheme comes the word as a unit. The word is a familiar unit but is hard to define. Words have traditionally been classed into eight parts of speech on a number of criteria. Fries's attempt at using one main criterion—the positions words occupy in sentences—has not been very successful. However, his dichotomy of words into content words (having referents) and function words (indicating relationship of content words) is useful. Content and function words differ in a number of ways. To cite one important difference, content words form an open system, while function words form a closed system with a limited number of members. This difference affects our speech processing, notably our ability to predict deleted words in a sentence.

There will be another chapter on the word.

3

Words—Psychological Investigation
In Quest of the Meaning of Word Meaning

Nothing, surely is more alive than a word.

J. Donald Adams (b. 1891)

There are two separable but related purposes for this chapter. The first is to acquaint readers with the uses of words as test material, and with word-based research tools useful for psycholinguistic experiments. Word association tests and the semantic differential scale, in particular, will appear in subsequent chapters as experimental tools. The second is to probe into what "word meaning" means. The meaning of word meaning is elusive, and we shall approach it from many angles, hoping to capture some of its varied aspects, if not its essence.

Diverse characteristics of words

The word is a unit of verbal behavior; it may be a unit of thinking or memory as well, but in none of these cases is it the only unit. The word also has many convenient features as a unit for psycholinguists. When a word is the stimulus in experiments with English-speaking subjects, speaker and subject are already aware of it as a unit and require no specific training. Furthermore, experimenters can easily count and classify words as response units. The word has long been one of the favorite units of investigation for psychologists, perhaps ever since psychology became an independent discipline about a century ago. The eminent English scientist Sir Francis Galton used the word as a unit about 90 years ago in his first attempt at word association to reveal his own thought processes, which he was too embarrassed to publish (1879–1880).

If words are to be extensively used as units in psychological experiments, we have first to learn about their various characteristics. Consequently, words, English words in particular, have been rated and scaled *ad nauseam*—they have been rated for vividness, definability, imagery, familiarity, pronounceability, meaningfulness, concreteness–abstractness, and what-have-you. Some of these word characteristics are highly interrelated; words that are easy to define tend to have good imagery, are concrete, are meaningful, are familiar, and are easy to pronounce, as Table 3–1 shows.

TABLE 3–1   Intercorrelations between Characteristics of Words

	I	C	m	F	P	TLF
D	0.703	0.640	0.522	0.495	0.402	0.279
I		0.816	0.561	0.202	0.308	0.164
C			0.372	−0.027	0.140	0.040
m				0.436	0.342	0.256
F					0.613	0.651
P						0.540

Definability; Imagery; Concreteness; Meaningfulness; Familiarity; Pronounceability; TLF = Thorndike–Lorge Frequency. Slightly rearranged from O'Neill, 1972.

On the other hand, concreteness does not seem to be highly correlated with familiarity, frequency of use, or pronounceability.

In Table 3–1, the entries are correlation coefficients (rs). A correlation coefficient expresses a relation between two sets of scores, and can range from 0 to ± 1.00. If r is 0, one set of scores does not at all predict another set of scores; if r is ± 1.00, one set of scores predicts another set perfectly, without an error. In +1.00, a high score in one test predicts a high score in another test, while in −1.00, a high score in one test predicts a low score in another test.

Ratings of different word characteristics are available as *normative* (or *standard*) *estimates*. Psychologists collect responses to different types of word from large groups of people to compile them. Some of the more important ones are scales from Spreen and Schulz (1966) and Paivio, Yuille, and Madigan (1968) on concreteness–abstractness; Kent and Rosanoff (1910) and Russell and Jenkins (1954) on word association; Noble and Parker (1960) and Noble (1961) on meaningfulness; Jenkins, Russell, and Suci (1958) on semantic differential ratings; Thorndike and Lorge (1944) and Howes (1966) on word frequency. These normative estimates are extremely useful when we want to prepare test material using words with particular characteristics. In this chapter we shall be talking about all these characteristics of words. Word frequency will be discussed in Chapter 5, where we consider the statistical structure of language.

Concrete and abstract words

Consider the words "soul" and "pencil." Which is abstract and which concrete? What is the difference between these two words? Concrete words such as "pencil" refer to specific objects and events that can be seen, touched, smelled, tasted, or heard—in short, sensed. We can point to whatever a concrete word refers to, and thus concrete words presumably derive their meanings mainly through association with concrete objects and events. Abstract words such as "soul," on the other hand, cannot refer to specific objects and events. They derive their meanings through association with other words. Concreteness or abstractness is never absolute, however; it is a matter of degree.

English speakers, and presumably speakers of other languages as well, can rate words according to their degrees of abstractness and concreteness. In one study (Spreen and Schulz, 1966) subjects rated 329 very frequently used English nouns on a seven-point scale. Here are six words from the study to illustrate the range of concreteness that words can have. The least concrete word scored 1, and the most concrete 7. "Courage" scored 1.41; "devil," 2.68; "burden," 3.18; "household," 4.30; "cattle," 5.39; and "telephone," 6.9. Such ratings are very reliable—similar scores occur over and over in repeated ratings with different groups of subjects.

When we distinguish between concrete and abstract words, we are really dealing with the meanings of the words. We shall discuss one aspect of meaning here.

Word meaning as an image

The idea that word meaning is an image of the object has a long history. But we shall start our discussion with the psychologist Titchener (1909), who suggested that the word "dog" has meaning because the perception of the word evokes the image of a dog. The word that is heard or read has meaning because it evokes in the receiver a "corresponding" image. The questions that come to mind at once are: Can everybody invoke images for most words? If somebody cannot conjure up images for some words, are they devoid of meaning for him? Apparently for Titchener no word, however abstract, failed to evoke an image. The image of the word "meaning," for instance, was the "blue-gray tip of a kind of scoop which has a bit of yellow about it (probably a part of the handle) and which is just digging into a dark mass of what appears to be plastic material" (p. 19). He suspected the origin of this image to be in the numerous injunctions delivered to him in his youth to "dig out the meaning" of Latin and Greek phrases.

Titchener was lucky to have such a vivid image of "meaning"; not many other people will have an image of "meaning" or of many other words. Titchener's life work was based on imagery, perhaps because he himself imaged so vividly. Titchener did not consider different types of words. In most people some words evoke images well, but others do not. Image-evoking words are generally concrete. Just try to conjure up an image for "soul" and then for "pencil." According to Paivio and associates (1968), concrete nouns are particularly effective stimuli for the arousal of sensory images because of their consistent associations with specific objects. They found a high positive correlation between concreteness and imagery scores ($r = .88$). In Table 3–1 imagery and concreteness show a similar high correlation.

Images could function as mediators of recall in verbal learning. In other words, a stimulus evokes an image, which in turn suggests a response word. Concrete words are easier to recall, learn, or recognize, and evoke more associations than do abstract words. Paivio (1970) points out that imagery in such verbal tasks is functionally linked to stimulus or task concreteness rather than to response concreteness. Further, imagery is specialized for the processing of spatial information, and not for the verbal system. The verbal system is characterized more by its capacity for sequential processing. For example, the pair "suger–lake" may evoke a compound image, such as a lump of sugar dissolving in a lake, and is learned more easily than pairs of nonsense syllables or, presumably, pairs of abstract words. In one experiment that compared concrete and abstract words in verbal tasks, Gorman (1961) found that for both common and seldom-used words, concrete words were recognized better than abstract words.

We should expect a concrete noun such as "pencil" to evoke a specific image very quickly in most people, while an abstract word such as "love" would not be so quick to evoke an image. For "love," we may have to choose among many possible images, such as an image of lovers kissing, of a mother hugging her baby, of God looking after us, and so on.

The meanings and images of concrete words seem to be stable and uniform for different speakers of one language as well as for speakers of different languages. Perhaps because of this, concrete words evoke the same words more often than do abstract words in both inter- and intralanguage word association tests. We shall examine one type of cross-language or interlanguage comparison of word association later in this chapter. In Chapter 7, we shall discuss another type of interlanguage word association in which bilingual speakers respond in, say, Spanish to an English stimulus word.

How are images acquired? According to Staats (1968) sensory responses evoked by an object transfer to verbal stimuli occurring in contiguity with the object. Images are conditioned sensory responses for which words function as conditioned stimuli.

Even though possibly all word meanings may in the end be related to a hierarchy of images, the concept of meaning cannot be very well elucidated by reference to images, except perhaps for some few very concrete words. Images are also hard to investigate directly. We shall search for other ways of looking at word meaning after considering some tests that use words.

WORD ASSOCIATION TEST (WAT)

The first word-based research tool we discuss is the word association test (WAT). The basic technique of WAT is very simple: provide subjects with a stimulus word such as "table" and ask them to think of the first word that comes to their minds. We examine the types and frequencies of response words, and sometimes the time subjects take to think of response words.

Word associations reveal verbal habits, word memory structure, thought processes, and sometimes even the emotional state of a person. Furthermore, once we know the typical association patterns of particular words, we can take them into consideration in choosing test words for some verbal experiments. For example, it is much harder to learn pairs of words selected at random ("letter–curtain"; "mutton–paper") than it is to learn pairs of words that are associates ("table–chair"; "man–woman"). In recalling test words, subjects may even include a word that was not in the list of words given to them, if it is strongly associated with the words appearing in the list. Deese (1964) had subjects read and then attempt to recall the following list of words: "bed, rest, awake, tired, dream, wake, night, eat, comfort, sound, slumber, snore." About half the subjects included the word "sleep" in their "recalled" list of words.

We also ponder about why a particular response word is given to a particular stimulus word—why is "chair" given frequently as a response to "table"? Let us start with some basic findings of WATs.

Basic findings of WATs

Characteristic response patterns In one of the earliest WATs, the German linguist-psychologist team Thumb and Marbe (1901) used eight subjects and 60 words of different types. They found the following general trends in response patterns: (1) Words of one type evoked a response of the same type. For example, words of family relation led to response words of another family relation ("brother" led to "sister"; a noun led to another noun, and so on). (2) More frequently preferred associations occurred more rapidly than less preferred ones. The relation between frequency of preferred response and response time is known as *Marbe's Law*, and is shown in Figure 3–1. (3) A given stimulus word often produced an identical response in different subjects. These three findings by Thumb and Marbe have been found time and again in different WATs, and are stable characteristics of word association response.

Kent and Rosanoff (1910) used 1,000 subjects and 100 stimulus words in the first large-scale WAT. They established a set of norms that has been of great use to this day, not only in English but in other languages as well. Table 3–2 lists six different WATs involving different sets of subjects at different times over a half century, each using the original 100 Kent–Rosanoff stimulus words.

Table 3–2 shows the primary response (the most frequently given response word), secondary (the second most frequent), and tertiary response words to "table" in the six studies. It shows that common responses ("chair" to "table") increased in percentage over the years. A list of all response words would reveal that idiosyncratic responses (such as "mesa," which was given to "table" by 1 of 1,008 subjects) became more rare. Concrete responses increased and abstract responses decreased. Jenkins and Russell (1952) attribute these new trends toward uniformity and concreteness to the influ-

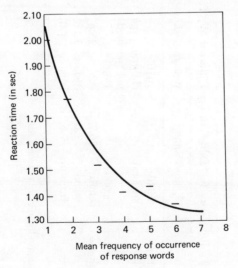

FIGURE 3–1   Response time for association as a function of the frequency of occurrence. Frequently occurring responses are given fast. (Adapted from Thumb and Marbe, 1901.)

TABLE 3–2 Responses to "Table" in Six Different WATs

	Kent–Rosanoff	Woodrow–Lowell	O'Conner	Russell–Jenkins	Rosenzweig	Entwisle
Year of publication	1910	1916	1928	1954	1957	1966
Type of subject	general	children (age not specified)	men from industry	Minnesota college students	French adults	children in first grade
Number of subjects	1,000	1,000	1,000	1,008	288	280
Primary response	chair 26.7	eat 35.8	chair 33.3	chair 84.0	chaise 53.4	chair 36.1
Secondary	wood 7.6	dishes 12.6	leg 11.6	food 4.1		eat 6.4
Tertiary	furniture 7.5	legs 7.0	wood 8.4	desk 2.1		sit 2.9

The response figures are percentages.

ence of mass media, of advertising, and of the standardization of school instruction. We are in the "group-think" age!

Stimulus words with different characteristics, such as abstract–concrete, evoke different patterns of response. Those given by 1,008 college students to the words "table" (frequently used concrete word) and "trouble" (frequently used abstract word) are shown in Figure 3–2.

We see that 83.3 percent of all 1,008 subjects in the Russell–Jenkins (1954) study gave the primary response "chair" to the stimulus "table." For "trouble," on the other hand, only 8.8 percent gave the primary response "bad," leaving 91.2 percent of subjects to give less probable responses. For the secondary response, 41 subjects who said "food" for "table" represented 34 percent of all subjects who had not said "chair," whereas 49 subjects who said "shooter" for "trouble" represented only 5.3 percent of those who had not said "bad." This pattern holds for all rank levels of responses. For example, the tenth most likely response to "table" was given by 6.5 percent of those who had not given the nine most probable responses, but the tenth

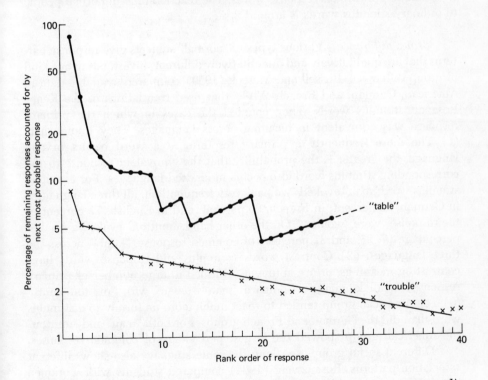

FIGURE 3–2 Word association responses to "table" (frequent, concrete word) and "trouble" (frequent, abstract word). (Based on data by Russell and Jenkins, 1954.)

most likely response to "trouble" was given by only 2.9 percent of those eligible. In short, the response set to "table" is more compact than that to "trouble" at all levels.

WATs can reveal the emotional state of a person. The Swiss psychologist Jung (1918) pioneered the use of word association in clinical diagnosis. He used emotionally loaded stimulus words to probe into patients' repressed images, wishes, or emotions. Both the time it takes for a person to produce a response word and the type of response word are supposed to reflect his emotional state. Here is an illustrative case. A 32-year-old surgeon, married and childless, with severe anxiety, who was being seen at the Menninger Clinic, responded to "breast" with "mammary gland," taking 4 min 5 sec. His diagnosticians' comment on this response was "neurotic intellectualizing." Out of 60 stimulus words only 12 elicited responses requiring specific comment (Rapaport, Gill, and Schafer, 1946). Note that in the clinical uses of WAT, we focus our attention on deviant rather than on standard or common responses (as we had been doing earlier). This patient took an unusually long time to produce his response words. The reaction time in normal people to ordinary stimulus words is around 2 sec.

Group difference   Various types of "normal" subjects give response patterns that are qualitatively and quantitatively different. Investigating one kind of group difference, Russell and Meseck (1959) compared available data in American, German, and French WATs that used translations of the Kent–Rosanoff stimulus words. They counted the cases in which the primary response was equivalent in meaning across languages. They found that: (1) The more frequently a primary response to a word occurs in one language, the greater is the probability that the equivalent response to the corresponding stimulus word also occurs in kindred languages. For example, stimulus word "man" evoked "woman" very frequently in all three languages: in German, 52 percent; in French, 66 percent; and in English, 77 percent of the responses were "woman." On the other hand, "mutton" evoked a smaller percentage (7, 25, and 37 percent) of common response, "lamb," across the three languages. (2) Contrast words (stimulus and response words have contrasting meanings, or are antonyms) formed a large number of primary responses in all languages. Compare "man–woman" with "mutton–lamb." (3) The American group tended to react much more uniformly to a stimulus word than did the German and French groups. For both "man" and "mutton" the American group showed the largest percentage of common responses.

Different social groups speaking the same language also show different association patterns. Rosenzweig (1964) compared students with workmen in two language communities, America and France. He found that American workmen and students showed many more responses in common than did French workmen and students. French workers were dissimilar to any other group in that they rarely responded to adjectives with adjectives. Rosenzweig points out that class differences between workmen and students are greater in France than in the USA, and differences in verbal habits are correspondingly larger.

Do men and women give different patterns of associations? Palermo and Jenkins (1965) found that female college students (1) give fewer different responses to each stimulus; (2) are more likely than male students to respond with one of the four most frequent responses to a stimulus; and (3) tend to give fewer *superordinate responses* (a superordinate response to "table" would be "furniture," the name of a class to which "table" belongs). Cramer (1968), after reviewing many studies on this topic, concludes that at every age female subjects may be characterized as more stereotyped.

To summarize group differences up to this point, women give more common responses than men, or women > men; English speakers in the USA > French or German speakers; American students > American workmen > French students > French workmen; 1952 > 1910. Is the giving of common responses related to verbal skills? This question is hard to answer from the above pattern. What we can say is that conformity-minded people or people who are exposed to uniform mass media are likely to show more common responses, or less richness, in their response patterns. All groups may be moving toward giving more common responses over the years.

Paradigmatic and syntagmatic relations

Language involves two basic, complementary relations: syntagmatic and paradigmatic. Linguistic elements are in a paradigmatic relationship if one element can substitute for the other in a given context, and in a syntagmatic relationship if one can relate directly to the other in a single context.

$$\begin{Bmatrix} my \\ the \\ his \\ that \end{Bmatrix} \quad \begin{Bmatrix} new \\ old \\ big \\ ugly \end{Bmatrix} \quad \begin{Bmatrix} car \\ book \\ pen \\ bag \end{Bmatrix}$$

In the above example, the phrase "my new car" consists of three elements (words). Any of the words listed in the same columns could substitute for them to make another equally valid phrase, such as "the new bag." Hence, "car" stands in a paradigmatic relation with "book," "pen," and "bag," because each of these words can occur in the context (or paradigm) "my new ——." "Car" stands in a syntagmatic relation with "my" and "new," because they combine to form the noun phrase "my new car."

Paradigmatic and syntagmatic relationships operate not only among words but among phonemes. The phoneme /b/ stands in a paradigmatic relationship with /p/ and /s/, because each of these phonemes can occur in the context /-et/, as in "bet" and "set," while the combination of /b/ and /-et/ to form /bet/ demonstrates a syntagmatic relationship.

Adults and children show an interesting difference in association patterns. Adults typically respond to a noun with another noun, to an adjective with another adjective; they give primarily *paradigmatic responses*. Children, on the other hand, respond to "soft" (adjective) with "pillow" (noun) —a word that follows the stimulus in a sentence, and usually belongs to another grammatical class. They tend to give *syntagmatic responses*. Cramer (1968) summarizes the findings of several WATs with children: syntagmatic responses decrease while paradigmatic responses increase from age 5 to college age. The change from primarily syntagmatic to primarily paradigmatic responses occurs between ages 6 and 8, while in 1910 such a change occurred between ages 9 and 12. Test-taking practice, linguistic sophistication through mass-media, and urbanization may be responsible for the modern trend.

How do paradigmatic responses develop? According to the father of word association, Galton, frequently evoked responses are words that have frequently been placed into contiguity with their stimuli. This theory explains syntagmatic responses but not paradigmatic responses. Paradigmatic responses are words from the same grammatical class; they are rarely placed into contiguity with stimuli but can replace the stimuli in speech.

Ervin (1963) tried to save the contiguity theory in explaining paradigmatic responses by pointing out that words in the same grammatical class can be placed into contiguity when a listener anticipates what he will hear next. Contiguity will occur when the listener's anticipations are *wrong*. If he hears "the hole is too . . . ," and anticipates "shallow," but hears "deep," the two adjectives will be placed into contiguity.

Ervin's explanation can be put in a testable hypothesis: the frequency of any particular paradigmatic response will depend on the number of times it has been erroneously anticipated for its stimulus. McNeill (1966a) tested the hypothesis by requiring his subjects to make overt anticipations of a given set of nonsense syllables to fit in a given set of sentence frames. In a subsequent WAT, McNeill did not find that the frequency of the subjects' overt anticipations was correlated with the frequency of their paradigmatic responses.

The concept of *semantic markers* (Katz and Fodor, 1963) might be useful in our effort to explain the origin of paradigmatic responses. For the time being, think of semantic markers as the components into which the sense of a word can be analyzed. For example, "man" has semantic markers (living), (human), (adult), and (male). A common paradigmatic response forms a minimal contrast with the stimulus—a shift in one marker causes the change of the word meaning. Thus when "man" is a stimulus, "woman" is often given as a response. "Man" and "woman" are both (living), (human), (adult), but differ on one semantic marker, (sex). "Man" and "woman" also share such syntactic features as [noun, count noun, singular].

According to McNeill, young children give relatively few paradigmatic responses because they have incomplete lists of semantic markers. If children do not know a sizable number of a word's markers and features, the set of words that minimally contrast with the stimulus may be so large as to include words in different grammatical classes. McNeill's notion seems to explain the finding that children's responses are often in grammatical classes different from stimuli, but it does not explain why the responses are the kinds of word that follow the stimuli in speech.

M. M. Taylor (private communication) has suggested a plausible explanation of adults' paradigmatic responses and children's syntagmatic responses. In adults a stimulus word weakly evokes many contextual associates, or images, in the first stage. All of these associates in turn may evoke response words in a second stage, and a few of these second-stage are actually evoked by many of the first-stage associates. The few will tend to be paradigmatically related to the stimulus word, since paradigmatically related words tend to occur in similar contexts. Among them the most likely response will be the one that most often occurs in almost the same context as the stimulus. Antonym pairs are good examples.

In children, the stimulus word evokes the context, but here association stops; one of the first-stage associates is given as a response. The children have not yet learned that there are other words that can also occur in that context. Word association is a two-stage event in adults and a one-stage event in children, as depicted in Figure 3–3.

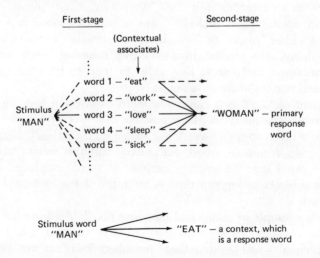

FIGURE 3–3   The underlying processes of word association. *Top:* Two-stage process in adults. *Bottom:* Single-stage process in children. (Suggested by M. M. Taylor.)

Ervin, McNeill, and M. M. Taylor are all emphasizing the role of contexts. Young children do not have many semantic markers and syntactic features, and hence do not give many paradigmatic associations. Their association patterns reveal their own experiences with words in limited contexts. For example, their syntagmatic associations seem to reflect the frequency of two-word sequences in the language, particularly in samples of language to which young children are likely to be exposed. Furthermore, the contexts in which words are first or only occasionally experienced would vary from child to child. Hence, syntagmatic associates are more varied than paradigmatic ones (Deese, 1965).

Associative meaning and meaningfulness

The sum total of the words a given person thinks of, or a whole group of people thinks of, in response to a given stimulus word can be considered as the associative meaning of that word. Thus, associative meaning, which is one aspect of word meaning, is the connection of a word to other words that constitute its verbal environment. Another aspect of the meaning of a word is its connection with extralinguistic behavioral or environmental events.

If there is associative meaning, there can also be similarity of associative meaning. Two words are similar to the degree that they share common associates. Deese (1962) noted that two stimulus words, although they fail to evoke each other as responses, can have a number of responses in common. "Piano" and "symphony" are intuitively related, but "piano" does not evoke "symphony" as an associate, nor does "symphony" elicit "piano." But "note, song, sound, noise, music, orchestra" are responses evoked in varying frequencies by either "piano" or "symphony" as stimulus words. Thus "piano" and "symphony" are similar in associative meaning. Such associatively similar words and the objects they refer to tend to be used in the same linguistic and nonlinguistic environments.

A variant of WAT is a *continued word association* test, in which the subject produces as many words as possible in a given time, say, 60 sec, in response to a given stimulus word. For example, the subject might produce "chair, top, leg, furniture, wood, eat" to the stimulus word "table." Noble (1952) suggested that the average number of words produced by a large number of subjects in a given time is an index of the *meaningfulness* (m) of that word.

Here is a sample of nouns and nonsense disyllables in order of increasing m values. "Gojey" (0.99); "quipson" (1.26); "rostrum" (2.73); "fatigue" (5.33); "kitchen" (9.61). Note that "meaningfulness" is not the same as meaning: m values do not tell us what a word means. The responses might reveal something about what a word means, but m values are calculated merely by counting the number of responses. It might sound paradoxical to talk about the meaningfulness of nonsense syllables, but they often have a certain degree (usually low) of meaningfulness, perhaps because their syllables occur in real words.

How does the meaningfulness of a word develop? Since meaningfulness is an index of the variety (more correctly, frequency) of experiences represented in the concept, the more varied or frequent experiences one has with a concept, the more meaningful the concept becomes. Noble (1953) asked subjects to rate the number of times they had come in contact with a particular word (never, rarely, sometimes, often, very often). Using the same words and nonsense syllables as those employed in his study on the number of associations, Noble obtained a correlation of 0.92 between this rating and the measure of meaningfulness, suggesting that these two measures are probably measures of just about the same thing.

We learn words better and faster when there is a variety of associated experiences with which to form connections. Kimble (Kimble and Garmezy, 1968), for example, found a functional relationship between the ease of learning and the meaningfulness of words: the more meaningful a word is, the faster it is learned as a part of a list. For the same reason, m values predict the ease of recall, recognition, and other verbal behavior.

To conclude, word association is a simple technique, yet it reveals a host of interesting verbal habit patterns, which change according to the types of subject, with the words used, and over time. One word of warning— as we show in the following two chapters, language is more than a chain of word associations, and word association cannot by itself explain how we acquire linguistic knowledge and skill.

SEMANTIC DIFFERENTIAL (SD)

Another useful word-based research tool is the semantic differential (SD). We shall discuss what SD measures and how it is constructed. In the process we may learn another aspect of word meaning.

SD measures connotative meaning

Connotative and denotative meaning   The denotative meaning of "father" is "a male parent," as most people would agree. Its connotative meaning can be "good, strong, big, gentle, loving," or it can be "bad, weak, violent, cruel, mean," depending on what one's experience with one's father has been. Dictionary definitions of words are usually denotative meanings, and there is better agreement among speakers on denotative than on connotative meanings. "Black," "Negro," and "nigger" have the same denotative meanings, but different connotative meanings for most people, while "father," "big brother," and "uncle" have different denotative meanings but may have similar connotative meanings for some people. In short, an event or a thing that a word refers to or denotes is its denotative meaning. A word also evokes emotional or evaluative responses in us due to our particular experiences with the word itself or with what it denotes. These emotional or evaluative responses are the connotative meanings of the word, and are measured by SD.

Figure 3–4 depicts the theory behind SD, as formulated by Osgood and associates (1957). The stimulus characteristics of an object such as a ball (its shape, resilience, weight, and so on) regularly lead to a particular behavior pattern of eye movement, grasping, squeezing, as well as the pleasurable associations of play behavior. The easily conditionable part of this total response is conditioned as an implicit or mediating response to the word "ball." This covert mediating response consists of only a part of the total overt response pattern to real balls: those parts that are most easily subject to conditioning, such as the glandular and emotional components of the total response. They require little effort and do not interfere with the ongoing process of the total overt response pattern. SD measures those implicit, physiological, emotional, covert mediating responses that constitute the connotative meaning of the word "ball."

How SD is constructed   SD is a set of rating scales. It is "semantic" because it has to do with (connotative) meaning, and "differential" because an individual differentiates words (or concepts expressed in more than one word) according to how they agree with one or the other of a pair of

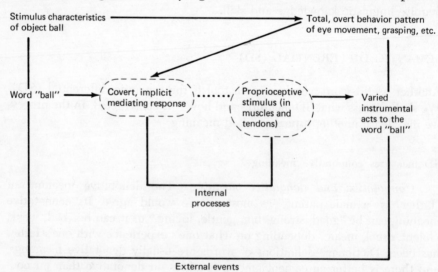

FIGURE 3–4   The theory behind SD, or process of conditioning implicit response. (Adapted from Osgood and associates, 1957.)

contrasting adjectives, which define a "scale." The scales are antonymous adjective pairs such as "good–bad." Typically about 20 are used, although the types and number of scales can be flexibly chosen to suit different purposes. An individual rater indicates the direction and intensity of his judgment on each of the scales by placing the concept under study at one of seven points from one extreme to the other. The experimenter randomizes the left–right position of the positive and negative poles (or adjectives with desirable and undesirable meanings) in the scales to prevent the rater from developing a particular set and then simply checking down the column.

To illustrate what SD looks like, and what an individual rater does, I show my own SD ratings of two concepts, "father" and "daddy," in Figure 3–5. Note that even though the two concepts "father" and "daddy" have the same denotative meanings, they show different SD profiles or ratings because of their difference in connotative meaning for me.

Osgood and his associates (1957) experimented with many and varied scales, but *factor analysis* always clustered a number of polar adjective scales around three independent dimensions of meaning, which they called evaluation, activity, and potency. In a factor analysis, the investigators start with a large number of scales, about 50 to 70, and see how these scales are correlated. For example, they find that scores on the scales of good–bad, pleasant–unpleasant, and sacred–profane are related and can mainly be explained by one factor, the *evaluative dimension*. Scores on another set of

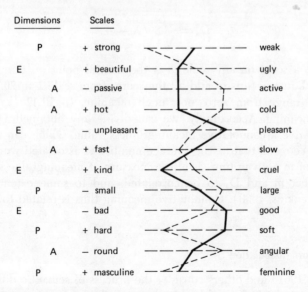

FIGURE 3–5 Taylor's SD ratings of "daddy" (solid line) and "father" (broken line). E = Evaluative dimension of meaning; P = Potency; A = Activity; +, Positive pole; −, Negative pole.

scales including strong–weak, large–small, and heavy–light are correlated among themselves, but not with scores on the scales of the evaluative dimension. These related scales are mainly concerned with the second dimension, called *potency*. Similarly, the scales of active–passive, fast–slow, and sharp–dull are related among themselves, but not much with the scales in the above two dimensions. Together they reduce to the dimension called *activity*.

Osgood and his associates claim that the scales always reduce to the same three dimensions over both changing subject and language populations, although each dimension may sometimes require different scales. For example, in Japan but not in the United States, vulgar–elegant is one of the important scales for the evaluative dimension. Carroll (1959) questions whether three dimensions exhaust the connotative meanings of words. How many dimensions one extracts from a factor analysis depends on the type and number of scales from which the dimensions are extracted. In the case of SD, the concepts for which the chosen scales have been tested also matter. In order to establish the dimensionality of a system one must adequately sample the total space for which one is seeking dimensions, and this is very difficult.

The extent to which a given concept deviates from a completely neutral profile is a measure of its connotative meaningfulness, and the geometric mean deviation is expressed as polarity:

$$D_4 = \sqrt{\sum_1^{20} (X - 4)^2}$$

where X is a score on any scale, 4 is the neutral point on the seven-point scale, and Σ instructs us to add all the scores from scale 1 to 20. The value of D_4 can range from zero, not much meaning, to 13.42 ($\sqrt{20 \times 9}$), maximal meaning. Accordingly, we can divide any obtained D_4 score by 13.42 to derive a connotative meaningfulness value, which can range from 0 to 1.00. We recall that m, the average number of associated words subjects can think of in a given time, is also a measure of meaningfulness. Thus, we might expect m and D_4 to be correlated, and to some extent they are: $r = .76$ (Jenkins, 1960). Connotative meaning thus is related to associative meaning.

SD and word association

Bousfield (1961) and others consider the process of semantic differentiation simply as a special class of highly circumscribed word association. Actual empirical analysis (Johnson, Miller, and Wall, 1965) does indeed show that the more extreme the location of a word on a semantic differential scale, the more likely it is that one of the polar adjectives defining that dimension will be included in its associative response set. Thus, they concluded that semantic placement reflects associative strengths, not mediational response evocation. However, as noted earlier, one may suggest that these two concepts are not really very different.

On the other hand, some experiments carried out by Staats and his associates (for example, Staats and Staats, 1957) show that nonverbal mediators are capable of affecting the verbal behavior measured in SD. In these studies, test materials were nonsense syllables. One, such as YOF, was paired once each with a series of meaningful English words such as "beauty," "win," and "gift." These words have divergent denotative meanings, but all have high loadings on the positive evaluative factor on SD. XEH, on the other hand, was paired with "bad" words—"thief," "ugly," "bitter," and so on. At the conclusion of these paired presentations, subjects rated the originally neutral nonsense syllables on the SD evaluative dimension. The syllables so conditioned came to produce evaluative ratings appropriate to the words paired with them. The diverse denotative meanings of the words did not matter. Most subjects were unaware of the conditioning process. This experiment again shows how connotative meaning may develop by conditioning.

Yavuz and Bousfield (1959) did a similar experiment but used real words. Subjects responded to unknown Turkish words with known English translations. A week later, the investigators examined how much the subjects had retained by giving them the Turkish words to translate. Subsequently, the subjects rated the Turkish words on the SD good–bad scales. Subjects were able to reproduce the good–bad connotations of the Turkish words even if they had not remembered the translations of these words. The Turkish words had acquired such connotative meanings by being linked with the corresponding English words, and the connotative meaning captured by SD was still present although the denotative meaning had been lost. The experiment demonstrates the existence of connotative meaning with or without denotative meaning.

SD as a research tool

Although there have been some misgivings about methodological aspects, SD has proven useful for comparing responses of different types of subjects to the same concept, responses of one type of subject to different concepts, or responses of the same type of subject to the same concepts at different times. The experiments described below as well as my own SD ratings earlier (Figure 3–5) are examples of such comparisons using SD.

In a test of cultural difference, we can ask: Do people of different cultures have different connotative meanings for words with a common denotative meaning? Sometimes they do. For example, speakers of Hopi, Navaho, and Zuni perceive differently the concept "coyote," as shown in SD ratings in Figure 3–6. Although anthropologists regard these three tribes in the southwestern United States as distinct cultures, the Hopi and Zuni cultures are more similar to each other than they are to the Navaho culture (Maclay and Ware, 1961). Note that Hopi and Zuni speakers are closer together in their semantic profiles than is either to Navaho. We can test in similar ways cultural differences in perceiving more important and interesting concepts such as "democracy," "death," or "old age."

SD can be used in measuring change of attitude over time. Mental patients' attitudes toward emotional concepts can be compared before and after psychotherapy. For example, whether the patient's evaluation of the mother has changed can be determined by SD. If it has improved, the ratings should have shifted from the predominantly negative poles on the evaluative scales to neutral or even to the positive poles. It would be interesting to see how SD profiles of Americans have changed over the last decade to such politically important concepts as "Communism," "Red China," or "politicians."

"Red" is often called the color of love (and hate). In western cultures a heart shape in red symbolizes love, and "seeing red" means anger. We can use SD to see whether profiles of ratings on "red" and "love" are similar. According to Hofstätter (1955) the correlation between the two ratings is as high as .89. Presumably one can carry on such tests with symbolism of other colors: yellow–cowardice; green–envy; black–evil; white–purity; purple–majesty; and so on. It would be interesting to investigate cultural differences in color symbolism using SD. In western cultures black clothes are worn at funerals, but in Asia the appropriate color is white. Consequently, the color symbolism of black and white might be different in these two cultures.

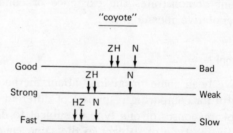

FIGURE 3–6 Cultural differences among Hopi, Navaho, and Zuni reflected in semantic differential to the concept "coyote." (Adapted from Maclay and Ware, 1961.)

MORE ABOUT WORD MEANING AND SEMANTIC MEMORY

We have so far looked at word meaning as an image of an object, as whatever a word denotes, as the emotional or evaluative responses a word evokes in us, and as the relationship a word has with other words. Let us look at it from yet other viewpoints.

Referent, reference, and context

Triangular model of signification   In a traditional dyadic scheme a word stands for an object or an event (referent), and has always only one fixed, true meaning. Ogden and Richards, in their classic book *The Meaning of Meaning*, (1923) were critical of this view of meaning. They warned that a word is not a part of its referent such that words have meaning in and of themselves. The conviction that every word must have one real or true meaning, driven to its logical extreme, leads to word magic. For example, in some societies a man who knows his enemy's name is expected, by means of it, to acquire magic powers over him. Use of the sentence "The Divine is rightly so called" shows that people really can have such a mistaken idea of a word. Every concept has many labels and every label refers to many things. As an example of the former, once I and my husband came to a highway when driving along a side road. He said, "There is the highway," and I said, "There is number ten," the name of the highway. We understood each other perfectly and instantly.

Something mediates between the word and the concept, and this mediator is called meaning or *reference*. Ogden and Richards conceived the relation among word, reference, and referent in a triangular model of signification, as in Figure 3–7. The mediating component, called reference or meaning, is the experience of perceiving referents in a context. Thus what meaning "really" is can only be grasped in a context of a verbal exchange. Words have no meaning as such; they get meaning from the way they are used by individuals in a particular context.

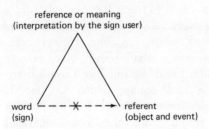

FIGURE 3–7   The relationship among word, reference, and referent: a triangular model. A word does not directly connect to a referent. (Adapted from Ogden and Richards, 1923.)

We thus have a vague feeling that word meaning is relative—it depends on the context of the utterance and the usage in a culture. According to the German philosopher Wittgenstein (1958) it becomes impossible to give for a word a meaning that holds in all contexts, because the contexts are continuously changing; the meaning is inconsistent outside the framework of the particular language "game" involved. To Wittgenstein, a language is a game that is played in some context for some purpose and has certain rules that permit certain moves but forbid other moves. Wittgenstein advised: "Don't ask for the meaning of a word; ask for the use."

A cognitive theory of semantics   Olson (1970) enters into the picture at this point to clarify these vague feelings we have about word meaning being relative. He asserts that words do not mean referents or stand for referents; they have a use—they specify perceived events relative to a set of alternatives; they provide information. The choice of a name reflects the most frequent differentiations that must be made by the language user. A ball may be called a baseball, an object, a sphere, a thing, that, it, one, or thingmabob, and so on, all depending on contexts. A theory of semantics has to specify those contexts. If there were two balls in the visual field, one rough and the other smooth, it should be entirely appropriate to say "Give me the smooth one." If there were several objects, but only one, the ball— the intended referent—smooth, it would be appropriate to say "Give me the smooth thing." If a cricket ball and a baseball are in the visual field, the speaker must say "Give me the baseball." If only one ball and nothing else is in the visual field, the speaker may simply say, "Give it (that) to me."

"Context" should include the knowledge about a topic the speaker and the listener share due to their knowledge of the world or preceding verbal exchange. But Olson focuses his discussion on the perceptual or visual field shared by the speaker and the listener at the time of their verbal exchange.

Consider the following paradigm, which specifies the relation of an utterance to an intended referent.

Case 1: A gold star is placed under a small wooden block. A speaker who saw this act is then asked to tell a listener, who did not see the act, where the gold star is. In every following case, the star is placed under the *same* block, a small, round, white, . . . one. However, in Case 2, there is one alternative block present, a small, round, black one. In this case the speaker would say, "It's under the *white* one." In Case 3 there is a different alternative block present, a small, square, white . . . one. The speaker's utterance would be: "It's under the *round* one." In Case 4 there are three alternative blocks present: a round, black one; a square, black one; and a square, white one. The speaker would say in this case, "It's under the *round, white* one." What should be an utterance in Case 5?

From the paradigm, Olson concludes that: (1) Words do not name things. In the paradigm case the thing is a block, yet few if any of the speakers so designate it. The speakers call the block "one," because the speaker and the listener already know that they are talking about the block, and that all of the objects are blocks. (2) Words do not name intended referents. In the paradigm case, the gold star is under the same block, the same intended referent, yet the utterances differ in each case, depending on the number and type of alternatives present. Words designate, signal, or specify an intended referent relative to the set of alternatives from which it must be differentiated. The meaning of an utterance is therefore the information provided by the utterance to a listener so that the listener can choose or differentiate among alternatives. The term "information" here means any perceptual or linguistic cue that reduces the number of alternatives to the intended referent.

Olson has two more conclusions, but for our purpose these two are sufficient. In Olson's particular paradigm certainly his conclusion seems to follow. However, I have set up a different paradigm next to his in Figure 3–8 to show that in some arrangements a word refers to a thing or a class of things, and that a word denotes an intended referent. In Taylor's paradigm

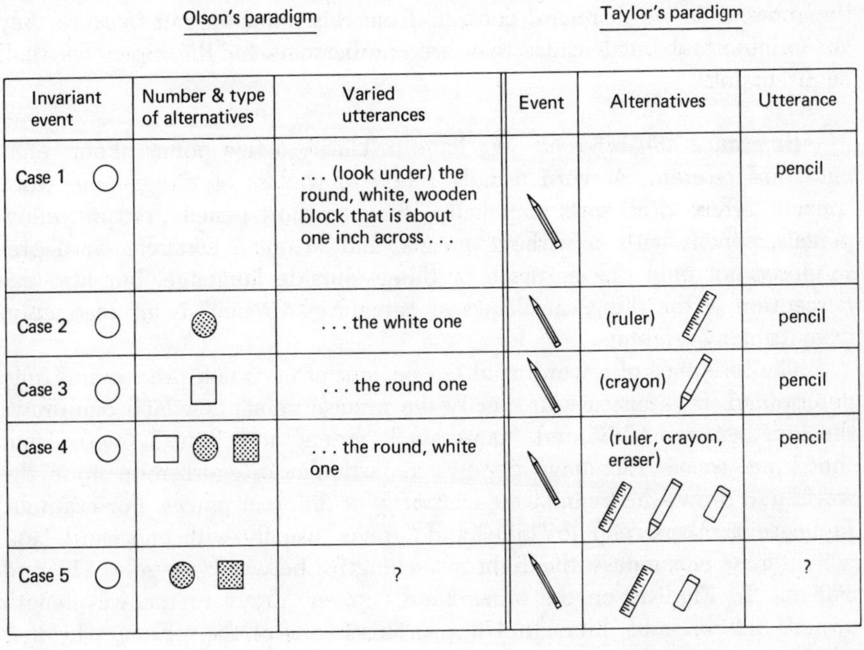

	Olson's paradigm			Taylor's paradigm	
Invariant event	Number & type of alternatives	Varied utterances	Event	Alternatives	Utterance
Case 1 ◯		. . . (look under) the round, white, wooden block that is about one inch across . . .	✏		pencil
Case 2 ◯	◉	. . . the white one	✏	(ruler) 📏	pencil
Case 3 ◯	☐	. . . the round one	✏	(crayon) ✏	pencil
Case 4 ◯	☐ ◉ ▨	. . . the round, white one	✏	(ruler, crayon, eraser) 📏 ✏ ▭	pencil
Case 5 ◯	◉ ▨	?	✏	📏 ✏ ▭	?

FIGURE 3–8 The relation of an utterance to an intended referent: compare varied utterances in Olson's paradigm to one invariant utterance in Taylor's paradigm. (Olson's paradigm based on Olson, 1970: case 5 added, and cases 1–4 rearranged.)

we have the word "pencil" for a particular object or referent, and whatever alternatives may constitute its context, we can always (from Cases 1, 2, 3, and 4) simply use the word "pencil" to let the listener know what we mean without any ambiguity whatsoever. It is conceivable that even "pencil" may be ambiguous in some other contexts, but in the contexts we are talking about as well as in many other contexts it seems unambiguous.

Here I am implying that some words may unambiguously denote their referents regardless of context, as long as these contexts are not out of the ordinary. Could it be that the more specific a word is, the less a context matters? A general or generic word with multiple meanings such as "thing," "one," or "get" certainly can be used unambiguously only in specified contexts. But note that even these words have certain, if vague, meanings by themselves. In the ensuing discussion, we shall assume that a word denotes a referent, and the word meaning can be discussed independently of contexts, at least for some words with only one or one dominant meaning. Stimuli in word association tests are usually given without contexts, yet evoke common responses from different subjects. The subjects may be responding to a set of semantic markers or critical features with which each word is associated and that set this word apart from other words whatever the context. So we disregard contexts from this point on, not because they are unimportant but because they are cumbersome for the topics we shall be discussing.

Reference and referent   We have to clarify a few points about reference and referent. A word usually refers to a class of things—the word "pencil" refers to all sorts of pencils—long or short pencils, red or yellow pencils, pencils with or without erasers, and so on. A concrete word presupposes not only the existence of things outside language, but also our perception of the things in classes or categories. "Pencil" is an abstraction from its many referents.

The reference of a word need not be, and often is not, precise and fully determined. It is not easy to specify the precise points at which one draws the line between "hill" and "mountain," "green" and "blue," "warm" and "hot," and so on. Language imposes a particular categorization upon the world and draws the boundaries arbitrarily at different places. For example, Japanese speakers refer to "blue" and "green" usually with one word "ao," which may encompass the light wavelengths between roughly 470 and 500 mμ. In English, on the other hand, "green" refers to the wavelength around 520 mμ, and "blue" to 470 mμ. This is one of the reasons why it is often impossible to establish lexical equivalences between different languages. This sort of nonequivalence happens within a single language, too. When I say "It's warm today," I may refer to a temperature of 15°C (59°F), while another person at the same time might say "It's freezing cold," using the term "warm" only of a temperature near 30°C (86°F), to which I might say "boiling hot." However, generally speaking, such imprecise categorizations of referents do not hamper our communication too seriously, at least not within a single language.

Semantic markers and semantic memory

Semantic theory in linguistics has not been as fully developed as syntactic theory. The modern trend in linguistics seems to incorporate semantics into a syntactic theory, as we shall see in Chapter 4 on grammar and speech. Here we shall merely learn a little about semantic markers, because they provide a useful framework for studying word meaning and appear several times in this book.

Linguists (such as Katz and Fodor, 1963) analyze the sense of a word into semantic markers. For example, the sense of "man" is the product of markers (living), (human), (adult), (male), and so forth. How many markers do we need to completely analyze the sense of a word and to distinguish that word from other words? This important question is difficult to answer, drawing linguists into debates (for example, Katz and Fodor vs. Bolinger, 1965, on "distinguishers"). For the sake of simplicity, we shall assume that there may be a handful of semantic markers that will set a particular word apart from most other words in most contexts. Our mental dictionary has to contain a sufficient number of semantic markers for each word. When we say we know what "man" means, or when we respond to "man" with "woman" in a word association test, we show that we have stored in our mental dictionary the above four semantic markers plus certain syntactic features such as "noun, count noun, singular."

If we store words with inappropriate and incomplete semantic markers we may use the words inappropriately in a sentence, producing *anomalous sentences*. For example, a child who has not yet stored the marker (inanimate) for "moon" may produce an anomalous sentence such as "moon is hungry." The most famous semantically anomalous sentence in psycholinguistic circles is Chomsky's creation, "Colorless green ideas sleep furiously." This sentence seems to have a good structure, but does not make sense. For example, how can "green" be "colorless"? But note that anomaly is also a relative concept. The above examples can be appropriate in poetry, dreams, hallucinations, "stream of consciousness" writings, jokes, or childish beliefs. These sentences are anomalous to the extent that they do not make literal sense, and are not found in "normal" speech.

One concern of psycholinguists is to see how we store semantic markers in memory, and how we acquire them. Leaving the second question to the chapter on language acquisition, let us tackle the first question here. In storing semantic markers, we must consider efficiency in terms of minimizing the storage space and the effort and time required for retrieval. First, we will examine a hierarchical organization model: there is a hierarchy such that various markers differentiate a word from other words at different levels. Taking an example from the memory structure hypothesized for "canary" by Collins and Quillian (1969), at the lowest level "canary" is yellow and can sing. At the second level, a canary is a bird and has wings and can fly. At the third level, a canary is an animal and has skin, eats, and so on. Collins and Quillian call "bird" a category name, and "has wings" and "can fly" two *properties* of "bird." Properties uniquely characterize a category name. Note that each word has stored with it a configuration of pointers to other words in the memory. This configuration represents the word meaning.

If Table 3–3 represents a configuration of word meaning, our time to answer the following three questions will be different.

1. Can a canary sing? (the lowest level)
2. Can a canary fly? (the second level)
3. Does a canary have skin? (the third level)

To decide "A canary can sing," one need only start at the node "canary" and retrieve the properties stored there to find the statement true. But to decide whether "A canary can fly," one must move one level to "bird" before one can retrieve the property of flying. Therefore, one should require more time to decide that "A canary can fly" than to decide that "A canary can

TABLE 3–3   The Hypothetical Memory Structure for a Three-level Hierarchy for "Canary"

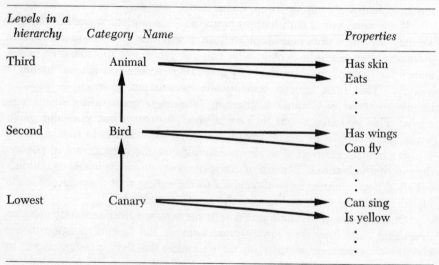

Levels in a hierarchy	Category Name	Properties
Third	Animal	Has skin / Eats / . / . / .
Second	Bird	Has wings / Can fly / . / .
Lowest	Canary	Can sing / Is yellow / . / . / .

Adopted from Collins and Quillian, 1969.

sing." Similarly, one should take still longer to decide that "A canary has skin," since this fact is stored with the node for "animal," which is yet another step removed from "canary." The experimental results seemed to bear out this prediction, on the whole: question (1) required the shortest time to answer; (2), an intermediate time; (3), the longest time.

Conrad (1972) later supported Collins and Quillian's hierarchical organization model but not their hypothesis of cognitive economy of storage, which proposed that those properties that do not uniquely define a word but are also properties of the word's superordinate category are stored only in the configuration that defines the superordinate. For example, the property "flies" is assigned only to "bird" and need not be repeated for "canary."

Conrad points out that Collins and Quillian used the properties they themselves generated on intuitive grounds, while she used properties collected from a large number of subjects. Thus Conrad could note that some properties were given more frequently than others by her subjects. Properties with a low frequency (such as "An orange is edible") would take longer to retrieve from memory than would those with a high frequency ("A banjo has strings"). In short, Conrad finds a hierarchy of organization based on frequency of properties, while Collins and Quillian find it based on the level of categories. Further, Conrad's experiments suggest that properties are stored in memory with every word they define and can be retrieved directly rather than through a process of inference. This finding does not support the hypothesis of cognitive economy of storage.

Anderson and Reder (1974) point out that the findings of Collins and Quillian are in fact subject to multiple interpretations. In one more possible interpretation, "canary" and "bird" are more similar (in terms of feature overlaps) than "canary" and "animal." Subjects can verify semantic relations of similar concepts more quickly than dissimilar concepts (Rips, Shoben, and Smith, 1973).

Rumelhart, Lindsay, and Norman (1972) have proposed and simulated on a computer a network model of cognitive structure that combines Conrad's and Collins–Quillian's approach. Properties are associated with both particular and general concepts by means of labeled relations, such as a "has" or an "is" relation. Think of the word "house." What kinds of information do we produce when describing its meaning? An important part of the meaning of a concept includes the following relationships.

House isa[1] dwelling. (The *class* of concepts to which it belongs)
House has rooms. (The *properties* which tend to make the concept unique.)
House is cozy. (Another property of house)
House is "Mon Repos." (*Examples* of the concept)

[1] "Isa" is a specific operator in the computer-based network grammar. Many such operators are involved in the total model.

Examples have the reverse direction of "isa," that is, examples are almost always related to class names: the two simply exchange positions. Hence, the last example could also have occurred in the form " 'Mon Repos' *isa* house." If a house is a dwelling, an example of a dwelling will be a house. "Isa" is a compound of "is" and "a," and it always connects with an object. "Isa" should not be confused with "is" in "house is cozy." "Is" is used primarily when the property is a quality.

We note that the words used in the definition are themselves concepts, and therefore defined in the same way. The result is an interlinking structure, like the one shown in Figure 3–9. The network model is not neat. But then Lindsay and Norman (1972) point out that real behavior is often complicated, confusing, and circular.

Lexical organization in memory—a hierarchical model

Now we talk about how words, rather than information about words, are organized in our memories. Word association tests reveal to us which words are organized closely together. The sorting tasks to be described here reveal more about word organization, and permit us to develop a hierarchical model of lexical organization. Before describing the experiments we have to understand what the experimenter (Anglin, 1970) means by *features*. Words have critical features—"book" has the critical feature that it refers

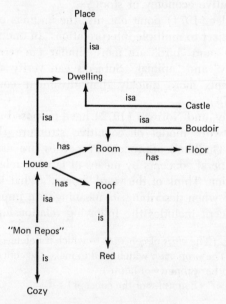

FIGURE 3–9   The definition of "house" in the network model. (Adapted from Lindsay and Norman, 1972.)

to a solid object containing pages that have print on them. In particular contexts, one can ignore its position, its coloring, its texture, its size, or its binding. The most important threads in an adult's lexical network are determined by features shared by a group of words. The set of features associated with a word represents a large part of its meaning. The extent to which two words share meaning is a function of the overlap of the two corresponding sets of features. Features are roughly similar to what Katz and Fodor (1963) call semantic markers. Words are not isolated, unrelated entities: they cohere in a system. A major basis for the organization of words within the lexicon results from the fact that the features of words can often be cast into a hierarchical or nested relation, as in Figure 3–10. Figure 3–10 constitutes only a frame upon which a host of "property" (Collins and Quillian, 1969) relations can be hung. Note the following relations among the words in Figure 3–10.

(1) "Boy" and "girl" are both human children.
(2) "Boy" and "horse" are both animals.
(3) "Boy" and "flower" are both living organisms or beings.
(4) "Boy" and "chair" are both physical objects.
(5) "Boy" and "idea" are both entities.

The relation between two words is closest in (1), and becomes less and less as we move to (5). At the same time, the level of abstractness increases from (1) to (5).

Anglin used a sorting task on 20 words to determine how close in meaning one word is to another. The proximity for a word pair is defined by the number of judges who sort the two words into the same pile. For a sorting task, typically the subject is given a deck of cards with a word and its

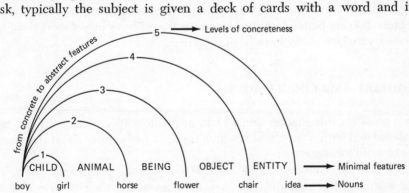

FIGURE 3–10 Hierarchical organization of nouns. The two nouns, "boy" and "girl" share the most concrete minimal feature (child), and are closely organized in memory. On the other hand, "boy" and "idea" share the least concrete feature (entity), and are not close together in memory. (Adapted from Anglin, 1970.)

definition on each card. The subject is required to sort the words into piles on the basis of similarity of meaning. There may be any number of piles with any number of words per pile. Sorting, better than any other technique, suggests adults' sensitivity to features, to equivalence relations, and to the hierarchical structure of the lexicon.

Adult subjects in Anglin's sorting task grouped verbs, adjectives, adverbs, and nouns separately. Most word associates of adults are the same part of speech as the stimulus, and confusion in memory tasks tends to be paradigmatic (Anderson and Beh, 1968). All these facts suggest that the words in our memories may be organized in terms of form class or parts of speech.

Within a given part of speech, the extent to which adults clustered two words decreased at greater levels of abstractness or generality. Considering the nouns, 98 percent of the adults put the words that both refer to children, "boy" and "girl," into the same pile; 45 percent of adults clustered word pairs "boy–horse" and "girl–horse," for which the minimal feature (the most concrete category label that applies to both words) is "animal"; 36 percent clustered the word pairs for which the minimal feature is "being." In short, adults often group words presumed to be concretely related; they seldom group words presumed to be abstractly related.

Children's clusters were smaller and more syntagmatic compared with adults' clusters; the children did not group words by parts of speech as much as did adults. However, oppositions ("boy–girl" or "above–below") had the highest proximities in all tasks for adults and children.

How semantic information and words are organized in our memories is an intriguing question. Both hierarchical and network models sound plausible, if simplistic. Old-fashioned library card indexes use both types of organization. It may be that different aspects of semantic memory and word organization are better described by one or the other, or by yet more complex models, of which many have been proposed.

SUMMARY AND CONCLUSIONS

Two goals for this chapter are: (1) to acquaint readers with words as test material and with word-based research tools; (2) to ponder about the meaning of word meaning.

Words are convenient test material for psychological experiments. To use words as test material, we have to learn about their diverse characteristics, such as frequency of use or abstractness–concreteness. Conveniently, there are normative estimates of several characteristics of words.

One of the word-based research tools is the word association test, which reveals our verbal habits, thought processes, memory structure, and even emotional states. We examined some characteristics of response patterns, such as Marbe's Law. Different groups of subjects (such as male/female) tested at different times show different response patterns, especially in their tendencies of giving common or uncommon responses.

Children tend to give syntagmatic, while adults give paradigmatic, association responses. A stimulus and a response word are in syntagmatic relation if they combine to form a larger linguistic unit. Two words are in paradigmatic relation if they substitute for each other in a sentence. Children have to experience words in varied contexts before they can shift to paradigmatic word association processes.

One variant of word association tests is a continued word association, in which the subject produces as many words as possible in a given time. The average number of words produced by a large number of subjects is an index of meaningfulness.

Another useful word-based tool is the semantic differential, which measures the connotative meanings of concepts. A semantic differential consists of about 20 scales, or adjective pairs with negative and positive poles, which can tap three independent dimensions of meaning. Using this tool, we can, for example, compare verbal behavior as well as attitudes of different groups of subjects toward some important concepts.

Here is a summary of what we have learned about the ever-elusive meaning of word meaning.

First, the word evokes an image of its referent. This is a limited definition of word meaning, because most people can conjure up images only for very concrete words.

A word also has an associative meaning, which is its relation with other words.

A word has denotative and connotative meanings. A word denotes an object or an event, and an image is a kind of a denotative meanings of a word. A connotative meaning is the evaluative responses a word evokes in us.

Ogden and Richards insist that what a word means can be understood only in the context where the word is used. Olson specifies the contexts that determine the choice of a word or an utterance.

Important as they are, we disregard contexts from this point on because they are cumbersome. The sense of a word can be analyzed into semantic markers (similar to "critical features," and the same as "lexical markers/ features").

Semantic information in our memories seems to be organized in a hierarchical manner. One hierarchical model says that a hierarchy is based on levels of categories ("animal"—"bird"—"canary"), while another model says that it is based on frequency of properties ("can fly" is one property of "bird"). A network model shows complex interlinkings of concepts: some concepts are used to define other concepts, which in turn are used to define the original concepts, and so on.

Word-sorting tasks show that words in adult memory are organized by parts of speech. With 1 each grammatical class, there is a hierarchy: the more concrete features any two words share, the closer they are in memory.

Both hierarchical and network models may be needed to describe word memory.

4

Grammar and Speech

. . . grammar, which rules even kings.
Molière (1622–1673)

A grammar is a description of how the three components of language—the sounds, the meaning, and the syntax—are used. A grammar is often codified as a set of rules. We learned about speech sounds in Chapter 2, and about word meaning in Chapter 3. In the first part of this chapter we shall learn mainly about syntax. *Syntax* comes from a Greek word meaning "putting together," and deals with the way in which words are put together in a sentence. In the second part of the chapter we shall examine some psycholinguistic experiments that test the ways speakers use and are influenced by syntactic rules. As the chapter progresses, we shall try to resolve the question of whether syntactic structures or semantic contents are more important in speech processing.

What is a grammar?

The study of grammar has evolved gradually over many years. Let us survey it historically in order to understand what a grammar is. In the process we may straighten out some misconceptions people sometimes have about grammar. The following brief survey is based on Lyons (1968).

Traditional grammar In the fifth century B.C., the Greeks classified words into various categories, which survive even today. Plato (429–347 B.C.) distinguished between nouns and verbs as follows: nouns were terms

89

that could function in sentences as the subjects of a predication, whereas verbs could express the action or qualify the predicate. Adjectives were included among the verbs. Aristotle (384–322 B.C.) added conjunctions, by which he meant all those words that were not nouns or verbs. He also noted that certain systematic variations in the forms of the verb could be correlated with such temporal notions as present or past. Thus the notion of tense was born.

Of the several different schools of Greek philosophy (grammar was a part of philosophy), the Stoics gave the most attention to language. They distinguished four parts of speech: noun, verb, conjunction, and article. Later members of this school separated common nouns and proper nouns, and classed adjectives with nouns instead of with verbs. The Stoics developed the classification of inflections, the relationships between such forms as "boy" and "boys." They gave to the term "case" the sense of its present usage, distinguishing between "upright" case (nominative) and "oblique" cases, derivations from the upright. They further distinguished between active and passive, and between transitive and intransitive verbs. In the late second century B.C., Dionysius recognized adverb, participle, pronoun, and preposition, in addition to the Stoics' four classes. All Greek words were classified in terms of case, gender, number, tense, voice, and so on.

In the medieval period, adjectives were recognized as a separate class. Latin, which was by then mainly a written language, was also a lingua franca (common language) in Europe, spoken by scholars everywhere. Thus the study of language was concerned with the universal grammar and with the written language. "Grammar is substantially the same in all languages, even though it may vary accidentally," said Roger Bacon (1214–1294).

The classical tradition in the study of language is eloquently expressed in the definition given in the dictionary and grammar of the French Academy (1932 edition): "Grammar is the art of speaking and writing correctly. . . . The grammarian's task is to describe 'good usage,' that is the language of the educated persons and writers who write 'pure' French, and to defend this good usage from all causes of corruption. . . ."

Indian grammar was meanwhile developing independently of the Graeco-Roman tradition. Pāṇini (? fourth century B.C.) is acknowledged as the greatest of the early Indian grammarians. He described nouns and verbs in Sanskrit in much the same way as Plato did for Greek. Sanskrit grammarians also recognized prepositions and particles. Their grammar was superior to Western grammar in phonetics and in the study of the internal structure of words. Spurred by the necessity of preserving intact the pronunciation of Vedic hymns, the Indian scholars classified speech sounds accurately and in detail on the basis of observations and experiments. In Europe, the scientific study of speech sounds did not start until the late nineteenth century. The discovery of Sanskrit by Western scholars at the end of the eighteenth century was one of the principal factors in the development of comparative philology in the nineteenth century.

Comparative philologists established the principles and methods of setting up language families, and developed a general theory of language change and linguistic relationships. We examined a few language families in Chapter 1. Comparative philology gave a powerful impetus to the development of phonetics, which contributed, in turn, to the formulation of more general and more satisfactory laws of sound.

Modern linguistics The founder of modern linguistics is generally considered to be the great Swiss scholar, Ferdinand de Saussure, whose lectures were published in 1916 as *Cours de linguistique générale.* The book has had a great influence on modern linguistics. First, following de Saussure, the contemporary linguist maintains that spoken language is primary and that writing is essentially a means of representing speech in another medium. We adopted this position in Chapter 1. Secondly, the linguist's first task is to describe the way people actually speak (and write) their language, not to prescribe how they ought to speak and write.

Thirdly, de Saussure distinguished between *diachronic* and *synchronic* study of language. Diachronic refers to the description of the historical development of a particular language through time: for example, the way in which French and Italian have "evolved" from Latin. The synchronic study of a language means the description of a particular state of that language at some point in time. The synchronic description is not in principle restricted to the analysis of modern spoken languages. One can carry out a synchronic analysis of "dead" languages from written records. Nineteenth-century comparative linguistics was more concerned with diachronic study, while twentieth-century linguistic theory is concerned more with synchronic study. Our coverage of linguistics in Chapter 2 and in this chapter is based on spoken language and on synchronic description (not prescription).

The most characteristic feature of modern linguistics is *structuralism:* each language is regarded as a system of relations, the elements of which— sounds, words, and so on—have no validity independently of the relations of equivalence and contrast that hold between them. We saw examples of this approach in the description of linguistic units in Chapter 2.

Another important distinction de Saussure made was between *langue* and *parole.* When we say that someone "speaks English," or is a speaker of English, we do not imply that the person is actually speaking English on any one occasion. A parrot "is speaking English" on a particular occasion, but it does not "speak English." All those who "speak English" share a particular langue, and the set of utterances they produce when they are speaking English constitute instances of parole. In short, langue (a near equivalent to "language") is the grammatical and semantic system represented in the brain of the speaker; parole (= "speech") is the actual acoustic output from one's vocal organs and input to one's ears. We shall use the distinction between language and speech where necessary in this book. A most influential contemporary American linguist, Noam Chomsky (1957, 1965), distinguishes between "competence" and "performance" in a similar but not identical way.

Competence and performance

According to Chomsky, competence is the idealized speaker-hearer's ability to produce and understand the native language, even though he may not be able to articulate this ability. "A person who has learned a language has acquired a system of rules that relate sound and meaning in a certain specific way. He has, in other words, acquired a certain competence that he puts to use in producing and understanding speech" (Chomsky, 1970, p. 184). As English speakers who possess this ability, we can constantly create new sentences, recognize more or less ungrammatical sentences, and see the connections among grammatically related sentences. Competence, the linguistic knowledge of an idealized speaker-hearer in a completely homogeneous speech community, is the main concern of a linguistic theory. One can say that the rules of the grammar describe the native speaker's linguistic competence, which linguists attempt to formulate. Why competence refers to "idealized" linguistic knowledge becomes clear when we discuss performance below.

Performance is the actual use speakers make of their knowledge in concrete situations. In performance, speakers may or may not use their competence fully. As Chomsky points out, psychologists have long realized that description of what an organism does (performance) and a description of what it knows (competence) can be very different things. He goes on to cite the inability of most of us to multiply 18,674 by 26,521 in our heads even though we grasp the rules of multiplication.

Look at our spontaneous speech: it is full of incomplete and ungrammatical sentences. Here, for instance, is a rather representative example produced at a conference of psychologists and linguists:

"As far as I know, no one yet has done the in a way obvious now and interesting problem of doing a in a sense a structural frequency study of the alternative syntactical in a given language, say, like English, the alternative possible structures, and how what their hierarchical probability of occurrence structure is . . . ." (Maclay and Osgood, 1959, p. 25)

Various psychological limitations and malfunctions may prevent us from speaking as we know we should. These limitations may involve limited memory, fatigue, preoccupation with the cognitive process of formulating the content of a sentence, emotion, time pressure, laziness, and so on. Even when an utterance is grammatical and reflects competence more faithfully, we still have to consider psychological variables in performance: Why is a particular utterance spoken on a particular occasion by a particular speaker? In short, in performance we consider the speaker's competence as well as the psychological variables; we consider how psychological variables influence the way the speaker's competence is put to use. Psychologists' main concern is naturally with performance.

If performance reflects competence imperfectly, how is competence formulated by linguists? The linguists abstract and idealize the native speaker's linguistic knowledge by observing many speakers on varied occasions. The abstracted and idealized knowledge must have a certain internal structure, and this structure becomes the description of the language.

Ultimately we would like to answer the intriguing question of whether a linguistic theory describing competence describes, or should describe, performance as well. If language users' intuitive knowledge is best described by a set of rules, then these rules must be represented in their minds, providing the basis for their usage of linguistic rules. In other words, the description of *what* the linguistic usage of native speakers consist of (competence) should apply also to *how* they operate when using language (performance). Many psycholinguistic experiments to be discussed in this chapter attempt to answer this question.

We can also ask whether a linguistic theory can be developed with no consideration of performance. A recent trend in linguistics seems to go the other way, to include performance. For example, some linguists attempt to impose purely performance constraints, such as memory limitations, on competence models. Some psycholinguists (such as Bever, 1970) even challenge the distinction between competence and performance, noting that a real grammar describes not an abstract linguistic world but rather a set of intuitions about "grammaticality" held by native speakers.

At the end of this chapter, especially in the Concluding Remarks, we may be in a better position to sort out the relationship between competence and performance. Meanwhile, let us learn more about competence, which is a speaker's internalized "system of rules that relate sound and meaning in a certain specific way"—in short, a grammar.

TRANSFORMATIONAL GENERATIVE GRAMMAR (TGG)

Traditional grammars give structural descriptions and classifications of linguistic items, but do not go beyond this to formulate *generative* rules of sentences: how we use language "creatively" to make infinite use of

finite means. Generative grammars that emerged in the mid-twentieth century deal with this important question.

There are a few different approaches to grammar today, but for a number of reasons we shall concentrate on Chomsky's transformational generative grammar (TGG). TGG is the most explicitly formulated grammar,
and perhaps because of its explicitness, attracted psychologists' interest as
no other linguistic theory has done. The structure of language as described
by TGG has an intimate relation with assumed innate properties or operations of the mind; this may be another reason why TGG is attractive to
psycholinguists. TGG revolutionized the scientific study of language by
redefining the goals and methods of linguistics. The primary object of
linguistic theory, as viewed by Chomsky, is to uncover principles underlying
the construction of sentences rather than to identify and classify minimal
linguistic units. TGG, whose description is formulated with mathematical
rigor and precision, looks more like a formal deductive theory than a
catalogue of linguistic units.

A generative grammar may be described by analogy. Consider the rule
(2^n) whereby the number 2 generates the set 2, 4, 8, 16. . . . It produces
powers of 2 and no other numbers. Similarly, a generative grammar is a
system of rules that generates all the infinite variety of possible grammatical
sentences of a language and no ungrammatical sentences. The number of
possible sentences is infinite because there is no way of setting a limit,
except in some arbitrary way, to their number. To take a simple example,
if one attempted to list all sentences, it would always be possible to produce
a new sentence by joining two listed sentences with a conjunction such as
"and" or "but." Another way of making an infinite set of sentences is by
reapplying a sentence-generating rule without a limit to produce such
embedded sentences as:

> The rat ran.
> The rat (the cat chased) ran.
> The rat (the cat ((the dog teased)) chased) ran . . . *ad infinitum.*

Because a grammar can generate an infinite number of sentences, no grammar can consist merely of a list of the finite number of sentences. A grammar
must be projective—it must contain rules that will generate all the infinite
number of possible grammatical sentences and no ungrammatical ones. A
language, as defined by TGG, is the set of all the sentences a particular
grammar generates.

TGG still is not a finished nor a perfect product—there have been
revisions and challenges since Chomsky's profoundly influential book *Syntactic Structures* appeared in 1957. Chomsky's *Aspects of the Theory of
Syntax* (1965) presents a modified version of TGG. We shall cover the
syntax put forward in both books, since both have been influential in psy-

cholinguistics. Our main concern in describing TGG is to be comprehensible rather than comprehensive.

TGG, like any grammar, consists of three major components: the phonological, semantic, and syntactic components. The three components are interrelated but are usually discussed separately for convenience. Our concern here is with the syntactic component, and with any semantic component that forms an integral part of it. First we shall study the original version of TGG, which consists of phrase-structure rules (PS-rules) and transformational rules.

In reading the following description of TGG, please forget about how you actually produce sentences but think of rules you might write for a machine that could generate an infinite number of sentences. A machine follows rules automatically, hence the rules you write have to be full, formal, and explicit. The goal of TGG is to formulate principles underlying the construction of sentences in this manner, as though the rules were intended for a machine.

Phrase-structure rules (PS-rules)

PS-rules are sets of *rewriting rules* that can automatically generate all possible grammatical sentences. In the process of generation, the rules assign to sentences their correct structural description. Sentence structure is described in "constituent structures." A *constituent* is a unit (say, a word) that combines with other constituents (words) to form a higher constituent or unit (a phrase). A phrase in turn combines with other phrases to form a still higher constituent, a sentence.

Let us learn about the constituent structure by actually analyzing the structure of a sentence. The string "The cat scratched the dog" constitutes a unit, in this case a sentence, that is called the top-level constituent. Figure 4–1 shows a *tree diagram* of the example sentence, and demonstrates its constituent structure at different levels in a hierarchical organization. The top-level constituent, sentence, can be broken down into two smaller inter-

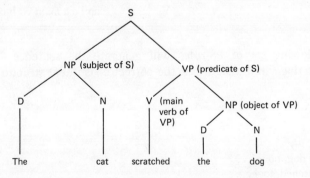

FIGURE 4–1   Tree diagram of "The cat scratched the dog."

mediate constituents: "the cat," a *noun phrase*, and "scratched the dog," a *verb phrase*. The noun phrase "the cat" consists of two constituents, determiner and noun. The verb phrase in turn has two subcomponents, "scratched," a verb, and "the dog," a noun phrase again. This second noun phrase also is broken down into determiner and noun.

A constituent then is any word (or morpheme) or sequence of words that functions as a unit in some larger construction. A constituent has a label or symbol such as NP and N. The sequence "scratched the" is not a constituent, and does not have a label.

Symbols such as noun phrase or verb designate grammatical categories of constituents, and are called *categorical symbols*. Notions like "subject-of," on the other hand, designate grammatical functions of, or relations between, constituents, and are called *functional notions*. Table 4–1 and Figure 4–1 show the relation between categorical symbols and functional notions.

TABLE 4–1   Relations among Constituents, Categorical Symbols, and Functional Notions

Constituents	Categorical symbol	Functional notion
a very old cat who is mean a very old cat the cat he	NP_1	can be a subject-of S
scratched the dog very gently scratched the dog scratched	VP	can be a predicate-of S
the very old dog the dog him	NP_2	can be a direct object-of VP
scratched	V	can be a main verb-of VP

The following set of PS-rules will generate the sentence "The cat scratched the dog," and assign to it the correct constituent structure.

1. S → NP VP
2. NP → D N
3. VP → V NP
4. D → {the, my, . . .
5. N → {cat, dog, bone . . .
6. V → {scratched, took, . . .

The arrow is an instruction to rewrite the symbol on its left as a string of elements that occur to its right. Brace brackets in the rules (4), (5), and (6) list a set of elements any one of which, but only one of which, may be selected.

The rules are applied in the following way. We start with the initial element, which is always S (sentence), and apply rule (1). This yields the string, NP VP. Inspect this string, and see whether any of the elements occurring in it can be rewritten. At this point, we can take on either NP or VP for rewriting. If we take up NP first, rule (2) rewrites it as D N. Rule (3) rewrites VP as V NP. This second NP can be rewritten as D N by reapplying rule (2). Finally, we have S rewritten as S{NP (D + N) + VP (V + NP (D + N))}. Actual words now substitute for the categorical symbols, generating the *terminal string*, "the + cat + scratched + the + dog." The set of seven strings including the initial string, the terminal string, and five intermediate strings constitute a derivation of the sentence, "The cat scratched the dog." The labeled bracketing, S{(. . .)}, associated with a terminal string is called a *phrase marker*. A phrase marker is usually represented as a tree diagram, as in Figure 4–1. It specifies a unique structure that underlies the structure of the sentence. The above rules can generate other sentences of the same structure, such as "My dog took the bone."

So far the rules indicated that the left-hand symbol can always be replaced by the right-hand symbols regardless of the context. But often rules have to be context-sensitive—restricted to certain contexts. For example, a verb in the present tense should be rewritten in the singular form in "The boy runs" but in the plural form in "The boys run." The rule is:

Verb→runs / in the context: NP singular
Verb→run / in the context: NP plural

Once again, a sentence is organized hierarchically by levels of constituents. The rewriting rules replace or rewrite a left-hand symbol by right-hand symbols, which are constituents one step lower than the replaced symbol in a hierarchical organization. This process starts with the top-level constituent or initial symbol, which is Sentence, and goes on until the lowest constituents, morphemes, are generated. In this way, a sentence is generated with an explicit structural description.

Transformational rules

As we have seen, PS-rules generate grammatical sentences and assign structural descriptions to what they generate. However, they do not describe certain relations among sentences. For example, we have an "intuitive feeling" that "The bat hits the ball" is related to its passive version "The ball is hit by the bat." At least the two sentences represent the same event. But even sentences that are not synonymous such as "The bat hits the ball" and "Did the bat hit the ball?" are felt to be closely related to each other. An English speaker can produce a negative version of "The bat hits the ball" if he is asked to. Additional rules called transformational rules take care of such connections among "related" sentences.

One single string can underly many related sentence forms such as active, passive, or question sentences. In that case, it is parsimonious to derive one underlying string by PS-rules, and derive the related sentences by applying *optional transformational rules.* Transformational rules may delete or permute certain items, or substitute one for another, or add a constant string in a fixed place, and so on. They are the rules that map one phrase marker onto another phrase marker; they operate after and upon the output of the PS-rules, that is, on a fully developed phrase marker. Transformational rules differ from the PS-rules in that they operate not on single symbols but on strings of symbols.

To illustrate how the transformational rules operate, "The man may have opened the door" is made into a passive by applying transformational rules to an underlying string, as follows.

$$NP_1 - Aux - V - NP_2 \rightarrow NP_2 - Aux + be + en - V - by + NP_1$$

The past participle suffix, *en,* is realized in such forms as "taken," but more generally as *ed* in forms like "opened." The plus signs tell us that *be + en* are to be attached to Auxiliary rather than to V, and *by* is to be attached to NP_1. Note that not just one element, but a string of four elements appears to the left of the arrow. The operations involved are:

1. Invert the two noun phrases so that NP_2 precedes NP_1.
2. Add the element "by" before NP_1.
3. Add a verbal auxiliary "be + en" before the main verb.

The final result is "The door may have been opened by the man."

Other transformations might express similar connections between "The car hit the tree" and any of the following sentences:

> Did the car hit the tree?
> The car did not hit the tree.
> When did the car hit the tree?
> The car's hitting the tree was a shock. (and so on)

The original abstract string that underlies all the above sentences is called a *kernel string.* A kernel string to which only *obligatory transformations* are applied is a kernel sentence, or simple active affirmative declarative sentence such as "The car hits the tree." Obligatory transformations take care of certain compulsory syntactic features such as number agreement between subject and verb, introduction and proper ordering of the element *do* into negatives and questions, and setting up word boundaries. Any nonkernel sentence such as a passive, a question, or a negative sentence is made from a kernel string by applying obligatory as well as optional transformations. A final group of transformations is generalized transformations, which join strings underlying two or more sentences so as to produce compound and complex sentences. For example, "The brown-haired man is honest" would result from a combination of two underlying strings "The man is brown-haired" and "The man is honest."

Here TGG seems to assume that the kernel sentence is linguistically "basic" in that its transformational history is simpler than that of nonkernel sentences. It is also "central" in that its underlying string is the source for other sentence forms. Because it is central, all sentence forms can appear in the active construction, while certain active sentences do not have corresponding passive forms (for example, a sentence with an intransitive verb such as "sleep"). In some languages passive forms seem to play minor roles. For example, in French "One speaks French here" is preferred to "French is spoken here."

The modified version of TGG

Chomsky subsequently (1965) modified his grammar. Two important points of revision seem to be that semantics is incorporated into syntax, and that the concept of "deep structure" is introduced.

In the 1965 version, the grammar has, as usual, three components: a syntactic, a phonological, and a semantic component. The syntactic component of the modified TGG consists of two major parts, a *base* and a transformational part. Figure 4–2 shows the syntactic component of the modified TGG.

Let us look at the base first. In addition to rewriting rules,[1] the base now contains a *lexicon* so that semantics can be incorporated into syntax. The rewriting rules generate a phrase marker that contains only a number of lexical "slots." These slots are then filled with lexical items taken from the lexicon, which lists lexical items along with their syntactic, semantic, and phonological information. We select (or a machine selects) from the lexicon an item with syntactic features and semantic markers compatible with the syntactic specification of the rewriting rules.

---

[1] To simplify my description, I have avoided such terms as "branching rules," "subcategorization rules," and "categorial component," which Chomsky used in his 1965 version.

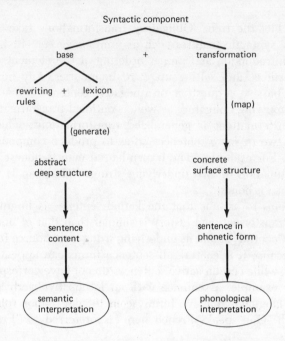

FIGURE 4–2   The syntactic component of the 1965 version of TGG.

The phrase marker for our earlier sentence "The cat scratched the dog" should now look something like Figure 4–3.

What advantages has the 1965 version over the old one? Since many features of lexical items are entirely irrelevant to the functioning of the rule of the base, and are highly idiosyncratic, the grammar can be simplified if they are excluded from the rewriting rules and listed in lexical entries. In a grammar, linguists always prefer simple rules to complex ones, other things being equal. It is now unnecessary to use rewriting rules to classify transitive verbs into those that do and those that do not normally permit object-deletion. Instead, the lexical entries specify that "eat" takes a direct object, while "sleep" does not. Further, both "eat" and "sleep" occur with animate subjects, but not with inanimate subjects. When this kind of syntactic and semantic information is not taken into consideration in selecting lexical items, there is a violation of selection restrictions; anomalous sentences such as "A tree reads an apple," which is syntactically correct but meaningless, can result.[2]

[2] Olson (1970) points out that semantic decisions are determined not (entirely?) by the syntactic or semantic markers that are exclusively a part of the linguistic system but rather on the basis of the language user's knowledge of the perceived and intended referent (see Chapter 3). He cites an example from McCawley (1968): syntactic

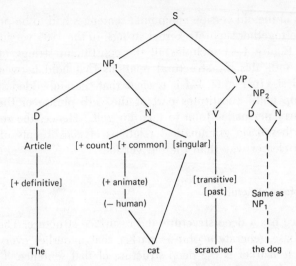

FIGURE 4–3 The phrase-marker (tree diagram) for "The cat scratched the dog" with semantics incorporated.

The second major part of the syntactic component is transformational rules. In the 1965 version, the role of transformational rules is not so much to generate related sentences (passives, negatives, and the like) from the kernel string, but to convert or map a deep structure into a surface structure through a sequence of transformations. The difference between a declarative and an interrogative sentence, or between an active and a passive sentence, is no longer described in terms of optional transformation, but in terms of a choice made in the base rules. For example, there might be a base rule of the following form:

$$\text{VP} \rightarrow \text{V} + \text{NP (Agentive)}$$

The selection of the element Agentive would distinguish the strings underlying passive sentences from the strings underlying corresponding active sentences. There would be an obligatory transformational rule, operating if and only if the input string contained the element Agentive. Transformations cannot introduce or delete meaning-bearing elements.

---

features of the verb "count" may specify that it demands a plural object "I counted the boys" and not °"I counted the boy." In "I counted the crowd," "the crowd" is singular grammatically but is plural in our knowledge of a crowd. The choice of the word "counted" depended on the plural aspect of the referent and not on the plural feature of the grammatical object.

Psychological relevance of the other syntactic component, rewriting rules and transformational rules, will be discussed at length.

Whereas in the old version compound sentences had to be produced by rules that join together separate kernel strings, in the 1965 version a phrase marker (see Figure 4–4) includes all the constituent strings (two kernel strings), and indicates the structural relations that hold between them in the final analysis. In Figure 4–4 it is clear that the embedded string, (S_2) "John takes up golf," constitutes part of the verb phrase of the complete sentence "Harry persuades John to take up golf." Hence, the revised 1965 version describes basic grammatical relations of constituents of an entire sentence in a clearer way than the old version.

Deep and surface structure

Every sentence has a deep structure and a surface structure. The rewriting rules of the base generate a phrase marker that underlies every sentence, and this phrase marker is the deep structure of that sentence. Transformational rules convert or map a deep structure into its surface structure. Compound or complex sentences may require a sequence of phrase markers, and a surface structure is mapped from the last phrase marker of the sequence. A deep structure contains lexical items, as well as structural information such as which word is the subject or the predicate, whether the sentence is affirmative or negative, whether it has one constituent embedded in another constituent, and so on. The intrinsic semantic content of lexical items and the manner in which they are related grammatically at the level of deep structure determines the semantic interpretation of a sentence.

In a simple sentence such as "John sleeps," surface and deep structure are the same. In a passive sentence such as "The apples are picked by John," the deep structure specifies that the agent of the action "pick" is John: John is the *logical subject*. The *grammatical subject* is "the apples," which governs

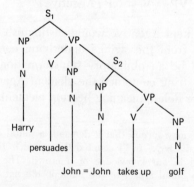

FIGURE 4–4   Deep structure of "Harry persuades John to take up golf." The logical subject of S_2 = the logical object of S_1 = John.

plurality of its verb, "*are* picked." A logical subject is the subject found in a deep structure, and a grammatical subject is the subject found in a surface structure. In "Harry persuades John to take up golf" (see Figure 4–4), one deep structure (S_2), "John takes up golf," is embedded in another deep structure (S_1), "Harry persuades John." Note that each of these two deep structures has its own logical subject and object.

In general, (1) a surface sentence and its deep structure may look different because of the changed ordering of words, as in the above passive sentence, or because of deletion of items in the surface structure, as in "I go, and (I) sleep." Another way in which the deep and the surface structures may differ is when a few separate deep structures are combined into a single surface structure, as in Figure 4–4. (2) Sometimes two different deep structures can appear identical in their surface structures, as in "John is eager to please" and "John is easy to please." The deep structure relation for the former is "John is eager to please someone," for the latter "Someone can please John easily." (3) An ambiguous surface structure can be "disambiguated" in two or more deep structures. "Teachers' marks are high" can be derived from either "Teachers give someone high marks" or "Someone gives teachers high marks." (4) Sometimes one deep structure can be transformed into two or more surface structures for stylistic or other reasons. "He looks up the number" can be "He looks the number up." (5) Finally, a sentence, if it is simple, can also be almost identical in its deep and surface structures, as in "I hit the girl." In general, the deep structure can be highly abstract; it may have no close point-to-point correlation to the surface phonetic realization. However, the deep and surface structures always stand in a specific relation to one another—a relation described by one or more transformations.

One level deeper, even before linguistic relations are worked out, a sentence may be conceived in terms of its ideas. Lindsay and Norman (1972) envisage both "Mother is cooking supper for Hubert" and "Hubert's supper is being cooked by mother" by one "deep structure," involving "mother" (agent), "supper" (object), and "Hubert" (recipient) all centered around "cook" (action). Their deep structure is close to what I call *concept structure*. Unlike a linguistic deep structure, a concept structure does not indicate different levels of linguistic units (NP, N, and so on) and how they are related—in short, it is not represented in a tree diagram. One concept structure may underlie several sentences of essentially the same content expressed in different linguistic structures, as does the Lindsay–Norman deep structure. But in the concept structure, action is no more central than agent, object, or recipient: any one of them may become central in different contexts (see Figure 4–5).

A speaker usually attempts to communicate the concept structure to a listener. Our spontaneous speech is often ungrammatical and incomplete

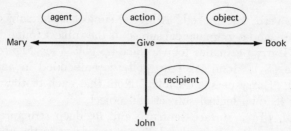

FIGURE 4–5   Concept structure for the sentences: "Mary gives a book to John." "A book is given to John by Mary." "John is given a book by Mary." "It is Mary who gives John a book."

but is understood, perhaps because the speaker and the listener are communicating at the deeper conceptual levels. A concept structure may refer to any or all of agent, action (or state), and recipient of action, regardless whether or not any of them is actually expressed in a sentence. In addition, it may contain information about where, when, for what, with what, and so on, a given event is taking place. At this deepest level, close to the meaning itself without a fully encoded linguistic structure, it is quite conceivable that different languages are very similar.

In Shank's (1972) elaborate theory of natural language understanding, a "conceptual base" underlies all natural language. Its elements are concepts and not words, because a given word in a language may or may not have one or more concepts underlying it. What is stored in memory is likely a conceptual base. Bilinguals presumably have one common conceptual base but different rules for mapping this conceptual base in each of their two languages. A conceptual base exists even in people without normal language use, such as deaf people.

Returning to Chomsky's linguistic deep structure, its status is currently hotly debated. Some linguists claim that languages are universal in deep structure but vary in their transformational rules in diverse ways to give their variety of surface structures. Other linguists (such as McCawley, 1968) reject deep structures as being superfluous. They argue that the generative power of a grammar is located totally in the semantic component, the rules of which operate prior to the operation of the syntactic component. That is, semantics generates the message, which is then related to some particular sentence by rules for syntactic interpretation. We may leave linguists to argue about the existence and the nature of deep structure, and proceed with our description of TGG.

To summarize TGG briefly, the original version consisted of PS-rules and transformational rules. The PS-rules generated an underlying phrase marker, which was made into a kernel sentence by application of obligatory transformational rules only. Optional transformational rules converted one phrase marker into other related phrase markers to produce passives, questions, and so on.

In the revised version, the semantics is integrated into a syntax. The base (rewriting rules + lexicon) generates deep structures, which provide the exclusive basis for semantic interpretation. The function of transformations is to convert deep structures into surface structures. Optional transformations no longer convert one sentence form into other related forms.

TGG IN PSYCHOLINGUISTIC EXPERIMENTS

Now that the difficult task of describing the main features of TGG has been completed, let us see how TGG (so far described) has been used, or misused, in psycholinguistic experiments. The basic question is: Does TGG describe performance? If by "competence" linguists mean a set of linguistic rules internalized in a speaker-hearer's mind, should not the speaker-hearer use these rules in producing and understanding speech? In other words, the rules of TGG should represent or reflect the way in which we produce and understand sentences. Chomsky himself seems to encourage using a grammar as a model of performance in the following statement: "He has . . . acquired a certain competence that he *puts to use* in producing and understanding speech" (1970, p. 184: italics mine). He also makes a statement that clearly discourages the equation of a grammar with a model of performance, as we shall see later. But the term "generate," Chomsky's occasional ambiguous statements, and the explicitness of the rules of TGG influenced some psycholinguists to think that TGG described performance.

Here we shall examine some experiments that have attempted to use TGG as a model of performance. Specifically, experiments have tested the following questions:

1. How are PS-rules reflected in speech?
2. Is a kernel sentence psychologically basic or central, as is suggested by its linguistic centrality?
3. Are transformational complexities reflected in speech processing?
4. Is speech processed according to its surface or deep structure?

How are PS-rules reflected in speech?

Do we perceive and process sentences in syntactic units, especially in phrases, as suggested by PS-rules? There are several ways to tackle this question. The simplest of these is a direct appeal to the intuition of the perceiver. Very often, adult subjects can report a reasonably consistent preferred segmentation of speech.

E. Martin (1970) used a word-sorting technique to see how ordinary users of the language organize words in a sentence into clusters. The subject was presented with a sentence and was asked to group its words into clusters. The test sentences differed in length, meaning, structure, and other characteristics. Subjects organized words of one type of sentence (Frame A) such as "Parents were assisting the advanced teenage pupils" as in Figure 4–6*a*. Note that the object phrase "the advanced teenage pupils" is a relatively compact constituent. Another clearly compact constitutent is the verb complex "were assisting." Note also that the verb complex clusters with the subject and not with the object phrase, thus yielding a subject-verb-object nesting of ((SV)O). The SVO organization is consistent; in all sentences of Frame A we observe ((SV)O); in none do we observe (S(VO), which is the way TGG would analyze the sentences. The other type of sentence, Frame B, ("Children who attend regularly appreciate lessons greatly") yielded (S(VO)), as shown in Figure 4–6*b*. Note that a Frame B sentence has a relative clause.

The experiment shows that subjective grouping of words may depart from linguistic phrasing for some sentences. What is the basis of subjective

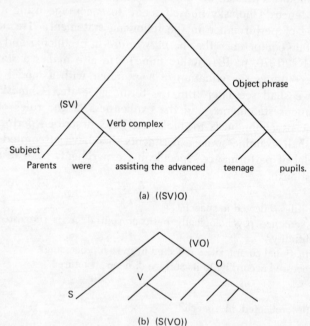

(a) ((SV)O)

(b) (S(VO))

FIGURE 4–6   (a) Subjective phrase marker for "Parents were assisting the advanced teenage pupils." (b) Linguistic phrase marker for the same sentence. (Based on Martin's data, 1970.)

phrasing? It can be semantic: (VO), "assist . . . pupils" in the Frame A sentence does not seem to make a coherent semantic unit, perhaps because three modifiers separate V and O. In a Frame B sentence, a relative clause (such as ". . . who attend regularly . . .") breaks up the close semantic relation between S and V. V and O are adjacent.

Another, more indirect and subtle, technique for discovering perceptual units is to examine the perceived timing of irrelevant sounds superimposed on sentences. Fodor and Bever (1965) asked subjects to listen to a sentence during which a click occurred, and immediately afterward to write down the sentence, indicating where they heard the click. They found that the click tended to be displaced toward major syntactic breaks. If a subject heard a click that occurred during a phrase as having occurred between phrases, it may be because the listener had to process the phrase as a unit that could not be broken by attending to the click.

A test sentence is shown below with a slash marking the major syntactic break, and apostrophes marking the loci where a click actually did occur in different recordings of the same sentence.

"That he was happy / was evident from the way he smiled."

In the above test sentence, subjects were most accurate in locating a click that occurred between the two major phrases of the sentence. A click that occurred elsewhere in the sentence tended to be perceived as occurring at the major break. Subsequent experiments (Garrett et al., 1966) have shown that acoustic variables such as pause and intonation, which tend to mark the constituent boundaries, are not the cues—the grammatical structure alone is the cue.

Reber (1973) points out that the click perception technique may introduce an attentional factor into the results. The sentential material and the click constitute two separate messages, only one of which is within the subject's attentional focus at any one time. With progress through a sentence, the subject would shift attention away from the channel containing the sentence to the channel containing the click; hence there is a decrease in error of click perception later in the sentence. However, within periods of increased or decreased attention, errors in click perception may still reflect linguistic structures.

Minor phrase as a processing unit

We have seen some experimental evidence about how we organize sentences perceptually into syntactic units. We also saw that subjective phrasing may depart sometimes from linguistic phrasing. At any rate, neither PS-rules nor the experiments so far described indicate what is the optimal size of a unit in speech processing. If units of speech processing are phrases, this is a good place to discuss the questions of optimal size of processing.

For a short sentence such as "The man / loves the pretty woman" (subjectively, it may also be organized as "The man loves / the pretty woman"), the two major phrases, NP and VP, seem to constitute the optimal processing units. What about a longer sentence such as "The very tall man / with brown eyes // loves the short woman / with blue eyes"? To process it as a single unit may impose an excessive load on the listener's short-term memory. Apart from the major NP/VP break indicated by the double slash, additional breaks indicated by single slashes will chunk this sentence into four minor phrases, each consisting of three to five words. As we shall see below, for some tasks minor phrases might be useful units of processing. However, no consistent procedure to chunk a long sentence into minor phrases has been described.

What about processing a sentence on a word-to-word basis? We have to agree with Miller (1962a) that we do not process speech in this way, because word-to-word processing involves too many separate decisions, hence is wasteful of processing time and effort. Nor is word-to-word processing the best strategy for getting the correct meaning. The meaning of an isolated word, even a content word, is often ambiguous. Within a phrase, surrounding words delimit or clarify the meaning and function of each word in a sentence. For this reason, a mechanical translation based on word-for-word substitution was so poor as to be nearly worthless (Yngve, 1962).

The optimal processing unit for some tasks seems to be about three to five words, if they form either minor or major syntactic units or phrases. In speaking of processing units, we have to consider the skill of the decoder as well as the difficulty of the material. A given person can process easy material in bigger units than difficult material. A skilled person may be able to process a given type of material in bigger chunks than can an unskilled person.

The following experiments show that we process speech at least in minor phrase groups. In reading aloud, the eye is usually ahead of the voice, because visual and cognitive processing is faster than the motor process of reading aloud. The span between the eye and voice, usually measured in words, is called eye-voice span (EVS). To measure EVS, a text being read is made unavailable (by turning off the light, for example) at some point, and a reader is asked to give as much of the text as possible beyond that point. Educated adults have EVSs of 4.4 words on the average, according to a very early study by Quantz (1897). The span can vary from 0 to 8 words. In a more recent study, Levin and Kaplan (1968) showed that EVS extended to a phrase boundary regardless of the age of the reader and the size of the phrase. The ages of their subjects ranged from about 7 years to adult, and the phrase sizes from 2 to 4 words. When readers inserted words that were not really in the text, their insertions usually completed phrases. Note that EVS involves reading aloud, which may require a different mode of information processing from silent reading.

In conclusion, syntactic units such as NPs or VPs consisting of a few words are used as processing units in a variety of speech behaviors. An NP or a VP is an efficient processing unit because it often conveys a relatively coherent meaning, less so than a full sentence but more so than a single word. If a linguistically defined NP or VP does not have a coherent meaning, then subjects may use meaning-based subjective units. Efficient processing probably always requires the partial processing of units having more and more coherent meaning.

We have discussed some ways in which surface structure affects speech processing. Later on we shall see that deep structure also affects how we process and organize speech units.

Are kernel sentences psychologically central?

Now we shift our attention from phrase units to the question of how we process different syntactic forms. Are transformational rules relevant to speech processing? According to the original version of TGG, a kernel string is transformed into such other sentence forms as questions or passives by optional transformations. A kernel sentence is a simple, active, affirmative, and declarative sentence (SAAD), which is derived from a kernel string using obligatory but not optional transformations. George Miller (1962b) was the first psychologist to translate this linguistic notion into a psychological one, by proposing that people remember a nonkernel sentence such as a passive by first transforming it into its corresponding kernel sentence, and then storing it along with a footnote about its syntactic structure. The transformational footnote, if remembered, enables people to make the necessary grammatical transformations from the kernel back to the nonkernel during recall. Such a model would increase the potential capacity of the human storage system. How has this eminently plausible model fared in psychological experiments?

One of the early experiments that support Miller's model neatly is that of Mehler (1963). He asked subjects to recall verbatim sentences such as "The man has bought the house" that varied in content and structural form. The subjects learned the active sentences significantly faster than the other forms, and most of their errors were syntactic errors. Moreover, the syntactic errors did not occur in a random fashion, but tended to produce a simpler grammatical form than the one given as a stimulus—for example, a passive sentence tended to be recalled in its corresponding active version. The experiment below by Savin and Perchonock (1965) also supports Miller's model, but in addition answers the following question.

Is transformational complexity reflected in psychological processing?

Exploiting the fact that our short-term memory storage is limited, Savin and Perchonock devised an ingenious experiment to test the effects of transformational complexity on sentence processing. They required subjects to recall both a sentence and a set of unrelated words. The number of unrelated words successfully recalled was the measure of the storage requirement for that particular sentence. In other words, assuming that the storage capacity is limited, a structurally simple sentence will require a small space, allowing many unrelated words to be stored, while a complex sentence requires a larger memory space, allowing fewer words to be stored. The test sentence in SAAD was "The boy has hit the ball," and other forms were transformations of this sentence into passive (P), negative (N), and so on. The experimenters assumed that passive + negative (PN) is more complex than either passive or negative alone, and passive + negative + question (PNQ) in turn is more complex than either PN or PQ alone. Table 4–2 lists the different sentence forms, all of which except NQ were tested by Savin and Perchonock. They further assumed that the content of the sentence was more or less the same while its structure changed in forms.

TABLE 4–2   Syntactic Forms of Sentences

Sentence form		Example
SAAD:	Simple-active-affirmative-declarative	The boy has hit the ball.
Q:	Question	Has the boy hit the ball?
P:	Passive	The ball has been hit by the boy.
N:	Negation	The boy has not hit the ball.
PQ:	Passive-question	Has the ball been hit by the boy?
PN:	Passive-negation	The ball has not been hit by the boy.
NQ:	Negation-question	Has not the boy hit the ball?
PNQ:	Passive-negation-question	Has not the ball been hit by the boy?

As predicted, the number of unrelated words recalled reflected structural complexity. That is, it decreased in order of the sentence forms listed in Table 4–2, except that slightly more words were recalled for PNQ than for PN. Also, the extra storage space needed for N was larger than for P, even though the model does not predict that any individual transformation is more difficult than another. In spite of these puzzling points, the experimenters concluded that sentences were remembered or perceived in terms of their underlying structures plus some specification of the operations required for generation of surface forms. The more complex transformations required more complex psychological processing. The sentence length had much less influence upon the task than did the transformational complexity.

Deep and surface structures in sentence processing

Does the deep structure of a sentence exist only as a technique of linguistic description? Do we process sentences in deep structure as well as in surface structure? The basic experimental paradigm in testing this question is to construct sentences that have different deep and surface structures, and then to see which of these two structures has a greater influence on our speech processing. Blumenthal (1967) required subjects to remember lists of two types of passive sentences: (1) "Gloves were made by tailors," and (2) "Gloves were made by hand." These two sentences are identical in surface structure—both sentences have "gloves" as the grammatical subject and "by + noun" as an adverbial phrase. However, the deep structure of sentence (1) is "Tailors make gloves" and that of sentence (2), "Someone makes gloves by hand." The experimenter aided subjects in recalling the sentences by giving them the final noun, "tailors" or "hand," as a prompt. Note that these two words have identical syntactic forms on the surface. Yet the noun corresponding to the underlying or logical subject, "tailor," was a more successful memory aid. Thus the experiment can be interpreted as showing that deep structure influences our speech processing.

Earlier in this chapter we talked about how the perception of click timing is influenced by surface phrase boundaries. A later experiment shows that the most effective structural division governing errors in click location is the point corresponding to the division into sentences in the deep structure, and is not directly related to the surface structure (Bever, Lackner, and Kirk, 1969). However, Toppino's (1974) re-examination of the same data argues that the influence of surface phrase boundaries is greater than that of deep phrase boundaries.

The deep structure should be, and is, relevant in the Dutch language as well. Levelt (1970) used the technique of having Dutch subjects judge word relatedness in a sentence. When the difference between the deep and the surface structure was minimal, as in "The boy has lost a dollar," the judgment was as the phrase structure predicts. However, when Levelt used a surface sentence that looked different from its deep structure, the deep structure influenced the subjects' judgment of word relatedness. Consider the following sentences: "Carla takes the book and goes to school." (The word order is the same in Dutch.) In the deep structure the sentence consists of "Carla takes the book" and "Carla goes to school." Note that the second "Carla" has been deleted in the surface structure of the coordinate sentence. How would a subject judge the relatedness between "Carla"—"takes" compared to "Carla"—"goes"? If one is taking the deep structure into account, one will discern the double role of "Carla" and judge these two pairs as about equally related. Levelt's Dutch subjects indeed gave these two pairs highly similar scores of relatedness.

These experiments seem to indicate that sentence processing can be influenced more by deep than by surface structures.

Re-examination of the relation between TGG and speech

So far I have listed, almost breathlessly, one experiment after another, each seeming to support the idea that a transformational generative grammar describes speech processing. At this point, let us pause and examine whether these experiments were appropriate in their procedures and in their interpretations. Specifically, let us re-examine the roles of the centrality of SAAD, transformational complexity, and deep structure in speech processing.

One of the common characteristics of the experiments we have seen is that they involved isolated sentences of short, well-formed, and simple construction. Such sentences are not representative of our spontaneous speech. However, the use of these materials was perhaps defensible because of the convenience they provide for experimental manipulations. Less defensible is the assumption of some psychologists that when a sentence form is changed from an affirmative-declarative to a negative or to a question, the content is held constant or unchanged. Are "I go," "Do I go?" and "I don't go" necessarily the same in content? We must remind ourselves that the purpose of using different syntactic transformations is to communicate some particular aspect of meaning. The least defensible procedure is asking subjects to memorize sentences verbatim, which certainly is not typical of everyday sentence processing. In verbatim memorization, subjects tend to bypass comprehension of sentence meaning and concentrate on memorizing individual words. Verbatim memorization is not a real test of the hypothesis that subjects have to decode sentences into kernels in order to understand them.

The investigators also overlooked the possibility that different sentence forms occur with varying frequencies in natural speech, which might influence our processing. How frequently do different sentence forms occur in our natural speech? We shall learn in the next chapter that common words are processed faster and better than uncommon words. We may find a similar phenomenon in processing different sentence forms. In Taylor's (1969) sentence-production experiment, the majority of the produced sentences were SAADs when the subjects were told to produce sentences in any form, in any length, without time pressure. There was a sprinkling of P, N, Q, Imperative (I), NI, but virtually no PNQ. Qs should be more frequent in dialogue situations.

Goldman-Eisler and Cohen (1970) collected samples of spontaneous speech based on about 1,000 clauses, uttered by speakers of various levels of intelligence, education, and mental health, in discussion, speeches, and interviews. SAAD constituted 80–90 percent of the verbal form, while N and P were in the range of 0.7 to 10 percent. PN or PNQ occurred very seldom. Thus we may conclude that differences in the difficulty of processing different sentence forms, as found in some experiments, may be a by-product of the fact that SAAD is very frequent, while N, P, PN, and especially PNQ are relatively infrequent and less practiced. Even when we consciously try to produce PNQ, we cannot produce it as easily as we can produce its "corresponding" PN or P. However, as we shall see below, there are semantic factors that also account for differential difficulties of sentence forms.

Incidentally, why is SAAD used so frequently? Brown and Hanlon (1970) ask whether our predominant use of SAAD is an instance of Zipf's (1949) principle of least effort—we prefer SAAD because it is the simplest sentence structure. I rather think that what form of sentence we produce is dictated by semantic consideration—our communication needs call for SAADs more often than any other sentence form.

In short, the experiments that supported TGG as a performance model used peculiar experimental procedures that may have led to peculiar experimental results where subjects seemed to be preoccupied with processing structure rather than content of sentences, and syntactic complexities alone contributed to processing complexities.

COGNITIVE APPROACHES TO SENTENCE PROCESSING

Now let us examine some experiments whose procedures do less violence to our ordinary speech processing. Investigators ask subjects to verify, recognize after delays, recall, or paraphrase a variety of sentences. Often the investigators provide linguistic and perceptual contexts for sentences tested. The subjects have to understand the meaning of test sentences to be able to carry out most of the experimental tasks. Hence, the following experiments test more real (less artificial) speech processing than the ones we have just discussed.

Verification

Slobin (1966a) required subjects to verify the content of sentences (true or false) with respect to pictures. The pictures presented situations that were either *reversible,* in that the object of action could also serve as the subject (as, "the cat is chasing the dog"), or "nonreversible," in that the object could not normally serve as the subject (as, "the girl is watering the flower").

Slobin investigated many variables and their interrelations, but we shall examine only three findings relevant to the present discussion. (1) Syntactically simple negatives took more time to evaluate than relatively more complex passives. Note that Affirmative → N involves a change of meaning while P → Active does not. (2) Making sentences nonreversible largely washed out the differences between active and passive sentences, making passives about as easy as kernels and passive-negatives about as easy as negatives. If reverse tranformation of P into a kernel is a necessary first step before meaning can be understood, any type of P should take longer to evaluate than its corresponding A. (3) True negatives (as, "the ball is not square") were more difficult than false negatives (as, "the ball is not round"), which in turn were more difficult than false passive-negatives. The false N performs the normal negative role of indicating a change of meaning, in the sense that it *denies* the situation shown in the picture. The true N performs the unnatural role of affirming what is in the picture.

Harriot's (1969) experiment also indicates that people do not always need to carry out a full transformational analysis to arrive at the meaning of a passive. He used sentences such as "The doctor treated the patient" and "The bather was rescued by the lifeguard." These sentences are reversible syntactically, but not semantically. That is, we do not expect, from our experience in the world, to hear a sentence such as "The patient treated the doctor." Subjects took about equal time to state the actor and the object of active and passive sentences in such semantically nonreversible sentences. However, in semantically reversible sentences such as "The brother hated the sister," passives took more time than actives. In short, subjects use flexible strategies for comprehending sentences, and when semantic cues are prominent they play a more important role than syntactic analysis. The passive transformation may take extra processing time only in the absence of clear cues.

These findings point out that if we have to attend to the content of sentences, processing difficulty is determined not by the syntactic complexity of the sentences alone but also by their semantic content. The results challenge sentence-processing models based exclusively on syntax—such as that each syntactic transformation takes a constant amount of processing time or that nonkernel sentences must be transformed back to kernel strings in processing.

Sentence memory

Sachs's (1967) experiment on sentence recognition was more analogous to sentence processing in everyday situations; she used passages of connected discourse consisting of longish sentences, which subjects had to recognize at various time intervals. What aspects of a sentence would subjects retain in such a task?

The four types of sentence used as test material were:

1. (the base sentence) He sent a letter about it to Galileo, the great Italian scientist.
2. (semantically changed sentence) Galileo, the great Italian scientist, sent him a letter about it.
3. (passive) A letter about it was sent to Galileo, the great Italian scientist.
4. (form changed or words rearranged, without changing the meaning) He sent Galileo, the great Italian scientist, a letter about it.

The concept structures sort out the relations among the agent, action, object of action, and recipient of action in Figure 4–7. These sentences were embedded in a contextual discourse. The subjects' task was to recognize whether or not a test sentence was identical to the original one that appeared in the preceding passage. Any one of the above four types of sentence could appear either as the original or as a test sentence.

The recognition memory for the form of a sentence declined much more rapidly than that for the meaning when tested with a varying amount of interpolated material between the original and tested sentences—0, 80, or

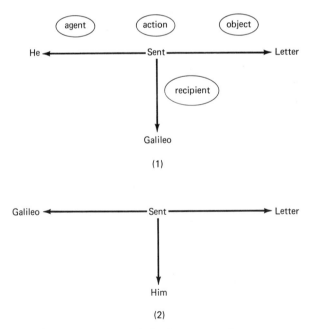

FIGURE 4–7   Concept structure of the four types of test sentence used by Sachs. Note that only (1) and (2) have different concept structures. (3) = (1) without Agent; (4) = (1).

160 syllables of connected discourse, which was a continuation of the passage. In other words, a change in meaning of the sentence was much more often recognized than change of form; the percentage of correct recognition for semantic change did not go down much over longer time intervals that accompanied different amounts of interpolated material. The passive/active change (3) gave results similar to form change (4). Changes from active to passive were no easier to recognize than changes from passive to active.

Sachs concludes that the original surface form of the sentence is stored only for the short time necessary for comprehension. When a semantic interpretation has been made, we store the meaning and not the syntactic form.

Here is a unique finding on the question of transformational complexity, deep structure, and sentence meaning. Bransford and Franks (1971) told subjects a story made up of individual sentences such as:

> The rock rolled down the mountain.
> The rock crushed the hut.
> The hut is at the river.
> The hut is tiny.

In actual presentation, these sentences were randomly interpersed with other sentences that were not part of the story, such as:

> The breeze is warm.
> The ants ate the jelly.
> The story is in the newspaper.
> The jelly is sweet.

The four sentences that comprise one story, or one complete idea set, must be extracted and put together from the entire set of sentences that actually are presented. Other sentences can be combined to form four different stories or idea sets.

About five minutes after all the sentences had been presented (during which the subjects did a short-term memory task), the subjects were asked to state whether or not they had actually heard the following test sentences before.

Test 1: The hut is at the river.
Test 2: The rock crushed the tiny hut.
Test 3: The rock crushed the tiny hut at the river.
Test 4: The rock which rolled down the mountain crushed the tiny hut at the river.

Only Test 1 actually had been presented to the subjects. Yet, when they were asked to say whether they recognized any of the four test sentences, they overwhelmingly selected Test 4, even though they had never in fact heard it. Test 3 was next in terms of the number of times subjects (falsely) recognized it as having occurred before. For both Test 2 and Test 1 (the only sentence actually presented), subjects usually denied having heard it before. Subjects were very accurate in rejecting a sentence created across idea sets rather than within an idea set.

In other words, when the subjects actually heard a series of short sentences—a series of deep structures, if you like, because the surface and deep structures were nearly identical—they combined them into one long, transformationally more complex sentence in their memories. How do we explain this remarkable finding? As one long, structurally more complex sentence, the meaning becomes clearer because four separate events are now logically and meaningfully connected to make one coherent, wholistic sentence meaning. The four events may be even stored as one visual image. This kind of spatial arrangement of concrete events should lend itself easily to image evocation (Paivio, 1970). However, Franks and Bransford (1972) used abstract sentences (as, "The arrogant attitude expressed in the speech led to immediate criticism") and replicated the findings of Bransford and Franks (1971). Griggs (1974) also replicated the above findings using a recall test. Ultimately, we extract and retain an idea or ideas expressed in sentences, not a discrete set of sentences.

If a sentence is processed according to its deep structure, one such as "French is spoken here" should be processed as "Someone speaks French here"—an actor is supplied, and the passive form is changed into an active form. Slobin (1968a) showed that a *truncated passive*, a passive without an explicit subject, is processed somewhat differently from a full passive. Truncated passives tend to be recalled verbatim, and not as full passives or as actives, while full passives are likely to be changed to active forms. But truncated passives are much more common in our speech, and are recalled with greater accuracy. Incidentally, in grammatical description, a truncated passive is generated from a full passive by deleting its actor, and hence has a more complex derivational history than a full passive.

In a recent experiment, Franks and Bransford (1974) pointed out that context can influence how we process truncated and full passives. If the context supplied information about the deleted actor, verbatim memory for the truncated passives decreased, and subjects tended to recognize alternate sentence forms (actives and full passives) expressing the meaning of the truncated passives plus the contextually given actor. An example of their truncated sentence was: "After the harvest a huge feast was served." (Context: "Mrs. Brown, who did it, was a very good cook.")

The investigators concluded that subjects often reconstruct information about syntax from semantic information. The sentence is not the basic unit of memory. This conclusion may be valid, but does not invalidate Slobin's finding that truncated passives are normally processed faster than full passives. We produce truncated passives to de-emphasize actors when actors are not important. Conversely, when we process a sentence like "French is spoken here," we can forget about actors.

Proposition

In what form is content of a sentence stored in long-term memory? Perhaps in "propositions." Anderson (1974b) defines a proposition as:

. . . an abstract memory representation which is structured according to certain rules of formation and which has a truth value. Although propositions are asserted by English sentences, propositions are not sentences nor are they made out of words. Rather, a proposition is a more abstract entity composed of concepts referenced by words. (p. 452)

Propositions are semantic interpretations of sensory experiences. (1974a)

According to Russell (1940), every valid sentence expresses a proposition, and every proposition can be expressed by a sentence. We may consider that a proposition is a fact, an event, or a state of affairs asserted or described by a sentence. But truth and falsity belong not to sentences but to propositions. "All triangles are trilateral" is an example of a proposition that is true, and "The earth is flat" is an example of a proposition that is false. The truth or falsity of the proposition "I feel sad" can be determined not by the sentence itself, but in relation with the state of my feeling. "The King of France is wise" spoken by a Frenchman living during the reign of Louis XIV and the same sentence spoken by a Frenchman during the reign of Louis XV will have different truth values (Chao 1968).

A sentence expresses a proposition, which is its sense. When two sentences have the same meaning, that is because they express the same proposition. The same proposition may be expressed in strikingly different sentences from diverse languages. Even in two related languages, French and German, we express the same proposition in different sentences: Défense de se pencher à la fenêtre"/"Nicht hinauslehnen" (Forbidden to lean yourself out of the window/Not to lean out) (a warning on the Orient Express). In translating from one language to another, especially to another unrelated language, the best strategy is to extract or recover propositions from sentences of the source language and express them in sentences of the target language.

Anderson (1974b) demonstrated that there are two modes of sentence representation in memory. Immediate memory of a sentence is in exact wording with retention of sentence form (passive or active). After a delay (about 2 min), the propositional representation comes to dominate and effects of sentence form diminish.

In Anderson's experiment, eight test sentences were parts of short, coherently structured stories (2 min for reading). Subjects had to indicate whether the probe sentence was true or false, and if it was true, whether it had the same form (passive or active) as the test sentence.

> Test sentence: "The boy hit the girl."
> Probe sentence: "The girl was hit by the boy."

In the delayed condition, subjects could still verify whether the probe sentences were true or false as well as they could in the immediate memory condition. But memory about the exact form of the test sentences was not as good as in the immediate memory. The propositional representation seems to have an active-like character, as indicated by the slow verifications of passive probes after delays.

Kintsch and Keenan (1973) showed that the number of underlying propositions influenced subjects' processing of sentences. They gave subjects sentences that differed in the number of underlying propositions from 4 to 9, but were equal in total number of words. The subjects had to read and recall the sentences immediately after reading.

Since there is no algorithmic procedure, or explicit step-by-step procedure, to analyze a given sentence into its propositions, the experimenters started with the propositional expressions themselves and translated these into English sentences, as follows:

> (took, Romulus, women, by force)
> (found, Romulus, Rome)
> (legendary, Romulus)
> (Sabines, women)

Each proposition consists of a relational term (written first) and one or more arguments, or things that are related. The above set of propositions is translated into one sentence: "Romulus, the legendary founder of Rome, took the women of the Sabines by force."

The subjects' reading time increased as more propositions were processed, and the number of propositions they were able to recall was related to processing time.

It appears that it is not the mere quantity of propositions that is important; the type of proposition also matters. It was found that all propositions were not equally difficult to remember: superordinate propositions were recalled better than propositions that were structurally subordinate. We can expect that the degree of difficulty in processing propositions may depend very much on content of the propositions. Kintsch and Keenan could not shed much light on this possibility because they used test sentences that dealt with familiar historical events; the test sentences had more or less equal familiarity. Compare the following two statements:

> The mass of a body in motion is a function of the energy content and varies with the velocity. (one of the statements of the theory of relativity)
> The price of a meal in a restaurant is a function of the meat quality and varies with the amount.

Which of the above two statements can you recall better after one reading? In a "difficult" proposition, constituting concepts and their relations are abstract and unfamiliar. Some sets of propositions are easy to integrate into one coherent story, while other sets of equal number are not so easily integrated. Hence the findings of Bransford and Franks (1971).

Paraphrasing

The following experiment shows step by step how we increase the derivational history of a sentence—which at the end turns out to be not relevant to speech processing. The main question Fodor and Garrett (1967) asked was: When and if we do recover deep structures, how do we do it? Increasing the distance from deep to surface structure by increased transformations tends to obliterate surface structure clues to deep structure. In one experiment they required subjects to paraphrase self-embedded sentences such as the one given below.

> "The shot (which) the soldier (that) the mosquito bit fired missed."

The investigators found that versions that included relative pronouns ("which" and "that") were easier to deal with than versions where the relative pronouns were deleted. According to the authors, this was the case because the relative pronoun provides a perceptual clue to semantically crucial deep structure relationships, especially relations between subjects and objects.

But the next series of experiments interests us more. The investigators added adjectives to the sentences in order to increase greatly the derivational complexity of the sentence. The above sentence, with two adjectives added, now looks like:

> "The *first* shot (which) the *tired* soldier (that). . . ."

A schematic deep structure tree for the sentence portion "the tired soldier fired the shot" is shown in Figure 4–8.

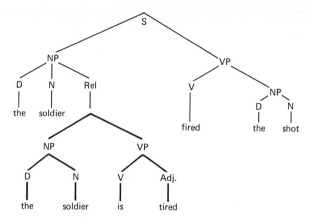

FIGURE 4–8   Schematic deep structure tree for "The tired soldier fired the shot."

The order of operations in the derivation is roughly the following:

1. Relativization applies to produce "the soldier who is tired."
2. "Who is" deletes optionally to yield the intermediate form, "the soldier tired."
3. Mandatory permutation of the adjective with the noun yields "the tired soldier."

An addition of one adjective involves the above three operations. Hence, two adjectives could add six more transformations to the derivational history of the sentence with relative pronouns, but they did not impair performance. On the contrary, the sentence "The first shot the tired soldier the mosquito bit fired missed" was actually easier than the version without adjectives. Retrieval of deep structures has been called a prerequisite for understanding of sentence meaning. Yet such retrieval has to depend on aspects of meaning and clues on the surface. Further, transformational complexity was not very relevant to processing difficulty.

The following two sentences may be considered paraphrases of each other—that is, they have identical semantic content expressed in different structures.

John	liked	the	painting	and	(John)	bought	it	from	the	duchess.
(sub. 1)			(obj. 1)		(omitted sub. 1)		(obj. 1)			

The	painting	pleased	John	and	the	duchess	sold	it	to	him.
	(sub. 1)		(obj. 1)			(sub. 2)		(obj. 2 = sub. 1)	(obj. 1)	

Subjects confused these two sentences in their memories (Johnson-Laird and Stevenson, 1970). Note that these sentences have different surface as well as deep structures but similar semantic representations. Once again, the level at which people process semantic content must be more abstract than a particular deep structure configuration.

Constructive approach

I have been more and more downplaying the importance of linguistic structures, even the sacred "deep structure," in speech processing. To culminate this trend, let us examine a "constructive approach" to semantic memory proposed by Bransford, Barclay, and Franks (1972). They argue against the common tacit assumption that sentences "carry meaning." They call such an assumption the "interpretive approach" to semantic memory: a semantically interpreted deep structure provides a sufficient characterization of what is stored in memory. Bransford and co-workers assert that people carry meaning, and linguistic inputs merely act as cues that people can use to recreate and modify their previous knowledge of the world. The act of comprehending a sentence generally involves considerably more than merely recovering the information specified by the input sentence; it involves constructing semantic information using the input sentence as a cue. A sentence is not merely a perceptual object that the listener may recall or recognize, but also a source of information that the listener assimilates to his existing cognitive knowledge.

They have devised a series of ingenious experiments to demonstrate their viewpoints. Consider the following two sentences.

1. Three turtles rested *beside* a floating log and a fish swam beneath them.
2. Three turtles rested *on* a floating log and a fish swam beneath them.

These sentences have identical deep structures that differ only in the lexical items *on* or *beside*, but the semantic situations differ in at least one very important way. The scene suggested by sentence (1) includes information about a fish swimming beneath the turtles. The scene suggested by (2) also includes this information, but it includes something additional. Since the turtles were on the log and the fish swam beneath them, it follows that the fish swam beneath the log. This information—the fish swam beneath the log—was not supplied by the linguistic input, however, but had to come from one's general cognitive knowledge of the world (in this case, knowledge of spatial relations).

Now, assume that subjects hear either sentence (1) or (2), and then hear a recognition sentence that merely changes the final pronoun specified in the input sentence, as in:

3. "Three turtles rested (beside/on) a floating log and a fish swam beneath *it*."

The two approaches to semantic memory, constructive and interpretive, make different predictions about the probability that the subjects will think they actually heard sentence (3) before. According to the interpretive approach, subjects store only the linguistic information underlying the input sentence. Hence subjects hearing either sentence (1) or (2) should be equally likely to detect the pronoun change in sentence (3). The constructive approach makes a different set of predictions. Subjects are assumed to construct wholistic semantic descriptions of situations. If they forget the information underlying the input sentence, they should not be reduced to guessing but should base their recognition ratings on the complete semantic descriptions obtained during acquisition trials.

In short, the constructive approach predicts that one's ability to detect the pronoun change in sentence (3) depends on whether one originally heard sentence (1) or (2). Subjects hearing sentence (1) should reject sentence (3), since it agrees with neither the actual input sentence nor the complete semantic description constructed. Subjects hearing (2) should be quite likely to think they heard sentence (3), since (3) is consonant with the complete semantic description presumably acquired. The experiment confirmed what the constructive approach predicted.

The following experiment by Johnson, Bransford, and Solomon (1973) also shows that subjects build patterns of meaning based on input sentences, or infer additional information not actually included in the input. Subjects were presented with concise English passages. In a subsequent recognition test, they falsely "recognized" sentences that introduced new information. Having heard "The boy pounded the nail to fix the birdhouse," they frequently reported recognizing "The boy was using the hammer to fix the birdhouse."

A thought on sentence-comprehension processes

What kind of sentence-comprehension processing can we suggest to explain these experimental results? Various elaborate models have been proposed. For example, Wason and Johnson-Laird (1972) have suggested a model for the processing of negative sentences, and H. H. Clark (1973) one for several forms of sentences. Glucksberg, Trabasso, and Wald (1973) and Olson and Filby (1972) discuss aspects of the sentence-comprehension process when sentence content has to be verified against pictures. In such tasks, at least the following stages of mental operations seem to take place:

Stage 1. Encode the sentence and the picture into comparable internal representations.

Stage 2. Compare the constituents of the representations.

Stage 3. If a mismatch occurs, a "truth index" is changed. In other words, people start off with a tendency to respond "true" and alter this response if necessary as processing continues.

Stage 4. Respond according to the final state of the truth index.

Stages 1 and 2 raise many controversies. Is the received sentence transformed syntactically (as, P → A) before further processing? Is the comprehension of sentence constituents based on surface structure or on deep structure? What is the order of processing constituents? And so on and so forth. The experiments by Glucksberg and co-workers indicate that context and task demands impose order on the list and lead to different operations on these structures. The depth of processing of sentences varies from simple lexical comparisons up to full encoding and use of syntactic and semantic features and case relations.

Sentences that can be verified against pictures seem to be special cases, and might involve special sentence-comprehension processes. How do we represent in a picture, constituent by constituent, "Do not waste your precious life away"? Sentences might involve different comprehension processes depending upon how concrete they are. Comprehension of concrete sentences depends heavily on nonverbal imagery, while that of abstract sentences, such as the above, depends more on verbal coding (Klee and Eysenck, 1973).

It is premature to propose one rigid model of sentence comprehension that can apply to all types of sentences. Here I will suggest an idea, not a model, about what mental operations we might go through in comprehending different sentence forms. This idea may apply to but one, albeit more general than picture verification, type of sentence comprehension. It incorporates some of the essential features of the models proposed by others.

When we receive a sentence, we compare it with a world event or experience that we habitually store in memory as "sentence information." This information is not in the form of surface or deep sentence structure— it is more akin to a concept structure, or sometimes to visual imagery. Taylor's (1969) sentence-production experiment (to be described shortly) showed that sentences about some extremely common topics may be as good as ready-made so that they can be produced with virtually no latency, but other sentences have to be formulated, and take varying amounts of latency. Such "ready-made" sentences may be considered as habitually stored sentence information.

If negative sentences are usually more difficult to process than their corresponding affirmative sentences, it may be because our habitual sentence information is in the affirmative form. Most of the sentences produced by the subjects in Taylor's experiment were in SAAD, but some were in P, NT, or Q. If "apples are good" is the habitually stored sentence information, in comprehending "apples are not good" we have to first compare the received sentence information with the stored one, and then negate it. Thus there are two processes involved, as opposed to one process in merely comparing a received affirmative sentence to the stored affirmative sentence information.

As for true negatives such as "The ball is not square," first we have to produce "The ball is square," compare it with the stored "The ball is round," and then negate it. On the other hand, to process a false negative such as "The ball is not round," we merely have to compare it with the stored information and negate it. Accordingly, Slobin (1966a) found that a true negative was more difficult to process than a false negative.

Wason (1965) found that in some contexts negatives are actually quite easy to process quickly and correctly, especially in the context of "plausible denial"—e.g., it is more reasonable to deny that a spider is an insect (once one has learned that fact) than to deny that a pig is an insect. (Who would have that stored?) "The train was not late this morning" would be obviously more pertinent when the train is normally late than when it is normally punctual.

In a plausible denial, let us say that the stored sentence information is "train is late," if that is the normal event. Now, if we receive "train is not late," the listener goes through the usual two processes. But suppose the train is punctual normally, and hence our stored information is "train is punctual." In this case, first we have to convert the stored sentence information from "train is punctual" to "train is late," to which "train is not late" is compared, and then negated. Thus three processes are involved, and hence "train is not late" is harder to process when the train is normally punctual than when it is normally late.

"Don't shout so loudly!" may be comprehended faster than its SAAD version, because the habitually stored sentence information seems to be in negative-imperative on this theme, as revealed in short latency in production (Taylor, 1969). For reversible passives, we may store two alternative sentence informations: "The girl kicks the boy" and "The boy kicks the girl." In nonreversible sentences we may store only one possible sentence, "The boy rakes the leaves" but not "The leaves rake the boy." Thus a nonreversible passive sentence is easier to comprehend than a reversible passive (Slobin, 1966a). Truncated passives also may be stored in that version rather than in full passive forms, hence are processed faster then full passives.

In short, we store sentence informations that reflect habitual events in the world. Sentence comprehension involves comparing a received sentence with habitually stored sentence information. Hence, speed and accuracy in comprehension are at least partly related to the degree of matches in forms between the stored information and a received sentence. Of course there are many events in the world for which there is no habitually coded information. Compare "The ball is round" to "The ball is red (or blue, or green)."

To conclude our discussion on sentence processing, sentences seem to be processed for, and stored in, their semantic content in terms of concept structures or propositions, which may lie at an even more abstract level than linguistic deep structure. Further, we comprehend and retain sentence meaning in relation to our knowledge of the world. Our habitually stored sentence informations on many events may be mostly in SAAD, but some may be in other forms.

When such linguistic notions as deep structure and transformational complexity appear to influence our speech processing, they may do so incidentally. That is, often deep structure may clarify grammatical relations of words in complex sentences, and sometimes transformational complexity accompanies semantic complexity. But sentence meaning can be more or less than is contained in deep structure. A transformationally more complex sentence may sometimes be a simpler or more practiced structure on the surface, in which case it will be easier to process than a transformationally simpler sentence.

PRODUCING SENTENCES

All the experiments on sentence processing we have examined so far are on sentence decoding—how we perceive, understand, and remember sentences we hear and read. We now ask: what processes does a speaker go through in producing a sentence? Does he go through the same operations as TGG describes? Chomsky himself says "no."

It would clearly be absurd to suppose that the "speaker" of such a language, in formulating an "utterance," first selects the major categories, then the categories into which these are analyzed, and so forth, finally at the end of the process, selecting the words or symbols that he is going to use (deciding what he is going to talk about). To think of a generative grammar in these terms is to take it to be a model of performance rather than a model of competence, thus totally misconceiving its nature (1965, p. 140).

Whether or not we are interested in testing TGG as a performance model, the question of how we produce sentences is an important one, but there are not many analytical experiments on it. Thus I have to describe my own experiment (Taylor, 1969) in some detail. In it I asked the question: in producing sentences, are speakers mainly concerned with content or with structure? If the structure is more important, then we can ask further questions, such as whether or not a speaker goes through the steps and rules of sentence generation as described in TGG.

Sentence production—content or structure?

To answer the first question, I gave my subjects one-word topics on which to produce sentences. By giving a new topic for each new sentence, I forced them to formulate a sentence theme at the moment of hearing a topic. This is a very useful procedure for revealing subjects' sentence-conceiving time as a function of either topic difficulty or the structural complexity of sentences to be produced. In ordinary sentence production, we may formulate our next sentence while we are still in the process of producing the current one. Thus pauses in connected discourse are hard to interpret: if there is a short latency, it may be because the speaker has already formulated his sentence while he was producing the preceding ones, not because the sentence to be produced is easy in content. The same thing can be said about a long sentence with many clauses—the speaker may formulate the theme of the next clause(s) while speaking the current one. In dialogues, a listener may be able to formulate his answer while listening to a question from the other person.

Producing a sentence on a one-word topic not only seems to simulate our everyday sentence production to some degree but also lends itself easily to experimental manipulation of the variables. For example, I could calibrate the one-word topics in difficulty, thus indirectly manipulating the content of sentences. I assumed that infrequent words are more difficult topics than frequent words, and that within each frequency range, abstract words are more difficult topics than concrete ones. Examples of topic words of different difficulty levels are:

> "car" (frequent-concrete)
> "soul" (frequent-abstract)
> "gesticulate" (infrequent-concrete)
> "phenomenal" (infrequent-abstract)

The subjects' sentences were examined for their structural complexities in two ways. One way was to draw a tree diagram of each sentence, and see how many nodes completely encoded the structure of the main noun phrase, the subject of the sentence. Of the two main constituents of a sentence $NP_1 + VP$, the speaker presumably first encodes NP_1 completely, storing VP in short-term memory for later encoding. This assumption follows from Yngve's "depth" model of sentence production, which will be discussed in detail later in this chapter. Thus, "you," "the pins," "the pins in the box," and "the pins in the box on the table" involve two, four, six, and eight structural encoding operations for this first component, the noun phrase, of the sentence (Figure 4–9). The smaller the number of structural encoding operations, the sooner can the speaker start sentence production, if the main

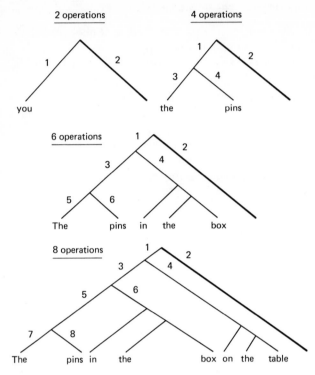

FIGURE 4–9   Structural encoding operations needed to produce sentence subjects of different complexity. (Adapted from Taylor, 1969.)

concern is structural encoding. A possible pause before VP may reflect the structural encoding of that constituent, but this question is worth pursuing only if we find a relation between presentence latency (the time between the presentation of the topic word and the subject's overt production of a sentence) and the structural encoding operation of NP_1. Another way to examine structural complexity very grossly is to compare the latency to produce different forms of sentences within a given difficulty level of the topic. Does a given speaker take longer to produce a passive or a negative than an active sentence?

Neither of the above two indices of structural complexity influenced the subjects' latency, but the topic difficulty (content) did. As expected, infrequent-abstract topic words had the largest mean latency, followed by infrequent-concrete topics, frequent-abstract topics, and frequent-concrete topics in that order. I concluded that speakers have to use their conceiving time more on content than on structure. We talked about the characteristics of abstract words in Chapter 3, and shall talk about infrequent words in Chapter 5. Abstract words may take longer to encode. Infrequent words may be low in our response hierarchy; they are less likely to be given as responses in word association tests, in word recall, and in other verbal behavior. These characteristics of topic words are all parts of the semantic aspects of sentences.

An interesting incidental finding in this experiment was that certain topics were more likely to be made into passive sentences, others into negatives, still others into negative-imperatives, and so on. Of course, the majority of the sentences were SAADs. On certain frequent topics the subjects often produced stereotyped non-SAAD sentences such as "Don't *shout* so loudly!", or "Is there a *soul?*" The italics were the topic words. These non-SAAD sentences were produced very quickly with short latencies. Passive forms, if they were produced at all, were usually on infrequent-abstract words: "*Phenomenal* discoveries have been made . . . ," probably reflecting the fact that both passive forms and infrequent-abstract words are prevalent in technical writings.

When is a sentence structurally so complex that a speaker has to be concerned with it? This is a good question to ask; one can argue that Taylor's experiment did not obtain a syntactic effect because of inappropriate indices of syntactic complexity. Rochester and Gill (1973) compared sentences containing *noun phrase complements* (NPC) and *relative clauses* (Rel C) in monologues and dialogues, and found that production of NPC was accompanied by more speech disruptions. They took filled pauses such as "ah," "um" or tongue slips as clues to decision-making. Examples of NPC and Rel C are:

The fact [that the woman was aggressive] threatened the professor.
   NPC   NPC

The book [which was written by Millet] was lauded by all.
   Rel C   Rel C

The investigators decided that NPCs were accompanied by more disruptions because they are structurally more complex.

Could these two types of sentence differ in semantic difficulty? The clause in NPC is a vital piece of information for the particular predicate, whereas the clause in Rel C is an incidental piece of information, so that an omission of the former is more disruptive semantically than an omission of the latter. Compare:

The fact threatened the professor.
The book was lauded by all.

We wonder if the vital piece of information contained in NPC perhaps required more cognitive planning than the incidental one contained in Rel C. All we can say is that the experimental findings of Rochester and Gill are hard to interpret, because they used natural, ordinary discourse without manipulating either the structure or the semantic content of the sentences.

Goldman-Eisler (1968) also investigated sentences produced in ordinary discourse. She manipulated content difficulty by giving subjects two different tasks: in one task they described, and in the other interpreted, a series of cartoons. The cartoons were taken from *The New Yorker* and had no captions. Interpretation presumably requires more cognitive activity than description, and should be accompanied by more hesitation pauses. Goldman-Eisler obtained the predicted results. Since she did not examine the structures of the produced sentences in the two tasks, we do not know whether the longer pauses accompanying the interpretive tasks are partly due to the subjects' tendency to produce more complex structures in that task.

Presupposition

In another type of sentence-production experiment, Osgood (1971) manipulated nonlinguistic, perceptual events, and then observed how produced sentences varied in form and content. College-student subjects observed the events and then described them in a single sentence to an imaginary child. The perceptual events were such as:

1. orange ring in the middle of the table
2. man stands holding black ball
3. black ball in the middle of the table
4. man stands holding red plastic cup in his hand
5. green plastic cup in the middle of the table

Even though each of the three critical demonstrations, 1, 3, and 5, is identical except for the particular object that is in the middle of the otherwise bare table, the types of sentences produced varied markedly, apparently being influenced by intervening events (event 2 precedes 3, for example). Event 1 produced typically "*An* orange ring is on the table" or "There is an orange ring on the table," whereas Event 3 produced "*The* black ball is on the table."

In general, perceptual events can create cognitive presuppositions in the same way that previously heard sentences do, and these presuppositions influence the form that descriptive sentences take. If a speaker has already seen a particular black ball, and assumed that his listener is familiar with it also, then it is absurd for him to say "the big, round, ball on the table is black" since it is its new location that is now informative, not its color or size. "The ball (or *it*) is on the table" is a more likely sentence.

Presuppositions are the stored knowledge used to interpret utterances, and normally contain information that the speaker assumes he and the hearer can both take for granted at that point in the conversation. They are old, shared information.

Osgood was able to influence the probability that subjects would refer to certain aspects of the situations and express the relations between these in a certain way. The subjects frequently used adjectives to identify an object at its first appearance or to distinguish it from similar objects. As objects became more familiar through repeated presentation, they tended to drop out adjectives; to use *the* ball instead of *a* ball; to use pronouns instead of nouns; to use negatives to express unfilled expectation, and so on.

Osgood's experiment is reminiscent of Olson's (1970) paradigm where a gold star being placed under the same, white, wooden block was referred to by the speaker in varied ways depending on what alternatives were present (see Figure 3–8).

Osgood concludes that what is transformed into a surface sentence is not another "sentence" (deep structure) but rather a momentary cognitive state (similar to a concept structure or a conceptual base?) that is not linguistic at all, yet has its own complex semantic structure.

Presupposition reflects a speaker's perceptual-cognitive activity. If this is so, then speakers of different languages should have similar presuppositions in any given situation. However, the ways these presuppositions are expressed differ across languages. For example, in English, a new thing and a thing known or in the field of attention for both speakers and hearers are distinguished by the choice of article: A new thing will be denoted by "a," and a presupposed one by "the." This distinction is not used in Chinese, Japanese, and Korean. Furthermore, these three languages normally omit agents of actions when the agents are presupposed, that is, are known to both speakers and listeners, or writers and readers. In written English, agentless sentences are considered "degenerate" or incomplete, although agents may well be omitted in everyday conversation.

Let us examine further the nature of presupposition in English sentences. According to Hornby (1974), "Richard has stopped getting drunk every night" involves two propositions: a presupposition that (R at one time got drunk every night), and a *focused proposition* or new information (R no longer does this). Depending on what a speaker wants to assume presupposed, and what he wants to focus, a sentence form can vary (focused prepositions in italics): "*It was John* who caught the thief" presupposes that the thief was caught and focuses on the fact that the one who accomplished this feat was John. On the other hand, the sentences "*It was the thief* that

John caught" and "What John caught *was the thief*" presuppose that John caught someone, and focuses on the fact that someone he caught was the thief.

Four linguists proposed rules for how we express presupposed and focal information in an English sentence using surface structure features. According to Halliday (1967), under normal intonation we present presupposed information earlier in a sentence while presenting focal information later in the sentence. The *by* preposition in the passive is considered by Fillmore (1968) to mark its object as focal, leaving the rest of the sentence as presupposed. In our example sentences that start with an introductory "*It is* . . ." the focus is in the earlier part while the presupposed information is in the later part of the sentence, according to Akmajian (1969). Chomsky (1971) proposed that the phrase which contains the locus of heaviest stress is marked as focal with the rest of the sentence as presupposed.

The kind of questions or queries that can be asked and answered differs according to which information is presupposed or focused. Only when "Richard at one time got drunk every night" is presupposed can the question "Has R stopped getting drunk every night?" be answered "yes" or "no."

We have seen that what information is presupposed and what information is to be focused determines some features of surface structure of sentences. They may also influence how hesitation pauses are distributed in sentence production. In processing sentences, difficulties might arise when presuppositions between the speaker and the listener do not exactly match. Breaking sentences into focused and presupposed information thus opens up a fertile area of research for psycholinguists.

I would like to end our discussion on presupposition with an old joke supplied by one of my editors. A ship's captain and his mate took turns writing up the daily ship's log. One day, angry, the captain wrote: "Mate was drunk today." Next day the mate saw this and took revenge by writing, "Captain was sober today."

Sentence-conceiving processes

Having examined a few experiments on sentence production, what can we say about a speaker's cognitive processes during sentence production? First, there is a topic (not necessarily in one word, of course) on which the speaker wishes to make a statement. Sometimes the topic is thrust upon the speaker; other times the speaker conceives it. The chosen topic may or may not be further elaborated into a brief central idea or theme of a sentence. It is risky to specify what a topic or theme might look like, because its form may differ from sentence to sentence. In sentence decoding, we extract and retain a theme from a given sentence, hence a theme in decoding is more specific than it is in encoding (see, for example, James et al., 1973).

I visualize sentence-producing processes as in Figure 4–10. The speaker is asked, "What do you think of Jim?" This question provides a topic to the speaker. The speaker thinks for a while (latency), and then conceives a theme, "Jim stupid." I put the sentence theme in a dotted enclosure to suggest its unspecifiable nature. Note that a conceived theme is not necessarily a deep structure, since it does not always have all the necessary lexical items, and linguistic relations among those that exist are not fully worked out. A theme may be even in a nonverbal state: just a vague feeling that the speaker does not care much about Jim, or an image of Jim with his usual stupid expression. Pick (1913) calls this stage "germ concept"; Erdmann (1908), "wordless thinking"; and Bühler (1908), "condensed thinking."

The conceived theme then is verbalized into a structured sentence, "He is rather . . . silly." During this verbalizing process, the speaker is selecting appropriate and specific words to express the theme in a full, communicable sentence. In Figure 4–10 note that the speaker has a hesitation pause before "silly," perhaps marking a search for an appropriate word. The speaker may weigh "stupid" against "silly," and decide on the latter because it is less offensive. (After all, the speaker has to take into consideration the fact that the inquirer and Jim are good friends.) We become conscious of word-selection processes under such circumstances.

Word-selection difficulty may also be revealed as a slip of the tongue rather than as a pause. Fromkin (1973) noted that when there are alternatives, synonyms or near-synonyms, speakers may be unsure of what word will best express their thoughts and in the moment of indecision may select

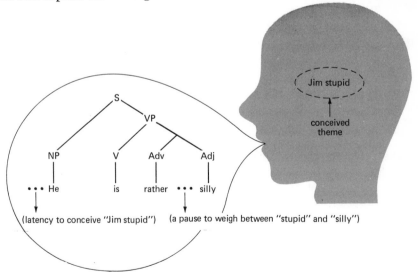

FIGURE 4–10   Producing the sentence "He is rather silly" to an inquiry, "What do you think of Jim?"

two words and blend them. An example is "splinsters," which is a blend of "splinters" and "blisters." This type of error reveals that the idea of the message is generated independently of, and prior to, the particular words selected from the mental dictionary to represent it.

At what stage is a syntactic structure made? According to Pick (1913), between a germ concept and word selection there is a stage where the syntax is completed; "the plan has to be completed before the building blocks can be inserted" (p. 235). This seems unlikely as a general rule. More likely the content implies the structure; the building is made to suit the blocks available. However, it is conceivable that decisions on certain features of surface structures—such as how presupposed and focused information are to be arranged, and whether a question or a passive form is to be used—have to be made before the first word of a sentence is uttered.

In an experiment investigating how far ahead we plan, Lindsley (1975) showed that subjects perform some verb selection before the initiation of S+V or S+V+O sentences. His subjects were presented with pictures depicting a man, woman, girl, or boy touching, kicking, greeting, or standing beside one of the others. The subjects had to use only these names in producing utterances whose lengths and grammatical forms were specified. The analysis used to obtain the result that verbs were selected before the sentences were spoken is quite complex, and the reader is referred to the original paper. It does seem to be valid for the specific experimental situation, however.

The highly constrained conditions of the laboratory task limit the extent to which we can talk about how we produce utterances outside the laboratories. If we come across a man drowning, surely "is drowning" is uppermost in our minds, and who it is in the process of drowning is less important. On the other hand, if the man who is drowning happens to be our own brother, the agent or subject catches our full attention. In this case, all we can utter, in great agitation, may just be "John, there, there!" One aspect of the new information is more important than other aspects, and has to be highlighted in our utterances. The aspect to be highlighted may be S, V, or O, all depending on contexts.

Other than such decisions on the general shape of a sentence, how much syntactic structure is completed before the word-selection stage? It seems unlikely that syntactic structures are completely encoded before verbalization of every sentence. If they were, presentence latency should have been partly related to structural complexities in Taylor's sentence-production experiment. Many syntactic decisions can be made while the earlier thoughts are being spoken. For example, in the sentence, "Yesterday, I bought a book, which . . ." the relative clause may or may not have been encoded before the sentence started. In "I opened the door, . . . with the key I found under the door mat," the adverbial phrase may have been an afterthought. If a structural plan is completed before words are inserted, sentences in our spontaneous speech would be well structured. But we know that this is not the case. A good example of a poorly structured "sentence" was given earlier in this chapter in our discussion of "competence and performance" (p. 92).

It is likely that a structure is encoded as a sentence is verbalized: structural encoding automatically accompanies verbalizing. The adverbial phrase "with the key . . ." may be an afterthought in both content and structure. The jargon speech produced by some aphasics may contain sentence melody, intonation, and sometimes grammatical structures (Weinstein et al., 1966). Some aphasics may not understand sentence meaning, yet may order constituents correctly in simple declarative sentences (von Stockert, 1972). These findings may be interpreted to mean that a syntactic process is a separable process. But the findings do not indicate at what stage in sentence production syntactic encoding occurs.

These findings on aphasic speech can also be interpreted to mean that encoding simple structures is such an automatic, overlearned, and stereotyped process that it can be retained even by severe aphasics. Syntactic encoding becomes automatic in normal sentence production, perhaps, because the speaker uses a handful of structures time and again to express constantly changing semantic content. The majority of our sentence forms would be SAADs, and some Qs. Sometimes various modifiers such as adjectives or adverbs might be included in sentences, increasing sentence lengths and complicating structures slightly. When we try to produce such uncommon structures as PQ, PNQ, the self-embedded, and sentences in foreign languages, we may become conscious of our process of structural encoding; producing such structures is not automatic and takes cognitive planning and time.

Yngve's "depth" model

Let us consider one more index of structural complexity. The following two types of sentence, one right-branching and the other self-embedded, differ in structural complexity but have equivalent content.

"She liked the man that visited the jeweler that made the ring that won the prize that was given at the fair." (right-branching)
"The prize that the ring that the jeweler that the man that she liked visited made won was given at the fair." (self-embedded)

Structural encoding   The self-embedded version has more *depth* than the right-branching one, according to Yngve (1960). Yngve suggested that a sentence is produced by expanding the nodes of a phrase marker, from

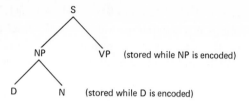

FIGURE 4–11   The nodes stored in sentence production, according to Yngve's depth hypothesis.

the top down, and left to right, in a binary (two-choice) fashion. In Figure 4–11, the leftmost categorical symbol in the last line of the already constructed derivation will always be expanded, while all the symbols to the right of it are postponed and kept in memory until the time comes to develop them. In Figure 4–11, NP_1 is expanded while VP is stored in memory; D is expanded while N and VP are stored, and so on. Postponed symbols therefore constitute a load on memory, and, given the limited capacity of short-term memory, this "machine" (sentence-generator) will severely limit the kinds of grammatical construction that can be achieved. The number of nodes stored in memory indexes syntactic complexity, and is called "depth." The number of nodes is limited to about seven. The depth, hence memory load, progressively increases in the following three sentences:

The family is leaving tomorrow.

The family [the woman told us about] is leaving tomorrow.

The family [the woman (we met yesterday) told us about] is leaving tomorrow.

The last sentence is about as far as we can carry the depth with our processing capacity. Structural encodings for the three types of sentence— left/right-branching and self-embedded—are shown in Figure 4–12. The left-branching and self-embedded structures have more "depth" than the right-branching one.

Essentially, Yngve's depth model says that our processing difficulty is determined by the structural operations that are anticipated and have to be stored in our short-term memory. The model has been criticized on many grounds. For one thing, it is exclusively concerned with surface structure and with left-to-right processing (see Chapter 5 for inadequacy of this processing). The model does not offer ways of expressing intuitive relationships among actives, passives, and so on. According to this model, all these different forms of sentence are derived independently.

Does the model predict processing difficulty, either in production or

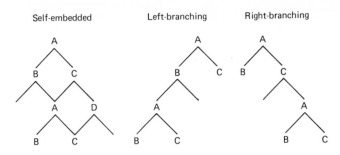

FIGURE 4–12   Structural encoding of three types of recursive element. Note where (A) recurs in the three types of sentence. There is no limit to the number of times the same rule (A) can be applied in the derivation of a sentence.

reception? Taylor's (1969) experiment showed that subjects' time to produce sentences was not related to the number of structural encodings specified by this model. The results can mean either that subjects do not use their cognitive processing on structural encoding or that the structural model of Yngve is not adequate.

Semantic memory load   Here we shall criticize Yngve's model for its neglect of semantic aspects. The model does not say anything about the already heard or produced semantic content of the sentence, which is the other side of the coin. If a sentence with great depth is difficult to produce, it may be partly due to an increased amount of semantic content that has to be stored in the process. Consider a simple noun phrase such as "the new club member." "The," "the new," "the new club" cannot be processed fully until the head noun of the phrase, "member," appears so that the noun phrase is completed and can be processed as a unit. The fragments of the noun phrase already heard or produced constitute a semantic memory load. Usually the greater the structural depth, the more words must be stored semantically.

Let us examine differential difficulties associated with right/left-branching and self-embedded sentence structures using a "semantic load hypothesis." A right-branching sentence has a series of subjects and their predicates, but each subject is closely followed by its own predicate, hence the semantic and structural memory load is small. That is, a subject is stored only until its predicate appears so that the subject and its predicate can be processed together as a sentence or a clause. As for left-branching, it has great depth structurally and should be hard to process, according to Yngve's model. However, from the semantic point of view all the relative clauses, or adjectives (in "My father's friend's dog's food's smell is awful") preceding or following the main noun are modifiers. Modifiers are by definition not essential for semantic interpretation of the main point of a sentence. We may store only those modifiers that may be directly relevant to the main point of the sentence, ignoring modifiers that modify other modifiers. Thus, the processing difficulty of left-branching is determined by how many semantically essential modifiers (structurally deep) are embedded in the sentence.

How do we process a self-embedded sentence? As processor, one has to store a series of subjects until one comes to a series of predicates. Furthermore, one has to make sure to match a subject with its correct predicate. To do so, one may have to rely on semantic content: It is the "jeweler" who "made the ring," however distantly these two items may get separated in a sentence. In a self-embedded sentence, a close semantic constraint between each subject and its separated predicate should make the processing task easier. Compare "the jeweler made the ring" to "the jeweler built the bridge." "The jeweler" and "made the ring" go together semantically, or have a close semantic constraint, so that the processor can easily find the right predicate among the string of predicates. Even if one has lost the track of the linguistic structure, one's knowledge about the jeweler and the jeweler's customary activity may help one to reconstruct the full sentence from the parts one remembers.

Schlesinger (1968) demonstrated that comprehension of nested sentences can be considerably facilitated if semantic cues are available. Subjects found it much easier to grasp the content of a sentence like "This is the hole, that the rat, which our cat, whom the dog bit, made, caught" as compared with a sentence with minimal cues about which noun goes with with which verb, as in "This is the boy, that the man, whom the lady, whom our friend saw, knows, hit." When the semantic cues are incongruous (as they are if you work it out in the above sentence about the rat, cat, and dog), subjects nearly always give an interpretation that is in line with semantic expectations rather than correct syntactic analysis.

The most important task of the sentence processor—either as a speaker or as a listener—is to keep track of the semantic content so that the sentence emerges with a coherent theme at the end. In short, a "deeply" self-embedded sentence is difficult to process due to both structural and semantic memory load. But even deeply embedded structures may be easily processed if semantic cues are clear.

In conclusion, semantic content is what we extract in sentence comprehension, and what we conceive in sentence production. The conceived content is abstract, and is put into actual words and a syntactic structure in the process of verbalizing. We examined how topics, perceptual events, presupposed information, and semantic memory load influence speed, difficulty, form, and content of sentence production.

CONCLUDING REMARKS: A GRAMMAR DOES NOT HAVE TO DESCRIBE PERFORMANCE

Some psycholinguists eagerly embraced the original version of TGG as a possible model of how we process sentences. But the initial enthusiasm inevitably gives way to a period of sober reevaluation. TGG itself has undergone some changes, and no doubt will undergo more changes. There are also other models of grammar than TGG. For example, a "categorical grammar" (Bar-Hillel, 1953) starts with the words and works toward a single symbol that represents a grammatical sentence; a generative grammar seems to move in the opposite direction. The categorical system seems to have all its grammatical rules included in the dictionary, whereas the generative grammar does just the opposite and includes the dictionary in its grammatical rules.

Still another kind of grammar is Fillmore's (1968) *case grammar*, which is based more on semantics than Chomsky's primarily structure-based grammar. "Case" in linguistics refers to syntactic and semantic relationships among parts of sentences. As we saw in "What is grammar?" in this chapter, the earliest grammars of the ancient Greeks used case concepts. In English, cases are primarily indicated by prepositions and by word order. Fillmore lists six cases of nouns, four of which are:

> Agentive (animate instigator of action)—"*John* opened the door" or "The door was opened by *John*."
> Instrumental (inanimate force causally involved in the action of verb)— "The *key* opened the door" or "The door was opened with the *key*."
> Dative (the animate affected by the verb)—"He murders *John*" or "It was apparent to *John* that he would win."
> Locative (the location of the action)—"*Chicago* is windy."

Note that there is no one-to-one relation between semantic and syntactic relations. For example, the Agentive case does not necessarily determine the grammatical subject; an Instrumental, Dative, or Locative noun can become a subject of a sentence. In this, Fillmore's case structure differs greatly from the "cases" of the ancient grammarians.

For Fillmore, constituents of a sentence are not subject and predicate, but "modality and proposition." A proposition is a tenseless set of relationships involving nouns and verbs. Modality includes such concepts as tense, mood, negation, and much more. Although Fillmore lists six specific cases, he admits that there could be several other cases (implying the possibility of endless proliferation of cases). Any inconsistency in usage of cases among various languages (which Jespersen [1924], among other linguists, noted) can be dismissed as a surface phenomenon; case relationships in "deep structure" are supposed to be universal, and perhaps innate.

If we tried to rely on a grammar to describe performance, we would have three entirely different models of performance, depending on which of the above three grammars we adopted. Thus, psycholinguists developing a performance model may have to maintain a certain degree of detachment from grammar, even though we certainly take it into consideration.

In what ways are a grammar and a model of performance different? Osgood (1968) listed four ways, which I reword and expand to eight in the ensuing discussion, hopefully without diluting his cogent arguments.

1. A real speaker depends on a finite memory, whereas a grammar does not. Thus a grammar can generate an infinitely self-embedding sentence, whereas the speaker cannot.

2. Speech is organized to some extent over time, whereas a grammar is time-independent. In a phrase-structure grammar, rewriting progresses from higher-level units to lower-level units. However, within the same level, the order with which each symbol is rewritten is immaterial. For example, the initial symbol S has to be rewritten into NP and VP. But at this level, whether NP or VP is taken up first for rewriting is immaterial. The speaker usually, but not always, progresses from an earlier item to a later item, that is, NP then VP.

3. The model of the speaker is a context-dependent device, whereas a grammar is relatively context-free. Each sentence is analyzed with little regard for other sentences in its context. Nor does it consider nonlinguistic contexts in which a sentence is produced and comprehended. When a human processes a real sentence, both the linguistic and the nonlinguistic contexts are of paramount importance, and are discussed extensively in this and following chapters. In this chapter we have emphasized how our knowledge of the world, presuppositions, and context influence our speech processing.

In many cases a literal interpretation of a sentence is not good enough; a listener has to understand what is implied, sometimes at the peril of being reprimanded for disobedience. H. H. Clark and Lucy (1975) cite two such examples: the sergeant who says to a private, "Do you see that cigarette butt there, soldier?" does not normally want an answer to the explicit question. He wants obedience to the implied order. Nor is Bertie Wooster merely making an observation about the atmosphere in the room when he says to his butler, "It's stuffy in here, Jeeves." He means for Jeeves to do something about the condition, perhaps open the window. Clark found some evidence in his experiment that the listener constructs the literal meaning before the implied meaning.

I will cite a few examples where listeners have to accept meanings opposite from what are expressed in sentences. "Sure, you are" (as a response to such brags as "I'm the smartest guy in my class") may have one linguistic description, but can be processed in many different ways, depending on its linguistic and nonlinguistic contexts. In one context, a listener may accept its literal meaning; in another context, he may take it as a sarcastic comment and accept its opposite meaning. Under certain circumstances, feebly uttered "No, I don't want it" must be taken to mean "Yes, I want it." What about lies that are correctly perceived to be lies? No amount of linguistic analysis, using either deep or surface structure, and TGG or case grammar, will tell us that utterances can be correctly interpreted to have opposite meanings; neither can they help to tell when we should interpret literally and when not.

Correct interpretation comes from shrewd perception of the speaking habits of the people involved, the truth value of the proposition, and many other contextual cues. In general, how quickly we interpret utterances for their implied rather than their literal meanings may depend on how salient contextual cues are on one hand, and how perceptive a listener is on the other hand. It is conceivable that when contextual cues are loud and clear, implied meaning can be instantly grasped, bypassing analysis of literal meaning.

4. A grammar is more concerned with the structure than with the content of a sentence, while the reverse is true in performance. Although grammars attempt to incorporate semantics into syntax, a grammar has not shown us why and how we produce a sentence with a particular semantic content. Let me dramatize the importance of content in speech once more: "Life is an empty dream," a simply structured, short sentence, SAAD, in fact. Surely a listener would not process it in the hurried and casual way he would process the similarly structured sentence "This is a red pencil." The original speaker of the first sentence probably did not produce it casually either: we can even conjecture that he must have contemplated life long and deeply (a long latency indeed!).

In a grammar, a prior syntactic analysis is required for semantic interpretation. In speech, when knowledge of syntax is severely limited as it is in young children and foreigners, sentences seem to be processed not through analysis of syntax but by attending to salient words (see Chapters 6 and 7). Syntactic analysis may be required in complex sentences, but not necessarily prior to—perhaps along with—semantic analysis.

5. The sentence is unquestionably a unit in a grammar, but not necessarily in performance. In speech we tend to omit linguistic items that can be easily inferred from contexts and include or emphasize those items that might give new information to a listener. This is one reason why our utterances are not always grammatical. Here is a typical informal dialogue between two friends, A and B.

A. How about dinner?
B. What, so soon?

A. Why not?

B. O.K., dinner, then.

None of the above utterances is a grammatically well-formed sentence, yet a message is obviously conveyed in this dialogue. In performance, "utterance-unit" seems to be more relevant than a sentence. We learned that a sentence is not necessarily a unit in long-term memory. At a deeper level, we can explore semantically based units such as a concept structure, conceptual base, or proposition.

6. A grammar is neutral with regard to encoding (production) and decoding (reception). After all, a normal adult is both a speaker and a listener, and hence a listener and a speaker should share an identical competence. But in performance, the ways the listener and the speaker put their competence into use may differ. In producing a sentence, the speaker has to conceive a theme of the sentence as well as choosing the right words to complete it. This process is reflected in hesitation pauses, which tend to occur before sentences as well as before content words.

The decoder, on the other hand, has a slightly different task; he has to extract a theme from the given words of a sentence. He carries out his task by listening and organizing what is heard in perceptual and processing units, which are usually phrases. Thus, the decoder's pauses may occur between phrases, and less before content words. This asymmetry in distribution of encoders' and decoders' pauses is demonstrated in J. G. Martin's experiment (1967). In it, encoders described Thematic Apperception Test (TAT)[3] pictures, and decoders (each one of whom was yoked with one encoder) attempted to reproduce what the encoders were saying.

Further examples of asymmetry between encoding and decoding can be seen in aphasia. We may distinguish roughly two types of language disorder—a predominantly receptive and a predominantly expressive disorder (see Chapter 11). In foreign language learning, it is possible to acquire receptive and expressive skills independently of each other.

7. In some ways speech is a skilled act, and like any skilled act, it should be influenced by practice. This is at least one reason why a handful of well-practiced, stereotyped structures require less cognitive planning than does the ever-changing content in sentence production. If we process a variety of sentence forms differently, this may be at least partly due to the overlearning of certain forms such as SAAD, as compared to such rare forms as PQ and especially PNQ. But there is no reason why a grammar should concern itself with how often a structure is used.

8. How humans acquire language and how we deviate from our com-

---

[3] TAT is a projective test of personality in which the subject makes up stories about pictures of ambiguous content.

petence in normal as well as pathological conditions are of major concern in a performance model, but not necesarily in a grammar.

In conclusion, a grammar is a formal device, intended to describe language treated as an abstract system. How much behavioral data should a grammar consider? One of Chomsky's favorite phrases is "abstracting away"—linguists abstract away deviations and imperfections in behavioral data and work with idealized data. According to Chomsky, no behavioral evidence is required to formulate competence or a grammar. A native speaker's (vaguely defined) intuition about grammaticality of sentences seems to be the only connection between a grammar and an actual speaker-hearer.

Other linguists, such as Derwing (1973), ask: "Of what significance is a 'generative explanation' for which no psychological reality is even claimed?" (p. 287). Derwing would like to see linguistics as a branch of psychology, considering that language is inherently a psychological phenomenon.

We psycholinguists are not sure whether we would like to welcome linguistics as a branch of psychology. Psycholinguistics and linguistics have somewhat different goals and subject matters. Psycholinguists are not concerned with *formulating "idealized" speaker-hearers' linguistic knowledge* but with *observing actual speech of language users*, with all their deviations from grammaticality.

In short, psycholinguistics should be interested in the grammars linguists develop so that we may describe observed speech adequately, but be wary of taking any grammar, especially structure-based grammar, as a model of performance. The primary function of performance is communicating semantic content, not producing grammatical structures.

A network grammar   Can we write a grammar that really describes speech? Remember, speech is an exchange of ideas between a speaker and a listener. Both the speaker and the listener bring a body of knowledge—a network of interlinked concepts—to a speech situation. A network grammar indicates where in the body of knowledge the individual concepts represented by content words are supposed to fit; it indicates where open links exist and just what concepts are needed to fill them.

"The book consists of three parts" may be "parsed" in terms of the linkage of the words, and what each word needs and implies for its fulfilment. This parsing, in contrast to that of structural grammars, can be done largely on one word at a time, since it deals with the relationships of the words with what has gone before and with what remains to be expected.

"The" indicates that a static concept such as an object or an idea that is known to both the speaker and the listener is to be expected. It ties the concept to come with something already known, and indicates to the hearer "this will not be new" (Fig. 4–13A). Note that "a book" and "the

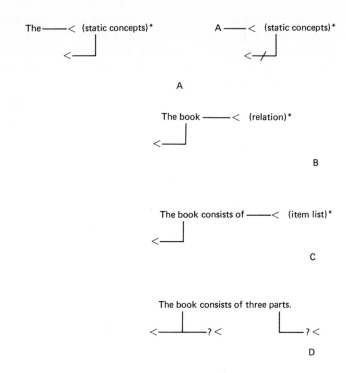

FIGURE 4–13   Parsing "the book consists of three parts" in a network grammar.

book" will have different description in the network grammar but not in TGG.

The word "book" fits the open link of "the" but leaves open links of its own. Something is going to be said about the book (Fig. 4–13B). "consists of" is a form of relation, and requires a list of constituents of the book to satisfy it (Fig. 4–13C). An utterance is parsed in this manner until the gaps in the pattern of knowledge are momentarily closed. A falling intonation pattern on "parts" if it is spoken, or a period if it is written, indicates that the utterance is closed. At the same time, a topic is left open for further discussion. The topic may be ambiguous, as it is in this case. We can depict this state as in Figure 4–13D. The next utterance may start something like: "It is . . . ," in which case we know that the "book" link is being filled, or "They are . . ." or "The first . . . ," in which case the "parts" link is being filled or partly filled (based on an unpublished paper by M. M. Taylor).

The network grammar seems to answer most but not all of the arguments I advanced against a linguistic grammar. Further, it should apply to any language, and does not require the usual linguistic distinction between deep and surface structures. However, this grammar, like any other, can provide only a frame of parsing; each utterance requires its own network. We can envisage hopelessly unwieldy and complex networks which can describe a long conversation between two sophisticated people on a complex topic. But then, the network grammar deals with the whole relation between language and knowledge, nothing less. All the same, it may be worth our while for us to develop a network grammar, not to replace any linguistic grammar but to supplement it.

SUMMARY AND CONCLUSIONS

The study of grammar is surveyed historically, starting from the ancient Greeks' attempt to classify words into parts of speech. Ancient Indian grammar also classified words. But in addition it studied phonetics and the internal structure of words, thus giving impetus to the nineteenth-century comparative philology. The classic tradition in the study of grammar was to prescribe how to speak and write correctly.

Modern linguistics since the early twentieth century describes, and does not prescribe, spoken speech. It also studies each language as a system of relations. It distinguishes between a system of linguistic items (*langue*) and instances of langue (*parole*). Chomsky distinguishes in a slightly different way between competence (linguistic knowledge possessed by an ideal speaker-listener) and performance (the actual use a speaker makes of that competence in concrete situations). Performance deviates from competence for various psychological reasons.

Chomsky developed transformational generative grammar (TGG) as a description of competence. The original version of this grammar consisted of PS-rules, which generated underlying phrase markers, and transformational rules, which converted one phrase marker into other related phrase markers to produce passives, questions, and so on.

In the revised version, the base of the syntactic component generates deep structures and from them the transformational rules map surface structures. Deep structures contain lexical items, as well as their structural relations, and provide an exclusive basis for semantic interpretation. One level deeper, there might be "concept structure," which is a conception of a sentence in terms of ideas, without linguistic structure.

One test of TGG as a model of performance was to see how PS-rules are reflected in speech. Experiments such as click perception show that major phrases defined by PS-rules seem to be processed as units. But word-sorting experiments show that subjective phrases may sometimes depart from linguistic phrases. The optimal processing unit may be a minor phrase consisting of a few words forming a syntactic and semantic unit.

The second test of TGG was to show that kernel sentences are psychologically central. In verbatim sentence recall, subjects' errors tended to be syntactic, and these errors tended to produce a simpler grammatical form than the one given as a stimulus. In the third test, increasing transformational complexity from SAAD to P to PQ and then to PNQ was reflected in storage requirements for these sentence forms.

The fourth test was to see whether we process sentences in deep and/or surface structure. In recalling two sentences identical in surface but different in deep structures, subjects seemed to be influenced more by deep than by surface structures.

To cite only two of several shortcomings of the above experiments, the investigators assumed that a SAAD and its "corresponding" N differ in structure only, and not in content; the experimental task was often verbatim recall of test sentences.

If experimental tasks resemble everyday sentence processing—verification of truth or falsity of a sentence, paraphrasing, or long-term memory—subjects pay more attention to sentence content than to structure.

Sachs's experiment shows that when a semantic interpretation has been made the meaning, and not the form, of a sentence is stored. In another experiment, after having heard a series of short sentences, subjects later falsely "recognized" a long, complex sentence as the one they had heard before. This is because one long and complex sentence unites isolated events, expressed in separate sentences, into one coherent meaning (Bransford and Franks, 1971). Sentences may be stored in long-term memory in propositions. A proposition is an abstract entity composed of concepts, which has a truth value and which can be asserted by a sentence.

Bransford and co-workers propose a "constructive approach" to semantic memory. The act of comprehending a sentence generally involves considerably more than merely recovering the information specified by the input sentence; it involves constructing semantic information from our knowledge of the world, using the input linguistic sentence as a cue.

Sentence comprehension involves a few stages of mental operation. One idea is that we compare a received sentence to habitually stored sentence information that reflects nonlinguistic events in the world. This stored information is often in SAAD, hence SAAD is processed faster than other sentence forms.

In sentence production, too, we are concerned with content. Taylor's experiment shows that subjects' conceiving time is related to content difficulty but not to structural complexities. Conceptually more difficult interpretive tasks require more cognitive activities than descriptive tasks, according to Goldman-Eisler. Perceptual events can create cognitive presuppositions, which influence the form and content of sentences describing the events. In a sentence, we express presupposed and focal information using surface-structure features such as word order.

Sentence-producing processes seem to involve, first, presence of a topic, which may be elaborated into a brief theme. The speaker selects words and constructs a suitable structure in the process of verbalizing the sentence. Since we use a handful of stereotyped structures to accommodate constantly changing content, our cognitive activity should be concentrated more on content than on structure.

A "deeply" self-embedded or left-branching sentence contains many structural encoding operations that have to be stored in short-term memory, according to Yngve's "depth" model. However, increasing structural "depth" is usually accompanied by increasing semantic content that has already been produced and has to be stored in short-term memory.

In concluding our discussion on the relation between grammar and speech, I enumerated eight items that show that we have to consider grammar and speech separately. To cite only two items, the primary concern in speech is meaning while in grammar it is structure; linguistic and non-linguistic contexts are vitally important in speech, but not in grammar.

We should explore network grammars, which deal with the whole relation between language and knowledge; they indicate where in the body of knowledge of a speaker and a hearer open links exist and what concepts will fill them.

5

The Statistical Structure
of Language

*Paris
in the
the spring*

Did you read "Paris in the spring"? That is wrong. If you did, it was because "Paris in <u>the</u> spring" is a very likely phrase. The sign in fact says "Paris in the *the* spring." This is an example of how the statistical structure of English can affect your perception.

Let us consider some more examples. Suppose you almost heard a word, /ca⚡/, but you could not make out the last sound clearly. Suppose the last sound seemed to be either of the easily confused sounds /t/ or /p/. You would be more likely to choose "cat" than "cap," if you heard it without context, because "cat" is more frequently used in English.

If you heard the word in the context of a conversation about animals, you would be even more sure that it was "cat." Here, the category "animal" narrows down the number of alternatives you have to consider for your word. Now, if you hear the same word in a context of a sentence, "A dog and a ca⚡ are two of the most popular pets," what is your chance of deciding on "cat" instead of on "cap"? In this case, even if the whole word had been obscured you could have guessed it without difficulty.

In all these cases, the listener does not rely solely on what is contained in the sound itself to recognize the word. We have learned not only the meanings of words and their grammatically correct use but also the structure of the language, which enables us to anticipate what we are going to hear and to reconstruct what must have been said in cases of difficulty. We shall

148

discuss three aspects of the statistical structure of language—relative frequency, number of potential alternatives, and sequential constraints—one at a time.

FREQUENCY OF OCCURRENCE OF VERBAL ELEMENTS

To find out how frequently words (or letters, and the like) are used, we take a fair sample of spoken speech from telephone conversations or interviews, or of written speech from newspapers or magazines. We count how often each of the items in the collected sample is used, and calculate their average frequencies. Tabulations of the frequencies of such verbal elements are of theoretical and practical importance. For theoretical reasons, we ask whether some items are used more frequently than others; which these frequently used items are; and why they are used frequently.

Psychologists running experiments often use the relative frequency of verbal elements as an independent variable that can influence such speech behavior as perception, solving anagrams and crossword puzzles, learning, and remembering. Psychologists also would like to know how and why variation in word frequency affects these events. Word frequency even influences speech disorders: stutterers or aphasics may have more difficulties with infrequent than with frequent verbal elements. Thus when frequency is not an independent variable, psychologists control for it by equating their test material for frequency across their different experimental conditions. For example, if one wants to see whether abstract and concrete words differ in the ease with which they may be learned, words of these two types must be chosen to be similar in frequency of occurrence.

Knowledge of the relative frequencies of words is extremely useful in preparing teaching material for children or for foreigners learning a second language. For example, books intended for young children or beginners of a second language should contain only frequently used words. It is easier and more useful for them to learn frequent words like "bread" and "water" than infrequent words like "stridulate" or "serendipity." Ogden (1934) prepared for foreigners learning English a "Basic English" word list that contains only 850 frequently used English words (600 of them nouns). He chose those 850 words carefully so that by combinations they could express most of our communication needs. Most of the combinations of easy words that served for difficult words were reasonable, such as "go down" for "descend," although some quaint expressions would be needed, such as "blood, body water, and eye water" for "blood, sweat, and tears."

In discussing the frequencies of verbal elements, I use mainly the

English language because there are more data available on English than on any other language. If certain types of verbal element are used frequently because of universal human characteristics, then intuitively such verbal elements should share a similar frequency pattern across different languages. Those few data cited from foreign languages bear out this expectation.

Before examining the frequencies of verbal elements, we must learn about some useful ways of counting words and other elements.

Type, token, and type–token ratio

Each occurrence of a particular item is called a *token*. Each group of identical tokens is called a *type*. In the sentence "What woman wants, God wants," there are five tokens, but only four types, since "wants" is a type that occurs twice. In general, to get word tokens, count all the words in a passage, and to get word types, count only the number of different words that occur in the passage.

When we determine the number of occurrences of each word type we usually express it as a percentage of the total number of tokens. In a passage of 1,000 word tokens, we might find 100 occurrences of "the," 10 percent of the total passage. Such a percentage value is referred to as the relative frequency of occurrence of the particular word type. The number of different words divided by the number of total words is a measure of the diversity in a sample, and is called *type-token ratio*, or TTR. In one English text, we may count 50,000 tokens or words, and find 5,000 types or different words. The TTR for this text will be .10.

Various factors affect TTR. For example, it is influenced by the mode of speech; oral speech has a smaller TTR than does most written speech. The length of the passage is also necessarily related; if the passage contains only one word, this word is one type and one token, yielding TTR $= 1.0$. As the length of the passage is increased, it becomes less and less likely that each added token represents a new type, because the word has probably been used earlier in the passage. Thus TTR gets smaller as the length of the passage is increased. Carroll (1964) suggests a measure of vocabulary diversity that is approximately independent of sample size: the number of different words is divided by the square root of twice the number of words in the sample, or Diversity $=$ Types $/ \sqrt{2 \times \text{Tokens}}$. Abnormal TTRs occur in the speech patterns of special types of speakers—schizophrenics, the deaf, and a certain type of aphasic may show different, most probably smaller, TTRs than normal adults. In one study (Chotlos, 1944), TTR was found to be correlated with the intelligence of speakers; speakers of higher IQ obtained higher TTRs than speakers of lower IQ.

Relative frequency of phonemes

Which are the frequent phonemes? Although we have about 38
phonemes in English, we do not use all of them equally often. We use some
phonemes and consonant clusters more than others. As psycholinguists, we
would like to know which they are, and why. According to Dewey (1923),
the most frequently used sound, /i/, occurs more than 100 times as often as
the least used sound, /z/.

Denes (1963)[1] obtained three different statistics from a wide sample
of spoken English. Two of them are the frequency distributions of phonemes
and phoneme *digrams* (pairs of phonemes occurring consecutively). Table
5–1 shows the frequencies of occurrence of consonants and vowels. According
to Table 5–1, the six most frequent consonants are /t, n, s, d, l, m/, which
are responsible for half of all consonant occurrences. All of them except /m/
have an alveolar place of articulation, and are distinguished only by their
manner of articulation. The place of articulation of /m/ is bilabial rather
than alveolar, but is still in the front of the mouth.

The digram frequency distribution shows that most of the frequent
consonant clusters consist of sound pairs with the same alveolar place, but
with different manners of articulation. Examples are: /nt/, /st/, /nd/. In
only a small proportion of cases is there a change of place with no change
in the manner of articulation, as in /kt/. Somehow English, at least, has
developed in such a way that differences in manner of articulation carry a
greater weight in speech than differences in place of articulation.

Table 5–1 does not consider the fact that different consonants are preferred in different positions of words. English speakers use /ð, w, s, h, t, m,
b/ frequently at the beginning, and /t, n, d, z, s, l/ commonly at the end
of words. /ð/ in the initial position is the most frequent of all consonants:
it occurs in only a handful of different words, such as "this" or "the," altogether about 30 in number, but these 30 are very frequent words in
English.

With regard to vowels, /ə, i, ai/ are responsible for half of all vowel
occurrences. Front vowels, /i:, i, e, a, a:/, are the most frequent; then the
central vowels /ə, ə:, ʌ/; and then the back vowels /o, o:, u, u:/.

Why are certain phonemes used frequently? First, let us contrast
consonants to vowels. Even though articulation of consonants is more complex than that of vowels, there tend to be more consonants than vowels in
many languages. The complexity of consonant articulation permits a greater

---

[1] Phoneme frequency counts by Dewey and Denes show highly similar but not
identical results. Dewey considered consonants and vowels together. Also, 40 years
separate the two counts.

TABLE 5–1   Frequency of Occurrence of English Phonemes

	% occurrence		% occurrence	Rank
ə	9.0445	t	8.4033	1
i	8.2537	n	7.0849	2
ai	2.8473	s	5.0893	3
e	2.8126	d	4.1767	4
i:	1.7878	l	3.6892	5
ou	1.7477	m	3.2890	6
ʌ	1.6701	ð	2.9927	7
o	1.5330	k	2.8985	8
a	1.5261	r	2.7697	9
ei	1.4956	w	2.5661	10
u:	1.4222	z	2.4927	11
o:	1.2007	b	2.0842	12
a:	0.7755	v	1.8515	13
au	0.7741	p	1.7698	14
u	0.7672	f	1.7283	15
ə:	0.6661	h	1.6729	16
cə	0.4335	j	1.5303	17
iə	0.2867	ŋ	1.2436	18
uə	0.1426	g	1.1619	19
oi	0.0872	ʃ	0.7021	20
Total	39.2742	θ	0.5955	21
		dʒ	0.5138	22
		tʃ	0.3684	23
		ʒ	0.0512	24
		Total	60.7256	

From Denes, 1968; rank order added.

variety of distinct consonants than is possible with the simple vowels. In Chapter 2, in discussing the motor theory of phoneme perception, we noted that the identification of consonants is more precise than that of vowels. We know of the rare and celebrated example of the Czech sentence that consists entirely of consonants (if /r/ is a consonant), "Strč prst skrz krk," but we do not know of a sentence of comparable length that consists of only vowels.

Are infrequent consonants difficult consonants? Poole (1934) prepared a table that shows the ages at which children master different consonants. When these data are compared with the frequencies of use found by Denes, as in Table 5–2, correlation between them is small. In other words, the sounds mastered late by children are not necessarily those sounds used in-

TABLE 5–2   Relation between the Age at Which Phonemes Are Mastered and Adult's Frequency of Use

Age	Phonemes mastered (Poole, 1934)	Rank order in frequency of use (Denes, 1963)	Average rank
3½	b, p, m, w, h	12, 14, 6, 10, 16	11.6
4½	d, t, n, g, k, ŋ, y	4, 1, 2, 19, 8, 18, 17	9.9
5½	f	15	15
6½	v, ð, dʒ, l, ʃ	13, 7, 22, 5, 20	9.4 .
7½	s, z, r, θ, hw	3, 11, 9, 21 —	11

frequently by adults. For example, /s/, which is the third most frequent consonant, is mastered at the late age of 7½. Some of the consonants that normal children master late, /ʃ, s, θ/, are also the most difficult sounds for a deaf child to acquire (Hirsch, 1966). We cannot order consonants for difficulty in a consistent manner, but in general, /p, m, t/ seem to cause least, and /s, f, θ, ʃ, ð, z/ most trouble to people acquiring speech sounds for the first time, and to people with speech disorders.

The difficult consonants are in general those possessing the sibilant or fricative and the continuant features. They involve adjusting the tongue and holding it for a short time without anything to rest on. "They require the use of more muscles, closer control of the amount and the timing of movement, and generally finer coordination" than do other sounds (Fry, 1966, p. 194). To produce stop consonants, one merely has to flip the right articulators and one has got it. If one did not get it, one was wrong; there is no partially right stop consonant. The lack of a neat correlation between frequency of occurrence and ease of articulation is perhaps due to the fact that once we have overlearned these "difficult" sounds, they cease to be difficult. However, the seven most frequent consonants and some of the most frequent vowels are produced with the tongue near the front of the mouth. We may wonder whether front sounds require less effort to produce than central or back sounds. Certainly the tongue-tip is more mobile than the root of the tongue.

Are frequent consonants easy for listeners to discriminate? We use the manner of articulation as a prominent discriminating feature of consonants. Recall the experiments in Chapter 2 that showed that English consonants produced in a similar manner, but not at the same place, are confused among themselves and judged to be closer to each other in psychological distance. Five of the six most frequently used consonants are produced at the same place but in different manners, thus ensuring easy discrimination among them.

In English we show a preference not only for certain sounds but also for certain syllables. For example, the most frequently used syllable /ðə/ occurs on average once in every 14 successive spoken syllables (Dewey, 1923). Although English has over 1,000 syllable types, only 70 syllable types account for half of our speech. From telephone speech in business, French, Carter, and Koenig (1930) obtained the relative frequencies of different syllables shown in Table 5–3.

TABLE 5–3   Relative Frequency of Occurrence of Syllables

Syllable structure	Example	Occurrence	Syllable structure	Example	Occurrence
CVC	cat	33.5%	CVCC	don't	7.8%
CV	go	21.8	VCC	ant	2.8
VC	an	20.3	CCVC	stem	2.8
V	a	9.9	CCV	ski	0.8
			CCVCC	skits	0.5

C = consonant;
V = vowel.
Based on data from French, Carter, and Koenig, 1930.

We prefer syllables in which consonants and vowels alternate. Vowels alone may be easy to articulate but are not easy to discriminate, whereas consonants alone are hard to produce. Consonants may be readily linked by intervening vowels. CVCC (nonexistent in Japanese), and CCV and CCVCC (not common in Ural–Altaic languages), are more complex to articulate than CVC and may not commensurately increase discriminability. Such syllables are far less common than CVC. Consonant clusters, especially in the initial positions, are difficult to articulate for young children and people with some speech disorders. Some aphasics may break up consonant clusters by inserting a vowel between normally linked pairs of consonants (Shankweiler and Harris, 1966). We observe the same tendency among speakers of languages without consonant clusters who try to speak languages that include them. For example, a Japanese rendition of the English word "strike" is "suturaiku."

Relative frequency of letters

We do not use certain letters frequently merely because they are easy to write! Rather, written-letter frequency has to reflect spoken language. However, if we are to devise a rational writing system, we should construct frequently used letters more simply (fewer strokes, perhaps) than infrequently used letters. In the English alphabet, as well as in alphabets of other languages, all letters are too simple to show much variation in ease of writing. Or are they?

After reading an early draft of this chapter, M.M. Taylor and Sharon Smith did a simple test: they measured the time it took to write different (cursive) letters of the English alphabet ten times. The longer it takes to write a letter, the more complex this letter must be. This letter complexity was then correlated with frequency of occurrence. There was a small negative correlation between these two variables. For example, e and n, which are two of the most frequently used letters in English, took the shortest times to write, 0.25 sec/letter and 0.38 sec/letter respectively. On the other hand, two of the least frequent letters, x and w, took 0.90 and 0.89 sec/letter respectively.

Chinese characters are ideal for studying the relation between the frequency of use and the complexity of characters. Chinese characters can range in complexity from one stroke to over 30 strokes. Figure 5–1 gives an example of a simple and a complex character. Is the complexity of Chinese characters related to their frequency of use? Table 5–4 is the result of a survey on frequencies of characters carried out by a leading newspaper in Japan, Asahi, in 1950 (Ono, 1967). This table is limited in scope because it reports on only 1,000 characters (Japanese use only a few thousand out of over 50,000 Chinese characters), and after the 20th rank, the rank progresses by units of 50 or 100. Be that as it may, the table shows the same general trend: simpler characters are used more often.

FIGURE 5–1   A simple and a complex Chinese character. Consider each of –, |, and ⌐ as one stroke. Left: a simple character (1 stroke), appropriately meaning "one"; right: a complex character (30 strokes), meaning "the sound of thunder."

TABLE 5-4: Frequency of Chinese Characters in Japan (from Ono, 1967)

Rank	Character	Frequency			
			18	事	72447
1	十	226176	19	人	70680
2	一	212040	20	六	68913
3	二	185535	50	開	42408
4	三	180234	100	点	30039
5	日	178467	150	立	20321
6	五	109554	200	判	14136
7	会	102486	250	早	12369
8	四	90117	300	渉	10792
9	大	86583	350	統	9719
10	本	84816	400	推	8835
11	中	83049	450	留	8735
12	田	83049	500	足	8645
13	出	81282	600	転	7068
14	国	77748	700	室	5586
15	同	75981	800	級	5396
16	長	75981	900	忙	4931
17	上	74214	1000	乳	4361

Now let us examine two other trends in the use of Chinese characters. First, simple characters are embedded in progressively more complicated characters, with more specific and probably infrequently used meanings. Table 5–5 is the result of my modest efforts at copying complex characters. Table 5–5 merely shows a discernible trend, not a rule. The second trend in the use of the characters is that the three languages that use them, Korean, Chinese, Japanese, have simplified forms for some rather frequently used characters. Figure 5–2 shows some simplified forms and their original complex forms. The simplified forms, and not their originals, seem to be exclusively used in modern Japanese. The mainland Chinese have simplified about 5,000 characters that are in frequent use.

English speakers have an implicit knowledge of letter frequency. Attneave (1953) asked his subjects to indicate how many times, out of a thousand letters, each of the letters of the alphabet would occur. The correlation between such judgments and an actual count of printed English was .79, indicating a rather high degree of accuracy on the part of the subjects. Our implicit knowledge of letter frequency helps us in solving crossword puzzles or in breaking simple codes.

The data on letter frequency were used in devising efficient stenography and in the original invention of the Morse code. Morse first tabulated the quantities of type for each letter found in a printer's office, and devised his code to reflect the relative amounts of the type, presuming these in turn to reflect the frequencies of the letters in English text. He gave the shortest and simplest code (• = e) to the most frequent letter and the longest and most complex code to the least frequent letter (− − • • = z), with a graded scale of length in between.

A typewriter is an indispensable tool for many of us. Yet the conventional keyboard arrangement of letters (Figure 5–3a) is very inefficient. The keyboard was, in fact, designed to be inefficient. That is, it was designed to slow down the typist in order to prevent jamming of the keys. In the early typewriters, if two keys close together were struck rapidly one after another they would jam, because the keys had no springs. Even with modern keys that spring back, the original inefficient arrangement of keys still remains.

Forty years ago the American educational psychologist Dvorak analyzed 38 million different letter sequences and frequencies, and studied slow-motion films of people typing. He then came up with the Dvorak Simplified Keyboard (DSK), which is shown in Figure 5–3b. The most important change is that most of the really common letters are on the easy-to-reach middle (home) row. Within this row, vowels rest under the left hand and the frequently used consonants are under the right hand. Infrequently used letters like *q*, *j*, *x*, *v*, and *z* are exiled to the bottom row, and frequent digrams are split between the two hands. With the new arrangement, a typist does 70 percent of the work on the home row, compared with 32 percent on the standard home row. DSK also redistributes the workload between the two hands and among the fingers. On the standard, the left hand does 50 percent of the work; on DSK, 44 percent. The result of all these changes in keyboard arrangement is that learning to type and typing are easier and faster, with less fatigue and mistakes. On the standard keyboard, 100 words a minute is a kind of magic barrier. One Dvorak student was clocked at 165 words a minute in an unofficial test. Unfortunately, DSK has not yet been commonly adopted (reported in *The Globe and Mail*, Toronto, December 1972).

Word frequency

The Oxford English Dictionary lists nearly half a million words. The average adult is said to have a use-and-recognition vocabulary of 30,000–60,000 words. We use some of this vast number of words more frequently than others. Thorndike and Lorge (1944) collected 30,000 of the most common types among 1,000,000 printed English words. The result of their effort is *The Teacher's Word Book of 30,000 Words*, which tells anyone who wishes to know about the frequency of a particular word in standard English text.

TABLE 5-5   Progressively More Complex Chinese Characters with Increasingly More Specific and Infrequent (?) Meanings

Character	Meanings	Character	Meanings
鳥	bird	女	women; a girl
鳴	the cry of a bird or animal; to sound	妃	imperial concubine
鶱	to soar high	姦	adultery
鷺	downy feathers of long-legged birds	嬲	lewd sports (the two flanking characters are "men")
纞鳥	argus pheasant; small bells hung on bridles	嬳	modestly
雨	rain	鼻	nose
雩	drizzling rain	鼽	to turn up nose
霝	the sound of rain	鼻及	to snivel
霖	a long-continued rain	鼻邕	a stoppage of the nose
雷雷	the sound of thunder	齉	to speak through the nose

Character	Meanings		Character	Meanings
虫	insects		言	words; to speak
虱	louse		訃	to announce death
螢	a glow worm		誓	to swear
蟓	a big caterpillar		讛	to speak in one's sleep
蠩	a short-legged spider		讞	to decide on judicial cases

For example, "car" occurs 1,000 times, "phenomenal" only once, in 1,000,000 words. Word usage changes somewhat over the years; in 1944 we did not have such currently fashionable words as "countdown" and "rip-off." A more up-to-date oral sample is Howes's (1966) "A Word Count of Spoken

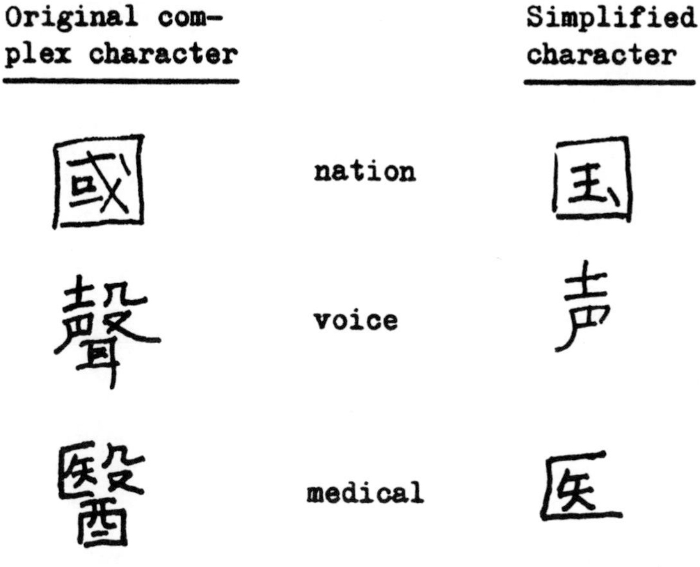

Original com-plex character		Simplified character
國	nation	国
聲	voice	声
醫	medical	医

FIGURE 5–2   Original complex Chinese characters and their simplified versions.

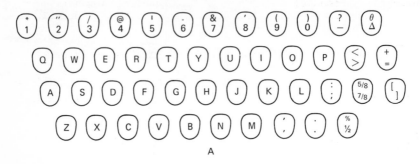

OLIVETTI KEYBOARD

A

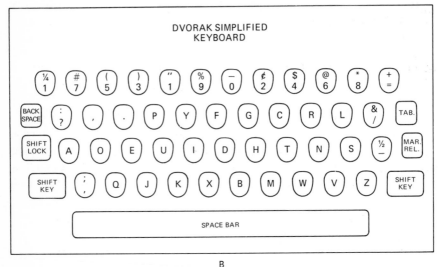

DVORAK SIMPLIFIED
KEYBOARD

B

FIGURE 5–3   *A*, An Olivetti typewriter keyboard with its conventional letter arrangement. *B*, Dvorak Simplified Keyboard—the frequently used letters are arranged in the home row.

English Words." An international word frequency count is also available for English, French, German, and Spanish (Eaton, 1961).

The 50 most commonly used types make up about 60 percent of our spoken word tokens and 45 percent of those we write. In other words, we do not need many different words to carry out ordinary oral conversations. The 10 most used English words in oral speech are: "I, the, a, it, to, you, of, and, in, he" (Denes, 1963), all function words. Their average length is 2.1 letters, or 1.9 phonemes. The 30 most frequently occurring words in German constitute one-third of all texts (Hörmann, 1971). Words such as "die, der, und, in, zu, den, das . . . ," almost all of them function words, with an average length of three letters, make up the 30 most commonly used German words. Oettinger (1954) found that the distribution of word lengths for written Russian has two peaks at lengths of one and seven letters. The one-letter words are practically all function words.

In English few long function words exist (such as "whereinsoever"), but the longer the function words, the less frequently they occur. Content words are longer than function words, and their probabilities of occurrence are not strongly dependent on their lengths. All the same, the most probable length of a content word is 3 letters. In short, as word length increases, frequency of occurrence decreases, the rate of decrease being more gradual for content than for function words (Miller, Newman, and Friedman, 1958).

Zipf (1935) observed that the majority of the commonly used words in many languages are monosyllables. We think of German words as being usually long and polysyllabic. Yet even in German 50 percent of a large sample, nearly 11,000,000 running words of written German, were mono-syllables, and words of four or more syllables formed only 8.4 percent (Kaeding, 1897). In Chinese, of course, almost all monosyllables can be words, though by no means are all words monosyllables.

Not only do we use short words frequently, but we also tend to abbreviate a long word when it comes to be used very frequently. "Gas, auto, exam" in the USA and in Canada; "petrol, telly, pub" in England, are shortened versions of "gasoline, automobile, examination, petroleum, television, public house." We also have shorter versions of frequently used long words: "ma" for "mother," "granny" for "grandmother," and "Meg" for "Margaret." We devise acronyms for frequently used long expressions: CARE, laser (light amplification by stimulated emission of radiation), and so on. IPA, TGG, EVS, and TTR are a few of many acronyms used in this book.

The more an English word is used, the shorter it becomes. Moreover, Baker (1950) points out that this is not a haphazard process, nor is the rate of decrease in word length a constant; the more often a word is used, the more rapidly it decreases in length. Further, he obtained highly similar trends for French, German, and Spanish.

The relative frequencies of words strongly affect many areas of speech behavior. We learn, perceive, memorize, read, or guess familiar words faster and more accurately than unfamiliar words. In one experiment that used frequency as an independent variable, Howes and Solomon (1951) showed that how fast we can recognize a word in a tachistoscope depends on how frequently the word occurs in general usage. A tachistoscope is an instrument that can present visual stimuli to subjects for a controlled time, usually for a very brief duration. As Figure 5–4 shows, the more frequently a word is used, the faster it is recognized. For example, a word that occurs once per million words requires about 500 msec, while a word that occurs 100,000 times per million needs only 50 msec to be recognized at 90 percent accuracy.

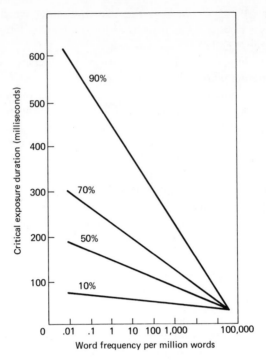

FIGURE 5–4   The relationship among word frequency, speed of tachistoscopic perception, and percent correct perception. (From Carroll, 1964; and Howes, 1961)

In Taylor's (1969) sentence-production experiment, subjects produced sentences more quickly for frequent than for infrequent words. Even the solution of anagrams is affected by word frequency (Mayzner and Tresselt, 1958). The usual interpretation is that high-frequency words are more readily evoked in a problem situation because they are relatively high in the subjects' response hierarchy. One verbal behavior that is not favorably influenced by word frequency is how well one recognizes words after having seen them before among other words in a list. Infrequent words are more distinct than frequent words, and it must be distinctiveness rather than familiarity that is important for recognition memory.

To summarize, we use certain phonemes, letters, syllables, and words more frequently than others. We seem to prefer verbal elements that require least effort to produce and/or cause least confusion to hear. The relative frequency of occurrence of verbal elements in turn influences our speech processing profoundly. In general, frequently occurring elements are easier and faster to process than infrequently occurring elements.

Zipf's Law

Phenomenon   Zipf (1949) found an interesting relation between the frequency of occurrence of words and their ranks. If the most frequently occurring word is given a rank of one, the second most frequent a rank of two, and so on, there should be a relation between rank and frequency, and the curve relating the two should slope downward. What is interesting is that when rank and frequency of words are plotted logarithmically against one another on a graph as in Figure 5–5, a smooth, straight line with a negative slope of 45° emerges. This function is referred to as Zipf's frequency-rank law, or standard curve, and implies that frequency × rank = constant ($f \times r = C$). Logarithmic coordinates are used in Figure 5–5 to make the points more easy to read and the relation more obvious. Curve *B* is based on a count of words in American newspapers that tallied 43,989 word tokens and some 6,000 types. Curve *A* is from Joyce's *Ulysses*, which contained about a quarter of a million word tokens and nearly 30,000 word types. The data on which *A* is based are shown in Table 5–6. Considering the divergent bases of these two counts, the two curves *A* and *B* are surprisingly similar.

Deviation from the straight line indicates abnormality in speech behavior. The hypothetical line *C* with a gentler slope indicates a diversifica-

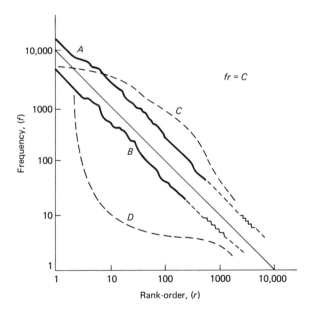

FIGURE 5–5   The rank-frequency distribution of words: *A*, James Joyce's *Ulysses*; *B*, American newspaper English; *C* and *D* are hypothetical. (From Zipf, 1949: *C* and *D* added.

TABLE 5–6   Arbitrary Ranks with Frequencies in James Joyce's *Ulysses*

I Rank (r)	II Frequency (f)	III Product of I and II ($r \times f = C$)
10	2,653	26,530
20	1,311	26,220
30	926	27,780
40	717	28,680
50	556	27,800
100	265	26,500
200	133	26,600
300	84	25,200
400	62	24,800
500	50	25,000
1,000	26	26,000
2,000	12	24,000
3,000	8	24,000
4,000	6	24,000
5,000	5	25,000
10,000	2	20,000
20,000	1	20,000
29,899	1	29,899

From Zipf, 1949; Column IV deleted.

tion trend—it would mean a larger vocabulary and a lower probability of occurrence of the most frequent words. Another hypothetical line with a steeper slope, D, indicates a simplification trend, a tendency to use fewer different words. In this case, the probability of occurrence of the most frequent word would be greater: a few words are used again and again. Such a trend might be found in children, speakers with low education and low intelligence, schizophrenics, and aphasics.

The graph shows the likelihood that a certain word will occur *on the average*. If we take into account the likelihood of the word's occurring in a specific context, we do not obtain the curve predicted by $f \times r = C$. For example, after "of" the most frequent word is "the," which occurs 10 times as often as any other word in that position. After "the," however, almost anything can happen, and there is a long list of nouns and adjectives that are about equally likely. Thus the curve of words following "of" has a steep slope, while the curve of words following "the" has a gradual slope, as Figure 5–6 shows.

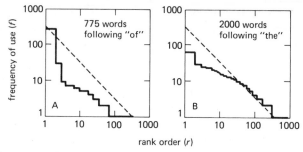

FIGURE 5–6 The standard curves for selected words. Left: The curve for all words following the word "of." Right: Words following the word "the." (from Miller, 1951)

In its most general form, Zipf's law states that the distribution of word frequencies calculated from any ordinary sample of language always has the same mathematical form, as long as the sample is from normal speakers. The data from many unrelated languages, and from texts covering a thousand years of history, have been found to conform to this equation. Even babies' babblings can be described with this equation. Written as well as spoken language on any subject matter shows this relation between frequency and rank. Since the equation depends on the number of words occurring with every possible frequency, it is not greatly affected by circumstances that increase the number of words occurring just once, such as lists of objects or names; they affect only a single point on the curve. The law applies to phoneme, syllable, or morpheme counts as well.

Interpreting Zipf's Law What mechanisms underlie this law? According to Zipf, human behavior in many spheres is founded on the principle of least effort. The organism strives to maintain as low an average level of exertion as possible. We have already seen this principle influencing our preference of certain syllable structures or the arrangement of letters on a typewriter keyboard. Zipf claimed that from the speaker's point of view language would be at its simplest if the speaker had only to utter the same word again and again, or in other words, if the language consisted only of a single word. With a single-word language, the speaker does not have to go through a selection process when he needs a specific word. Moreover, this one word is so overlearned that it requires very little effort to produce. From the listener's point of view, on the other hand, the language would be most rational and most convenient if every distinctive meaning had its own word. In language these two tendencies confront each other; one to say things as economically or effortlessly as possible, and the other to be explicit for the listener's benefit. Zipf's standard curve can be viewed as the equilibrium between these two tendencies.

The mathematician Mandelbrot (1952) later advanced a different interpretation of Zipf's standard curve. According to Mandelbrot, Zipf's curve is merely one way to express a necessary consequence of regarding a message source as a *stochastic process*. A stochastic process is any system that gives rise to a sequence of symbols or events to which a probability law applies, such that after a certain sequence, the probability of each other possible event or symbol can be assessed. A sequence of letters and words making up texts of English or of any other language is a good example. A sequence of musical notes written by a specific composer is another example. So is the sequence of numbers that win at roulette. Only because language can be regarded as a stochastic process can we have the present chapter on the statistical structure of language.

If we have a message-generator producing some very long and random sequence of letters, where "space" is considered to be a letter, and if we define a "word" in this product as any sequence of letters that occurs between spaces, then there will necessarily be more occurrences of particular short than of particular long words. Shorter sequences of letters are more likely to be the same as each other while longer sequences are more likely to differ. We can create only 26 possible one-letter "words," but there are 26^2 (676) possible two-letter words, 26^3 (17,576) three-letter words, and so on. To put it in another way, the same short words occur frequently while each of the long words occurs infrequently. The result will be a demonstration of Zipf's Law.

Zipf's Law has implications for the type-token ratio, since the number of types is fixed once the number of tokens is known and vice versa. Zipf's Law states that $f \times r = C$. Mathematically, this implies that the number of tokens is approximately $C \log_e C$ and the number of types is C. If Zipf's Law holds, one can plot the number of types to be expected as a function of the number of tokens, as shown in Figure 5–7. This relation actually holds over quite a wide range of token numbers, though it generally underestimates slightly the number of types in a given text. Both the newspaper sample of some 40,000 words and the quarter-million word sample from *Ulysses* have about 1.15 times as many types as would be expected from Zipf's Law. Chotlos's (1944) children, with samples only in the range of 2,000 words, show an excess of types by about a factor of 1.5. Carroll's suggestion of an index of TTR independent of text length quoted earlier (Diversity = Types/$\sqrt{2 \times \text{Tokens}}$) does not correspond to Zipf's Law at all.

To summarize, Zipf's standard curve expresses an interesting relation between frequencies of verbal elements and their ranks: $f \times r = C$. The curve can be interpreted as a balance of two forces—unification and diversification. It can also be interpreted as a consequence of regarding a language as a stochastic process and as an efficient communication channel.

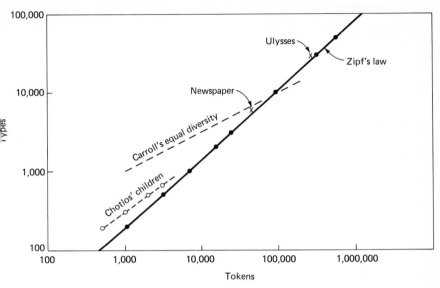

FIGURE 5–7   The number of types expected as a function of the number of tokens, if Zipf's Law holds. Note that *Ulysses* and newspaper counts roughly fall on the same function relating types and tokens, while Carroll's measure of diversity does not.

THE NUMBER OF ALTERNATIVES AND SPEECH

Information theory: A bare outline

Information theory or communication theory has exercised a strong influence on a number of different fields of science, including psychology and linguistics. It developed from engineers' and mathematicians' concerns over how to transmit signals from an information source to a destined receiver. Signals have to be transmitted with as little loss of information as possible through channels of communication that are usually "noisy." In the frame of information theory, signals have an information content by virtue of their potential for making selections. In telegraphy, the function of the source of information is to select letters successively from an alphabet and to transmit them as signals over a wire or by radio to a receiver. At the receiver, the signals are used to select letters from the same alphabet. The signals form a coded representation of the message; thus, messages are sent and received via a code. Language similarly forms a coded representation of concepts that are to be transmitted from one mind to another.

All communication rests upon the possibility of choice, of selection from a set of alternatives. If there are no alternatives at the point of choice, no information is communicated. If your professor has said that a grade of A will be handed out to everyone in your class, you will gain no further information when the final grades are announced. If on the other hand you were told that the grades could range from A to D, you will anticipate your grade with uncertainty and even anxiety. When the grades are announced, your uncertainty is removed and you gain information. In general, *information* is that which removes or reduces the uncertainty that exists when more than one alternative is possible. The more alternatives from which a choice has to be made, the more uncertainty there is about the outcome of the choice, and the more information is communicated when the choice is made known. In the example of the grades, if your professor told you that you ranked in the lower half of the grades (C and D) rather than the upper half (A and B), the amount of information you gained would not be as much as if you were told the specific grade you made. A choice among two alternatives answers the question "Is my grade in the upper or the lower half?," while a choice among four alternative answers the question "Is it A, B, C, or D?"

The amount of information should not be confused with the content of the information. Your actual grade, say C, would remain the same whether your professor told you that you belonged to the lower half or that you made C. And the point that a B average is required to get into graduate school does not enter this problem at all. That is "semantic" information, or meaning, and is quite different from the technical concept of "information."

The amount of information can be measured using an equation formulated by Hartley (1928) and developed by Shannon (1948) and numerous successors. In this equation, the amount of information is expressed as the logarithm to base 2 of the number of alternatives, or $\log_2 2 = 1$ bit (from *bi*nary dig*it*). The answer to one binary question such as "Is it in the upper or lower half of the grades?" will remove all uncertainty if the alternatives are two. If the alternatives are four in number, two binary questions are required ($\log_2 4 = 2$ bits): the first question determines that you belong to the lower half of the grades (C and D), and the second question decides between C and D.

According to Hartley's equation, the occurrence of 1 out of 10 possible alternatives carries half the amount of information that is carried by the occurrence of 1 out of 100 (10^2) alternatives, and only a third as much as by the occurrence of 1 out of 1,000 (10^3) alternatives, as $\log_2 10 = 3.32193$; $\log_2 100 = 2 \log_2 10 = 6.64386$; and $\log_2 1{,}000 = 3 \log_2 10 = 9.96578$ (bits). The stimulus itself, the actual physical event that occurs, could be identical in the three situations. The only difference would be how many other possible events might just as readily have occurred instead of the one that did occur.

Speech as a process of choice

Psychologists have adopted from information theory such useful concepts as "selection of a symbol from a set of alternatives," "amount of information," "noisy channel of communication," and "redundancy." Here we shall consider the first and the second concepts, "selection of a symbol," and "amount of information." Recall from Chapter 3 what Olson's (1970) cognitive theory of semantics says about word meaning: words do not "stand for" referents, but have another use—they specify perceived events relative to a set of alternatives; they provide information. In producing a sequence of words, too, we make a choice from a set of alternatives at each point of the sequence. Of course, the number of alternatives fluctuates, and the alternatives are not necessarily equally likely. A selection process may be reflected in spontaneous speech as hesitation pauses: speakers may show hesitation pauses at the points where they must consider a large number of alternatives. According to this view, hesitation pauses are analogous to an increase in reaction time in perceptual tasks or decision-making when a choice has to be made from an increasing number of alternatives. Speakers may show hesitation pauses preceding the first word of a sentence (Taylor, 1969) or of a clause (Goldman-Eisler, 1968). These pauses may be used to formulate the content of the entire sentence as well as to choose the first word. The speaker may also be choosing one way of expressing the sentence theme among a few alternative ways.

Hesitation pauses that occur within phrases or clauses seem to reflect the difficulty of choosing a word out of many alternatives. Goldman-Eisler found that pauses occurring within phrases preceded content words, long words, and words of high information value. Words that had been preceded by a pause when originally uttered by one speaker proved to be significantly harder for another person to guess later. Both pausing and guessing may reflect difficulty in choice because at that point there are many alternatives. Stutterers seem to have more stutterings at the places where normal speakers would have hesitation pauses, possibly for the same reason. This problem is discussed in the chapter on speech disorders (Chapter 10).

Decoders (readers) tend to make pauses not, like speakers, before the words of high information value but rather at grammatical junctures, where they may pause to assimilate what they have heard so far (J. G. Martin, 1967). Actors must learn to put the pauses at the places that are natural for free speech, not for reading.

The listener must go through the same selection procedure as the speaker. The listener's selection must be based on the sounds he hears, although it may be partly self-generated from his expectations. In ordinary verbal interaction, the topic, the situational context, and the speaker's talking habits all act to confine the alternatives listeners have to search through in their anticipation of what is to come. If anything outside the expected set is spoken, we tend to miss it, especially when the listening conditions are less than ideal. When I first started attending lectures in America, my English was even poorer than now, and I used to understand the lectures but not the professors' jokes. Jokes often rely on an unexpected twist of word or context.

Investigating the size of the alternative set as it influences our speech behavior, Aborn, Rubinstein, and Sterling (1959) asked subjects to restore words deleted at different positions in sentences of various lengths. They found that how well the subjects could guess words of different grammatical classes reflected the size of the class of the omitted word. In English, the sizes of grammatical classes differ—we have more nouns than verbs, and more verbs than adverbs. Function words such as articles and pronouns are few. Thus, missing nouns are harder to predict than verbs, and verbs in turn are harder to predict than adverbs. Prediction of missing function words is easiest of all.

Using words in isolation, we can demonstrate the effect of the size of the alternative set on perception, independently of the effect of sequential constraint. Miller, Heise, and Lichten (1951) demonstrated that our ability to identify a spoken word through a considerable amount of noise is inversely related to the logarithm of the number of different words from which we have to choose the stimulus, as shown in Figure 5–8. The sound patterns falling on the listener's ears were in all cases quite comparable. In other words, a word chosen out of a small set of alternatives was easier to identify than the same word chosen from a large set of alternatives. The difference lies not in what words were spoken, but in what words *might* have been spoken.

We can predict deleted letters far better than deleted words, because there are only 26 letters plus space instead of the large set of words. Even if we consider only very frequently used words, they still greatly outnumber the letters. We can predict deleted vowels more easily than consonants, again partly because we have fewer vowels than consonants, and partly because vowels tend to start function words. Try to decipher the following two strings:

$$—i— i— a —oo— a— a —e—i—$$
$$Th–s –s a b—k –nd – p–nc–l$$

In sum, choice of a symbol out of a number of alternatives, and the amount of information as formulated in information theory, are useful concepts in discussing speech processing. Speech processing is a constant series of choices from sets of alternatives. The more alternatives there are, the harder the choice, and this difficulty is reflected in pauses on the part of speakers, and in errors of prediction on the part of guessers. The same effects are found at every level of language—letter, sound, word, clause, or sentence.

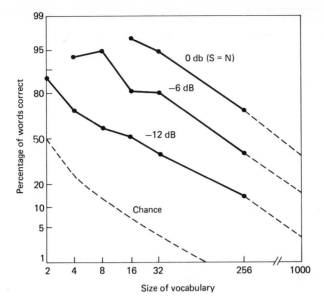

FIGURE 5–8   Percentage of words correctly identified as a function of the size of the vocabulary from which the words have to be selected, for various signal-to-noise ratios. At 0 dB, the signal strength is equal to the noise strength. At −12 dB, the signal is 12 dB below the noise level. (From Carroll, 1964; and Miller, Heise, and Lichten, 1951)

SEQUENTIAL STRUCTURE OF LANGUAGE

It is easier to perceive d after the sequence "b, c, –" than after "y, z, –," or after a random sequence such as "t, x, –." d is even better perceived in the middle of a patterned sequence, such as the blank in the middle of "c, –, e," and a longer sequence, "a, b, c, –, e, f, g" is even more helpful than "c, –, e." Here we shall try to concentrate on the third aspect of the probability structure of language, sequential constraint, which perhaps is the most important factor that influences our speech processing.

Sequential redundancy

Try to guess the last letter in the following five sequences:

(a) AAAA–   (b) CAND–   (c) CAKE–   (d) TAKE–   (e) PXRN–

You note that the missing letters in sequences (a) and (b) are almost completely predictable; they are almost 100 percent redundant. In (c), any of the letters S, R, Y, or D is possible; and in (d), N, R, or S; and in (e), any of the 26 letters in the alphabet is possible. The kinds of sequence we commonly find in ordinary language are (b), (c), and (d). Sequential redundancy is the constraint operating on single letters at the end of (long) sequences of letters.

One technique of measuring sequential redundancy is a *guessing game*. Shannon (1951) showed subjects a succession of (say) ten letters, and asked them to guess what the eleventh letter had been. The subjects were urged to continue to guess until they came up with the correct answer. The constraints of spelling, grammar, or idiom make it possible for a subject to predict with some accuracy what the eleventh would be. Shannon counted the number of guesses required. If all guessers hit the correct letter at the first guess, the constraining influence of the sequence of ten letters upon the eleventh would be 100 percent. Shannon's data and other confirming studies indicate that the English language is highly redundant. The average letter in English is approximately 50 percent determined by what has preceded it; less than one-half of its information is new. This technique gives the lower-bound estimate of redundancy, because subjects may or may not have perceived and put to use the total redundancy of the language.

According to Burton and Licklider (1955), printed English might display higher redundancy if very long-range constraints were considered, such as the influence of subject matter, style, level of presentation, and dynamics of the situation reported or described. Using paperback novels as test material, and graduate students of high verbal skills as subjects, they obtained letter redundancy values as high as 80 percent. Redundancy increased as the number of letters known to the subject increased up to 32 letters. Beyond 32 letters redundancy remained at 80 percent. Because printed English usually consists of passages of more than 30 letters, the constraining influences in printed English are such that any letter is 66–80 percent determined by what preceded it.

Words are considerably less predictable than are letters. However, the influence of contextual constraint on words is similar to that on letters. For example, a deleted word is best predicted at the middle of a sentence, and the more words that are given as context, the better the prediction, up to a certain point. Most of the effect of context occurs within 5 or 10 words, or between 23 and 45 letters (average word length is 4.5 letters), which is similar to the limit of 32 letters given by Burton and Licklider (Aborn et al., 1959). Of course, sometimes contexts can have effects at much longer ranges, but these rare cases do not much affect the conclusion because of their rarity.

It is possible to demonstrate the effect of sequential structure independently of the effect of the number of alternatives. In a memory experiment, Miller's (1962b) subjects reported grammatical sentences like "Don brought his black bread" more accurately than ungrammatical strings like "bread black his brought Don." Even subjects who were extremely familiar with the restricted set of words used in the experiment and the order in which they could occur performed in this way. This effect may be due not directly to the sequential structure of the sentence, but to the fact that the sentence has meaning and can be reconstructed correctly from its meaning without being recalled word by word, as must the disorganized group of words.

The statistical structure of language influences not only the way we perceive but also the way we pronounce utterances. We tend to pronounce with less care those words or phrases that we expect our listeners to anticipate well. For example, we note that among different grammatical classes of words, function words that carry little information seldom get stressed in our enunciation. In one study (Allen, 1972), linguists marked stress levels of each syllable in the following string.

$$\overset{10}{\text{Talks}} \;\; \overset{0}{\text{in}} \;\; \overset{7}{\text{terms}} \;\; \overset{0}{\text{of}} \;\; \overset{5}{\text{getting}} \;\; \overset{0}{} \;\; \overset{0}{\text{a}} \;\; \overset{10}{\text{name}} \;\; \overset{0}{\text{for}} \;\; \overset{1/2}{\text{him}} \overset{4}{\text{self,}} \;\; \overset{5}{\text{so}} \ldots$$

The figures over the syllables are the total stress-mark scores each syllable received from all five linguists in two sessions. The figures reflect roughly the relative importance of the syllable in the string.

P. Lieberman (1963) studied the relation between redundancy and pronunciation. He had three speakers read the following meaningful grammatical English sentences aloud at a fast rate.

(a) The number that you will hear is nine.
(b) A stitch in time saves nine.

He then isolated the word "nine" from the recordings of sentences (a) and (b), and played the "nine" samples to 43 listeners for identification. The listeners correctly identified "nine" samples isolated from (a) 61 percent of the time; from (b), 26 percent. That is, the speakers pronounced "nine" in (a) with more care than in (b), in which they expected their listeners to predict it easily. The redundancy calculated using the guessing technique was 0.85 for "nine" in sentence (b), but 0.1 in (a).

Order of approximation to English text

We have some implicit knowledge of the *transitional probabilities* of the English language: given the word "goes," we know that "down" follows it with high probability, and given "down," "here" comes with higher probability than "roses" or "electromagnetism." Of course, such variations in transitional probability occur in letter sequences too: in English, u is almost certain to occur, while k is highly unlikely, after q. Using our knowledge of transitional probability, Miller and Selfridge (1950) constructed strings of words with different amounts of sequential constraint, ranging from zero to sequential constraints ranging over several words.

To construct a zero-order approximation to English (a string with no sequential dependency among the words), they chose words at random from a dictionary without considering frequency. One result is:

combat callous irritability migrates depraved temporal prolix alas pillory nautical . . .

For the first order of approximation, words were chosen at random, but from a population with probabilities of occurrence proportional to their frequencies in larger samples. To achieve this, they wrote each word on one or more slips of paper, put all the slips into a huge urn, scrambled them, and drew. There were many more slips with the word "the" on them than there were slips with "calisthenics." This way, the relative frequency of words is made the same as the relative frequency in ordinary English. One result is:

day to is for they have proposed I the it materials of are its go . . .

High-order approximations cannot be constructed by selecting according to the real frequencies of word groups in English, since these frequencies cannot be counted. Rather, one must use intuitive knowledge of what these frequencies must be. One gives a subject a word string and asks for a word that naturally might follow. In general, the order of approximation is determined by the number of words given to the subjects before they add the next word. Thus to generate the fourth order, give three successive, sequentially structured words to the subject, who adds a fourth word to the string. Take the last three words from the new four-word string, and give it to another subject, and so on. One result is:

we are going to see him is not correct to chuckle loudly

and depart for home . . .

As the order of approximation gets higher, the word string becomes more and more redundant. In a way it becomes textlike, although even with very high order approximations the content of the string rambles like a dream. Also, structure may not be very grammatical.

How do different orders of approximation influence our speech processing? Speed and accuracy of reading, writing, telegraph transmission, and other processing are greater in sequences of higher-order approximation than in sequences of lower orders. For example, Sumby and Pollack (1954) instructed subjects to copy written material with the least possible number of glances. A glance was necessary for every 3 words of the zero-order approximation, but only one for every 10 words in ordinary prose. Miller and Selfridge showed that learning also is better for higher orders of approximation. However, immediate recall of words did not improve beyond about the fourth order.

Coleman (1963) correctly pointed out that the technique used to generate approximations to English produces higher-order approximations that are more complex and grammatically deviant than lower-order ones. If a person is faced with a long sequence such as "humble because they have no electricity," he has to resort to a complex and far-fetched sentence to incorporate it, especially because he is not allowed to use punctuation. Thus in his own experiment Coleman matched all test passages for frequency of occurrence of words and for syllabic length. With this procedure, he was controlling the test passage for one obvious variable. With such material there was no leveling off at fifth-order approximations. The mean number of items correct continued to increase up to the ninth order, the highest order Coleman studied. Coleman also ordered recall of words according to different sizes of sequences—correct single words, two-word sequences, and so on, up to correct 17-word sequences. The advantages for the higher-order approximations became greater as recall was scored in longer sequences. At higher-order approximations, sequential constraints package words into familiar phrases and clauses.

On the level of letters, Erdman and Dodge showed as early as 1898 that we can correctly read from a single brief exposure (100 msec) 4 to 5 unconnected letters, but 12 to 20 letters that form familiar words. We also can read a word at a distance at which individual letters are unrecognizable. Miller, Bruner, and Postman (1954) examined this phenomenon more systematically. They prepared 8-letter sequences of different orders of approximation to the statistical structure of English, as follows:

zero-order sequence	YRULPZOC
first-order	STANUGOP
second-order	WALLYLOF
fourth-order	RICANING

The investigators presented these 8-letter sequences, or pseudowords, to subjects in a random order in a tachistoscope. The subjects wrote the letters they saw in their correct order in the eight blanks on the answer sheet. It was found that the higher the approximation order, the higher the percentage of letters correctly placed: we perceive more letters in familiar sequences.

As with words, getting more letters does not necessarily imply getting more information. Since the information per letter is less for the higher-order approximations, perhaps the same amount of information per exposure was perceived for all orders of approximation. It seems that we can handle only so much information in a given amount of time. Experiments on different orders of approximation to English demonstrate that we have acquired the habits of ordering phonemes, letters, and words in proper sequences in English. We transfer these ordering habits even to novel arrangements of verbal elements in laboratory experiments. In any transfer of learning habits, the more similar the materials are to our original learned material, the greater is the degree of transfer. Our ordering habits are so strong that an unfamiliar letter sequence is likely to be misread as a more familiar sequence, as was shown in an early experiment by Wilkins (1917). The words typed in two lines and exposed briefly (50–100 msec) were:

RENAISTECTURE
ARCHISANCE

but were misread, as you can guess, as "Renaissance Architecture."

Language is not a Markov chain

A grammar that produces sentences considering only the transitions between successive words from left to right is a *finite-state grammar* or finite-state *Markov process*. A sentence-producing machine begins in the initial state, runs through a sequence of states (producing a word with each transition), and ends in the final state. The sequence of words that has been produced is a "sentence." We assign a probability to each transition from state (word) to state. The Markov process is named after A.A. Markov, who in 1913 published a statistical study of Pushkin's poetic novel, *Eugéne Onégin*, in which he considered only digrams. A stochastic series in which the probability of each sign depends only on the immediately preceding sign is a Markov chain. Chains in which the sign depends on several preceding characters are sometimes called higher-order Markov chains.

Markov chains have several inadequacies for describing language. As we have seen, if we choose each word in a string with only the immediately preceding word taken into consideration, the emerging string is not necessarily a sentence with a coherent theme. There are also discontinuous dependencies; a word may be effectively independent of its next-door neighbor while strongly constraining one farther away, although on average the more affected words are likely to be closer. Consider the example of embedding a clause within a sentence: "The dog, while the clock struck ten, barked . . . ," where "dog" constrains "barked," much more than it constrains "while." The maximum constraint in a particular case may occur at any length.

It is about time to remind ourselves that language is hierarchically organized; smaller units are combined into bigger and higher units—words into phrases, phrases into clauses or sentences. In "To have two wives is a burden," one entire phrase, "is a burden" is constrained by another entire phrase, "to have two wives." Note especially that there is no dependency between the two adjacent words "wives" and "is." Sequential constraints may operate across sentences as well. After the sentence "It is raining," "I need a raincoat" is probable but not "I must have a sunbath." Experimentally, E. E. Miller (1956) showed that recognition thresholds for sentences presented in a tachistoscope were improved if the various sentences were given in a meaningful rather than a random order. In well-written prose, sentences within the same paragraph should have more mutual constraints than sentences chosen from random paragraphs.

So far we have talked about constraints that operate forward—that is, earlier items influence later ones. Now we examine constraints operating backward, that is, instances where the later items influence the choice or perception of earlier ones. In this sense, too, language is not Markovian. In sentence production, a particular word is sometimes chosen according to what is to follow. For example, in "There is/are a book/books," the choice "is/are" depends on whether later on in the sentence you want to refer to one book or to more than one book. Again, the constraints can operate over several words backward. For example, in processing the spoken form of

$$\text{Rapid} \begin{Bmatrix} \text{righting} \\ \text{writing} \end{Bmatrix} \text{with his uninjured hand saved the contents}$$

$$\text{of the} \begin{Bmatrix} \text{burned message} \\ \text{capsized canoe} \end{Bmatrix}$$

the listener cannot determine the meaning of "righting/writing" until several seconds after it had been heard.

W. Bryan and N. Harter in the 1890s observed highly skilled telegraphers listening to Morse code. The telegraphers did not transcribe the auditory signals that constituted a word until some 6 to 12 words after the signals were heard. If subsequent portions of the message could not provide helpful context, as in the case of stock quotations or transmissions in cipher, the telegraphers changed their strategy and copied the message much more closely in time. Such messages were much more difficult to receive and had to be transcribed slowly. Telegraph companies even in the last century charged higher rates for sending such messages precisely because they lacked redundant context (reported by Warren and Warren, 1970).

What are the sources of sequential constraints? Constraints that exist within words are mostly due to phonological rules (for example, consonants and vowels usually alternate) and articulatory constraints. There are two sources, syntactic and semantic, for the constraints that exist among words, phrases, and clauses. After "The tall . . . ," usually adjectives or a noun will follow, although other parts of speech are permissible.[2] Any number of

---

[2] "The tall must stoop, but the short can walk upright here."

adjectives is possible, but sooner or later we must have a main noun to complete our noun phrase. We then must have a predicate at some point to complete our sentence. Semantically, we choose a word that can be described by "tall": "man" and "tree" are possible while "river," "road," and many other words are excluded in a normal type of speech. After "tree" is chosen, we know from our knowledge of the world what things trees can be or do. We can produce "The tall tree is majestic," but not (except poetically) "The tall tree loves me." Between-sentence constraints are largely semantic; the meanings of sentences should relate to each other.

Cloze procedure

Using the basic notion of redundancy, Wilson Taylor (1953) developed a tool measuring reading ease (*readability*) of text and the degree of comprehension of readers. The tool is called the *Cloze procedure*, the word "Cloze" coming from the Gestalt notion of closure—our tendency to perceive an incomplete form such as a circle with a gap as complete, or closed. In speech processing, we fill in missing or incorrect letters or words to perceive a complete and meaningful utterance. We expect that such filling in may be more difficult in some sentences than in others. Try to fill in the missing words in the following two sentences:

(a) Two of the most popular ———— pets are dogs and ————.
(b) The identification response is ———— similar to acoustic ————.

Sentence (b) is taken out of a psychology journal article, and the missing words are "formally" and "stimuli."

To obtain a Cloze score, every fifth word in a written or oral message of approximately 250 words is deleted. The number correctly restored is the Cloze score. We can use the same procedure for measuring a receiver's comprehension of a message. A person who correctly fills in many words must be comprehending the message better than the person who fills in only a few. High Cloze scores might be obtained in *Reader's Digest* articles, and low scores in material from law or technical books.

Another well-known readability index is the *Flesch count* (1946, 1962). A difficult text, by the Flesch count, consists of long words and long sentences. Writings of Gertrude Stein will be found "easy" by this count because they consist of short sentences with short words. The difficulty of her writings comes from a peculiar, idiosyncratic use and arrangement of words, as the following sample of her writing shows.

. . . In this way mouth is a mouth. In this way if in as a mouth if in as a mouth where, if in as a mouth where and there. Believe they have water too. (from "Three Portraits of Painters—Cezanne")

Words deleted from such a text will be hard to predict, and Cloze scores will be low. Thus the Cloze procedure, which takes account of all aspects of the statistical structure of language, as well as of extralinguistic knowledge of the subject matter, makes a better readability index than does the Flesch count.

Coleman (1965) developed four readability formulas, based on the correlation of Cloze scores with four measures of ordinary prose that are related to the Flesch count: the number of one-syllable words (X_1 in his formulas); the number of sentences (X_2); the number of pronouns, not including possessives (X_3); and the number of prepositions, not including "to" in infinitives (X_4). The counts are normalized to 100-word texts. One of his formulas includes all four measures, as in:

$$X' = -26.01 + 1.04X_1 + 1.06X_2 + 0.56X_3 - 0.36X_4$$

To obtain X', count X_1, X_2, X_3, and X_4 of a text, and insert the obtained values in the formula. The higher X' is, the easier is the text. X' for articles in *The Reader's Digest* might be 70–75 percent, while articles in law journals might be 25–30 percent. Essentially, this formula says that prose will be more readable, with a higher Cloze score, if it contains many one-syllable words, short sentences, and pronouns, and few prepositions.

Finally, a word of warning: Kincaid and Delionbach (1973) report that lowering the level of writing below the reading ability of the reader will not improve its readability.

How redundant should language be?

One way to define redundancy is to say that a message is redundant if we use more symbols than absolutely necessary to communicate it. Consider expressions such as "yellow jaundice," "repeat again," "red blood." In "I am a man," four separate features indicate that the subject is singular: "I" instead of "we"; "am" instead of "are"; "a" instead of "two"; and "man" instead of "men." The equivalent sentence in Chinese is "I man," whose plural would be "we man." Sometimes a Chinese sentence is so economical that it sounds cryptic to English-speakers. The great Chinese sage Confucius (551–479 B.C.) advised us:

> Know, know; don't know, don't know—that is know.

To paraphrase it in redundant English, "To know what you know and to know that you don't know what you don't know—that is the characteristic of one who knows." (from *The Wisdom of Confucius* by Lin Yutang 1938).

Even in English, if we have to save space and money we can cut down the redundant symbols and features, as we do in newspaper headlines and telegrams. From this morning's paper (*The Globe and Mail*, Toronto, May

9, 1973) I found the following three titles that lack function words. As you can see, they are not at all ambiguous.

LIBYAN AIRLINER CRASH TOLL NOW 107
WINDSOR RACEWAY BRIBE RUMORS PROBED SECRETLY
EAST-WEST SPLIT PARALYZING VIETNAM TRUCE BODY

Some linguists believe that languages evolve from long, elaborate phonetic patterns with little communication content toward short units combined according to rules so as to convey much content per element. In statistical terms, with evolution a language shows a progressive decline in redundancy. The American etymologist J. H. Tooke (1777, mentioned in Flesch, 1962) observed that what once took a whole sentence or clause to express can now be compressed into a single word. We now have a single word "tooth" for "that which tuggeth" and "memorandum" for "that which ought to be remembered." More obvious to us is a word like "singer," a person who sings, or who can sing, or who lives by singing.

What kind of language are we going to have in the future? A grammar may be streamlined over time by elimination of the patently redundant features. Shedding long and cumbersome inflectional endings is one way and requiring fewer grammatical features is another. Recall that the Chinese language gets along well with "I man/we man." Frater, one of the planned linguae francae (international languages) based on Latin and Greek roots, is similar to Chinese in this respect. The deaf's sign language also lacks many of these grammatical features. A deaf person can say a short sentence with one hand signal. Sign language is rapid, and can be as much as three times as fast as normal speech. Of course, the sign language misses intonation and the other subtle information-carrying nuances of spoken speech.

I am not suggesting that redundancy is wasteful and should be completely eliminated from language. Human language at any time anywhere should contain a certain amount of redundancy. Otherwise communication would become a strain. We could not miss even a single phoneme, syllable, letter, word, or grammatical feature and still get a message correctly. The speaker or writer would have to be excessively careful in his enunciation, spelling, and expression. With redundancy, information on any point is spread out over the communication, and momentary lapses of attention or noise bursts do not destroy it all.

Garner (1962) assumes that redundancy exists in the printed language not just as an accident; in the course of development the amount of redundancy may have increased (or decreased in some cases?) to satisfy some realistic criterion. The criterion being satisfied is one of 100 percent constraint for single letters in the middle of reasonably long sequences. There is a good reason why unilateral sequential redundancy should be approximately 50 percent: this is the lowest value of redundancy that can allow us to detect and correct isolated errors in the middle of long sequences with almost 100 percent accuracy.

So redundancy is useful for gaining accuracy. When we give our name to a stranger on the telephone, we sometimes deliberately increase redundancy in order to gain accuracy: "T for train; A aim; Y yes; L lord; O O.K.; and R rain" will introduce my name. Communication between pilots and a control tower at an airport has to be accurate, but the environment is very noisy at airports. Here technical personnel resort to a highly redundant language—they use a restricted set of words or phrases. The language used by the operator of a control tower at a military base is made up of "sentences" like: "Air Force 5264. Ready number one in take-off position. Over," or "Extend your base. We have C–54 on final" (Frick and Sumby, 1952). Many of these sentences sound unintelligible to us, but not to the pilots. These messages form a subset of the set of all possible English sentences, which in turn is a subset of all possible English letter sequences. The pilots are thoroughly familiar with all the possible messages—13 message units—that comprise this subset of subsets. Also, the pilot knows whether he is landing or taking off, and this situational context further restricts the set of possible messages. By asking 100 Air Force pilots to predict tower messages, Frick and Sumby calculated the redundancy of control tower language to be 96 percent. In other words, pilots can pretty well anticipate what messages they are going to receive from the tower. Thus, for so noisy an environment high redundancy is useful, especially since errors in transmission of messages are costly at places like airports.

If noise pollution is going to be an unavoidable part of our future environment, then we have all the more reason to keep a certain amount of redundancy in our language. We have to strike a nice balance between economy and accuracy in communication.

SUMMARY AND CONCLUSIONS

Three aspects of the statistical structure of language influence our speech processing. The first is the relative frequency of verbal elements. We use certain phonemes, syllables, letters, and words more frequently than others. We seem to prefer verbal elements that require least effort to produce and, at the same time, are least confusing to hear. We also devise our letters and other code systems in such a way that frequently used items will be simpler. Frequently used Chinese characters also tend to be simpler or have simplified versions. Frequently used words tend to be, or to become, short.

The relative frequencies of verbal elements influence our speech processing profoundly. We can identify, read, memorize, or learn frequent verbal elements faster and better than infrequent ones.

Zipf's Law states that there is a relation between frequencies of verbal elements and their rank order such that (frequency $\times$ rank) is constant over words. Three interpretations of Zipf's Law were discussed.

The second aspect of statistical structure discussed was the way the number of potential alternatives influences our speech processing. This is explained in the framework of information theory, which says that all communication rests upon the possibility of a choice from a set of alternatives. The more alternatives from which a choice is made, the more information that choice conveys. Experiments show that the size of the alternative set influences our ability to guess deleted items or identify words through noise. Pauses in spontaneous speech may also reflect selection processes.

The third aspect is sequential constraint. English text is highly redundant, which means that we can easily guess a missing letter or word in a context, or anticipate a letter or word after a patterned sequence. Such guessing is best for the middle of a sequence, and the longer the sequence the better the guessing, up to a point.

We can construct strings of words (or letters) with different orders of approximation to real English text. The higher the order of approximation, the more closely the string resembles a natural language sequence and the better it is processed.

There is a strong linear constraint between two adjacent words or letters. But constraints can exist between higher linguistic units too. Strong constraints can also exist between discontinuous elements or can operate backwards. All these points show that a text or utterance is not strictly a Markov chain.

The ease of guessing deleted words in a text makes an excellent readability index, called the Cloze procedure. Coleman's formulas relate the Cloze procedure and the Flesch count by showing that Cloze scores will be high and the text usually readable when it contains many one-syllable words, short sentences, and pronouns, and few prepositions.

Redundancy is inefficient or inelegant when we use more symbols than necessary. But a certain amount of redundancy is necessary to combat errors in communication over "noisy" channels. Evolving languages seem to be slowly reducing redundancy.

6

Language Acquisition

"P'raps it was John, but p'rapser it was Mary."

Spoken by a child

Infants (from Latin: in = not, fari = speaking) have no language, but they soon acquire it with little specific training. Moreover, they learn their language in a regular sequence that is similar for all languages. Non-human animals do not learn human language even when subjected to intense, prolonged, and ingenious training, although they may learn some rudimentary approximation to language.

PHYSICAL EQUIPMENT FOR ACQUIRING LANGUAGE

Infant's brain

The human brain at birth has about 24 percent of its adult weight, while a chimpanzee starts life with a brain that already weighs 60 percent of its final value (Lenneberg, 1966). The infant has its full quota of nerve cells, but *synapses*[1] are changed by activity, and the cells themselves grow bigger with age. Nerve fibers become *myelinated*—a fatty substance forms a sheath about the fiber, with the result of faster transmission of nerve impulses, and possibly better insulation between fibers. Fibers also branch out in many directions. Some if not all of this branching depends directly on

[1] Synapses are connecting points that mediate the transmission of nerve impulses between adjacent neurons.

experience. *Glial cells* multiply around the nerve cells, to which they give nutrient support. The human brain grows slowly in weight as well as in complexity of function, and matures fully only in the early teens. The human therefore has more opportunity for complex learning than does the chimpanzee. Corresponding to the slow maturation of the brain, language development is also gradual. At birth the infant has no language; soon it shows the primitive beginnings of language, which eventually develop into full-fledged language at about age five. At five a chimpanzee is fully mature, but a child still has a lot of growing and a lot of learning to do.

Although human neonates have no language, there is ample evidence that they are born with physical equipment well suited for acquiring language. The human brain's two hemispheres—the right and left hemispheres—are connected by a thick bundle of nerve fibers. Usually, but not always, the *left hemisphere* is the dominant one for speech. Anatomically, a particular part of the language-processing area in the left hemisphere is already larger at birth than the corresponding part in the right hemisphere (Witelson and Pallie, 1973).

There is also some behavioral evidence that newborn babies are already "tuned" to human speech sounds. Eisenberg (1965) found that babies respond differently to sounds at the speech-sound frequencies than to those at higher frequencies. They respond differently also to patterned, as compared with constant, acoustic stimuli. Condon and Sander (1974) report that the newborn infant, as early as the first day of life, makes precise and sustained segments of movement that are synchronous with the articulated structure of adult speech that it can hear. Babies 1 to 4 months old respond differently (vary nonnutrient sucking rates) to synthetic [b] or [p] (Eimas et al., 1971); and to natural speech versions of [a] or [i] and [i] or [u] (Trehub, 1973). Finally, infants learn quickly to respond to speech; within a few months after birth they already respond vocally to a human "speaking" to them.

Critical period

There may be a critical period for acquiring language, while the brain is still *plastic*. Most areas in the infant brain have no specific functions, and whatever happens early to the brain may influence the way it develops later. For example, if the left hemisphere is removed in infancy, the right hemisphere develops speech functions. The concept of a critical period implies that language may be acquired readily during this period but not so readily later. The exact time span of the critical period is ill defined for language acquisition, but may last until the early teens, when the brain completes its functional organization. Thus it coincides with the period of neural plasticity rather than with the period of full maturation and complete organization of the brain.

What behavioral evidence shows that language is not readily acquired after the end of the critical period? The so-called *"wolf"* and *"attic" children* are supposed to have been abandoned in early life to be raised by wolves in forests, or by deaf-mute adults in attics, without exposure to human language. These children did not possess human language when they were found in their late childhood. After their capture, they learned a modest amount of language only with special training. Recently Fromkin and co-workers (1974) described a 15-year-old girl who was kept in diapers like a baby until she was found at age 11, and could utter only grunts. In a few years she advanced to the speaking ability of a child of 2–2½ years under a university-backed linguistic program. It is hard to predict whether she will ever reach the level of "normal" children of her age in her linguistic development.

For other evidence on the existence of a critical period, let us look at the effects of brain damage, deafness, and mental retardation in childhood. We begin to observe behavioral evidence of cerebral organization at around age 4. If damage to the dominant hemisphere occurs before this organization is completed, the nervous system adjusts and language develops normally or nearly normally, whereas damage after the completion of organization results in more lasting language disturbance. Deaf children respond well to language training if deafness occurred after some maturation of the brain and some exposure to language, whereas if deafness started too early, language training is very difficult. The mentally retarded show a slow improvement in language acquisition until their early teens. At this age progress is arrested regardless of the amount of training, and the retarded will speak a sort of baby-talk forever after (Lenneberg, 1967). Finally, most adults can learn a foreign language only with considerable effort, and then imperfectly, although the process may be easier if other foreign languages were learned in childhood.

As evidence that language is acquired readily during the critical period, note that a normal child acquires a language or languages not through special training but mainly through "exposure." A child who is exposed to more than one language during this period will become a multilingual without much effort and with a good accent in each language (see Chapter 7). Children can learn and unlearn languages in a short time, depending on what language environment they find themselves in. Drastic environmental deficiencies such as having no parents, having deaf parents, or being institutionalized may retard the rate and reduce the quality of language development, but they do not affect the general sequence of language acquisition.

Table 6–1 is a rough summary of language acquisition during the critical period and beyond.

Table 6–1 also enumerates the topics to be discussed in the rest of this chapter. The phonemes mastered at different ages are taken from Table

TABLE 6-1 A Summary of Language Acquisition

Ling. Stage	MLU[a]	Age	Sample Utterance	Phonology	Vocab.	Semantics	Word Order	Syntax	Piaget's Stage
	1 mor-pheme	12–16 mos.	/bɔ:/; Mon-mon; there; up; no; man/ chair/ coat/ suitcase	Intonation? Most vowels & easy consonants	1–5 words "nénin"	Referent; Concrete content and function words; →Superconcrete feature		Single words in isolation or in juxtaposition; Holophrase?	Sensory motor intelligence
I	1.8	19 — 27	Mommy sock. No pocket.	Intonation	"fa-fa"	Agent-object; Possessor-possessed; Nonexistence →Abstract flowerness	OV or VO; later SV	S → N+N (as, sub. + obj.); S → Nom {Neg} {NP}{VP} Pivot grammar?	
II	2.3 — 3.5	20 — 40	He no bite you. Why not he eat?	Master /b, p, m, w, h/	270 "dog"	Modulation of meaning; Judge anomalous sentences; →Abstract four-legged property	Interpret 2Ns & IV strings as SV or VO	Master (-ing), "in, on"; Plural, possessive, article	

186

			Phonology	Vocabulary	Semantics	Grammar	Cognition
III	4	26—42	I didn't did it. Does the kitty stand up?	Basic phonological rules	1,000	"Sweet" in physical sense only; 2-factor semantic space?	3rd person singular, past tense, copula, auxiliary	Symbolic thought
		4–6 yrs	(Like adults in simple sentences)	Master /d, t, n, g, k, ŋ, y, f/	2,000	Syntagmatic to paradigmatic word association	Mastered the basics of grammar, but can't produce passives	Intuitive thought
		6½–9 yrs	Is the ball hit by the bat? Did he not already funny?	/v, ð, dʒ, l, ʃ, s, z, r, θ, hw/ Subtle phonological rules		Dual meanings of "sweet"; 3-factor semantic space	Interpret 2Ns & IV strings in SVO, SOV or VSO	Produce PQ; regularizing peters off; can't distinguish grammatical & logical subject; can't put a complex concept into a sentence	Concrete operation (relation)
		11–15 yrs	(Like adults even in complex sentences)			Dual meanings of "sweet" and their relations	Can't sort words into four parts of speech	Formal operation (abstract thinking)

ᵃ MLU = mean length of utterance.

5–2 in Chapter 5. Brown (1973) distinguishes five stages of linguistic development; these are collapsed into three stages in the table. Klima and Bellugi (1966) also use three stages.

Students of language acquisition (such as Brown; Klima–Bellugi; Bloom) equate stages of linguistic development not with age but with mean length of utterance (MLU) measured by the number of morphemes in the utterance. Children acquire language at varying rates, though in uniform sequences. Most emerging linguistic sequences relate to increases in MLU; the addition of bound morphemes (–s, –ed), the addition of negative forms and auxiliaries used in interrogative and negative sentences, and embedding and coordinating all occur with longer average utterance length. Two children matched for MLU are much more likely to have speech that is at the same level of constructional complexity than are two children of the same age but different MLU. Note that morphemes rather than words are used as units: the emergence of bound morphemes reveals linguistic development. MLU loses its value as an index of linguistic development by the time the child reaches stage III in Table 6–1.

COGNITIVE BASES OF LANGUAGE ACQUISITION

So far we have seen that children are born with the equipment necessary for language acquisition. The physical equipment, especially the central nervous system, matures further, enabling the children to develop their perceptual-cognitive capacities. With developing cognitive capacities the children can notice prominent things in their environment. They also note recurring and regular patterns in verbal inputs. From these perceptual-cognitive activities, children eventually learn to code their cognitive representations in linguistic forms. It is obvious that children have to have a certain knowledge, perhaps very limited at first, of an object *ball* before they can refer to it in their utterance. The child may note that the object exists; it bounces; has a round shape; feels not too hard, and so on. This elementary knowledge of the ball comes mainly from sensory-motor manipulation of the object. The child may not yet know that it is made of rubber; or that different sizes make a difference in how well a ball bounces; or that air inside the ball makes it bounce. But the child can make it bounce, and that is all a 2-year-old needs to "know."

Cognitive development, according to Piaget

The Swiss psychologist Jean Piaget (see, for example, Piaget, 1952; Flavell, 1963) divides cognitive development into the following stages, which provide a broad cognitive background for language acquisition. Though

Piaget gives age limits to these developmental stages, he recognizes that they are only approximations. The transition from one to the next is continuous, but the sequential ordering of the stages is invariant. Moreover, these stages are found in every culture. There is a universal sequence for the development of language, and a universal cognitive developmental sequence may underlie it.

Piaget's stages may be summarized as follows:

1. *The sensory-motor stage* (birth to 2 years). The child starts noticing the existence of objects. Objects are separate from the self. An object is conceptually "permanent," in spite of its changing movements, orientations, and locations. Manipulating objects is the chief means of interaction with the environment. The child's thinking seems concerned only with the actual entities in the immediate environment.

2. *"Preoperational thought,"* which is divided into two substages.

2a. *The stage of symbolic thought* (age 2–4). The child elaborates symbolic function in play and integrates it with language acquisition. The child differentiates between an object and its internal representation, a symbol. The symbol is an object or action that comes to stand for other objects or actions by exhibiting some objective similarity to them. An example is the pebble that is used as a "pretend" candy in a child's game; he does not eat the pebble, because he realizes the symbolic nature of the pebble. Words are also signs, but their relationship to significates (objects) is arbitrary and conventional. Words are social signs, and are sharply differentiated from the private signs of the child. At first language is assimilated to the child's private symbolism; but as the child's symbolic function is slowly weaned from its initial egocentricity, so the child's use of language becomes increasingly socialized. The use of language in social contexts plays an important part in this weaning. But to Piaget, the symbolic function originates independently of language.

2b. *The stage of intuitive thought* (age 4–7). This period is not clearly distinguished from the previous one. Language and the symbolic function are not integrated so that the child thinks "in language"; the child's thinking and use of language are egocentric. Since words have been assimilated to a private, even idiosyncratic symbolic function, the child attaches private meaning to public signs and is unaware of the fact. Social experiences are not yet rich enough for the child to realize that others do not share these private meanings. Thinking is centered upon one relationship at a time.

3. *The stage of concrete operations* (age 7–11). The concrete operational level of thinking is reached when the child is able to vary two or more relationships simultaneously. The child solves *conservation problems* by compensation—one beaker gains in height what is lost in width, and another beaker gains in width what is lost in height, hence the two beakers come out containing equal quantities (Figure 6–1). But the child still

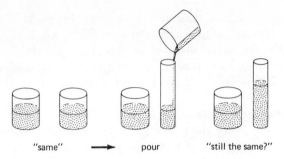

"same"   ⟶   pour   "still the same?"

FIGURE 6-1   Piaget's conservation problem with liquid.

remains fixed upon the concrete qualities of objects and the immediate present.

4. *The stage of formal operations* (age 11–15). The child makes the final steps toward abstract thinking, and is capable of hypothesis-testing; is able to consider rationally the *form* of an argument, as distinct from its content; can ignore the factual correctness of a proposition, and focus on the consistency and validity of a logical chain. A 12-year-old will accept and think about the following problem: "All three-legged snakes are purple. I am hiding a three-legged snake. Guess its color." This stage is only partially attained. All people, even the most intelligent, remain to some extent dependent on the content of a logical argument (see, for example, Wason and Johnson-Laird, 1972).

Let us now turn to the processes of language acquisition. We shall see that the gradually developing cognitive capacities allow children to acquire more and more complex, adultlike competence in all aspects of language.

Children find rules

At the outset we should note that children are not merely accumulating their speech sounds, vocabulary, and sentences, as earlier researchers in language acquisition tended to assume. Speech is a creative process in the sense that we produce and encounter novel sentences with almost every speech act. With our limited memory capacity, it is more sensible for us to acquire a vocabulary and a set of rules that we can apply to new utterances, than to try to memorize all possible utterances. Linguistic rules are seldom spelled out and taught to children. Children abstract and internalize the rules from the speech around them; their cognitive ability to note regular patterns in constantly changing linguistic data enables them to do so. As their cognitive capacity matures, children can abstract more and more complex rules. Slobin (1971) distinguishes several levels for children's rules, ranging from weak to stringent, as follows. I add a few more examples from other sources.

1. Not all possible word combinations actually occur in children's two-word utterances; there is some regularity and nonrandomness in word combinations. For example, at about 2, a child might say "baby high-chair," but not "high-chair baby."

2. Children have a *regularizing tendency,* or they extend regularities to new instances, rightly or wrongly. For example, they would say "goed," "comed," and "sheeps." "P'raps it was John, but p'rapser it was Mary" (Jespersen, 1922, p. 130).

3. In the normative sense of "rules," children are able to judge whether an utterance is correct with respect to some linguistic standard—they have a sense of grammaticality. During spontaneous speech, when children stop and correct themselves, one can infer that they are monitoring their speech against some notion of correctness. By age 3, self-corrections are frequent: "She had a silly putty like me had . . . like I . . . like I did." A German child, not yet 2, said: "Papa, hast du mir was mitgebringt—gebrungen—gebracht?" ("Papa, have you brought me something?") almost in a breath (Jespersen, 1922). Here the child used its own rules as the standard. The child also detects deviations from the norm in the speech of others. When C. Smith (1970) gave sentences such as "*Mine* old green coat has holes" to 3- to 4-year-olds to imitate, the children changed it into a more common sentence, "My old . . . ."

4. A more stringent criterion of grammatical judgments is a response to a direct question. One can ask the child if it is "better" or "more correct" to say "two foots" or "two feet." An ability to answer such questions develops late, and it is of little use to ask them of very young children. Brown and Bellugi (1964) report the following exchange between an interviewer and a child:

> Interviewer: "Adam, which is right, two shoes or two shoe?"
> Adam (2-year-old): "Pop goes the weasel!"

5. The most stringent test is that the indivdual can state explicit rules, but even adults fail this test. To begin with, no complete and adequate grammar of English or of any other natural language has been written. We have seldom been told specific rules, but have abstracted them ourselves. We behave as though we knew the rules, but this knowledge is inarticulate; we just do it right. In Messer's (1967) study children were able to discriminate between sound sequences that followed English phonological rules and sequences that did not. When asked to explain their choice, the children merely answered: "cause," or the equally unhelpful "I just did." Adults would often be no better able to answer.

Since children seem to acquire rules, we may now examine how they acquire phonological, semantic, and syntactic rules. These aspects are interrelated to some degree, and are discussed separately only for convenience.

PHONOLOGICAL DEVELOPMENT

How do children acquire phonemes and rules for combining sounds into pronounceable sequences? Let us consider some stages in the process.

Early vocalization

Random vocalization and crying: birth to 6 months   A new born baby's birth cry is more a reflex than an act of communication, and we need not dwell upon it. Lewis (1963), however, observed that within a few hours of birth mothers can already differentiate whether crying is caused by acute and mild discomfort. Mothers can also distinguish sounds other than crying as comfort or discomfort sounds. Discomfort sounds are narrow, tense, and nasalized sounds, and are results of contraction of the facial muscles, and narrowing of the mouth cavities. Comfort sounds are produced when an infant is relaxed with its mouth slackly open so that phonation simply appears at the end of expiration. These phonations are usually /ɔ/ or /ʔ/, a throat sound.

In the second and third months, an infant often responds vocally to an adult voice. If the mother makes a sound chosen from the infant's repertoire of sounds, it will respond with a similar sound. Thus the mother and the infant can occasionally carry on a "dialogue." During this period the baby engages in more or less random vocalization that bears little relationship to the sounds contained in its linguistic environment.

Babbling: 6–12 months   We can distinguish babbling from random vocalization in a number of ways. One type of babbling is segmented into pieces consisting of several syllables, and we can observe changes in pitch and stress, such as rising intonation patterns as if asking questions. During the babbling period the sound repertoire of the infant increases. At this stage children in different linguistic environments have similar sound repertoires. Nakazima (1962) found that there were no differences in the speech-sound repertoires of Japanese and American children even through the stages when words and phrases were beginning to appear. The first words of both groups of children were very similar in phonetic composition. Babbled utterances can be analyzed into syllables, but most of them are not recognizable as words. Once in a while, eager parents may recognize "words" in babbling, such as "mama," "papa," or "nana."

Is babbling a preparatory exercise for speech? Allport (1924) claimed that children develop a phonemic system by matching the sounds they hear to the sounds they produce in babbling. We can only conjecture what the possible benefits and purposes of babbling might be. Babbling may be used (a) to explore the possibilities, and to learn to control the output, of the vocal mechanism; (b) to take pleasure in vocal performances. There is no way either to confirm or refute benefit (a). As for (b), Lenneberg (1966) found that even congenitally deaf children vocalize. The quality of the deaf children's voices was quite similar to that of hearing children up to 6 months. If there was any difference, it was that the deaf children tended to engage in certain types of noise more persistently, while hearing children would go through a wide range of different types of sound, as if to run through their repertoire for the sheer pleasure of it. At around 9 months, lacking auditory feedback, the deaf children cease to babble. Since deaf children do not hear the sounds they make, they cannot associate muscular sensations from articulatory movements with the particular sounds.

Development of a phonemic system

Jakobson's law of universal sequence   The linguist Jakobson (1941) proposed an interesting notion about how children all over the world might develop a phonemic system. He claimed that the sequence of phonemic development is invariant and universal among children everywhere. Since phonemic development is closely tied in with physical maturation, this "law" is reasonable. The child learns early only those sounds that are common to most world languages, while those phonemes that distinguish its mother tongue from the other languages of the world appear later. /P, m, t/ are three consonants acquired early, and are found in many languages. Phonemes that are relatively rare, such as /θ/, are among the last phonemes acquired by children exposed to languages that contain them. Sounds that occur rarely in languages, and that are acquired later by children, also tend to disappear first in aphasia (this point will be considered in chapter 11). The phonemes acquired first have the greatest articulatory and auditory contrasts, and should occur in any efficient language. As languages require more sounds, they have to use phonemes with more subtle distinctions, the kind of phonemes that children master late.

Here is the detailed sequence of early phoneme acquisition, as described by Jakobson. In the first stage, children acquire /a/ and /p/, the two phonemes with the greatest mutual contrast. The vowel /a/ is an optimal vowel having maximum opening of the mouth; voicing; the greatest acoustic energy; no time limitation; and energy concentrated in a relatively narrow frequency range (*compact*). In contrast to /a/, /p/ is an optimal consonant having maximum closure of the mouth; production at the front of the mouth; voicelessness; minimum energy; and an extreme limitation in the time domain (a brief burst of noise), without any great concentration of energy in a particular frequency band (*diffuse*). At this stage the syllable CV /pa/ is possible.

At the next stage, an infant splits first the consonant and later the vowel into distinctive alternatives. Most frequently, the oral stop /p/ obtains a counterpart in the nasal consonant /m/. The opposition /m/:/p/ may be preceded by the split of the /p/ stop into two opposites, labial and dental, /p/:/t/. In the labial /p/ the lower end of the frequency spectrum predominates (*grave,*) and in the dental /t/, the upper end is the stronger one (*acute*). At this stage the pole of high and concentrated energy, /a/, contrasts with the low energy stops /p/ and /t/. Figure 6–2 left shows how these three contrasting phonemes form a "primary triangle."

Next the primary triangle splits into two triangles, one for the vowel and the other for the consonant. On the vowel side, the single compact /a/ finds its opposite in a diffuse vowel /i/. Then /i/ splits into /i/ and /u/, and the acute/grave contrast emerges. (See Figure 6–2b, the upper triangle.) The consonant group duplicates this originally vocalic (vowel) opposition by including the velar stop /k/. In other words, /k/ and /p/ or /k/ and /t/ are contrasted on the energy dimension as compact/diffuse, while /p/ and /t/ contrast in frequency as grave/acute (Figure 6–2b, the lower triangle.)

The consonantal opposition nasal/oral, which is the earliest acquired

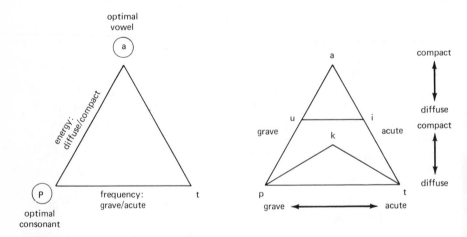

FIGURE 6–2   The sequence of phoneme acquisition. Left: The primary triangle. Right: The two-dimensional pattern: the vocalic (top) and the consonantal (bottom) triangle. (Based on Jakobson, 1971.)

by the child, occurs in all languages of the world except for some American Indian languages; it is ordinarily the consonantal opposition most resistant to aphasia. No language lacks the oppositions grave/acute and compact/diffuse, whereas any other opposition may be absent in some languages.

Jakobson's law of phonemic development of children has brought order into the bewildering array af facts accumulated by observation, which seemed to lack a common denominator until his broad principle was applied to them. Investigators who applied the law to their observational and experimental data involving different languages have found it substantiated, at least in its broad outlines. Menyuk (1968), for example, notes that the early acquisition order of distinctive features by both English- and Japanese-speaking children was identical: both groups acquired the features nasal, grave, voice, diffuse, continuant, and strident, in that order.

Babbled syllables Since /p/, /m/, and /a/ are among the first phonemes babies acquire, some of the earliest babbled syllables are [pa], [papa], [ma], [mama], and so on. It is not by accident that in many languages of the world "mama" is used for mother and "papa" for father. Incidentally, why is "mama" used for mother and "papa" for father? The anthropologist Murdock (1957) surveyed 531 words for mother and 541 for father in world languages, and found that 55 percent of the words denoting mother and only 15 percent of the words denoting father used /m/, /n/, or /ŋ/. Again Jakobson has an explanation.

Often the sucking activities of a child are accompanied by a slight nasal murmur, the only phonation which can be produced when the lips are pressed to mother's breast or to the feeding bottle and the mouth is full. Later, this phonatory reaction to nursing is reproduced as an anticipatory signal at the mere sight of food and finally as a manifestation of a desire to eat, or more generally, as an expression of discomfort and impatient longing for missing food or absent nurse, and any ungranted wish (1971, p. 216).

While we are talking about "mama" and "papa," let us have a look at other "baby words." They are imitations of babbling both in phonetic composition and in their rhythm of reduplicating syllables. Examples from different languages are: "dyadya" (uncle), "nyanya" (nanny), "teta" (aunt) from Russian; "mamma" (food), "poppa" (kiss), "buba" (piggy-back) from Korean; "nenne" (sleep) from Japanese; "nanna" (cradle) from Tuscan; "puppe" (doll) from German; "daddy, papa, bye-bye, dindin, tata" from English. Note that these baby words from different languages sound similar, even though they mean different things.

Children acquire most of the phonemes of their language by age 5. But some of the children do not master some of the "difficult" consonants until the age of 8 (see Table 6–1).

Phonological rules

Children must learn not only individual phonemes, but also the rules for using them. "Sporn" is not a word in English, but it could be a word, while "tporn," "kporn" or "nporn" could not. Other languages, of course, have different phonological rules.

How early do children observe the phonological rules of their language? To find an answer, Messer (1967) studied 13 children aged between 3.3[2] and 4.3. Messer gave the children pairs of monosyllables containing English and non-English initial and final consonant clusters, and asked them to tell him which of two things sounded more like a word. The children tended to select as possible words those syllables that were constructed according to English phonological rules. For example, all 13 children chose [trisk] and none chose [tlidk'] as a possible word. They mispronounced the impossible syllables more often than the possible, but the mispronunciations usually involved only one distinctive feature change that made the group more nearly possible. Examples are [ʃkib] changed to [skib] and [tʃluf] to [ʃluf]. This is another piece of evidence that children remember certain aspects of a phonemic segment rather than the segment as a whole. For example, [ʃ] and [s] share six features and differ only on one feature, according to Table 2–3: [ʃ] is +diffuse or +anterior while [s] is —diffuse or nonanterior.

However, there is ample evidence that children by age 8 have by no means mastered all the phonological rules completely. To cite one experiment, Anisfeld, Barlow, and Frail (1968) studied four groups of subjects, aged 6, 7, 8, and 19. The subjects had to choose between a pair of artificial words—"narv" or "narp"—as a preferred plural for a corresponding singular word, "nar." Singular CVC words ended in /l/, /r/, or /n/. To form plural words, the investigators added to the singular words any of the following sounds: /m, p, v, f, k, g, t, d, n, tʃ/.

Subjects' ages mattered in this task. The first- and second-grade subjects and adults preferred the sounds /f, v, tʃ/, which share with the appropriate plural markers /z/ and /s/ the features +continuant (not /tʃ/) and +strident. The features +diffuse, —grave, +voice, and —nasal also characterize the appropriate /z/, but the two features preferred by the older subjects are more important because they distinguish /z/ from other consonants more than any other features. Six-year-old kindergarten children did not show this pattern of preference—in fact, they showed no significant preference for any feature.

In sum, children first acquire phonemes with gross and distinct feature contrasts, and move on to learn phonemes with more subtle and finer contrasts. Phonemes are combined according to specific rules in a language, and children early show evidence of having acquired these rules.

---

[2] 3.3 = 3 years 3 months old.

It is perhaps because of this early acquisition of phonemes that older people have difficulty in learning a second language in a phonemically correct manner. But children do not reach an adult level of mastery until age 8.

SEMANTIC DEVELOPMENT

We deal with several questions here. How do children: (a) acquire a vocabulary? (b) use words? (c) acquire semantic markers and syntactic features? (d) develop lexical organization? (e) develop the connotative structure of meanings?

Vocabulary and use of words

Vocabulary A child rapidly learns about the world from sensory-motor experiences. Soon children start to assign labels—names—to the things with which they are already familiar—toys, family, and their own activities. There is nothing intrinsic or lawful about the relation between words and the things they designate, and a child simply must find out what each thing, if it is a concrete object, is called. The child associates the object *milk* with the word "milk" because the word is often used in the presence of the object. After children have learned the word "milk," they can say it whenever they want milk, and be rewarded with what they want. Alternately, a child may by chance happen to utter a word-like sound sequence such as [mamma] and receive food from its mother. In this way the mother can reinforce selectively and specifically some of the child's spontaneous vocalizations. "Mamma" ("food" in Korean), "mama" or "papa," and other baby words are perhaps shaped in this way by *instrumental conditioning*. Probably only a small portion of the early vocabulary is acquired through such a shaping procedure, however.

A child may acquire abstract words in a slightly different way, since abstract words cannot be related to specific objects. Understanding abstract words such as "soul" or "life" is beyond the cognitive capacity of young children. Children may learn such words by encountering them in appropriate verbal contexts, and by having adults explain them.

By various means, children keep increasing their vocabulary throughout their lives, but the rate of increase is perhaps fastest in early childhood. Children start with a few words around age 1, then increase their vocabulary size to an average of 270 words at age 2; 900 at 3; 1,520 at 4; 2,060 at 5; and 2,550 at 6 (Lenneberg 1966).

Use of words Young children may use words in ways different from adults while their semantic development is still immature. We shall see how semantic development proceeds, as revealed in the early use of words.

There is a controversy as to whether semantic development is a generalization process or a differentiation process. According to Anglin (1970), semantic development is essentially a *generalization process* in which the child first appreciates the similarity among small groups of words and only later sees the similarity among increasingly broad classes. At first a child might see that roses and tulips are flowers; oaks and elms are trees; and collies and poodles are dogs. Somewhat later the child might realize that the objects classed as flowers are similar to the objects classed as trees in that both are plants. Later still there might form even more general and abstract concepts of living things, and finally, entities that would apply to most nouns (see Figure 3–10). Development in the other parts of speech would proceed in a similar fashion.

E. Clark (1973) assumes an opposite direction of acquisition, namely *differentiation*. If the features that make up the meaning of a word are related to each other hierarchically, the most general, "top," feature is acquired first and all objects sharing this feature are classed together (for example, "tick-tock" (watch) extends to clocks → gas-meter → fire hose wound on spool → bathroom scale with round dial). The other features are acquired in the order of their level in hierarchy. A narrowing-down process occurs toward the end of this extension period. As new words are introduced to take over subparts of a semantic domain, the child will gradually add more specific features that differentiate the meaning of one word from another.

Leaving this controversy unresolved for the moment, let us trace semantic development as revealed in early use of words by children. Bloom (1973) describes three phases.

Phase I: Guillaume (1927) reports the following referents for "nénin" (breast) as used by his young son (11–12 months?).

> To ask for the breast, also a biscuit;
> The red button of a piece of clothing;
> The point of a bare elbow;
> An eye in a picture;
> His mother's face in a photograph.

Phase II: Lewis (1959) observed the use of the word "fa-fa" (flower) in a child. This stage appears to begin midway into the second year.

> Yellow jonquils growing in a bowl;
> Flowers of a new species and a different color but still in a bowl;
> Pictures of flowers in a book, lacking odor, texture, and tridimensionality (17–24 months);
> Embroidered flowers and sugar flowers on a biscuit (22–26 months).

Phase III: In the last half of the second year, the child typically labels all four-legged animals as "dogs" and all vehicles as "trucks" or "choo-choo."

Bloom does not seem to offer a plausible explanation for the three phases. M. M. Taylor (personal communication) explains the semantic development as follows: The succession between these phases can be understood in terms of a single process, which one might call *feature definition.* The concepts of "generalization" and "differentiation" are not needed, and may well be confusing a simple issue. Consider the examples of things called "nénin." Each has some aspect in common with the original "nénin," a breast. The common feature may be shape, color, affective impact, or almost anything else. "Nénin" is used when something occurs that is similar to the original in any of many different features. The features are very concrete, and do not interact in groups. Either the object has the proper shape (elbow tip) or the proper coloration (red button) or the proper pleasant impact (mother's face) or something else. If *any of these features occurs,* that is enough to make the thing "nénin." E. Clark's example of extension, "tick-tock," seems very similar to "nénin"; the object needs only the round shape and/or dial to be called "tick-tock."

Later, at the "fa-fa" stage, the concepts are less concrete. Only flower-like things are "fa-fa." All the features that we relate to flowers must be simultaneously present. The child has learned to abstract "flowerness" out of masses of features. It is not enough that there be a yellow blob; there must also be a stem, perhaps leaves, and so forth. This stage is more abstract, though less diffuse, than the "nénin" stage. *All features must co-occur* in order for the abstraction of "fa-fa" = "flowerness" to be valid. It is about the stage of abstractness that we adults dignify with the label "concrete."

Still later, the feature definition has proceeded further. One particular *selected group of features together* can now *define a property.* The word used to describe this property may well be a word adults use in a more restricted way, but this does not imply that the child uses the word wrongly by its own lights. When a child says "dog," for example, to refer to a sheep, it is only an error because it is not an adult usage. The child has abstracted the four-legged-animal property and labeled it "dog." We do the same, but label it "animal."

We cannot deny that the child has a separate concept for dogs and sheep, any more than we would deny that adults differentiate among books just because we label them all "book." If a child calls dogs, cats, and sheep "dog," it may well be because no one has yet provided a word for the abstract idea, or even conveyed the notion that abstractions can have labels. The abstract idea, after all, cannot be demonstrated by single examples, and neither can it be labeled so long as the child continues to allow only one label for a single object. Bilingual children should have an advantage in this, because they are accustomed to calling one object with two names.

It must be conceivable to children that something can at the same time be a "dog" and an "animal" before their language could show an adult hierarchy of abstraction. The use of "dog" for "animal" suggests that abstractions are easy to label.

Throughout the "nénin"—"fa-fa"—"dog" sequence we see successive refinements in the definition of critical features and increasing sophistication in their recombination into more and more abstract concepts.

After surveying the literature on children's semantic development, Palermo and Molfese (1972) point out that even a slightly older child may have a vocabulary including a substantial set of words with meanings different than the same words have for adults. Asch and Nerlove (1960) presented children aged 3–12 with a series of objects and asked if any of the objects could be called sweet, or cold, or crooked, and the like. Note that these terms have both a physical and psychological meaning—they may refer to both physical characteristics of objects and psychological characteristics of persons. A child who could identify correctly objects physically associated with the words then was asked if a person could be "sweet." Children who used the word in the psychological sense were asked about the relation of that meaning to the physical meaning.

Children aged 3 and 4 could correctly use the words with respect to the physical objects, but with the possible exception of "sweet," they had no idea that the words could be applied to people. In fact, they denied specifically that these words could be so used. The 7- and 8-year-old groups, however, correctly applied about half of the words to people, but could not relate the physical meaning of the words to the psychological meaning with any great success. By 9 to 10 years of age, half of the children could correctly use all of the words in both functions, and could indicate the relation between the two uses. While the 11- and 12-year-old groups did not perform perfectly, they did show marked advances in the comprehension of the dual functions of the words.

The authors conclude that children first master the object reference of double-function words, then the psychological sense of these terms as independent meanings, and finally the dual or relational aspects of the words. In their use of words children thus seem to move from the ability to conceptualize primarily in terms of concrete operations to more abstract levels at about 11 or 12 years of age, a finding in agreement with Piaget's stages of cognitive development.

Semantic Markers and Syntactic Features

Semantic markers To use words appropriately children must learn semantic markers (Chapter 3) and syntactic features for each word. A full mental dictionary entry for the word "bread" would have to include at least the following syntactic features: [noun; mass noun; gender if applicable] plus a collection of semantic markers such as (inanimate), (edible), and (beige-color). For example, "bread," being a noun, is not usually used in *"It breads." Being an inanimate object, it cannot be literally used in "Bread cries." Children often produce anomalous utterances like these because they have not yet acquired complete and appropriate sets of syntactic features and semantic markers. They often fail to distinguish between animate and inanimate objects. For example, a 2-year-old French child produced: "n'a pas faim la lune" ("The moon isn't hungry") (Kahane et al., 1958).

How are semantic markers acquired? Children must abstract them by experiencing the object and the word in varied contexts. Their perceptual-cognitive capacities mature with increasing age, enabling them to understand increasingly abstract semantic markers. Young children are more likely to notice that bread is (edible) than that it is (inanimate), which is a more general and abstract marker than (edible). In fact, the contrast between (inanimate) and (animate) seems to be one of the last markers children acquire. Many groups of humans never acquire this distinction at all, endowing each rock and tree with its own spirit.

How can we demonstrate what semantic markers children have at different ages? De Villiers and de Villiers (1972) asked children aged 2–3 to judge whether simple imperatives such as "Throw the sky" or "Throw the stone" were right or wrong. Even children not linguistically well developed could judge semantically anomalous sentences as wrong. If I were to do such an experiment, I would introduce different degrees of anomaly. If children develop semantic markers gradually, they may be able at certain ages to reject grossly anomalous sentences but not slightly anomalous ones. "Throw the sky" is very anomalous but "Throw the house" is less so in that a house is potentially throwable, even though one does not usually throw houses around.

Syntactic features How are the syntactic features of a word acquired? Jenkins and Palermo (1964) proposed a *mediation process* for learning grammatical classes—a child learns grammatical classes of words through their verbal contexts. The child learns that "doll" and "bottle" belong to the same grammatical class from hearing them in equivalent sentence frames: "Here is the doll" and "Here is the bottle." Or, "Give me the doll (or bottle)." Sentences such as these, which occur frequently in the child's linguistic environment, teach the child that "doll" and "bottle" belong to the same class and can be used in the same way. Thus upon hearing the new sentence "Here is the book," the child can regard the "book" as belonging to the same class as "doll" or "bottle." The child eventually comes to develop a rule that any word which fills the blank in "Here is the _____" is a noun. Of course sentence contexts are not always so simple and uniform as this, but the kind of sentence to which young children are exposed is often of this type. Because even very simple sentence contexts are quite varied, children take some time to master grammatical class.

Glucksberg and Cohen's (1965) experiment shows that a CVC nonsense syllable may function like a noun or a verb in a word-association test after it has appeared in sentence frames where it functioned as a noun or a verb. This is what the mediational theory would predict—nonsense syllabels acquire "nounness" or "verbness" through the mediation of sentence frames.

Anglin's (1970) analysis of word-sorting tasks (Chapter 3) presents the following picture of lexical growth. North American children as old as eighth-graders cannot sort test words into four parts of speech, even though the notion of grammatical class is taught in their English lessons from the second grade on. Young children treat words bound by concrete relations as do adults. However, they do not appear to appreciate, as adults do, the more abstract features that relate words. They cannot grasp the abstract semantic concepts in terms of which the parts of speech are taught. These conclusions may not hold in educational systems that place strong and early emphasis on formal parsing, as in Great Britain. Lexical generalization appears to be an extremely gradual process that may never be completed. The *syntagmatic–paradigmatic shift* (Chapter 3) that occurs in word association between the ages of 5 and 7 should not be interpreted as a quantal shift in lexical organization, but rather as the important beginning of a process that will continue for many years. The word association task appears to tap only the kinds of relation that are acknowledged by both adults and children in the clustering studies—concrete ones.

With regard to connotative meaning, Di Vesta (1966) had children in the second and seventh grades rate a large number of concepts on the semantic differential scales. Connotative meaning appeared to be securely formed by the time the child was in the second grade; the child's semantic space corresponded closely to that of adults, and was largely described by the same three meaning dimensions—evaluative, potency, and activity. There seemed to be a progressive refinement and differentiation of the meaning system of children, as in the other aspects of language development. A two-factor system comprised of evaluation and dynamism (potency and activity collapsed) emerged before the three-factor systems. Remember, however, that the number of factors recovered from a semantic differential experiment depends more on how well the subjects can do the experiment than on the structure of their language. If they are erratic in their responses, only the strongest dimensions can be recovered from the experiment, even though other dimensions of meaning may be important in determining their actual usage of words.

In short, children acquire concrete features first, and gradually learn more and more abstract features of words. As they learn abstract features, they learn to use and organize words like adults.

ACQUISITION OF SYNTAX

Eventually a child must learn how words are arranged in a sentence so that it can express complex ideas unambiguously. Children must learn the syntactic forms used in their language to express subject-predicate relationships, modifier-head noun relationship in a noun phrase, affirmative-negative, question-interrogative-declarative, and so on. Such relationships are basics of communication, and are found in almost all languages, but the means of expressing them are different. In this section, we shall see that children initially do not use these linguistic relationships properly, and acquire them only gradually. We shall trace the gradual acquisition of syntax.

Many of the recent data on early syntactic development have been obtained in *longitudinal studies* of a small group of children who are just beginning to make primitive utterances. The children's syntactic development is followed up to ages 4 or 5, when they seem to have mastered the basics of syntax. In these studies psychologists, and occasionally linguists, sample the children's speech periodically over a number of months or years. Then the investigators attempt to describe the structures of collected utterances in some frame, such as transformational generative grammar or case grammar. They collect the children's utterances in natural settings, usually in dialogues between mother and child, but occasionally supplement the natural observation with tests.

Everybody who has observed young children gets the impression that they show signs of comprehending speech before they can produce it. But young children's comprehension is hard to investigate. How much can we attribute to contextual cues and how much to genuine comprehension of syntax? The following discussion is mainly on children's speech production, and occasionally on comprehension.

Single-word utterance (10–20 months)

I once observed a 15-month-old-baby uttering /bɔ:/ (ball) in a falling pitch contour, with his arm stretched to the bag that contained the ball. What was he trying to say? Was he confusing the bag with the ball? Was he saying "I want my ball" or merely "There is my ball"? We can only infer his intention from the situational context. In this case, even the context allows at least the above three possible interpretations.

Here are some more examples of one-word utterances. De Laguna (1927) noted a French girl uttering:

"Mon-mon" ("Raymond"), pointing to the slippers that belonged to her brother Raymond;
"Mon-mon" ("Raymond has made me unhappy"). R had been teasing the girl and she ran crying to her papa;
"Maman" ("mommy"). A child banished from the kitchen by her mother went to her father and complained.

Pitch contours   Menyuk and Bernholtz (1969) examined some one-word utterances of a child for their pitch contours. The two examiners attempted to classify the isolated utterances as declarative (D), question (Q), and emphatic (E) on the basis of pitch contours. They had 81 percent agreement on their classification, and all the disagreements involved E. In *spectrograms*, D ends with a falling fundamental frequency contour, Q with a rising one, and E with a sharp rise and then a fall. Figure 6–3 shows the various pitch contours.

Such sentencelike intonation contours were once taken as evidence that one-word utterances were sentences, or *holophrases* (*holo* = complete, *phrase* = phrase or sentence). Bloom (1973) points out that there is no behavioral evidence that children intend a Q or D—both intonation patterns apparently occur in the same situational contexts. The agreement between listeners in Menyuk and Bernholtz's study may not have represented agreement with the child's intention. Ultimately, situational contexts provide us clues to the children's intentions. Bloom goes on to cite Weir (1966), who was unable to find any systematic differences in the use of different intonation patterns in the syntactic speech of her 2-year-old son. Similarly, Miller

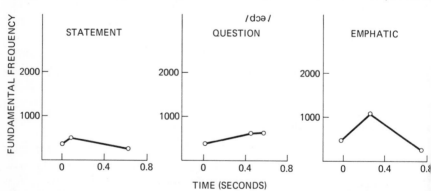

FIGURE 6–3   Measurement of fundamental frequency at beginning, peak, and end of the utterance /dɔə/ as a statement, question, and emphatic. (From Menyuk, 1971.)

and Ervin (1964) were unable to find intonation patterns used contrastively until the development of the grammatical system was well under way after 2 years of age. Bloom concludes that children learn to use intonation patterns in their speech in an adult way only after they learn that basic grammatical distinctions are signaled by word order in English, that is, after they learn to use syntax. Her daughter did not use sentence intonation at 20 and 22 months when she was learning to use syntax, but it had appeared by 28 months.

The intonation patterns of single-word utterances are not too reliable as clues to different intents of a child's utterances, even though the patterns can sometimes be reliably differentiated by adults, as shown in Figure 6–3.

The function of single words   As McNeill (1970) points out, if "nana" (banana) is uttered in presence of a banana, we might suspect that it is used as a label. If a child says "nana" pointing to the top of the refrigerator, the usual place for finding bananas even though there were no bananas at the time, we can be sure that "nana" could not have been used just as a label. McNeill interprets the single words uttered by Greenfield's (1967) 16-month-old subject as expressing the following grammatical relations:

"door," meaning "close the door"—"door" is used as the object of verb;
"eye," meaning "water is in my eye"—"eye" is used as the object of prepositions;
"baby," meaning "the baby fell down"—"baby" is used as the subject of sentences.

McNeill notes that the words above are "nouns"; verbs are completely missing. Because all grammatical relations are implicit, nouns can be used in every available grammatical relation without endangering the comprehension of adults.

Do single words express well-defined grammatical relations? First of all, Bloom (1973) notes that the seven most frequent single words used by her daughter Allison (16 months) were "there, up, more, down, no, gone, baby." Note that they are not all "nouns" of adult language. Bloom convincingly argues that single-word utterances are not sentences. Children produce one word at a time primarily because they do not yet know the linguistic code. But they have begun to know considerably more about the world of objects, events, and relations.

According to Braine (1974), one-word utterances seem to have been constructed by choosing a word that singles out one salient feature of the perceptual-cognitive complex the child wants to communicate. Considering one-word utterances in this manner is more reasonable than considering it to be a holophrase expressing well-defined, though implicit, grammatical relations. As we have seen, "Mon-mon" or "Maman" can be used in referring to a variety of rather complex situations. Except for one salient feature (to which children can refer using one word or even pointing), young children may perceive each complex situation rather vaguely. Their cognizance may be akin to the way an adult conceives the theme of a sentence before it is uttered (see Chapter 4). Unlike adults, children have not learned syntactic means to express this vague cognizance in a full grammatical sentence. A single word is a sentence with implied grammatical relations only from an adult's point of view. In comprehending a single-word utterance, adults do not necessarily construct an unequivocal sentence with well-defined grammatical relations; they may merely take cognizance of a complex situation, using a child's single word (or pointing) as a cue.

Occasionally children may use two or more words in juxtaposition, but not joined in syntactic combination. Bloom's best example is:

> (Allison, looking at man waiting in airport,
> sitting, with coat and suitcase)   man/chair/coat/suitcase

The intonation pattern unmistakably distinguished such sequences of words as this as series of single-word utterances. Each word occurred with terminal falling pitch contour, and with relatively equal stress. There was a variable but distinct pause between them, so that utterance boundaries were clearly marked. Utterance groups like this appeared to indicate that Allison recognized more than one aspect of a referent, or recognized the relationship between aspects of a referent, before she could use a linguistic code for expressing such occurrence or relationship. The use of successive single words seems to refute the hypothesis that the reason sentences do not occur at this stage is lack of vocabulary.

Two-word utterances (18–24 months)

As soon as children produce an utterance containing two or more words we may examine the relationships between the words. One kind of relationship, based on semantics, has already been discussed. Here we talk about possible syntactic relationships between the words.

What is a pivot grammar? Many students of language acquisition once used to accept Braine's (1963) placement of the two words in *pivot* and *open* classes. Braine classified the words as pivot or open according to their functions and positions in the utterances. A word is called a pivot because other words may be attached to it. The pivot class is a small, closed class, and each of its members is used frequently. The membership of his class is stable and fairly fixed; only a few pivots are added each month. All other words in the child's vocabulary at this stage belong to the open class. Open-class words are numerous and may occur as single-word utterances. According to this description, children's words of the two roughly differentiated classes may be combined in a few well-defined ways.

The pivot grammar admits the following constructions:

Structure	Utterance
$P_1 + 0$	See boy
$0 + P_2$	Boot off
$0 + 0$	Mommy sleep
0	Mommy

P_1 {see; pretty; my; more; bye-bye; no; . . .}
P_2 {it; off; by; come; . . .}
O {boot; hot; boy; mommy; sit; sleep . . .}

The pivot grammar does not admit the following structures:

$$P$$
$$P_1 + P_2$$
$$P_2 + P_1$$

The basic phrase-structure grammar here is: $S \rightarrow$ pivot $+$ open. The English data on two-word combinations correspond remarkably well with the data from a number of other languages, including German, Russian, Luo, and Samoan (Slobin, 1971). The growth of such two-word utterances is at first slow, but rapidly accelerates.

Is there a pivot grammar? Brown (1973), after re-examining studies by several researchers on diverse languages, criticizes the pivot grammar on structural grounds. Even though some high-frequency pivotlike constructions were used by all the children Braine and other investigators (such as Miller and Ervin, 1964) studied, these constructions only approximated the pivot grammar. No investigator has observed all combinations allowed by the rules, while many combinations that should be allowed are never used by children. The simple rules, $P_1 + O$ and $O + P_2$, that summarize the utterances obtained also predict a large number of others, such as "My hot" ($P_1 + O$); "Mommy it" ($O + P_2$), that have not been reported by investigators in the ten years since Braine's original proposal of pivot grammar. On the other hand, P ("more") and P $+$ P ("Want more"), which were not allowed by the pivot grammar, did occur, though rarely.

The positions of particular pivots were not fixed; "Bye-bye boy" as well as "Papa bye-bye" occurred.

Park (1970a), who studied his daughter learning Korean, points out that both pivot and open classes were made up of the same sorts of words—nouns, verbs, adjectives, and adverbs.

S → *noun + noun*   As with single-word utterances, there is a question about what functions these two-word combinations may serve. At this stage the intonation patterns may be somewhat more contrastive in function than they were earlier. "What beads?" with a rising tone, or "More pencil!" with a contour that rises first and then falls may function as Q and E respectively. Ervin and Miller (1963) noted that "Christy room" means either "Christy's room" or "Christy is in the room," depending on which part of the utterance is stressed. If the first vowel is stressed, the child means the former, and if the third vowel is stressed, the latter. Utimately, intonation patterns have to be interpreted by their situational context.

Bloom (1970) analyzes in some detail the construction S → open + open, or more specifically, S → noun + noun. This construction appears later than pivot + open, according to Braine (1963), and is one of the most common constructions, according to Bloom. Bloom notes that it specifies the following grammatical relations (given in order of frequency), as inferred from the situational contexts.

1. Subject-object ("Mommy sock" = mommy putting Kathryn's sock on Kathryn) Kathryn, one of the three children Bloom studied, was 21 months old with mean length of utterance (MLU) of 1.32 morphemes at the time.
2. Genitive ("Mommy sock" = Mommy's sock)
3. Attributive ("bread book" = a cookbook for baking bread)
4. Subject-locative ("sweater chair" = sweater is on the chair)
5. Conjunction ("umbrella boot" = umbrella and boot)

The noun + noun constructions do not express:

> Identity ("mommy [is] lady")
> Disjunction ([either] "bread [or] book")
> Direct-indirect object ("mommy [gives] sock [to] Kathryn)

Bloom's conclusion is that the notion of "pivot grammar" describes children's utterances in only a most superficial way. Constructions 1 and 2 are identical on the surface, but imply different semantic interpretations. "Mommy" fits the definition of a "pivot" class, as it occurs frequently in a fixed position in a construction. But it occurs with variable grammatical functions in relation to the other constituents with which it is juxtaposed. A pivot grammar makes no distinction among the five (noun + noun) onstructions and underestimates the child's knowledge. In Bloom's opinion, pivot grammar is not a universal first step in syntax but is one possible rst strategy in English.

All things considered, pivot grammars are not universal either cross-nguistically or with the American English community for the full eriod from MLU of 1.0 to 2.0.

This stage (Braine's pivot-grammar; S → noun + noun of Bloom; tage I of Brown; MLU 1.0–2.0) is linked with a corresponding stage of e child's sensory-motor intelligence as described by Piaget. The child an learn about enduring objects in immediate space and time through ensory-motor intelligence. Grasping more abstract relations such as dis-inction (either . . . or) or causality (. . . because) has to wait for a more ature stage of cognitive development.

Vord order

Greenberg (1963), after examining a number of widely different languages, oted that every language has classes of subject (S), verb (V), and ob-ect (O). The order SVO (as, the boy meets the girl), SOV, VSO (sub-ects always precede objects), but not OSV, OVS, VOS, occurred. Some ighly inflected languages may allow rather free orderings of S, V, O, but ven such languages have the permissible orderings as preferred ones. The niversal word orders of SVO, SOV, and VSO are supposed to be innate—hildren put words in these orders as soon as they can produce two or ore words.

In production   As we have seen in the preceding section, words in oung children's spontaneous utterances are put in some order that allows easonable semantic interpretation on the part of adults. In English declara-ive sentences, order will distinguish subject from object, modifier from ead, subject from locative, possessor from possessed even when such tructural signs as the possessive inflection, the copula verb, and prepositions re missing.

However, there are some "odd" word orders in children's spontaneous peech and in the sign language of the deaf. Young children do not use vord-order information adequately in interpretation. Are there then uni-versal and innate word orders?

Jespersen (1922) describes an interesting case of twin boys aged 5.6 who were shamefully neglected by their mother and lived with a deaf old woman, who also neglected them. The boys did not speak Danish ut developed their own language. Most of the words were evidently Danish words, but much distorted and shortened. Their words were put to-gether without any inflections, and the word order was totally different from

Danish. An example: "trousers Maria brother water," which meant "brother trousers are wet, Maria." A Danish child of 2.1 said: "Oh papa lamp mother boom," when his mother had struck his papa's lamp with a ban (Jespersen). The garbled masterpieces of Burling's (1959) daughter are "Nono falling Nono jammies pant," or "Reading a mommy a book Nono Leopold's (1971) daughter at age 2 produced "Meow bites Wauwau" apparently meaning "Wauwau bites Meow." As her father commented, syntax begins with anarchy!

Bloom (1970) also points out that Gia, one of her three subjects, produced "book read" and "read book" in virtually identical speech environments. Earlier Gia had produced object nouns before verbs—"balloon throw." The grammatical relations of subject-object did not exist in the sentences that Gia and Eric (another of her three subjects) produced in the earliest texts. Gia learned the subject-object relation first; Eric, the verb-object. Both children subsequently (by the end of stage I?) learned the subject-verb relation—the structure that was least common in the utterances of all three children Bloom studied.

Park (1970b) says that among the three German-speaking children he studied ungrammatical orders were actually more common than grammatical ones. In Korean, where order is "as free as it ever is,"[3] Park (1970a) daughter used one order only: SVO ("Su–sin look-at cap").

Deaf people before they are taught verbal language would be useful as informants to test for the existence of universal and innate word order Schlesinger (1971a) studied the sign language of the deaf in Israel before they were taught Hebrew. He found that the deaf did not express the concept of "bear holding monkey for man" in one particular sentence structure. Users of the sign language did not employ any rule consistently to distinguish between the subject, the direct or indirect object, and the verb. The order was also haphazard except that the verb did not appear in an initial position, and that adjectives followed their nouns. For example they might use, "bear monkey give man" or "bear monkey man give" but not "give . . . ." Here the deaf may be trying to avoid ambiguity: the sign denoting the action becomes "meaningful" only in connection with a sign standing for the agent. A similar explanation may apply to the finding that the adjectives always followed the nouns modified by them. Communication between the deaf was not too successful. Schlesinger concluded that SVO, VSO, and SOV are not innate sentence structures.

Two of the three "universal" orders, SVO and VSO, are not used in Japanese or Korean. In these two languages, the important point is that

---

[3] This is Brown's (1973) description. The word order is not completely free in Korean. The most common order would be SOV, and a less common but possible order would be OSV. Park's daughter produced an order which was ungrammatical in her native language, just as his German subjects did.

V comes after O and S; S and O can interchange their orders, or even be omitted. Should SVO and VSO then be considered universal orders? Any linguistic universals must be expressions of our desires for effective communication, and be reflections of characteristics of human perceptual-cognitive processing. The similarities among diverse languages cited in Chapter 1 are examples of such "universals," based on characteristics of human information processing. Schlesinger claims that his deaf subjects avoid putting a verb at the beginning of an utterance for effective communication. Whether the nonoccurrence of V at the beginning of a basic sentence form is a universal feature has yet to be determined.

In interpretation Sinclair and Bronckart (1972) studied French-speaking children in Geneva to see whether they interpreted sentences in any particular order. They asked children aged 2.1–7.0 to guess the meaning of deviant three-word utterances, resembling utterances spontaneously produced by very young children. All the three-word combinations were presented in the six possible orders.

According to age, the children chose different strategies to interpret the utterances. The earliest type of solution was to consider the utterances as consisting of two parts only: name of a person and his action (agent + action) or an action and the person on whom the action was done (action + patient)[4]. The word order played little part except that NVN (noun-verb-noun) items elicited transitive ("hit him") types of solution earlier than VNN or NNV.

The subsequent type of solution considered three parts: an agent, an action, and a patient; here the proximity of the noun to the verb rather than the word order played an important role. For example, in NNV, the second N could be the agent and the first, the patient. At older ages the first N was taken to be the agent, the second the patient, whatever the position of the verb for all different word orders. This strategy resulted in SVO, SOV, or VSO, namely the three candidates for universal word orders. The SO rules had become established.

Sinclair-de Zwart (1973) comments that differentiations between the subject's own action and the object acted upon on the one hand, and the child who is speaking as an agent and some other person or object as agent on the other, give rise to the first grammatical functions of subject-predicate and object-action. She emphasizes that in this analysis the SVO structure is established through and around the verb.

De Villiers and de Villiers (1973) report that young children were unable to use the word-order information in acting out either active or

[4] Agent: someone who acts; patient: someone on whom an action is done. These terms express the semantic or real-world roles nouns play in sentences. Their grammatical roles would be subject and object in an active sentence.

passive reversible sentences. The majority of responses at this stage (MLU = 1.0–1.5 morphemes) were in the form of "child as agent." Given the sentence, "Make the cow kiss the horse" (active reversible sentence), the child kissed the cow or the horse or both. There was no tendency to prefer either the first or second noun as an object.

In sum, word order is a linguistic means to express semantic relations among words in an utterance. If the word order is incorrect, children's utterances are often difficult to comprehend; if they have the correct order, they are understood even when telegraphic. In English the word order is meaningful, and most children pay attention to it. They use it in a consistently appropriate fashion in their spontaneous speech and as a guide to comprehension, as long as an utterance is short, consisting perhaps only two words. However, Stage I children do not easily use word order information in utterances with three or more words. The correct use of word order in longer utterances develops with age.

The order of SV, or agent before its action, seems to code semantic information unambiguously. If an utterance contains both S and V, SV rather than VS seems to be preferred in many languages, by children, and by deaf people.

Acquiring morphological rules

In English we inflect words for person, number, tense, and so on. The final phoneme of a word affects the way in which some of these inflections are marked (see Chapter 2). Do children acquire these morphological rules, or learn which words require which suffixes? If they learn rules, at what ages do they learn what rules?

Studies using nonsense syllables   Jean Berko (1958) reasoned that if children have acquired rules, they should be able to apply the rules to novel sequences or to nonsense syllables. She made up nonsense syllables following rules for possible sound combinations in English. Pictures to represent the nonsense syllables were then drawn on cards. For example, a 4-year-old shown a picture of a man who is swinging something around his head is told: "This is a man who knows how to *gling*. He *glings* every day. Today he *glings*. Yesterday he _____?" The child can immediately supply the most probable word: "glinged." Adults have much difficulty in deciding on the appropriate response and seem to be torn among "glinged, glang, glung," and even "glought."

Berko used similar test materials to test the mastery of rules for forming comparatives of adjectives and the progressive tense of verbs (-ing). In all cases, the children showed that they had learned rules which they could apply to novel sound sequences. Between two variants of plural morphemes, the children tended to be more correct on /-z/ than on /iz/, and among three variants of past tense morpheme, on /-t/ and /-d/ than on /-id/. In other words, the rules that are general in application are used first and more correctly than the rules that apply only to restricted cases.

Spontaneous speech   How do English-speaking children acquire bound morphemes? Brown (1973) has made a detailed analysis of the spontaneous speech of three children, Adam, Sarah, and Eve. When Brown and his associates at Harvard University started their longitudinal study of these three children in the early 1960s, the children were not at the same chronological age: Eve was 18 months, and Adam and Sarah were 27 months old. Eve and Adam were only children when the study began. They are the children of college-educated parents, while Sarah has high-school-educated parents. Even though their ages were different, their stages in language development were similar. The three families were totally unacquainted, and each child heard a different set of sentences as an input.

The researchers noted the first appearances of noun and verb inflections and of such little words as articles, spatial prepositions, copula and auxiliary *be* forms in Stage II (see Table 6–2). None of these grammatical morphemes is acquired suddenly and completely. Each is for a considerable period of time sometimes present and sometimes absent in ordinary contexts. The proportion of times a form is present gradually rises with time. The researchers have taken as a criterion of acquisition a form's presence in 90 percent of all obligatory contexts for three successive two-hour samples. The orders in which the three children acquired 14 morphemes were approximately the same, and are given in Table 6–2.

TABLE 6–2   Mean Order of Acquisition of 14 Morphemes Across Three Children

Mean order	Morphemes	
1	Present progressive	-ing
2–3	Spatial preposition	in, on
4	Plural	-s
5	Past irregular	came, fell, sat
6	Possessive	-s
7	Uncontractable copula	am, is, are, be (as main verbs)
8	Articles	the, a
9	Past regular	-ed
10	Third person regular	-s
11	Third person irregular	does, has
12	Uncontractable auxiliary	am, is, are, be (in progressive)
13	Contractable copula	-m, -s, -z, -r
14	Contractable auxiliary	-m, -s, -z, -r

The third column added to Table 38, Brown, 1973.

The three inflections requiring (-s) do not appear at the same time; hence, phonemic development does not govern the order of morpheme acquisition. Bellugi (1964) noted that the possessive (-s) was the least frequently occurring inflection in a mother's speech. This suggests that possessive (-s) is not often called for, especially when we have other means to express the same function—"of" or possessive pronoun such as "my." As for the other endings, (-ing) occurs before the third-person (-s), perhaps because a child has more occasions to refer to actions in progress and to plural nouns than to a third-person-singular verb. The third person is not likely to be present when the child is talking, or if present, is not likely to be the center of the child's interest. The third person (-s) is also conceptually hard to grasp for young children. After all, "he" or "she" makes the same action as "you" and "I." Why should "he" or "she" require an extra (-s)? On the other hand, an action in progress and plural objects are concrete and easy to grasp for children. Take plural nouns—the child can see the difference between one candy and two candies.

The order of acquisition depends upon relative complexity, grammatical or semantic, and not simply upon the frequency of the morphemes in parental speech or phonemic complexity.

The grammatical morphemes add number, tense, specificity or nonspecificity (articles), containment or support ("in," "on"). Brown (1973) characterizes the semantics of all of the morphemes as "modulations" of meaning—they modulate or modify the more "basic" relational meanings of Stage I, agent-action, recurrence, and so on. "Modulation" suggests a class of meaning somehow subordinate, less than essential. Modulations can be acquired only after the content words and rules of combination and order of Stage I have been acquired.

How are bound morphemes acquired in languages other than English? Russian has a complex inflectional system that includes gender and several cases for nouns and adjectives. Accordingly, Russian children master their morphological system relatively late. Slobin (1966b) gives the following picture:

Age 3 for gender agreement between nouns and verbs in the past;
Age 6 or 7 for the declension of masculine and feminine nouns ending in palatalized consonants (such as /tʃ/);
Age 8 for the distinction between count and mass nouns.

Slobin (1973) cites Omar's (1970) dissertation on the acquisition of Egyptian Arabic. The Arabic rules for plural formation are so complex and irregular that in Omar's study children as old as 15 erred in pluralizing even familiar nouns. One of the peculiar rules is that the numerals 3–10 take the noun in the plural, while numerals above 11 take the singular.

We can only envy Chinese children, who do not have to cope with all these contraptions.

The tendency to generalize regular inflectional endings to all sorts of words is rampant in young children. Children at some ages love rules in all aspects of their life, and produce such rule-governed, but wrong, words as "comed" and "foots." This *regularizing tendency* is again convincing evidence that children abstract rules, rather than imitate and memorize individual items. Children initially produce the correct "strong" forms ("came," "took," "feet") as independent vocabulary items, not realizing the relation between "come" and "came." Later, when their cognitive faculties are more developed, they notice the relation between "cry" and "cried," and generalize this relation to other words. Sometimes children know strong forms as independent words, but at the same time know the rule that verbs inflect for past tense. The result is that my 6-year-old son produced "took*en*," and my daughter at age 7 produced "took*ened*." Such a regularizing tendency seems to be overridden by knowledge of the correct forms for common irregular words around age 8. However, if the irregular form is not known, the regularizing tendency persists throughout life. How many people say "hippopotamuses" for "hippopotami"? Each is probable, and both derive from a rule. What is the plural of "shoe"? Until quite recently, around the time of Shakespeare, it was "shoon."

Transformation rules

Children eventually have to learn to express relationships among different forms of sentences by syntactic means. The linguist-psychologist team Klima and Bellugi (1966) tried to find some basic regularities in children's negations and questions. First they listed sample questions and negations from the protocols of Eve, Adam, and Sarah, the subjects of longitudinal studies by Brown and his associates.

The investigators examined the three children's syntax in three stages of development. The first stage was from the first month of study (MLU = 1.8 morphemes); the last was from the month when the MLU approached four morphemes for each of the three children; and the second stage was between the two (MLU = 2.3–3.5). We shall examine only a few utterances of one type at each stage that seemed to show the developmental trend particularly well, along with their grammatical descriptions.

Negation—Stage I (MLU = about 1.8 morphemes)

Utterance	*Structural description*
No heavy.	
No sit there.	[Nucleus—no] S
Wear mitten no.	

A nucleus can be used alone as an affirmative counterpart. Note that there are no negatives within the nucleus, nor are there auxiliary verbs. The element that signals negation is "no" or "not," and this element either precedes or follows the rest of the utterance.

While Klima–Bellugi's emphasis is more on structural aspects, Bloom (1970) again considers the semantic content of the utterances. According to the surface structure, the following three negations produced by Kathryn (MLU = 1.32) are identical. But the contexts enabled Bloom to interpret them in three ways.

"No pocket"—nonexistence
(denies the existence of pocket; Kathryn is unable to find a pocket in mommy's skirt.)
"No dirty soap"—rejection
(the soap *exists*, and it is dirty. Kathryn pushes away a piece of worn soap.)
"No dirty"—denial (Oh, that's not a dirty one.)

Negations in adult speech can be organized in terms of the same three semantic categories.

Bloom's structural description of negative sentences at this stage is:

$$S \rightarrow \text{Nominal (negative)} \begin{Bmatrix} \text{NP} \\ \text{VP} \end{Bmatrix}$$

The linguistic operation of negation had a limiting effect on the structural complexity and length of Kathryn's utterances. That is, an inclusion of the negative element caused replacement or deletion of other forms. In the earliest sentences, the negative element did occupy the initial position in the surface structure of sentences. However, this occurred as a consequence of the deletion of other constituents, namely, sentence subjects. In the subsequent texts, there were sentences that contained both subjects and negative particles ("Kathryn no shoe"). Negative sentences could not be constructed as simply a positive sentence with a negative sign attached outside the sentence, as described by Klima–Bellugi.

One kind of negative sentence, "No Kathryn playing self" (K did not want to play with the slide and went into the playpen to play alone), was produced by Kathryn at MLU = 1.92; by Gia, at MLU = 2.30; and by Eric, at MLU = 2.63. Bloom calls it "anaphoric"—"no" did not apply to the remainder of the sentence, which was an affirmative statement. The second type of negative sentence produced by Bloom's subjects at this stage of development was "Kathryn no shoe" (K was not wearing shoes); the "no" occurred before the predicate that was being negated. These two types of sentence were the most complex negative sentences the three children produced, precisely because of the inclusion of sentence subjects. Bloom's description of the children's linguistic development ends when Kathryn's MLU = 2.83; Eric's = 2.84; and Gia's = 2.75. In terms of MLU, this stage is comparable to Klima–Bellugi's stage II.

We now get back to Klima–Bellugi's description of both negations and questions. We bear in mind that their description is mainly on structural aspects, and not too much on semantic contents.

Negation—Stage II (MLU = 2.3–3.5)   *Structural description*

    I can't catch you.
    Touch the snow no. $S_{(neg)} \rightarrow NP—(Neg)—VP$
    He no bite you.

The auxiliary verbs appear in the negative forms "don't" and "can't." Since there is no corresponding affirmative use of "can" or "do" in their protocol —there is no "I can do it"—Klima–Bellugi concluded that the children must be using "don't" as a single item. Children must encounter "don't" a lot more often than "do." The negatve "no" is now found within the sentence, but not connected to any auxiliary verb. There are now pronouns, articles, and adjectives.

Negation—Stage III (MLU = 4.0)   *Structural description*

    I didn't did it.
    You don't want some supper. $S_{(neg)} \rightarrow NP—Aux—VP$
    Ask me if I not make mistake.

The negative auxiliary verbs are no longer limited to "don't" and "can't," and auxiliary verbs now appear in declarative sentences and questions. Auxiliary verbs can now be considered as separate from the negative element of the sentence. Indeterminates—"some"—appear in affirmative sentences, and are used incorrectly in negative sentences. Past tense and progressive (-ing) are marked.

Question—Stage I (MLU = 1.8)   *Structural description*

    Fraser water?
    What doing? $S_{(q)} \rightarrow Q^{wh-}—NP$ $\left\{ \begin{array}{l} (doing) \\ (go) \end{array} \right\}$
    Where horse go? $S_{(q)} \rightarrow Q\ yes/no$

Yes/no questions are marked by rising intonation only. There are many *wh-* questions, which no doubt are useful for children in exploring the world.

Question—Stage II (MLU = 2.3–3.5)   *Structural description*

See my doggie?
Why you smiling? $S_{(q)} \rightarrow \left\{ \begin{matrix} Q \text{ yes/no} \\ Q^{wh-} \end{matrix} \right\}$ Nucleus
Why not he eat?
You can't fix it?

Pronouns, articles, and modifiers are more often present, and some inflections (present progressive and plurals) occur. There is no inversion of auxiliary and the subject.

Question—Stage III (MLU = 4.0)   *Structural description*

Does the kitty stand up?
Where I should put it when I make it up? $S \rightarrow (Q(wh-))NP—Aux—VP$
Can't it be a bigger truck?

There is now a class of verbal forms that invert with the subject in certain interrogatives (yes/no questions), and may take the negative particles along. Notice, however, that the auxiliary verbs are not inverted with the subject noun phrase in *wh-* questions: it seems as though children can perform only a few grammatical operations at a time. That is, if they have to introduce *wh-* question morphemes, they must forgo the inversion operations. But they can carry out inversions when this is the only grammatical operation needed. There are now relative clauses and other embeddings for the first time. Sentences are getting longer, and as a whole, becoming more like adults' speech.

To summarize Klima–Bellugi's data, the different grammatical operations seem to emerge roughly in the following sequence.

1. Intonation.
2. Adding "no" or "not" and *wh-* to a nucleus.
3. Each of "why not," "can't," or "don't" appears as a single item.
4. "No" or "not" appears inside a nucleus.
5. Auxiliary verbs appear.
6. Auxiliary verbs and subjects are inverted where needed.
7. Relative clauses and embedded sentences appear.

The children's utterances are primitive in the sense that they are not expressed in full and adequate linguistic structures. Further, one primitive surface structure may imply several different semantic contents. But their utterances have some structures that are syntactically deviant from the language they hear in regular ways, as if constructed according to a different, simplified set of rules, constrained by their limited cognitive faculties. Shortly, we shall discuss what kind of grammar fits children's speech.

Telegraphic speech

Either in spontaneous productions or in imitations of adults' speech, children aged around 2 to 3 produce utterances that are short and lack many function words, inflectional endings, auxiliary verbs, and copulas. Such speech is called "telegraphic." Unlike adults' telegrams, the "telegraphic" speech of children may omit some content words and retain some function words. Pronouns are omitted less often than other function words such as articles, prepositions, and conjunctions, but more often than content words. We have seen, and shall see, many examples of telegraphic speech throughout this chapter.

Why do children produce short utterances? Why are certain items selectively omitted? We know that children have a short memory span. But their utterances are short in both spontaneous and imitated speech, hence limited memory alone is not responsible for telegraphic speech. Memory span may be responsible for the fact that children retain the last word of an utterance in imitation. But then, the last word is usually a content word. Brown (1973, Table 11, p. 76) prepared a table listing 13 model sentences imitated by six children aged 25–35 months. Two children at 32 and 35 months imitated almost all of the model sentences correctly. Other children imitated in telegraphic speech most of the time ("I showed you the book" → "I show book"). Among 52 telegraphic imitations, all but one retained the last word, and all the last words were content words.

The children know hundreds of words, hence limitation of vocabulary alone cannot be the cause either, especially for the omission of content words. However, as discussed under semantic development, the children may have certain vocabulary items in their repertoire with incomplete and inappropriate syntactic features and semantic markers. Bloom (1970) describes Kathryn (MLU = 1.32) reporting to her mommy "Jocelyn cheek" (Jocelyn, K's friend, had bruised her cheek on the playground.) Here "hurt," a content word, is not uttered but may have been implied. Kathryn had used "hurt" in other appropriate contexts (talking about chapped hands). Bloom suggests that Kathryn might not have learned the complex symbol features of "hurt" as a verb that can appear both before and after nouns. A more appropriate explanation is that a young child can keep only two or three concepts in mind at once. "Jocelyn" and "cheek," the two most salient concepts for K's message, happen to fill K's mind, leaving no room for another less salient word.

Children more commonly omit function words, inflectional endings, auxiliary verbs, and copulas. Why? Such items indicate grammatical relations among words in sentences. Their meanings are varied, nonspecific, abstract, and nonessential. For example, the preposition "to" can take on many varied meanings depending on how it is used in sentences ("Her rise to fame";

"Dance to the music"; "I go to school"; "To cry is cowardly"; "Give it to me"). We cannot attach a specific meaning to "to" as we can to a content word such as "milk," which refers to specific object. Thus, the meaning of "to" or "for" is hard for children to grasp. Function words also tend to be less stressed in speech, thus not attracting children's attention. Function words occur seldom at the end of an utterance; in short-term memory, the last item tends to be retained because of its recency. Some function words seem to have "concrete" reference as used in simple utterances. Consider "Boot off" and "Boot on." The two prepositions "off" and "on" occur at the final positions, and also may be stressed because they alone signal the contrast in meaning between the above two utterances.

Finally, we must consider the effect of telegraphic speech on communication. As in adults' telegrams, most of the items dropped in telegraphic speech are redundant items that would not affect too seriously the main point of a message. Of course, the children (or adults, for that matter) do not calculate the amount of redundancy, but they can conceptualize particular points of their message in terms of a few important content words (or even function words), such as "Jocelyn cheek" or "Boot off." They can then assess whether or not they have conveyed the main point of their message. As long as the content of their messages is short and simple, as long as they preserve word order to some degree, and as long as the situational contexts are clear, children fare well with their telegraphic speech.

A kind of telegraphic speech occurs also in Black English (Chapter 1), pidgin English (Chapter 7), and aphasic speech (Chapter 11), for similar reasons and with similar effects as in children's speech.

Imitation, expansion, and modeling

In Brown and Bellugi's (1964) records, only about 10 percent of children's speech at 28–35 months is imitative. Imitated speech is not an exact copy of the speech model; it reflects the children's developmental stages in spontaneous production. Both spontaneous speech and imitated speech are short and telegraphic.

C. S. Smith (1970) asked 3- and 4-year old children to repeat a variety of sentences. She found that there were more structure-violating errors in repeating structures that were not in the children's spontaneous speech. For example,

(stimulus) "Mommy could have lost her purse."
(response) "Mommy lost her purse." (reduction)
(s   ) "Not Jane, but Betty, called you."
(r) "Betty called you." (confusion?)
(s   ) "The boy who was running fell down."

(r)   "The boy was fell down." (lack of understanding)
(s   )   "Mine old green coat has holes."
(r)   "My old green coat has holes." (normalization)
(pp. 126–127)

We see that imitation makes an excellent test of a child's level of syntactic development.

Bloom, Hood, and Lightbown (1974) consider that imitation plays a useful role in a child's linguistic development. The authors made an extensive comparison of imitative and spontaneous utterances in the naturalistic speech of six children (MLU = 1.0 to 2.0). There was intersubject difference in the extent of imitation, but each child was consistent in the tendency to imitate or not to imitate across time. Imitating children imitated only words and structures in the model speech that appeared to be in the process of being learnt. They tended not to imitate words and structures that they themselves either used spontaneously and so presumably knew, or did not use spontaneously at all and so presumably did not know.

The authors conclude that imitating the model utterances provides experience in encoding the relevant aspects of the situation to which the utterance refers, so that the mapping or coding relation between form and content can be affirmed. They agree with Piaget that imitation is always a continuation of understanding.

The resistance of children to new forms sometimes goes to extravagant lengths. Consider the following exchange between one mother and her child from McNeill's (1966b, p. 69) record:

Child: "Nobody don't like me."
Mother: "No, say, nobody likes me."
Child: "Nobody don't like me."
(after eight repetitions of this dialogue)
Mother: "No, now listen carefully; say 'nobody likes me.'"
Child: "Oh! nobody don't likes me."

The mother repeats her child's utterances rather more often than the child imitates its mother, according to Brown and Bellugi. In repeating the child's utterance the mother expands it to test her hypothesis about what the child is saying, rather than to teach correct grammar. In her expansions the mother typically preserves the word order but adds the parts she judges to have been omitted. There are usually several possible adult sentences available as expansions of any one telegraphic utterance. "No fall" could mean "I am not falling," "I don't want to fall," or "Don't fall," for example. But the intonation and the situational context indicate what the child intends to say, and that sentence becomes the expansion. If the child's intended meaning is correctly grasped, the mother's expansion expresses in proper surface structure the semantic content the child intended. Brown and Bellugi find that middle-class mothers expand the child's utterances approximately 30 percent of the time.

How effective is expansion in the child's syntactic development? Feldman and Rodgon (1970) compared "contingent expansion" (only clear utterances were expanded) to "noncontingent expansion" (all utterances were expanded). The contingent helped more than the noncontingent expansion, and both types of expansion were superior to "modeling." In modeling, everything said by a child is commented upon rather than improved upon. For example, "Doggie bite" becomes "Yes, he's biting" in expansion, but "Yes, he is very mad" in modeling. Expansions are particularly effective when children imitate an expansion itself. Slobin (1966c) examined utterance by two of Brown's subjects and found that about 15 percent of their imitations were repetitions of expansions or responses to expansion questions. About 50 percent of these imitations of expansions were themselves partial expansions of the child's original utterances. That is to say, the child's second utterance, like the parental expansion, is longer or more complex than the first utterance.

Syntactic development beyond age 5

So far we have discussed children's acquisition of a "basic" syntax, which is supposed to be accomplished by age 4 or 5. Further language development goes on beyond age 5. There is a general but gradual consolidation of language structures from kindergarten to seventh grade, and usually there are also abrupt shifts in performance between kindergarten and first grade and between the fifth and seventh grades (Menyuk, 1964; Loban, 1966).

Other studies show that children aged 5–9 have a great deal of difficulty producing passive constructions even when the experimenter provides passive examples in the context of describing a picture. If the passive sentences are negated, the child's difficulty is compounded, but if the passive is truncated (without an explicit subject; see Chapter 4), the difficulty is reduced (Hayhurst, 1967).

Children over age 5 also have difficulty in understanding subtle points of grammar. Carol Chomsky (1969) showed that children do not fully understand the differences between deep-structure subject (logical subject) and surface-structure subject (grammatical subject). For example, a blindfolded doll was in front of a child, who was asked, "Is the doll easy to see or hard to see?" Note that the deep-structure subject in the sentence is "someone"—"Someone sees the doll easily." However, Chomsky's subjects misunderstood the sentence to mean "The doll sees," as the following sample protocol shows.

Lisa, aged 6.5:
Q. Is this doll easy to see or hard to see?
A. Hard to see.
Q. Will you make her easy to see?
A. If I can get this untied.
Q. Will you explain why she was hard to see?
A. (To doll) Because you had a blindfold over your eyes.
Q. And what did you do?
A. I took it off.

At age 5, 22 percent of the children answered this question correctly, but by age 9, 100 percent of them answered correctly.

Using slightly different procedures Cromer (1970) replicated Chomsky's experiment. Children aged between 5.3 and 7.5 had to show, using puppets (a wolf and a duck), who is biting in the following three types of sentence:

"The wolf is *happy* to bite" (S-adjective—the deep and the surface subject coincide);

"The wolf is *tasty* to bite" (O-adjective—the surface subject is not the deep subject but the deep object);

"The wolf is *nice* to bite" (A-adjective—the interpretation of the deep subject is ambiguous, and depends on context)

Many children consistently answered every unambiguous adjective type by showing the named animal to be the one doing the biting. They seem to have answered on the basis of a "primitive" rule of identifying the deep subject as being the surface subject, thus correctly interpreting those sentences using S-adjectives, but incorrectly assigning the subject for those with O-adjectives. A second group, the Intermediates, gave mixed answers— sometimes giving the named animal and sometimes giving the other, some of these being wrong. The third group, Passers, consistently answered correctly, giving the surface subject when an S-adjective was used, and giving the other when an O-adjective was used.

All of the Passers were over age 6.7, but there were some Intermediates and even some primitive-rule users above this age, with some primitive-rule children as old as 7.4. The three groups of children divided into three mental age groupings on the basis of the Peabody Picture Vocabulary Test: All children below mental age 5.7 were either Primitive-rule Users or Intermediates, predominantly the former; all children with mental ages between 5.9 and 6.6 were Intermediates; and almost all children above mental age 6.8 were Passers.

My son, approaching age 9, produced "Did he not already funny?" The concept he was trying to express was rather difficult: Chaplin, as a burnt-out clown in the film *Limelight*, has already ceased being funny.

In summary, a child starts with single-word utterances around age 1. These utterances may consist of two or more words spoken consecutively but separately. At around age 2 children can utter two related words to express a variety of semantic intentions, which can be inferred from word order and situational contexts. However, Stage I children do not easily use word-order information in utterances with three or more words. An English-speaking child acquires inflectional endings and function words gradually in Stage II, starting from conceptually less complex ones. The child at the same time acquires syntactic means to express negations, questions, and other sentence forms. Children may master a "basic" syntax by age 5 and subtle points of syntax by age 9.

SOME VIEWS ON ACQUISITION OF LANGUAGE

Empiricism vs. rationalism

There are two main opposing explanations of how children acquire language, particularly syntax. The empiricist says that no linguistic structure is innate, and has to be learned. Verbal responses are a subclass of responses in general, and have to be learned through the establishment of connections between stimulus and response. Hence the general laws governing learning, such as reinforcement, frequency, and contiguity of occurrence, can explain verbal responses. The innate abilities required are relatively simple ones such as the ability to form associations between stimulus and response, to generalize among stimuli, and to discriminate different stimuli. This ability is not unique to humans.

Of the several versions of the learning-theory account of verbal behavior, Skinner (1957) gives the simplest: verbal responses are directly attached to stimuli without any need for intervening variables such as meaning or grammatical rules. Osgood and his associates (1957) give a somewhat more complex account. They propose a mediational learning theory that treats meaning as a mediation process (see SD and connotative meaning in Chapter 3). The stimulus-response approach, like information theory (Chapter 5), is concerned with the probability that a particular stimulus will initiate a particular verbal response because of previous conditioning.

Chomsky (for example, 1965, 1968) is a leading advocate of the opposing rationalistic approach to language acquisition. According to this view, the structure of language is to a considerable degree specified biologically. The function of experience is not so much to teach as to activate the innate capacity, to turn it into linguistic competence. Chomsky proclaims, ". . . a grammar is no more learned than, say, the ability to walk is learned." He argues that acquisition of stimulus-response probabilities would be a wildly uneconomical explanation of language acquisition. The number of different grammatical sentences is potentially infinite, since it is always possible for a speaker to produce some new combinations of words not spoken before. It is hard to believe (for Chomsky) that a child learns a language by experiencing all possible sentence strings, and by becoming aware of the probabilities that relate successive words in a sentence.

Chomsky further believes that a grammatical theory must develop an account of linguistic universals and attribute tacit knowledge of these universals to the child. Throughout this chapter, we have seen that psychologists and linguists tend to consider what is universal automatically to be innate. Chomsky distinguishes "formal" and "substantive" linguistic universals. *Formal universals* are strong similarities in the way a language is put together that are found in all languages. For example, the syntactic component of a grammar must contain transformational rules, even though the particular transformations that appear in different languages may vary. The distinction between deep and surface structures is another example of a formal universal.

Substantive universals are the linguistic elements shared in all languages; items of a particular kind in any language must be drawn from a fixed class of shared items. Jakobson's "distinctive features" (see Chapter 2) are examples of substantive universals in the phonetic domain. Other examples are syntactic categories such as noun and verb, which are found in all languages, although the concepts encoded by them may vary.

According to Chomsky, real progress in linguistics consists in the discovery that certain features of a given language can be reduced to universal properties of language, and explained in terms of these deeper aspects of linguistic form. The rationalistic approach to language acquisition states that the linguistic universals are intrinsic properties of the language acquisition system of children. Chomsky states:

It seems plain that language acquisition is based on the child's discovery of what from a formal point of view is a deep and abstract theory—a generative grammar of his language. . . . A consideration of the character of the grammar that is acquired, the degenerative quality and narrowly limited extent of the available data, the striking uniformity of the resulting grammars, and their independence of intelligence, motivation, and emotional state, over wide ranges of variation, leave little hope that much of the structure of the language can be learned by an organism initially uninformed as to its general character (1965, p. 58).

Let us discuss the arguments advanced by Chomsky and by some psycholinguists who support his position. First of all, we shall take up Chomsky's point that acquisition of stimulus-response probabilities would be a wildly uneconomical explanation of language acquisition. We may argue that stimulus-response connections made through conditioning might adequately explain the learning of some words where the "creative" aspect of language is not very relevant. In learning syntax, too, children do not have to experience all possible probabilities that relate successive words in a sentence. A relatively small sample can serve to establish estimates of the probabilities. When content and structure are considered together, sentences children encounter may change constantly. However, the children encounter a handful of the same structures, simple and short SAADs, Qs, Is ("Eat it") and NIs ("Don't touch!") time and again.

What is innate and what universal?

Among psycholinguists, McNeill (for example, 1970) embraces Chomsky's view wholeheartedly. McNeill claims that children are born with basic linguistic information that, among other properties, contains the basic grammatical relations of subject and predicate; the modifier and head of the nouns phrase; the main verb and the object of the verb phrase, and so on. These linguistic relationships are all in the base or deep structures of sentences, and are applicable equally to the acquisition of any natural language.

As evidence of his claim, McNeill cites the fact that these linguistic relations appear in the child's earliest sentences—before it has learned the various language-specific rules for constructing sentences according to the specific grammar it eventually acquires. At this early stage, moreover, children everywhere produce similar utterances. These patterns of relationship are expressed even though they are deep structure relations and are not overtly shown in surface structure.

Is McNeill's evidence convincing? First, of the possible syntactic devices—intonation, word order, selection of the grammatical categories of words, alteration in word morphology, production of different sentence forms, and transformations from deep to surface structures—perhaps the first two may be used by young children, but even these two are not always used consistently. The number and consistency of syntactic devices used increase gradually with age up to age 9. Simply because children eventually use these syntactic devices does not allow us to infer that the infants had them all along.

Grammar of children's speech   Secondly, let us consider the deep structure in children's speech. According to Schlesinger (1971b), the components of the structural relationships expressed by children's utterances are semantic concepts like agent, object, action, and their relations, rather than syntactic notions like subject and predicate. The semantic concepts like agent or object do not reflect specifically linguistic knowledge, but rather are determined by the more general innate and universal cognitive capacity of the child. Children acquire language by learning *realization rules* that directly translate semantic intentions into surface structures. Realization rules order the concepts in a relation among themselves, and also assign them to grammatical categories such as nouns or verbs. To Schlesinger, no such abstract syntactic level as deep structure exists. He thereby solves the problem of how children can learn something that is never directly represented in speech by arguing that they do not have to.

Schlesinger and Bloom represent Stage I utterances as in Figure 6–4. In Bloom's representation, a deep structure lies between the semantic level and the surface-structure level. The deep structure contains X of VP, which is deleted on the surface by a reduction transformation. Bloom thus attributes a more complex cognitive operation (conceive the third concept V in its proper relation with the other two concepts or nouns) and linguistic operation (reduction transformation) to a young child than does Schlesinger. In Schlesinger's representation, semantic concepts and their relations are directly translated or mapped on the surface structure, bypassing a deep structure. Schlesinger's representation is more in agreement with our earlier explanation of "Jocelyn cheek" (see "Telegraphic speech")—a young child can keep only two or three concepts and their relations in mind at once. "Jocelyn" and "cheek," the two most salient concepts for the child's message, happened to fill her mind, leaving no room for another less salient concept, "hurt."

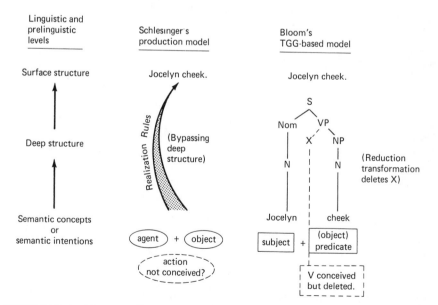

FIGURE 6–4   Two possible grammars for Stage I utterances.

Interpreting two-word utterances in terms of salient concepts ties in with Braine's interpretation of single-word utterances (see "Single-word utterances"). If two-word utterances are derived through a reduction transformation, there is no reason why single-word utterances cannot be similarly derived. This explanation of single-word utterances would attribute even more complex cognitive operations to a young child than it attributes to older children with their two-word utterances. It is hard to imagine that a one-year-old child conceives three concepts, "Jocelyn, hurt, cheek," plus their relationships, and then drops two of them—how does the child decide which ones to drop?

An eloquent example of a young child processing a complex sentence by noting salient words is provided by Guillaume's (1927) 19-month-old child. The child was told to pass on: "Va dire à papa de venir chasser les mouches pour que tu puisses dormir, quand tu auras mangé à ta soupe" ("Go tell papa to come and get rid of the flies so that you can sleep when you have finished your soup"). The child translated: "Papa!—Soupe—Peït (his name)—Némir—Tape—Moute" ("Papa—soup—Peït—sleep—smack—fly").

In short, deep structure seems a superfluous concept which attributes to a young child unnecessarily complex cognitive and linguistic operations. In Chapter 4 on grammar and speech, we have seen that even in the adult's speech processing linguistic deep structures probably do not play important roles.

McNeill, Bloom, and Schlesinger are all attempting to write a grammar for children's speech—a set of formal, explicit rules that describe and generate children's utterances. McNeill and Bloom rely on Chomsky's (1965) transformational generative grammar, with its emphasis on grammatical deep structure. Schlesinger's production model is not as fully formulated as Chomsky's and is more semantically oriented.

Another semantically based grammar is Fillmore's (1968) case grammar (see Chapter 4). Brown (1973) attempted to fit this grammar for Stage I speech, and found it adequate for describing some aspects, but inadequate for describing others. All six case concepts (such as Agentive, Instrumental) Fillmore posited as universal and "presumably innate" are to be found in Stage I speech, except one doubtful case. In case grammar, a sentence consists of two constituents: sentence → modality + proposition (relationships involving agent-action). Stage I sentences consist of "propositions" and, except for simple negative, interrogative, and imperative, no modalities (similar to Brown's "modulations"—modifiers of the more basic propositions). In other words, Stage I speech expresses relationships between agents and actions, without marking tense, mood, number, or the like. But Brown points out that nothing in case grammar suggests why the irregular verbs *be* and *have* are omitted in Stage I speech.

It seems to me that Stage I speech such as "Wear mitten no," "Book read," and "Jocelyn cheek" lack either the agent or the action. Unless we invoke "deep structure," such utterances do not express propositions but may express a modality such as negative. Negation is perhaps as "basic" as a proposition in that it codes existence/nonexistence of an object, which Stage I children can cognize with their sensory-motor intelligence. Stage I children need primitive negatives also to express their vital communication needs for approval/denial or rejection. Recall that "no" is one of the most frequently used words during the period of single-word utterances (Bloom, 1973).

It is just as difficult to fit a grammar to children's speech as it is to fit one to adults' speech (see Chapter 4).

Why do children talk alike? The observation that young children's utterances are similar in every language is sometimes advanced as a powerful argument for the innateness of linguistic information. Here are some examples of two-word utterances that are highly similar across several languages:

there book (English)
Buch da (book there; German)
Tosya tam (Tosya there; Russian)
tuossa Rina (there Rina; Finnish)
Keith lea (Keith there; Samoan)

(Slobin, 1971)

Here we shall not dispute the observed similarity but question the possible reasons for it. Are the children's utterances similar because children are born with innate and universal linguistic information, or with innate and universal cognitive capacities that underlie linguistic capacities? Children everywhere undergo a similar sequence of physical maturation, including brain maturation. This similarity of physical maturation may underlie a similarity of cognitive development, which in turn underlies linguistic development. Piaget's extensive work (see Flavell, 1963; Piaget, 1952) on cognitive development convincingly demonstrates that the sequence of cognitive development in childhood is uniform and universal.

Brown (1973) makes a reasonable observation on the relationship between cognitive and language development:

. . . perhaps there are fixed analytic patterns, processes of information analysis, which are released by any materials having the universal properties of language. And perhaps these processes succeed one another in a relatively fixed order and produce the invariant features of the development of language in relation." (p. 116)

Slobin (1973) proposed some specific universals in language acquisition and related them to underlying perceptual-cognitive processes. For example, the ends of words are perceptually salient, especially if they are stressed. Little children often imitate only the last part of a word, as in *raff* for "giraffe" and *cause* for "because." This perceptual-cognitive observation accounts for the fact that where the same linguistic function is signaled either by postpositions[5] (and suffixes) or by prepositions (and prefixes) in different languages, postpositions are acquired earlier than prepositions. Slobin cites a bilingual child who acquired a Hungarian locative which is always at the end of the noun but not the corresponding Serbo-Croatian locative which is marked by a preposition.

Not only are they perceptually salient, but postpositions may also be linguistically simpler than prepositions. To look at postpositions used in Korean and in Japanese, almost all nouns in a sentence must have postpositions. Hence they may be perceived as integral parts of words. Furthermore, postpositions (again in Korean and in Japanese) are far fewer in number and more consistent and clear-cut in their functions than prepositions in some Indo-European languages.

We can think of many other reasons than cognitive development for the similarity of children's utterances everywhere. One trivial reason is that simple and short things have a much better chance to resemble each other than do things that are complex and long. Utterances that are one-word, two-words, or three-words long and are expressed using only a handful of primitive syntactic devices have good chance to be similar.

Not only do children undergo similar sequences of acquisition but also their speed of acquisition more or less agrees across languages. Children everywhere are supposed to have mastered the basics of their language by age 5, which is considered to be an "astonishing" speed of acquisition. How do they achieve such a feat?

The lives of "normal" children everywhere seem suited to the task of acquiring a language. The children spend all their waking hours in a speech environment, day after day, year after year. Their main activity is not earning a living but acquiring a language and knowledge about the world. They carry out this important activity with warm emotional support from their close family members. In most societies, the family members in turn gear their speech to young children, hence children everywhere are exposed to speech that is simple in concepts and structure. Most important, children everywhere have a compelling need to communicate for their well-being, if not for their survival.

The above reasons for similarity in sequence and speed of acquisition should apply equally well to Chomsky's claim that language acquisition is

---

[5] Postpositions are attached to nouns to indicate grammatical functions of nouns in a sentence, as in the Japanese "Paul-ni" ("to Paul"). See Chapter 1.

independent of intelligence. Dale (1972), in support of Chomsky's position, points out that the mastery of the linguistic system does not vary greatly across individuals of differing intelligence. If language is the result of general learning abilities, linguistic competence should be a function of learning ability, that is intelligence. Dale comments: "The variation which does occur is far less than the mastery of, for example arithmetic, which is much less complex than language" (p. 65). We merely have to ask: Are children exposed to arithmetic as constantly as they are to speech? Do they have as compelling needs for arithmetic as for speech?

As long as favorable conditions for language acquisition are available, children can acquire with relative ease not only just one but two or three languages (see Chapter 7). Acquiring the "basic" syntax of a language or languages in favorable conditions may be relatively independent of intelligence. However, further refinements of linguistic knowledge and verbal skills depend on intelligence to some degree. Recall that the children's ability to identify a deep-structure subject was related to the children's mental ages (Cromer, 1970). Some mentally retarded children learn the basics, but not more advanced skills. Beyond their early teens, they speak a sort of baby-talk (Lenneberg, 1967). We note that people do not have as compelling needs for advanced skills as for basic skills.

Is exposure necessary and sufficient for acquiring language?

Nobody questions that exposure to a language is necessary in order that a child may acquire it. A very simple rule such as that for traffic lights—green for "go" and red for "stop"—can be extracted by any mature person who is "exposed" to traffic for a few minutes at an intersection. In a similar way, children, when exposed to speech, extract linguistic rules. But linguistic rules are vastly more complex and numerous than the rules for traffic lights, and a child needs a few years' concentrated exposure to acquire them. Let us see whether exposure is sufficient, and how much and what kind of exposure children need for them to acquire a language.

To what kind of speech are children exposed? There seem to be some differences between the speech patterns adults use among themselves and those they use in speaking to children. Adults "talk down" to young children. While babies babble, adults talk to them in baby-talk that uses similar sounds and rhythm structures. To slightly older children, parents still tend to talk in short, simple, and fairly grammatical sentence structures about simple matters of life. I observed a French woman talking to a 10-month-old baby. She would say slowly and clearly, "red," "yellow," "orange," or "Look, this one has a hole," holding appropriately colored and shaped toy objects. Furthermore, she repeated the whole sequence two or three times. I could understand everything she said in French to the baby, but could catch only odd words or messages when she was talking to the baby's mother in rapid, normal French.

In talking to young children Chinese adults may repeat essential words, as in "Chy fann-fann" ("Eat rice-rice") or "Put on shoe-shoe" (Chao, 1968).

What happens if children are exposed only to adult speech spoken at a normal adult speed? The Japanese linguist Hattori (1965) observed that his baby daughter learned very quickly the Japanese words her grandmother taught by pronouncing them clearly and repeatedly. But she was unable to learn the Tartar language which Hattori and his wife spoke in normal, rapid conversation, even though the child was interested in the conversation. This brief description given as a footnote in an article on another topic merely whets our curiosity—how long was the child exposed to Tartar? Could she perhaps understand, if not speak, some Tartar? How did Hattori know that the child was interested?

Berko Gleason (1973) observed five well-educated families with young children aged from infancy to 8 years. The adults adopted a baby-talk style in talking to the babies, raising the fundamental frequency of their voices, using simple short sentences with concrete nouns, diminutives, and terms of endearment, and expanding the children's utterances. One mother, for instance, spoke in a normal voice to her husband, a high voice to her 4-year-old, a slightly raised voice to her 8-year-old, and when she talked to her baby she fairly squeaked. A mother might place the food in front of a child while saying, "Hot, hot!" In a similar situation, a hostess might say to adult guests, "Watch out for this dish—it's just out of the oven."

In support of innateness of linguistic knowledge, Chomsky often (for example, 1965, p. 58) cites the fact that children are exposed to "degenerate" speech samples, and yet develop linguistic competence. Degenerate as the speech samples may be, they are not without certain regularities and patterns. When I draw a series of circles freehand, each circle will be erratic, since it is impossible to draw a perfect circle without a tool. Further, every circle will differ from every other circle. However, any person can see that I am drawing a series of circles, or trying to draw one perfect circle: an observer abstracts "circleness" out of the series of erratic circles. This ability to abstract a pattern from erratic samples may be part of innate cognitive capacity. The same cognitive ability may enable children to abstract linguistic patterns and regularities. Each sample is likely to contain an aspect or portion of the hypothetical "perfect and complete" sample, and this aspect or portion is likely to recur in almost every real sample. Children can abstract the pattern because it recurs and is regular.

Feedback   Not only is "exposure" long and concentrated, it also includes "feedback." Children need to test out the extracted rules to be sure of them; they monitor the effect of their utterances on a listener. If a child can establish effective communication by using its tentative rules, the rules are reinforced, and the child may use the same rules in other similar situations. If communication fails, the tentative rules are not reinforced, and the child must find new and additional rules. After all, communicating messages is the main purpose of speech for children as for adults.

Brown, Cazden, and Bellugi (1967) observed that when Eve expressed the opinion that her mother was a girl by saying "He a girl," the mother merely answered "That's right." On the other hand Sarah's grammatically impeccable "There's the animal farmhouse" was disapproved because the building was a lighthouse. This observation is often cited as evidence that children do not receive positive reinforcement for their grammatical sentences and negative reinforcement for their ungrammatical sentences.

I use the term feedback and reinforcement to refer to the fact that children's utterances are understood and responded appropriately if they make sense, regardless whether they are grammatical or ungrammatical. Remember that many ungrammatical utterances make sense and are understood (reinforced) in appropriate contexts. Children sometimes do get frustrated because their grossly deviant utterances are not understood by adults. "Nono falling nono jammies pant" can be understood, if at all, only in an unambiguous context, and only by Nono's (if that is a name) own parents.

Dale (1972) discounts the role of reinforcement in children's acquisition of syntax by pointing out that the children can communicate well with "mi" or "want milk" to their understanding mothers. The child produces "I want milk" before the mother might begin to disapprove more primitive forms. In other words, according to Dale, children acquire syntax in absence of communication pressure—there is no need for, hence no reinforcement in, speaking in syntactically complex and correct manner. Why then do children bother to acquire syntax?

We must note that when an infant says "mi," the infant can be talking about only a few salient and essential things. The infant's mother is well aware of these few. Moreover, the indulgent mother is highly attentive to her infant's needs and utterances. When the child is old enough to say "I want milk" or more properly, "I want a glass of milk," the conditions that enabled effective communication between the infant and its mother are no longer there. Can a child communicate unambiguously to a milk–man such complex idea as "Please give me a jug of 2 percent milk instead of the usual 1-Qt. skim milk" by saying "mi" or "want milk"? As children get older they want to express more and more complex ideas, which must be put in conventional linguistic structures if they are to be communicable outside the immediate family circle in the absence of situational contexts.

Would the child's skill develop normally if the child were exposed to speech, but prevented from seeing the effect of the speech?

Practice and latent learning   Is practice also part of exposure? Students of language acquisition (for example, McNeill, 1970) insist that overt practice of response items is not essential. What may be important is not so much the practice of a particular item, as the practice of applying rules and patterns in varied contexts. Children do not have formal sessions for linguistic pattern drills such as those that adult learners of foreign language go through. However, such pattern drills must be going on informally and unobtrusively. Weir (1962) caught her 2.6–year–old son engaged in presleep monologues that are full of linguistic play–practice. Here is an example:

> "What color?"
> "What color blanket?"
> "What color mop?"
> "What color glass?"

and another:

> "Like it."
> "Don't like it."
> "Like it daddy."

Jespersen (1922) reports on a 2.9–year–old Danish child practising, again in bed, the use of "little":

"They are called small hands—little hands—small hands—little hands, no small hands." (In Danish *lille* is not used with a plural noun.)

Every time children speak or listen to speech they are practising some aspects of speech. We observe that when we do not constantly use a newly learned foreign language we tend to forget it. Young children quickly forget even their "native" tongue if they move to a new environment where another language is spoken (see Chapter 7).

As practice can be subtle, so can be learning. Hebb, Lambert, and Tucker (1971) point out that some learning is latent. Leeper (1935) first demonstrated latent perceptual learning: undergraduates' perceptions of an ambiguous figure were modified by the prior examination of a related figure. The learning was latent, with no discernible primary or secondary reinforcement. Such perceptual learning in infancy may have a lasting effect.

There is also a form of transient one-trial learning without reinforcement that can be called simply the acquisition of information. In Cromer's experiment on the deep and surface subjects (1970; see "Syntactic development beyond age 5"), children who had the adult rule (Passers) were able to assign the correct meaning to new adjectives given in the test sentence on the basis of a single instance of having heard these words in one differentiating frame! When we hear or see something and remember it, even for a short time and even if we make no response at the time, that is learning. Much of our learning may involve this type of subtle learning.

We suspect that some form of learning is involved in language acquisition, but not because we can always identify stimuli, reinforcement, responses, and their relationships. Speech is far too complex to be analyzed in this way. Sometimes we have to consider memory and semantic intentions, which occur internally and are difficult to observe directly; at other times we have to consider social and perceptual contexts, which are external but usually complex. Then speech itself is complex. But if we believe that learning is involved, we may at least have a reasonable frame within which to explore the different variables that may be involved. To claim that language acquisition is innate is to explain away a complex phenomenon. The question now comes back to what evolutionary pressures could have given rise to this complex innate structure.

In summary, language is used to express only what a child perceives and cognizes. As Piaget says, symbolization of the external world develops independent of, and prior to, linguistic symbolization. Children probably cognize far more than they can express with their limited linguistic means.

In all aspects of language—speech sound, semantic system, and syntax—the language-acquisition process is gradual and has a pattern. Children everywhere master linguistic rules, forms, and functions in the following pattern:

> essential before less essential;
> simple and short before long and complex;
> few before many;
> gross and distinct before subtle and finer;
> salient before less salient;
> concrete before abstract;
> isolated items individually before items in relation;
> regular before irregular (unless irregular items are common and simple);
> forms with more general application before forms with restricted application;
> basic functions before particular details of forms to express the functions.

This kind of pattern may occur in acquisition of other cognitive tasks than language.

Children need at least five years of exposure to a language before they become reasonably proficient. Mastery of the finer points of syntax, vocabulary, and speech sounds improves beyond age 5, perhaps up to age 9—or 90. Can we safely attribute to "innate knowledge" something that takes so long to develop fully, and which develops only in the right environment?

SUMMARY AND CONCLUSIONS

Humans are born with the physical equipment necessary for acquiring language. However, an infant starts life without any speech, and with a brain that is not fully developed. During the period when the brain is developing, but before its functions are completely organized, the infant acquires language(s) readily; beyond this "critical period," languages are more difficult to acquire.

Children develop cognitive knowledge of the world as they mature. Piaget divides stages of cognitive development into sensory-motor; pre-operational thought; concrete operation; and formal operation. Such cognitive development underlies linguistic development.

In acquiring language, children extract rules rather than merely copying adult speech or accumulating response items. One of the several lines of evidence for this is that children correct their own speech as well as that of others to conform to their own norm, even though it may differ from the community norm.

In phonological development, children go through periods of random vocalization and babbling. They first acquire phonemes with gross and distinct feature contrasts, and move on to the phonemes with more subtle and finer contrasts. Phonemes in a language are combined according to specific rules, and children early show evidence of having acquired some simple rules. They take longer to acquire more complex rules.

In semantic development, a child starts with a few words, and rapidly builds a vocabulary, initially perhaps through conditioning. The child uses words in ways different from adults. For example, one word may refer to several things for which adults would have separate words. Even an older child may not realize the dual functions of certain words. By experiencing words in various linguistic and situational contexts, children learn the semantic markers (from concrete to abstract) and syntactic features of each word, and becomes able to organize words in memory by grammatical classes, as adults do.

English-speaking children learn 14 morphemes in an order that is governed not so much by factors of phonemic difficulty or of frequency of occurrence, as by conceptual difficulty. Thus, plural (-s) emerges before the third-person verb (-s). Children may learn the morphological rules so well that they generalize the rules even to inapplicable words.

The acquisition of syntax is usually studied by observing a few children longitudinally. A child starts with single-word utterances at age 1. At this stage it may utter a few words in succession, but without any linguistic structure. At age 2, children combine a few words in an utterance in certain patterns. Both single-word and two-word utterances imply a variety of semantic contents that are inferred from word order, intonation, and situational context. The one or two words chosen in such utterances refer to salient features of the situation a child wants to communicate.

English-speaking children use interpretable word orders most of the time, but not too consistently at the beginning. The word order in more complex sentences seems to gradually approximate the "universal" SO order. SV also may be a "basic" order that codes semantic relations between S and V unambiguously.

Children eventually acquire transformational rules to express negations, questions, and so on. They can perform only a few grammatical operations (such as inclusion of auxiliary verbs and inversion of these with subjects) at a time, and some rules they know may be omitted if others must be simultaneously used. Children's sentences are telegraphic while they are acquiring syntax. By age 5, children have acquired the basics of syntax and their sentences start to resemble those of adults. But further refinement goes on beyond age 5. For example, producing complex passives or identifying deep-structure subjects in complex sentences develops between ages 5 and 9.

There are two opposing theories of the acquisition of language, in particular of syntax. The rationalistic approach says that there are linguistic universals and children are born with them. The empiricist's approach says that language is learned by establishing stimulus-response connections through conditioning.

The observation that sequence and speed of acquisition are uniform everywhere is cited as evidence for innate linguistic information. However, the uniform sequence of cognitive development and similarly favorable conditions for language acquisition everywhere can also explain this observation.

The early acquisition of underlying deep structures is cited as another piece of evidence for innate linguistic information. However, the deep structure may be superfluous: very primitive one-word or some two-word utterances may merely refer to salient perceptual-cognitive features, while slightly longer utterances may be expressions of semantic intentions such as agent-action-object rather than of syntactic deep-structure relations such as subject and predicate.

Children abstract rules if they are exposed to speech, even though each sample of speech may be "degenerate." Exposure is concentrated and may include feedback, informal practice, and subtle forms of learning. Rule-abstraction seems to be facilitated if speech is geared to the child's conceptual and linguistic level.

The rationalistic and empiricist approaches seem to complement each other. But what is innate may not be specific linguistic information, but rather perceptual-cognitive capacities, which enable children to acquire any language efficiently in an appropriate environment.

7

Bilingualism

*You are worth as many men as you
know languages.*

Charles V, Holy Roman Emperor, 1500–1558

Have you ever marveled at a fluent bilingual who communicates freely in either of two languages? The other language hardly interferes at all. In this chapter we shall learn about bilingualism, the ability of a person to use two languages. Bilingualism is far more widespread in the world than an average English-speaking American realizes. Cases of fluent bilingualism are often found in Canada, where many people speak both English and French. Any educated Hollander speaks at least three languages, Dutch, English, and German, of necessity. English is a second language to many people all over the world.

Two main questions are raised in this chapter: (1) What practical problems does a bilingual encounter in learning and using two languages? (2) What kind of information-processing and storage mechanisms must be developed?

First we must find out who is a bilingual.

Who is a bilingual?

A bilingual is a person who can speak two languages that differ in speech sounds, vocabulary, and syntax. As described in Chapter 1, sometimes the differences are large, as between two unrelated languages like English and Chinese; sometimes they are small, as between German and English.

In a special kind of bilingualism called *diglossia* (Ferguson, 1959), a "high" or standard language is used for formal communication (as in religion, education, national broadcasting, and other aspects of high culture), while a "low" or relatively unschooled dialect or language is used for more intimate communication—everyday pursuits of hearth, home, and work. When a New York Puerto Rican discusses business in English—even with other Puerto Ricans—but uses Spanish for home affairs, he is engaging in diglossia.

We also have varied styles of speaking (Dillard, 1972): formal (I do not know); semiformal (I don't know); informal (I donno); and intimate (a series of unspellable nasal sounds, usually accompanied by a shrugging of the shoulders and intelligible to the immediate family of the speaker). Styles and social class may interact in such a way that people from high social classes normally tend to use formal and semiformal styles while people from low social classes tend to use informal and intimate styles. In fact, there are endless variations in styles of speech. Even among our intimates, we talk differently to babies, to older children, and to our spouses.

To reiterate, a bilingual is a person who speaks two (or more) languages, dialects, or styles of speech that involve differences in sound, vocabulary, and syntax. Often, bilinguals have a dominant (native) language and a weaker (second) language. The questions raised in this chapter are pertinent to all types of bilingual. Naturally, some questions may be more pertinent to one type than to others.

Now, let us turn to our questions. The first question is how a person becomes bilingual.

ACQUISITION OF TWO LANGUAGES IN CHILDHOOD

Berlitz has run an ad showing the face of a Chinese four-year-old, with a caption that reads: "If he can speak Chinese in four years, so can you!" This ad by a leading commercial language school is misleading. In fact, the process of acquiring first languages is so different from the process of learning second languages that the two must be discussed separately. Note that I use the term "acquire" in early childhood, and "learn" in late childhood or adulthood, and that I use plurals for both first and second languages.

In Chapter 6 we learned that children are born with physical equipment well suited for acquiring language(s), and all "normal" children acquire their native tongue—some faster than others, to be sure. If children are exposed to more than one language during the critical acquisition period while the brain is still "plastic" (brain organization is not completed), they become bilinguals as easily and naturally as others become monolinguals. In acquiring two languages they have to acquire an increased number of speech sounds, words, sentence structures, and linguistic rules. But there is no ground to think that such an increase strains a child's acquisition capacity. Children master their native tongue whether it contains 10 or 70 speech sounds, and whether it contains a complex system of inflections or no inflections. Of course there is a peculiar problem of keeping separate two distinct sets of linguistic items and rules, instead of merely acquiring an increased number of items.

Let us examine what acquisition processes a bilingual child goes through.

How does a child acquire two languages?

Acquiring two languages at once An American linguist of German origin, Leopold (1939–1949), kept a detailed diary of his daughter's progress in acquiring German and English. Leopold's daughter Hildegard was born to German parents living in the United States, and was exposed to German at home and to English outside home. The family made a few visits to Germany, where they spoke only in German. During the first two years Hildegard learned to understand both languages, but when she talked she used an indiscriminate mixture of German and English words. For example, at age 20 months she had clearly German words such as "Baum" (tree), "dunkel" (dark), and clearly English words such as "big" and "egg," along with words that could pass as either German or English, such as "dies," "this"; "Haus," "house." Sometimes she put English words in a German sentence structure, as in "What grade is man when man nine years old is?"

German prevailed at first, but gradually gave way to English, which in the end far outweighed German. Not until she was 3 years old did she realize that she spoke two languages. At age 5, during a half-year sojourn in Germany, she seemed to forget English and spoke only German. Her German, however, was not the same as that of a native. After she came back to America she continued to use both languages, but spoke like a native only in English. She developed normally in every way, and progressed well in school.

Another linguist, Burling (1959), observed his son acquiring Garo (a language that belongs to the Tibeto-Burmese Family) and English. Stephen was 16 months old when Burling's observations started. The child began to use Garo words within a few weeks of arrival at Garo Hills in India, but his English vocabulary also grew steadily. It was several months before Garo became clearly dominant, probably due to the hospitalization of his mother, who was his most important model for English. His father frequently spoke to him in Garo.

At age 2, Stephen was not aware of the existence of two languages, although he did recognize that there were two words for certain things, such as "milk," which is "dut" in Garo. He incorporated English morphemes and words in Garo sentences. Soon he learned who spoke Garo and who spoke English, and switched easily from one language to another. For instance, he spoke to his father in English and immediately repeated it in Garo for someone else's benefit. Later, when he did consciously have two linguistic systems, the two never appeared to interfere with each other.

Within six months after his departure from India late in his third year, Stephen was already having trouble with the simplest Garo words. At age 5½ he was in kindergarten in the United States, speaking English perhaps a bit more fluently than most of his contemporaries. The only Garo words still used were the few that had become family property.

Here then are good examples of young children acquiring two languages as easily and naturally as other children acquire one language. The two bilingual children had an equally compelling need to communicate in each language during their early childhood. They had some language mix-ups, but these did not last. They certainly did not develop into schizophrenics with split personalities! Each eventually used one of the two languages as a native tongue; each acquired this major language as well as, if not better than, other children acquire their native tongues as monolinguals.

Unused languages are forgotten   Note that Hildegard seemed to forget English during a half-year sojourn in Germany at age 5, and Stephen forgot Garo almost as soon as he left the Garo Hills. Children forget a language as quickly as they learn it. One linguist observed a 6-year-old Spanish girl who was suddenly placed in a completely French environment. After only 93 days she seemed to have lost her Spanish completely. On the other hand, in less than a year she acquired a knowledge of French equal to that of the neighborhood children.

"Forgetting" of linguistic materials has its own peculiar characteristics. Burtt (1941) studied a child who was read selections from classic Greek when he was a baby. Years later, the child could memorize those same selections much faster than equivalent new material. In this study, the investigator read three Greek selections a day to a baby of 15 months, repeating the same selections daily for three months. Each selection consisted of 20 lines of iambic hexameter. At the end of three months another set of three selections was repeated daily for three months. The procedure was continued until the child was 3 years old, and 21 selections had been read. The baby had at the time no understanding of the Greek texts that were read to him.

When the boy was 8, 14, and 18 years old, he was tested to see how fast he could memorize the Greek selections, as compared to other selections from the same text. He had not studied Greek in the meantime. At age 8, he could learn the familiar selections with about 30 percent fewer repetitions than equivalent new material, and by age 14, with 8 percent fewer repetitions. By age 18, he learned the old and new materials with a similar number of repetitions.

Similarly, a language acquired in early childhood, even when "forgotten" from long years of disuse, may leave some residue in the mind, making later learning of the same language easier. If Stephen ever went back to the Garo Hills, would he learn Garo in shorter time than an English-speaking boy who had never been exposed to Garo in his life? This is an intriguing question.

Children sometimes acquire their mother tongue at home and then learn a second language at school. This second language is a foreign language to them, in contrast to the situation for children who acquire two languages at once. An effective way of learning a second language at school is an *immersion* program, in which the second language is used as a medium of teaching. In the United States, the Bilingual Education Act encourages the use of any minority language such as Spanish as a medium of teaching for economically underprivileged children. In bilingual Canada, French is used as a medium of teaching to predominantly English-speaking children at selected schools.

More commonly, children learn a second language as a school subject. English–speaking children may take two or three periods of French per week in primary schools. This method of learning is not as effective as the immersion course, but learning French in primary school is better than learning it in adulthood, no matter what the method.

Let us summarize some advantages of childhood language acquisition. Young children acquiring two or more languages at once during the "critical period" of language acquisition enjoy the same favorable neural, attitudinal, and social conditions as young children acquiring one language (see Chapter 6).

With respect to second-language learning in primary schools, the second language may not compete with the first, which has a head start but is not yet firmly established. Children learn foreign sounds and intonations very well, thanks to their imitative impulse. They also are not very self-conscious about trying a foreign language and making mistakes. They have less fixed mental sets than do older children or adults, and easily identify with others. Above all, they do not ask that disturbing question: "Why do I have to learn a foreign language?"

In short, in acquiring languages, children enjoy neurological, attitudinal, and social advantages over adults.

The effects of bilingual schooling on IQ and academic progress

Is early bilingualism detrimental to a child's intellectual, linguistic, and emotional development? What happens to a child's academic progress if a second language is used as a medium of teaching?

Apparently unfavorable effects   Some of the early American studies (such as Graham, 1925; Mead, 1927) seemed to show that on intelligence tests, particularly on verbal tests, bilingual children achieved less than monolingual children. The tests were likely to have been standardized on English-speaking children, and then translated into other languages for testing bilingual children. Many of the bilingual children tested were children of immigrants of low socioeconomic class. Such children, even monolinguals, typically score low on these tests. Further, the children were tested before they had adequately mastered English, and their mother tongue was merely a home language, not a literary language properly taught at school.

In Great Britain, Welsh-English bilingualism has been a subject of many studies. One large-scale study by Saer (1923) compared 1,400 monolingual and bilingual children in rural areas using the Stanford-Binet IQ test. The bilinguals were inferior to the monolinguals, and their inferiority became consistently greater with each year from 7 to 11 years. Such bilingual inferiority was not found in urban areas. According to the author, the children in rural areas learned English slowly and laboriously at school before they had completely mastered Welsh, while the children in the urban areas learned English at play effortlessly. Thus there is a possibility that the bilingual children in the rural areas were not proficient in English when they were tested. Their English experience was probably not unlike that of the immigrant Americans.

By trying to learn two languages, children may end up learning neither of them well. Jespersen (1922) asks: Has any multilingual ever become a great poet? Vladimir Nabokov writes beautifully and poetically in Russian, English, French, and German. The Polish-born Joseph Conrad became a great English writer, and Kahlil Gibran wrote elegantly and eloquently both in his native tongue, Arabic, and in his second language, English (for example, *The Prophet*, 1960). There could be linguistic disadvantages in learning more than one language, but these disadvantages are surmountable.

Let us move on to a slightly different topic in linguistic development, stuttering. Do bilingual children have more speech problems than monolingual children? Some people suspect that early bilingualism may cause mental and linguistic confusion, and might therefore lead to stuttering. To test this idea, Travis, Johnson, and Shover (1937) conducted a large-scale survey of close to 5,000 children, and found that there were fewer stutterers among English-speaking monolinguals (1.8 percent) than among bilinguals (2.8 percent).

If we examine these bilinguals, we find that they were immigrant children who had diverse languages as their mother tongues. These children were undergoing economic and emotional instability associated with changes in their environment and language. Not surprisingly, in 26 percent of the total group of bilingual stutterers, the age of onset of stuttering coincided with the introduction of a second language. This study may not show so much that bilingualism leads to stuttering as that emigration leads to (temporary perhaps) economic and emotional instability, which may be manifested partly in stuttering.

Favorable effects   In Canada, French-English bilingualism is of national concern, and many long-term, systematic researches on bilingualism have been carried out. We shall discuss some work of Lambert and his associates (Bruck, Lambert, and Tucker, in press) at McGill University in Montreal, mainly on English-speaking children taking French immersion programs. These programs, which started in 1965, have been thoroughly examined and have served as a model for similar programs in other localities.

The procedures of the programs were as follows. English-speaking children in St. Lambert, a suburb of Montreal, entered a 2-hour-per-day kindergarten where French was used exclusively from the first day. In first grade teachers introduced reading, writing, and arithmetic exclusively via French. With each successive year a larger proportion of class time was taught in English, until it reached 50 percent in seventh grade.

Lambert's team compared these children's IQ and academic progress from year to year for seven years against that of two control groups. One control group consisted of English-speaking children following the traditional English-language program; the other of French-speaking children following the conventional French-language program. These two control groups were similar to the immersion group in social-class and intelligence. Here are their findings in capsule:

1. The immersion group's English (in varied aspects—listening, reading, and the like) was as good as the English controls' even though they learned English formally only on a part-time basis beginning in second grade.

2. By the fourth or fifth grade the immersion group attained a functional bilingualism that permitted them to read, write, comprehend, and speak French fluently and naturally. However, in some details, such as pronunciation or conceptual vocabulary, they were not as good as native speakers of French.

3. In computational and problem-type mathematics and in science, the immersion group's performance was similar to or slightly higher than that of the English controls.

4. By fifth grade the immersion group performed better on an English-based measure of verbal intelligence than did the controls. In "creativity" tests the immersion group performed as well as or better than the controls.

5. Mathematical concepts and reading skills transferred between the languages. That is, mathematical concepts taught only in French or only in

English were used equally well in either language. This important finding may show that we solve simple mathematical problems without using any natural language. Of course, highly advanced mathematics or physics can be talked about only in a specialized language. It is true that the multiplication table we memorize in one language can be "automatically" recited only in that language. But automatically reciting the multiplication table is more a motor response than a problem-solving activity.

The finding that reading skills also transfer between languages shows that reading involves some basic skills that can be used in any language. Some of these might be a skill of associating visual objects, letters, with speech sounds, even though bilingual readers have to learn to associate different letters to different sounds in two languages. In silent reading, readers have to learn to pay more attention to important content words and less attention to function words. For obtaining maximum information with minimum time and effort, this strategy will be useful in reading any language.

6. What happens to bilingual children's attitudes toward themselves and toward French speakers? The immersion group's self-views were favorable, as optimistic and healthy as those of the control groups. They considered themselves to be both English and French Canadians without psychological conflict.

In other localities involving other pairs of languages, Malherbe (1969) found favorable effects from using English as a medium of teaching for Afrikaans-speaking children in South Africa. In the United States, Cohen (1974) and Richardson (1968) report success stories involving Spanish and English.

The story is different when one of the languages involved in bilingual education has low prestige. In the United States in 1968, President Johnson signed into law the Bilingual Education Act, intended primarily for economically underprivileged children whose mother tongue might be Spanish (Mexican or Puerto Rican) or one of a variety of American Indian languages. These children often suffer in academic achievement because of their limited ability in English, the medium of teaching. The act encourages the use of any of the minority languages as a medium of teaching for these children, as a "bridge" to English.

Gaader (1970) points out that minority languages seem to be woefully neglected in these so-called bilingual programs. For example, the projects depended on the teaching services of bilingual aides who were usually drawn from the community, rarely literate in the non-English tongue, and were paid low wages. Gaader also notes the lack of community support for bilingual education. A child is not expected to become vigorously literate in his mother tongue if that vigor and literacy are not found in public places and in the home.

In conclusion, most bilingual education carried out in recent times in Canada, South Africa, and the United States seems to be successful in the sense that children mastered two languages adequately, and their academic achievement did not suffer because of bilingual education.

Bilingual cognitive functioning

In Chapter 8 we shall learn that one language is better than no language in cognitive functioning. Then, are two languages better than one language?

As described earlier, English children with seven years of French immersion scored slightly higher than monolingual controls in "creativity" tests. One of the test items was to think of as many unusual uses of common objects (such as a rubber band or tin can) as possible. Bilingual children do better on this type of test—perhaps because they have two language systems representing two sets of cultures and experiences; to put it crudely, bilingual children may look at common objects in more ways than do monolinguals. For the same reasons, bilingual children also score higher than monolingual children in "cognitive flexibility," in which a child has to list all the different things each of eight displayed designs could represent. For a sinuous design, the child might see a snake, an umbrella handle, a swan, and so on.

From a real language situation, Morrison (1958) gives an example of a Gaelic-speaking boy of 11 who had just taken the Raven Matrices Test (a nonverbal IQ test). When asked whether he had done his thinking in Gaelic or in English the boy replied, "Please, Sir, I tried it in the English first, then I tried in the Gaelic to see would it be easier; but it wasn't, so I went back to the English" (p. 288).

Some psychologists speculate that flexibility may be also due to habitual switching between two languages, but a bilingual may possess two perspectives even when he does not constantly switch languages. After all, bilinguals, unless they are professional translators, do not normally switch languages constantly.

Peal and Lambert (1962) found that French-English[1] bilingual children scored higher in nonverbal intelligence tests that required reorganizations of relations and concepts such as figure manipulation and picture arrangement. The authors call this ability also "flexibility," and attribute it to a bilingual's tendency to separate the sound of a word from its referent. As evidence of such a tendency, Leopold observed that unlike monolingual children, who will correct their parents on wording of stories, his bilingual daughter Hildegard cared only about the content and had no objection to

---

[1] Often when a bilingual's native and second languages are known, his native language is written first.

word changes. Even her own memorized material would change wording without altering the content. Leopold writes: "I attribute this attitude of detachment from words confidently to the bilingualism. Constantly hearing the same things referred to by different words from two languages, she had her attention drawn to essentials, to content, instead of form" (p. 188). Burling's Garo-English bilingual son Stephen, however, was sensitive to any word change in the stories read to him. We do not know whether the fact that Stephen was younger than Hildegard has something to do with such differences. At any rate, these differences alert us to possible individual differences among bilingual children, as among other children.

Ianco-Worrall (1972) tested Leopold's contention that bilinguals separate word sound from word meaning earlier than do monolinguals. She used a semantic and phonetic preference test, a two-choice test in which similarity between words could be interpreted on the basis of shared meaning or shared sounds. A test item might be: "I have three words—'cap,' 'can,' and 'hat.' Which of 'can' and 'hat' is more like 'cap'?" She compared Afrikaans-English bilingual children aged 4–6 and 7–9 to monolingual children in either language. The bilingual subjects indeed tended to separate word sound from word meaning two or three years earlier than the monolingual children.

Bilinguals' reputed detachment from words may allow them to solve the following "rule-discovery" problems faster than monolinguals. Bain (1974) asked French-English bilingual children and monolingual children to find a suitable number to follow 31 in the series of numbers— 1, 3, 7, 15, 31, ? . One of the "creativity" test items Lambert and co-workers used is also similar to this problem. In Bain's experiment the child has to subsequently use the discovered rule in solving further problems of a like nature, that is, has to transfer the discovered rule to a novel situation.

We solve such problems by manipulating numbers directly without the use of natural language. Bilinguals who can think outside languages may solve perceptual (as in Peal and Lambert's tasks) or number problems better than monolinguals. Simple mathematical concepts transfer readily between languages because they are often solved without the use of any natural language.

Is there any other area, besides creativity or flexibility, where bilinguals are better than monolinguals? Peal and Lambert (1962), as well as a few other researchers (such as Cummins and Gulutsan, 1974), found that bilinguals scored higher even on the verbal parts of intelligence tests. Peal and Lambert speculate that the overlap of English and French vocabularies allows positive transfers between the two languages. I would speculate that there could be bilingual superiority in verbal intelligence even when bilinguals speak two unrelated languages. People who learn and use two or more languages are bound to contrast and compare languages, and may develop a certain "feel" or understanding about words or linguistic material in general. If so, this may be one of the reasons why people who have learned one foreign language easily learn additional foreign languages. But only people who have a good command of two languages may develop such understanding.

In short, researchers seem to agree that early bilingualism has no harmful effect on a child's linguistic and cognitive development. But they do not always agree about the association of bilingualism with cognitive and verbal superiority. When researchers find superior performance by bilingual children, they can only speculate on the reason. Meanwhile, why do we not consider that two sets of language and context are great assets whether or not they increase cognitive flexibility and verbal intelligence?

Two languages, two personalities?

Do bilinguals assume different personalities when they speak their two languages? We start with an anecdotal account from a French-born American writer, Julian Green. Attempting to translate one of his own books from French to English, he failed and had to sit down and write an entirely new book. He remarked: "It was as if writing in English, I had become another person" (1941, p. 402). I doubt the literal truth of that statement; rather, he adjusted his linguistic and attitudinal set from French to English.

Turning to experimental evidence, bilinguals make up different stories in their several languages on Thematic Apperception Test (TAT) cards, cards that contain pictures with ambiguous content. People are assumed to project their own motives, feelings, and personalities when they make up a story on each of the TAT cards. Ervin (1964) asked adult French-English bilinguals living in the United States to tell stories on two occassions, one in French and the other in English. To Picture 4 in the Murray Series, a 27-year-old woman told a French story, a part of which was:

. . . they certainly seem angry. . . . He wants to go see someone and he wants to get in a fight with someone, and she holds him back. . . .

In this story, aggression and striving for autonomy were identified as the main themes. The same person responding in English said:

. . . He keeps on working and going to college at night some of the time . . . and he's very discouraged and his wife tries to cheer him up. . . . (p. 504)

The theme in this case was the heroine supporting the husband in his achievement strivings. Stories were usually longer in French, perhaps because French was the subjects' mother tongue. On three out of nine themes there were significant differences between the stories in the two languages. The "achievement" theme was common in the English stories of female subjects, while verbal aggression against age peers and autonomy or withdrawal from others were more common in the French stories.

Using a sentence-completion test, Ervin-Tripp (1968) again found a content shift between two languages in Japanese-English war brides in the United States.

1. When my wishes conflict with my family's . . .
   "It is a time of great unhappiness." (Japanese)
   "I do what I want." (English)
2. I will probably become . . .
   "A housewife." (Japanese)
   "A teacher." (English)
3. Real friends should . . .
   "Help each other." (Japanese)
   "Be very frank." (English)

A control group of women who did not change languages but were instructed to give "typically Japanese" or "typically American" answers at the two sessions could not simulate such a content shift. A bilingual thus seems to change in attitude and outlook on life upon switching to the second language.

Whether or not a person changes in basic personality in changing languages is a separate question. Does a balanced bilingual change from an extroverted, impulsive, and gregarious person to an introverted, inhibited, and reserved person in changing languages? If we can indeed change personality by changing languages, think about what this possibility might imply. We have to devise an experiment that is really relevant to the question of personality (not merely outlook-on-life) change. For example, the behavior of bilinguals might be observed in the same setting once while they are speaking one language, and again while they are using another language. Judges could rate various items of behavior, such as how they cope with frustration, interact with other people, and solve problems, and assess possible personality changes. Again, if reasonably balanced bilinguals' writings in the two languages are compared, would we find that they are witty, erudite, and terse in one language, but dull, obtuse, and verbose in the second language, when writing about the same topic? We do not know.

LANGUAGE LEARNING IN LATE CHILDHOOD AND ADULTHOOD

Many people miss the golden period of early childhood for acquiring plural languages, and have to learn their foreign languages as older children or adults, usually at schools. Older learners do not learn languages as naturally as do young children. Furthermore, some learn languages faster and better than others. Aptitude, motivation, and teaching methods influence how well and fast older learners master foreign languages.

Aptitude for language

Some people seem to have a gift for languages, just as some other people have gifts for mechanical skills or drawing skills. People who are exceptionally gifted for languages can learn several languages well. The nineteenth-century English explorer Sir Richard Burton (Farwell, 1963) claimed to have spoken more than 40 languages and dialects. According to *The Guinness Book of World Records*, the most accomplished linguist ever known was Cardinal Giuseppe Mezzofanti (1774–1849), the former chief keeper of the Vatican library in Rome. He could translate 114 languages and 72 dialects, and spoke 39 languages fluently, 11 others passably, and understood 20 more, along with 37 dialects.

Closer to home, we observe that some students get high grades and other students get low grades in any language class. Such differences in grades appear as early as in elementary schools. In a typical elementary school, we may find that about 20 percent of pupils are excellent learners; 65 percent good to fair learners; and 15 percent poor learners. This breakdown may roughly reflect the distribution of three aptitude levels in the general population.

Aptitude for languages may consist of several distinct abilities. Let us see what they are.

Learning speech sounds   Speech sounds are the basic building blocks of any language. The ability to pronounce foreign sounds accurately is obviously a part of language-learning aptitude. To pronounce sounds accurately, first we must hear and discriminate the sounds accurately: we must have a "good ear." We must also reproduce sounds accurately by remembering them over periods longer than a few seconds.

Although having a good ear is an obvious part of language aptitude, it is only one of many components of aptitude. In fact, we sometimes come across people who pronounce sounds of foreign languages accurately, and yet have little command of these languages. Professional singers often do not fully understand the foreign songs they sing with such authentic pronunciation and feeling. Singing and pronouncing may share the requirement of having a good ear for sounds. In one study, a language teacher's ratings of accents were correlated ($r = .64$) with pitch discrimination, which is a subtest of the Seashore Measure of Musical Talents (Blickenstaff, 1963).

Good pronunciation seems to be related to certain personality traits as well. A person with a firmly established, rigid, and authoritarian personality seems to be less likely to learn authentic pronunciation than is a more relaxed person. Being less rigid than adult males, children and women usually pronounce foreign languages more authentically than adult male learners. Some adults even consider their "foreign" accents as marks of distinction.

A team headed by Guiora (see Guiora, 1971; L. Taylor et al., 1971) in the United States undertook an extensive research project to see whether "empathy" is related to authenticity of pronunciation. *Empathy* refers to one's sensitivity to cues in interpersonal situations, one's ability to put oneself in the other person's shoes, to share another person's feelings and thoughts. Empathy was indeed correlated ($r = .72$) with correct Japanese pronunciation by English speakers. One of the simplest and most reliable tests of empathy is "micromomentary expressions." The test consists of showing silent film slips at various speeds. Subjects indicate each observed change in facial expression in the film.

In short, a good ear for sounds and empathy are important for learning good pronunciation.

Vocabulary learning   Foreign vocabulary learning means associating a foreign word to the proper concept, or to an equivalent word in the native language; we learn to associate "pomme" with "apple," "drapeau" with "flag," and so on. Sometimes we may associate a foreign word, if it is concrete, directly to an object or action rather than to an English word; "paella" may be directly associated with that dish, and "courir" (French) with the action of running.

We do not always have to learn a foreign vocabulary by pure rote memory, as suggested by the above paired-associate learning; we can use some rational devices. We can take advantage of the fact that related languages have many *cognates*, words that are derived from the same origin. English "prince" = French "prince" = German "Prinz." But watch out for misleading cognates: "le crayon" is "the pencil". If we note that some French words begin with an [e] that does not occur in the English cognate, we can recognize such words as "*e*stomach" and "*e*space." We may also learn common suffixes and prefixes. The suffix (-tion) changes a verb into a noun, and the prefix (in-) changes a word meaning to the negative, in many Indo-Euopean languages.

Various "tricks" or mnemonic devices can lighten the burden of rote learning when foreign words are truly like nonsense syllables. One Latin primer suggested that a learner should remember "hasta" means "spear" by thinking of the warning not to be "hasty" with it.

Vocabulary should be learned in context, not as a list of paired associates between English and foreign equivalents. For one thing, words from different languages do not always have exact translation equivalents. A context specifies correct meanings of words and allows us to actively guess meanings of new words. When we learn a few languages at once, learning the vocabulary of each language in its own linguistic and cultural context will prevent us from mixing up words of different languages.

To speak over 40 languages and dialects, linguistic geniuses like Sir Richard Burton must have memorized a staggering number of words. Burton apparently had a phenomenal memory for words, but he worked hard at the task of memorizing them, and learned words in context.

Vocabulary learning requires a good memory, hard work, and rational devices.

Grammar learning   To learn how words are put together in sentences means to learn a grammar, or to be more precise, a syntax. We must become sensitive to the grammatical functions of words in sentences and discover grammatical rules from sentence patterns. Sometimes this requires an analytic mind. By analysis we sort out subject, object, predicate, and main verb of a sentence, especially if it has a complex structure with relative clauses.

Learning linguistic patterns by analogy saves a lot of time and effort. In Japanese,

>"to go" is *ikimasu*; "not to go" is *ikimasen*
>"to come" is *kimasu*; "not to come" is *kimasen*
>"to sleep" is *nemasu*; "not to sleep" is ___?___

On reading Japanese, you might know the first two, and then encounter *nemasen* for the first time. From the words you know, you can infer that it means "not to sleep."

Unfortunately, many grammatical rules are arbitrary and have to be memorized. In French, the gender of nouns is quite arbitrary: we cannot think of any logical reason why "la table" is feminine and "le livre" (book) is masculine. And yet, whether a noun is masculine or feminine will determine how adjectives will decline: "la grande table" but "le grand livre." Moreover, many grammatical rules have exceptions. In English we add the suffix (-s) to a noun to make it plural, but plural "sheep" does not require (-s). Sometimes rules are not fully and precisely formulated for how certain items have to be used grammatically. Examples of such items are English "the" and "a."

In addition to special abilities to learn sounds, vocabulary, and syntax, one has to be interested in linguistic materials to be a good language learner. Some people are interested in any kind of linguistic material— word puzzles, word origins, Scrabble, strange writings, foreign words, and even "foreign" accents. Perhaps people who display resourcefulness in vocabulary and syntax learning would score high on a test of interest in linguistic materials, if there were such a test. The phenomenal language learners we read about must have had a keen interest in languages. Take Burton, for example; although he learned most of his 40 languages because he needed them for his exploration and his anthropological studies, he learned some of them purely from curiosity about languages. In Africa, he compiled a vocabulary of an obscure language spoken by a small tribe merely to determine that it was not related to Arabic.

Aptitude testing

We can use tests to determine whether a person has a high or low aptitude for language learning. A good test has to be easy to administer and score. Most important, it has to have high *reliability* and *validity.* A reliable test will yield similar test scores wherever, whenever, or by whomever the test is conducted. A valid test has to measure what it is supposed to measure— a language-aptitude test should predict well how a testee will do as a language learner or user. The two aptitude tests that meet these requirements are the Modern Language Aptitude Test (MLAT) and the Language Aptitude Battery (LAB).

Two American psychologists, Carroll and Sapon, developed the MLAT in 1959 after extensive research. The MLAT is commercially available in a short (30 minutes) and a long (70 minutes) form, and comes with a manual and statistical information. It consists of the following five subtests, each measuring a distinct ability:

1. *Number learning.* The student is tested for his rote memory in recalling numbers expressed in an artificial language. Example: Write down in figures the number given in words in the new language.

2. *Phonetic script.* The student is tested for his ability to associate sounds with written symbols. This ability is related to the ability to learn and to mimic speech sounds. Example: Underline the word you hear— tik, tiyk, tis, tiys.

3. *Spelling clues.* The student selects a synonym to a key word from a set of choices. For example, the key word "luv" is a disguised spelling of "love." The test measures verbal knowledge to a considerable extent. Example: which choice is a synonym of the word pronounced like this: *luv*— carry, exist, affection, wash, spy.

4. *Words in sentences.* The student chooses a word or a construction similar to a model one. This test seems to be the most valid and robust of the battery. It is a test of grammatical sensitivity. Examples: Which italicized part of 2 corresponds syntactically to the italicized part of 1:

1. John sold *DICK* his bicycle.
2. If their *work* is up to *standard*, I will guarantee *them* a bonus at the *end* of
       A   B   C   D
the *week.*
    E

5. *Paired associates*. The student's rote memory is tested using Kurdish vocabulary, with emphasis on visual rather than auditory memory this time.

The Language Aptitude Battery (LAB) (Pimsleur, 1968) is similar to the MLAT in that it tests several different abilities. One test called Language Analysis is unique. Students see a series of foreign words and their English equivalents. From these they are to conclude how other things would be expressed in this language. This test seems to tap an ability to infer grammatical patterns using analogy.

How adequately do the MLAT and the LAB measure the distinct abilities that make up language aptitude? For convenience, both have to be pencil-paper tests that can be given to a large group of people learning any foreign language. Because of such practical considerations, neither test measures how accurately a student can pronounce foreign sounds. Both the tests measure vocabulary learning in a list of paired associates— in other words, as pure rote memory. The MLAT does not test linguistic interests, while the LAB tests a type of interest different from the one we discussed; it asks students to indicate, on a five-point scale, just how interested they are in learning a foreign language. In spite of these shortcomings, the two aptitude tests measure most of the distinct abilities and are very useful.

When neither the MLAT nor the LAB is available, one can roughly predict a child's achievement in language learning from IQ scores and various school grades normally available at schools. According to Pimsleur, language grades in class correlate .46 with IQ scores, .62 with average of school grades, and .72 with average of school grades + aptitude test (LAB).

Motivation

Reasons for learning languages   To be a good learner, a person has to have good reasons for learning languages, because learning is a long, expensive (sometimes), and arduous process. Reasons for learning may be utilitarian. Some professionals such as diplomats, missionaries, Peace Corps workers, intelligence personnel, anthropologists, and traders must have good speaking knowledge of the languages of people they deal with. Even tourists may find it useful to speak a little of the languages of the countries they visit.

For native speakers of other languages, English is a highly desirable, almost indispensable, second language to learn. English is often one of the official languages at international conferences. At the United Nations, English is one of the five official languages, with Chinese, Russian, French, and Spanish. There are more technical publications in English than in any other language. Furthermore, technical journals in non-English languages often carry abstracts in English. These hard facts explain why native English speakers are notoriously poor language learners while people from non-English-speaking countries, especially from small countries, are avid language learners.

There are other intangible or less utilitarian, albeit worthwhile, reasons for learning languages. Reluctant English-Canadians are coerced to learn French for the sake of promoting national unity, French being one of the two official languages. Equally reluctant Americans are required to study languages at schools for the sake of promoting international good will or becoming "well-educated" persons. Latin is learned not for its usefulness but because of the belief that it "trains minds." Learning Latin does not train minds any more than learning Swahili does. However, if Latin teaching focuses on the derivation of many Indo-European words from Latin roots, it may help students' vocabulary learning. We can also consider an apt point made by Goethe: "A man who does not know foreign languages is ignorant of his own."

Attitudes People may feel proud to speak one language, and ashamed to speak another. The extent to which the white man's language has prestige over the Bantu vernacular in Africa is illustrated by what a prominent chief in Transkei told Malherbe (1969, p. 43) when the chief encountered a plea for mother-tongue instruction: "Yes, it is good to learn one's mother tongue. If I know that, I am like a chicken pecking inside a hen-coop. But when I know the white man's language, I can soar like an eagle!"

Multilingual Israel is a good place to study the prestige values of different languages. Herman (1961) presented 84 students in Israel with a list of the major languages spoken in that country. The students rated the languages according to prestige value in their own eyes. The order from high to low prestige that emerged was: Hebrew, English, French, Russian, German, Arabic, Spanish, Yiddish, Polish, Ladino, Hungarian, Turkish, Rumanian, and Persian. How do these ratings correlate with achievement in language skills? Herman notes that in Israel when people are asked what languages they speak they tend to answer Hebrew, English, and Arabic in that order, even when Arabic is their most fluent language.

People also evaluate speakers of different dialects or languages. Lambert and his associates (1960) asked a sizeable group of English-Canadian university students (ECs) to evaluate the personalities of a series of speakers, actually male bilinguals speaking in either Canadian-style French or English. ECs rated the speakers in their EC guises as being better looking, taller, more intelligent, more dependable, kinder, more ambitious, and as having more character. This evaluational bias was just as apparent among judges who were bilinguals as among monolinguals.

The authors presented the same set of taped voices to a group of French-Canadian (FC) students whose age, social class, and educational level were matched to ECs. To the authors' surprise, FCs showed the same bias, evaluating the EC guises significantly more favorably than the FC guises on a whole series of traits. For example, they viewed the EC guises as being more intelligent, dependable, likeable, and as having more character! Only on two traits did they rate the FC guises more favorably, namely kindness and religiousness. Not only did the FC judges generally downgrade representatives of their own ethnic-linguistic group, they also rated the FC guises much more negatively than the EC judges had. This pattern of results may reflect a community-wide stereotype of FCs as being relatively second-rate people, a view apparently fully shared by certain subgroups of FCs.

Tucker and Lambert (1969) found a similar result with Southern blacks in the United States. The blacks have more favorable impressions of people who use Standard English than they do of those who speak with their own style. However, the blacks are more impressed with their own style than they are with the speech of educated, Southern-accented whites, or of blacks who became too "white" in their speech by exaggerating the non-black features and overcorrecting their speech.

Peal and Lambert (1962) noted that 10-year-old French-English bilingual children and their parents had a more sympathetc attitude toward English speakers than did monolinguals.

All these studies indicate that attitudes may influence achievement in a second language, although the pattern of influence is not clear. Sometimes favorable attitudes may induce people to learn a language, and other times people may develop favorable attitudes to a language because of having learned it. Favorable attitudes may be a helpful influence when people learn a second language voluntarily. On the other hand, there have been many cases in history when the conquered, the vanquished, the weaker, a minority, are forced to learn the language of the conqueror, the victor, the stronger, or a majority. In those cases people may of necessity learn the conqueror's language in spite of all their unfavorable attitudes toward the language as well as toward its speakers.

Methods of teaching, and learning strategies

Older children and adults learning foreign languages will benefit a great deal from good teaching methods. There are three major approaches to teaching foreign languages (based on De Camp, 1969). The *translation*, or *indirect, method* is an old-fashioned method in which students learn the target language chiefly by translating from or to their native language.

The teacher, who is not a native speaker of the target language, lectures in the student's own language on the grammar of the target language. The teacher allows the students little or no opportunity to use the language, and seldom speaks it. Naturally, the students seldom learn to speak the language or to understand speech, though they may learn to read by this method.

The *direct method* arose as a revolt against the translation method. It is still practiced in commercial language schools such as Berlitz. The teacher, who is a native speaker of the target language, forbids the students to use anything but the target language from the beginning, and uses audio-visual aids, gestures, and stage props, instead of written material or translations. The teacher avoids grammatical explanations, but drills in oral skills. This method has been successful in helping students achieve oral mastery of the target language in a short time, but at high cost. There is no control of sentence patterns and the students are immediately exposed to the entire bewildering range of the vocabulary and syntax of the language. Older learners may find this method tedious and boring because it does not make full use of their already developed thinking power and knowledge of the world.

The *linguistic method* gained impetus in World War II, when a large number of students (military personnel) had to learn foreign languages rapidly. Some esoteric Asian languages that had seldom been seen or heard in Europe or America had to be taught. This method combines active practice in the language with careful control and grading of the grammatical patterns of the teaching material. The students learn the language rapidly and fairly accurately. The method teaches various aspects of the language in five stages.

Stage 1. Recognition: The student learns to discriminate between two similar but different utterances. Typically the difficulty is to make phonemic contrasts that do not apply in the student's mother tongue. For Spanish students learning English, a *minimal pair* (see Chapter 2) such as "beat : bit" has to be contrasted.

Stages 2 and 3. Imitation and Repetition: The student learns to imitate a single word in the context of a sentence, with appropriate gestures, facial expressions, and intonations. Students repeat it until their response is reduced to a motor habit.

Stage 4. Variation: In substitution drill, the student holds the basic structure of the sentence constant and substitutes new words of vocabulary, one at a time. In transformation drill, the vocabulary is constant, and the sentence is changed to different but related forms. In combination drill, two simple sentences are combined into a more complex pattern by a conjunction or a relative clause.

Stage 5. Selection: The student learns idiomatic use of particular expressions, such as the subtle distinction between "tall" and "high" and that between slang and formal language.

Recently there has been some testing and thinking about the so-called "two major theories" of language teaching (for example, Carroll, 1966). One theory, the audio-lingual habit theory, has three principles: (1) Since speech is primary and writing is secondary, the habits to be learned must be learned first of all as auditory-discrimination responses and speech responses. (2) Habits must be automatized as much as possible so that they can be called forth without conscious attention. (3) The automatization of habits occurs chiefly by practice, that is, by repetition.

The cognitive code-learning theory, on the other hand, says that learning is a process of acquiring conscious control of the phonological, grammatical, and lexical patterns as a body of knowledge. The theory attaches more importance to the learner's understanding of the structure of the foreign language than to facility in using that structure.

The audio-lingual method is none other than the method that has been used in the direct and the linguistic method, while the cognitive code-learning method is a modified grammar-translation method. A language is a rule-governed, patterned system, and adults learn better when they understand rules, or what and why they learn. On the other hand, a language is a well-learned skill, and a skill can be acquired best by drills. Hence, any foreign language teaching for older people should combine these two theories or methods.

Adults learning a second language lack many of the advantages children enjoy. But the picture is not altogether dismal. Adults have longer attention and memory spans than children; they can learn rules from grammar books and find words from dictionaries; and they can develop their own learning systems that suit their own needs, aptitude, backgrounds, and time available.

Sir Richard Burton claimed to have developed a system that enabled him to learn a language in only two months. Actually, he spent far more than two months on Arabic and Hindustani, which he learned to speak fluently. At any rate, what was his system?

First he bought a simple grammar and vocabulary and underlined the words and rules he felt should be remembered. Putting these books in his pocket, he studied them at every spare moment during the day, never working more than fifteen minutes at a time. By this method he was able to learn 300 words a week. When he acquired a basic vocabulary, he chose a simple story book and read it, marking with a pencil any new words he wanted to remember and going over these at least once a day. Then he went on to a more difficult book, at the same time learning the finer points of the grammar. When he came across a new sound not found in any of the other languages he knew, he trained his tongue by repeating it hundreds of times a day. . . . When native teachers were available, he claimed that he always learned the "swear words" first and laughingly said that after that the rest of the language was easy. (Farwell, 1963, p. 30)

Burton's system is eminently sensible. Our only regret is that, except on sounds, he does not elaborate on making use of language similarities.

To conclude, older people learning second languages require aptitude, motivation, good teaching method, and learning strategies (and hard work!).

STORAGE AND PROCESSING OF BILINGUAL INFORMATION

So far we have examined various practical problems bilinguals face in learning and using a second language. We now consider memory problems. Alternately using two languages, a bilingual faces a peculiar problem in storing and retrieving linguistic information. How does one keep one's two languages apart? How and when do two languages interfere with each other? These questions ask what happens in a bilingual's brain and are studied indirectly. They are of theoretical interest.

Coordinate and compound bilingualism

The linguist Weinreich (1953) identified two possible types of bilingualism, which may have relevance to the separated and fused uses of two languages. In the first type, interlingual translations such as "casa" and "house" are treated as separate signifiers (words) with separate significates (objects), as in Figure 7–1A. Here we have two parallel, or coordinate, systems. Separate language acquisition contexts lead to such coordinate systems: Language 1 (L_1) is learned at home, L_2 at school; L_1 from father, L_2 from mother; L_1 in Canada, L_2 in Spain, and so on. Coordinate bilinguals keep the meanings of translation-equivalents different in their two languages. For the compound type, one set of significates is associated with signifiers in both languages, as in Figures 7–1B. In this case, the speaker learns a second language with the help of the first language (through translation) in one context, and the two languages are fused: the meanings of translation equivalents are identical or similar.

The psychologists Ervin and Osgood (1954) suggested a simple experiment to demonstrate the difference between coordinate and compound bilinguals: the ratings on a semantic differential scale of the same words given in two languages may be closer in compound than in coordinate bilinguals.

Lambert, Havelka, and Crosby (1958) took up Osgood and Ervin's

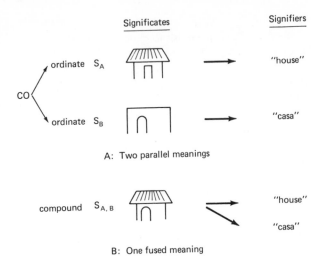

A: Two parallel meanings

B: One fused meaning

FIGURE 7–1   The relation between significates and signifiers in (A) coordinate bilingualism; (B) compound bilingualism.

suggestion. Coordinate bilinguals indeed showed a greater difference in the meanings of translated equivalents than did compound bilinguals on the four test words used. However, the coordinate bilinguals formed two subgoups: one subgroup learned the two languages in two geographically separate cultures and the other learned them in separate contexts but within one geographical region. Only the geographically separated subgroup showed the difference in ratings of meaning.

The experimenters compared the two types of bilingual on other measures, includindg facility in switching languages. The two types did not differ on this measure, even though the compound bilinguals, by definition, had learned their two languages in contexts that encourage translation and should therefore have been more facile at language switching.

Lambert and Rawlings (1969) set out to explore yet another difference: how compound and coordinate bilinguals work their way through chains of associations. The two types of bilingual subject had to find the core concept, "table," that integrates a set of associations: "chair," "food," "desk," "wood," and so on. If the list of words included words from two languages—"chaise," "food," "bois," "manger" . . .—would French-English compound bilinguals be more successful than coordinates in finding the solution?

Their experiment answered "yes" to the question. Here we must note that the definitions of compound and coordinate bilingualism in the published paper seem to have changed somewhat from the original definitions so that the comparison with other experiments is not easy. Special weight was given in this experiment to the age at which the two languages were acquired: compound bilinguals now had to have learned both languages in infancy and to have become fluent in both by the age of 6.

In ordinary situations, coordinate and compound bilinguals do not form a clear dichotomy, but form two poles of a continuum. Even Lambert and associates (1958) had difficulty in classifying some of their 32 subjects as one type of bilingual or the other. How often can we segregate language acquisition contexts into two neat types? Can one parent speak consistently in one language while the other parent speaks in the other language equally consistently? Many people may have learned a second language by the translation method in school (which is supposed to lead to compound bilingualism), but once they attain some proficiency in the second language, they may use their two languages in a coordinate fashion.

The factor that seems most important in keeping two language systems apart in a bilingual is a geographic-cultural distinction associated with the two languages. This factor is relevant both to the acquisition context and to the current use of the two languages. Recall that among the coordinate bilingual subjects only the subgroup who learned their two languages in different geographical contexts showed differences in the meanings of translation equivalents, judged on the semantic differential scale. Lambert and Rawling's new definition of compound bilinguals as those who have learned two languages fluently before age 6 practically assures that the two languages were learned within the same geographical-cultural context. Kolers's (1963) subjects, who were foreign students in the United States, gave distinct association patterns in their native tongue and in English. Ervin-Tripp's (1968) subjects, who were Japanese war brides in the United States, have different outlooks on life when they speak in Japanese and in English. These types of subject are likely to have learned English at school, probably by translation methods, and should be compound bilinguals by the original definition, but coordinate bilinguals by the new definition. Whatever labels may apply to them, their two languages are associated with two distinct geographical-cultural settings both in acquisition and in usage.

In short, the distinction between coordinate and compound bilingualisms looked promising when it was first described, but in the end, is neither clear-cut nor useful.

Linguistic independence and language switching

Penfield and Roberts (1959) hypothesized that the neurological systems underlying the two languages of a bilingual are functionally separated in such a way that when one is on, the other must be off. Penfield says that such a switch would be akin to a conditioned reflex: given a signal for language L_1, a bilingual will respond in that language. Many instances of linguistic interference (to be discussed below) indicate that there is not a simple switch for L_2 that is completely shut off while L_1 is on. In simultaneous translations, a translator has to switch on L_1 for reception while switching on L_2 simultaneously for speaking. One of the signals for switching on L_1 could be a word of L_1. In Taylor's bilingual continued word association tests (1971), subjects were allowed to give their first associations in either French or English to equal numbers of stimulus words in the two languages. If the English stimulus word turns on an "English switch" the first association would be expected to be in English. In many cases this happened, but not always. A switch, if it exists, is "leaky"—it is not on or off completely.

Macnamara and Kushnir (1971) propose a two-switch model of bilingual functioning—one switch to govern the selection of linguistic systems for input, the other for output. This model is applicable at least to simultaneous translation. The output switch is subject to voluntary control; the input switch is automatic. Though the input switch operates automatically, it does not work instantaneously; it takes an observable amount of time to operate. A mean figure for language switching in either input or output was close to 0.20 sec, which adds up to 0.40 sec if both are required. According to the authors, this finding implies that the input and output switches tend to operate sequentially and independently.

Kolers (1966a) obtained a similar switching time. He presented unilingual passages in English or in French, and mixed passages made up of some English and some French words. In one of the mixed passages the word order was in English, and in the second it was French, but the syntax of the two languages was similar. An example of a mixed passage with English word order is: "His horse, followed de deux bassets, faisait la terre resonner under its even tread . . . ." Bilingual subjects took longer to read aloud mixed passages than unilingual passages. The switching time, calculated by comparing times to read the mixed and the unilingual passages, was about 0.3 to 0.5 sec. Macnamara and Kushnir point out that Kolers's figures correspond to their own input-plus-output switching time.

To show that anticipation of switching reduces switching time, Macnamara (1966) presented two lists of money to one group of Irish-English bilinguals. Both lists were mixed in language, and involved the same number of switches, but the pattern of switches in one list was regular, while it was random in the other list. The random pattern took significantly longer to read aloud than did the regular one. In the regular switch pattern, subjects could anticipate a switch while speaking, and even though they did not know what the next response would be, they knew in which language it would be. Macnamara suggested that anticipation explains how bilinguals insert a word, a phrase, or a quotation from their other language in normal discourse without seeming to pause. An alternative explanation is that the switching pause is lost among the pauses of natural discourse.

Anticipation no doubt reduces language-switching time. However, switching time can be reduced for other reasons as well. In the case of normal discourse, bilinguals probably sometimes switch to the other language for a word or a phrase that is overlearned in that language or is more appropriately expressed in that language. A Japanese-English bilingual may switch to Japanese to refer to "shoji," which can be translated only into an unfamiliar, awkward, and ambiguous "a sliding paper screen door." The speaker may in fact save time by referring to "shoji" in Japanese, providing that the listener is also a Japanese-English bilingual. If I may add my own anecdotal evidence, I switch to Japanese (my primary-school language) when I count or do arithmetic. This switching occurs automatically, and sometimes I realize only in the middle of overt counting that I have made the switch. Introspectively speaking (!) no time is lost in switching, and no anticipation is involved. Contrary to Macnamara's contention, an output may not always be under voluntary control, and an input switch may not always operate automatically. We multilinguals have experiences in which we have to make some conscious adjustment when we are addressed in an unexpected language, even though it is a familiar one. Sometimes this involves a conscious search among various possibilities.

Among the factors that trigger one language system rather than the other in everyday use may be the topic, listener, or other environmental context, such as locality, that is associated with a particular language.

Ervin-Tripp (1968) set out to test the above observation. She asked Japanese war brides in the United States to explain or describe in English a set of 14 topics. The topics designed to be associated with English were the husband's work and leisure activities, American housekeeping, American cooking, and shopping for food and clothing in the United States. Another set of topics was designed to be more Japanese: Japanese festivals, Japanese New Year's Day, Japanese cooking and housekeeping, the Doll Festival, and street storytellers. The last two topics in each set were accompanied by photographs of the event to be described. The combination of a Japanese receiver and a Japanese topic, even in the American setting, almost always demands the use of Japanese in a normal situation. The effect of artificially violating this rule was that the women's speech was disrupted. They borrowed more Japanese words, had a more disturbed syntax, were less fluent, and had more frequent hesitation pauses than when discussing the American topics.

Linguistic interference

Bilinguals sometimes have to fight a tendency for the phonological, lexical, and syntactic systems of one language to intrude on those of another. Usually the dominant language intrudes upon the weaker. Also topics that are strongly associated with L_1 are not easy to talk about in L_2, and in talking about them L₁ may intrude on L₂. The degree of similarity between the two languages does not seem to be related to the amount of interference. However, to some extent the types of interference may be predicted by examining the similarities and differences between the two languages. The followng examples of interference have been actually observed, but they might have been predicted by comparing the phonological, lexical, and syntactic systems of two languages.

We can almost always tell foreigners by their foreign accents, which constitute the most glaring phonological interference from the dominant language to the weaker language. Sometimes foreigners' accents reveal their mother tongues. A French-English bilingual may pronounce English words starting with /h/ such as "house" in the French manner, /aus/. With many Chinese learners of English, /l/ can occur only before vowels, /r/ only after vowels. Thus, one lecturer, in trying to say "Rice grows near the river," came out with "Lice glows near the liver" (Chao, 1963). In rhythm or stress, a French-English bilingual may use a French stress pattern in English: "I think só" instead of "I thínk so." In word usage, Leopold's daughter Hildegard used an expression, "She will laugh me out" from the German "auslachen" (sneer). As for syntactic intrusion, Hildegard used the German word order in "Which grade is man when man nine years old is?"

According to Weinreich (1953), "The more numerous the mutually exclusive forms and patterns in each, the greater is the learning problem and the potential area of interference" (p. 1). This is not a helpful statement. Consider Japanese and English; the types and amount of interference will not be symmetrical between the two languages. For example, Japanese speakers learning English will have great difficulty and serious interferences in mastering the English sound system, because their own language involves fewer sounds and simpler sound combination rules (for example, no consonant clusters) than the English sound system. English speakers would not experience comparable difficulties in mastering the Japanese sound system, although they may with other linguistic aspects. Sometimes subtle rather than distinct differences can cause persistent interference. For example, Germans may master /θ/, which their language lacks, but may persist in pronouncing /dʒ/ in "judge" close to /tʃ/ in "church."

Storage and processing of bilingual information

The problems of coordinate bilingualism, language switching, and linguistic interference all suggest that the two language systems are stored separately in a bilingual's memory, but that separation is not always complete. Let us examine more direct tests of the degree of separation and of the types of word that are stored separately.

Common vs. separate storage Kolers (1963) tested two alternate hypotheses: (1) Experiences are coded once, in common, and each of the bilingual's languages taps this common store. (2) Events are coded specifically and separately in the language in which they are experienced. To test the two hypotheses, he designed intra- and interlanguage word association tests to give to Spanish-English, Thai-English, and German-English bilingual students studying in the United States. There were four types of word association—intralanguage or common language, with English stimulus words requiring English responses (E-E) or Spanish stimuli requiring Spanish responses (S-S); inter-language word associations, English-Spanish (E-S) and Spanish-English (S-E).

About 55 percent of the bilingual subjects' responses were unique and not shared between their two languages, while only about 20 percent were shared responses. Slightly over 10 percent of responses were scored as either native or English. The response "blanco" to "house" in the English-Spanish test differed from the response "window" to "house" in the English-English test, and they were scored as "unique" responses, while answers of "reina" and "queen" to "king" are translations and were scored as "shared" responses.

Kolers concluded that experiences and memories of various kinds are not stored in common in some supralinguistic form, but are tagged and stored separately according to the language a bilingual uses to define the experience subjectively. Compound and coordinate bilinguals did not differ in their association patterns.

There seem to be particular kinds of stimulus word that evoke unique responses. In the above experiment Kolers found that abstract words ("freedom," "justice") evoked more unique responses than concrete words ("table," "lamb"), but less than words of feeling ("hate," "jealousy"). In Ervin-Tripp's (1968) word-association test with Japanese war brides, she used culturally loaded stimulus words, which evoked unique responses in Japanese and in English. Compare the Japanese-English bilinguals' responses to the same stimulus words given in the two languages in Table 7–1.

Cognates and similar words in related languages also may evoke common responses. Let us examine this possibility, which would suggest that words may be stored in part according to their form rather than their language.

The word similarity factor in bilingualism Some words from related languages are similar because of both their common ancestry and the extensive loaning of words over the years. The degree of similarity in words ranges from very high to very low. "L'address" and "la cigarette" are examples of French and English words that are practically the same in pronunciation and in written forms. At the other extreme, words with no

TABLE 7–1   Japanese-English Bilinguals' Responses to Stimulus Words from the Two Languages

MOON		NEW YEAR'S DAY	
Japanese	*English*	*Japanese*	*English*
moon viewing	sky	pine decoration	new clothes
zebra-grass	rocket	rice cake	party
full-moon	cloud	feast	holiday
cloud		kimono	
		seven-spring herbs	
		shuttlecock	
		tangerine	
		footwarmer	
		friends	

Based on data from Ervin-Tripp, 1968.

apparent similarity are: "acheter" (buy) and "maintenant" (now). Since our interest is in apparent phonetic and visual similarities between French words and their English equivalents (regardless of how they might have originated), let us henceforth use the term "similar words" rather than "cognates."

The question is whether such different degrees of similarity between words from two related languages influence the speech behavior of bilinguals and language learners. Specifically, are similar words more similar in associative meaning structures and meaningfulness than dissimilar words?

Taylor (in press) tested the above question in continued word-association tests given to English-French bilingual children and adults. Subject 1 (child) responded to "la carotte" and "carrot" as in Figure 7–2. For this bilingual, the first associate was the same in the two languages, and there was a high degree of overlap in the remaining associations. The numbers of associations produced in the two languages were the same. Both children and adult subjects showed such a pattern of response, namely more similar responses to the similar than to the dissimilar stimulus words as measured on the three characteristics scored. Of the three, the overlap was the most sensitive in revealing differences in response to the two types of stimulus word. Concrete stimulus words, independent of their similarities, produced more similar response patterns.

Intralanguage associative link   In a bilingual's memory, are intra-language associative links stronger than interlanguage links? Is an English word more strongly linked to another English word than it is to a French

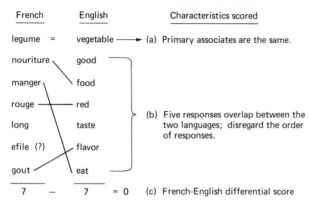

FIGURE 7–2   One subject's associations to "la carotte" and "carrot." (From Taylor, in press.)

word? To answer this question, Taylor (1971) gave continued word-association tests to English-French bilingual students, using an equal number of English and French stimulus words. Subjects were asked to produce as many associates as possible to each word in 90 sec. There were five language-switching instructions to the subjects: unilingual (stick to one language); free switching (switch languages when you wish); switch on every fifth response word; switch on every third response word; and switch on every word. The reasoning behind the design was that if words were organized by languages, the unilingual condition would evoke the largest number of responses. Free switching would evoke at least as many responses as in the unilingual condition, because subjects would switch only when ready, or when they had temporarily exhausted the supply of words from one language, thus not disrupting the organization of word groups by languages.

The free switching indeed produced as many words as the unilingual condition, while in the other switching conditions the more frequent the switches, the fewer were the responses. More direct evidence of strong intralanguage links is that the average switching probabilities in free switching between languages were low, well below 0.5. The switching probability would be 0.5 if the probability of remaining in the current language were equal to the probability of switching to the other language. In short, subjects preferred to remain in the current language rather than to switch into the other language.

Such strong intralanguage links may be explained by the fact that a word is learned and used in the context of its own language. In other words, a bilingual speaker does not learn or speak "Une red pomme is délicieuse," but "A red apple is delicious" or "Une pomme rouge est délicieuse." Nor is the speaker, in ordinary situations, likely to switch languages from one sentence to another. Thus, some separation in the storage of words from different languages is efficient for retrieval, whether there be two or more languages, or whether a speaker is a coordinate or compound bilingual.

Are words coded by meaning or by language?   The following experiments show that the meanings rather than the forms of words are perceived, so long as the bilingual subjects' task is reception and not overt production. Kolers (1966b) showed that repetition of items in translation is just as helpful for recall as repetition in the same language. Presenting "fold" twice and its French translation "pli" twice had the same effect on the recall of either word as presenting either one four times. "Fold" and "pli" neither look alike nor sound alike, and hence subjects did not see and store the words individually as visual or phonetic forms; they perceived and stored them in terms of their meanings. Information repeated in different languages is as well retained as information repeated in a single language.

In another experiment that was described earlier in the chapter, Kolers (1966a) prepared unilingual passages either in English or in French, and mixed passages that were made up of some English and some French words. French-English bilinguals had almost identical scores on comprenhension tests following silent reading of the unilingual and mixed passages.

In contrast to the above experiments, Kintsch and Kintsch (1969) *forced* their bilingual subjects to give different responses to a word and to its translation. They had German-English and English-German bilinguals learn eight-item paired-associate lists with four English and four German adjectives as stimuli and the digits 1–8 as responses. They used four German and four English translation equivalents as stimuli for the experimental list, and eight unrelated words—four German and four English—for the control list. The experimental list might include "schwarz–5" and its English translation "black–4." The control list might include "luftig (airy)–5," and an unrelated English adjective "murky–4." The requirement to make explicit distinctions between the members of translated word pairs on the experimental condition produced an increase of 53 percent in the subjects' error rate. With such an experimental requirement, they could not simply use word meaning independently of the language in which the word was presented; they had a harder time learning translated words than unrelated words both because of interlingual confusions and because they had to use special coding operations to avoid such confusions.

Perhaps the following experiment by Kintsch (1970) may shed further light on the question of whether words are coded by meaning or by language in a bilingual's memory. He required bilingual subjects to recognize

German and English nouns in three ways. Group 1 subjects identified each item either as new, as repeated in the same language, or as repeated in the other language (they responded either to semantic cues or to language cues). Group 2 subjects responded YES only if an item was repeated in the same language (language cue alone). Group 3 responded YES even when items were repeated with a language change (semantic cue alone). Performance in terms of percentage of correct responses was poorest for Group 1 and about equal for the other two groups. Group 2 subjects were unable to disregard an earlier presentation of an item in another language. Group 3 subjects were unable to treat translated words like non-translated words. Kintsch concluded that bilingual subjects can code words either in terms of language-specific cues or in terms of general semantic cues, as the task requires. But they cannot completely disregard either set of cues; language-specific cues intrude when they are concentrating upon word meanings, and word meanings interfere with recognition of language-specific forms.

From studies on the effects of brain damage or electrical stimulation of exposed cortex on bilingual speech, Penfield and Roberts, (1959) observed that there are no separate brain areas that subserve different languages. Thus, within the same neural area(s), words from two languages may be stored by language, by meaning, or by form and can be retrieved by cues appropriate to any storage method. Since two languages are coded within the same area(s), intrusion of one language code into another or one meaning code into another in certain conditions is possible.

Figure 7–3 is my attempt at visualizing word organization in a bilingual's memory. To make the model simple, word organization in a multilingual's memory is not described. In Figure 7–3, E_1 "table," is more closely associated with E_2 "chair," and less strongly with E_3 "leg," all within one language, English. "Table" is at the same time associated interlingually with f_1 "la table" or f_2 "la chaise" by meaning and by form. The association networks in English and in French to "table" and "la table" respectively may be similar, but need not be always identical; hence E_1—E_2—E_3, but f_1—f_2—f_4. In discrete interlanguage association tests, E_1 may evoke f_1, but E_2 may evoke f_3 instead of f_2. Word organization in bilinguals' memory is necessarily more complex than in monolinguals, because words have to be organized not only by meaning but also by language. Further, there are more words to be stored in the bilingual's brain. But thanks to an efficient organization, interference between languages is not rampant in ordinary situations, especially when there are distinct contextual cues associated with different languages.

Segalowitz (in press), after reviewing a body of literature, concludes that there is only one semantic system in the brain. It serves all the languages of the multilingual, and the languages of the multilingual become

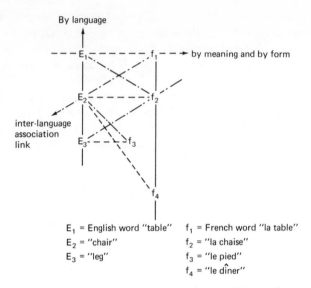

E_1 = English word "table" f_1 = French word "la table"
E_2 = "chair" f_2 = "la chaise"
E_3 = "leg" f_3 = "le pied"
    f_4 = "le dîner"

FIGURE 7–3   A model of word organization in a bilingual's memory.

functionally separate only at the speech-production end of the language system. This conclusion is attractive because of its simplicity. But as with everything else in life, things may not be as simple as we would like to have them.

Speech production must reflect some aspects of the stored semantic system. Why do bilinguals experience conflicts in speaking about some topics but not about other topics? As we have seen, some concepts (culturally loaded; abstract) are coded uniquely only in one language and are not easily talked about in another language. Further, if there is only one semantic system for two languages, why do association patterns for some stimulus words vary according to the language?

It is true that sentences expressing the same proposition from two languages, however different they may appear on the surface, can be translated into each other. However, note that different numbers and types of concept are combined in different ways to express the more-or-less same proposition in Chinese and English in Figure 7–4. Can we consider that the semantic systems of concepts in the two languages are one and the same?

Recently, Obler and associates (1975) reported some neurological evidence that words from two languages are processed somewhat differently. Ten normal, right-handed subjects who were fluent in Hebrew and English took dichotic listening tests. The words presented to the two ears were from one language, but different words were given to the left and the right ear.

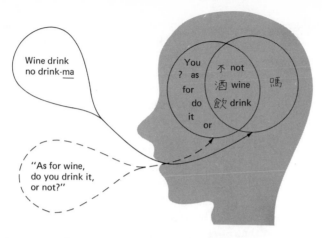

FIGURE 7–4   A model of a Chinese-English bilingual's word storage and sentence production. Most words, but not all, are stored separately for the two languages. Note the differences in surface structure between the Chinese sentence and its "equivalent" English sentence. A more natural English sentence would be "Do you drink wine or not?"

The left–right ear differences for one language (not always the same language) were greater than those for the other language in seven out of ten subjects.

A bilingual's semantic system must be more complex than that of a monolingual: some aspects of the semantic system must be unique to each of the two languages. How extensive the unique aspects are depends on the kind of relationship between the two languages—the more separated they are linguistically, culturally, and geographically, the more extensive the unique aspects must be.

Sentence processing   "Questo èssere molto bello pittura Mechelàngelo." This is a sentence spoken by an Italian guide showing foreigners around churches and museums (Hall, 1966). If one has never studied Italian, how would one comprehend this sentence? The guide is showing off a picture, and all interpretation must be guided by this context. Thinking of my own comprehension (as a non-Italian-speaker), I look for any recognizable words. A few of the words in the sentence are decipherable because I know other languages related to Italian—"molto" should mean "very"; "bello," "beauty"; "pittura," perhaps "picture"? Mechelàngelo is of course Michelangelo. Although I do not know Italian syntax, knowing these words and the context in which the sentence was spoken, I can say that the sentence is about a very beautiful picture by Michelangelo. The sentence in fact says literally, "This be very beautiful picture [by] M." In this sentence, grammatical gender is lost, the infinitive is used instead of an inflected form of the verb, and the preposition *di* "by, of" is not used before M.

The guide used a simplified syntax for the benefit of foreigners. Pidgin English, greatly simplified English, was born partly because English-speakers talked to native people in "baby talk," and partly because natives attempting to talk English injected their own syntax and at the same time simplified the English syntax. An example of Chinese pidgin English is: "Too much dust table topside" /tumətʃi dəst tebəl tápsaid/. To paraphrase, "There is a lot of dust on the table" (Hall, p. 85). Another example: "No can pei dog chicken bone" ("[You] can't give (pay?) [a] dog [a] chicken-bone" (p. 81). The point here is that when knowledge of the foreign language is limited, both speakers and listeners use minimum syntax, and the message is conveyed mainly by salient content words and by context. The pattern is similar to that of speech between adults and very young children (Chapter 6).

Even after students of a foreign language have learned a little about the syntax of the target language, there may be a period in which they process foreign sentences in their native syntax. We have seen in this chapter that children acquiring two languages simultaneously had a (temporary) tendency to utter sentences in their dominant syntax. In a study by Lance (1969), adults showed the usual array of problems arising from processing English through their native Spanish syntactic rules. However, the author made the important observation that from one-third to two-thirds of the deviant features of the foreign students' speech could not be traced to identifiable features of Spanish. Ervin-Tripp (1973) also found that a large percentage of adult (French-English?) bilinguals' errors had no clear relation to French. She considers that some of these errors are slips of one sort or another; others are learner's simplifications. But it is not clear how to regard "slips" in this kind of analysis. The errors must come from some phase of the language processing. To call them "slips" is merely to admit ignorance of what the processing problem is.

In the light of the above observations, how are we to take Ervin-Tripp's following suggestion?

The assumption is that in [foreigners] learning to interpret English sentences the basic processing heuristics which permit identification of subject, verb, and object, and modifier-head units must be developed very early to permit even primitive communication to take place. In these respects the adult seems like the child learning his first language (1973, p. 124).

This emphasis on the priority of syntax seems to conflict with much of the evidence adduced above, and with current ideas on first- as well as second-language learning. The syntactic analysis Ervin-Tripp describes may occur in intermediate or advanced learners. The more complex foreign sentences are, the more analysis must learners go through.

We do not know much about how a bilingual processes sentences from his two unrelated languages. Chinese and English sentences appear very different on the surface, as shown in Figure 7–4. How do such differences influence processing of sentences from the two languages by Chinese-English or English-Chinese bilinguals? As discussed in Chapter 4, what is conveyed in any utterance is a concept structure or proposition. Hence sentence processing in all languages may be basically similar. This observation does not mean that surface structure differences are totally irrelevant: they may affect efficiency of extracting concept structures, and they may affect the nuances of messages beyond their basic propositions.

SUMMARY AND CONCLUSIONS

A bilingual speaks two (or more) languages, dialects, or styles that involve varying degrees of phonetic, semantic, and syntactic differences. One of the bilingual's two languages usually is a native tongue, the other a second language.

Some children acquire two languages simultaneously in infancy as naturally as other children acquire one language. Bilingual children have temporary language mix-ups, and are not aware of dealing with two languages. Eventually, the two languages are segregated, and one of them becomes the child's dominant language. Unused languages are quickly forgotten, but may leave residues in the mind.

A second language may be acquired after the first has been established, either in an immersion program or as a school subject. All things considered, young children enjoy neurological and attitudinal advantages over adults in learning languages.

The effects of bilingual education on intelligence, school achievement, and stuttering were once considered unfavorable. Subsequent, better-controlled studies show favorable results. In some studies bilingual children score higher than monolingual children in cognitive flexibility and creative thinking, perhaps due to their two perspectives about things and their ability to detach concepts from words and languages.

Bilinguals seem to adopt different outlooks on life when they speak different languages. In sentence-completion tests, Japanese war brides in the United States showed more self-assertive content in English than in Japanese. However, the basic personality may or may not change in speaking two languages; the question has not been experimentally tested.

Older children and adults with high aptitude (good memory, sensitivity to grammar, and a few other distinct abilities) and high motivation (strong utilitarian reasons for learning) are good language learners.

People's evaluation of languages or dialects and their speakers reflects a stereotype of these speakers held in a community. People's attitudes toward foreign languages and speakers of these languages have complex relations with learning achievement.

We have discussed three teaching methods: translation (the target language is approached through the native tongue); direct (the spoken target language is used exclusively); and linguistic (through principles of linguistics). A method that combines the audio-lingual habit theory (mechanical drills) and the cognitive code-learning theory (understand rules) may be the best.

The foremost theoretical question in bilingualism is how a bilingual keeps his two languages apart. Does learning two languages in a common context lead to compound bilingualism, and in separate contexts, to coordinate bilingualism? Two languages may be kept separate in a bilingual if they are associated with two distinct geographical-cultural settings, regardless of how the two languages are acquired.

Switching languages takes time, as shown in such tasks as reading mixed-language passages aloud and emitting words in continued word-association tests. Switching to overlearned items in another language may not require time. Switching is not always complete, so that a bilingual experiences intrusions of the dominant language into the weaker language.

A bilingual must have a complex semantic system, storing some concepts uniquely according to each of the two languages and other concepts in common for both languages, depending on the concepts. Words from the two languages can be organized either by language or by meaning, but the two organizing methods may not be completely segregated in some cases.

In sentence processing, a "bilingual" with severely limited knowledge of foreign syntax relies on salient words to get the sentence meaning. In production, the speaker arranges the foreign salient words in native syntax at first, but after gaining some knowledge, may syntactically analyze complex foreign sentences and produce foreign sentences with the correct syntax.

8

Language and Understanding the World

Language is the parent, not the child, of thought.

Oscar Wilde

The mutual interdependence of thought and word makes it evident that languages are not really means of representing already known truth: they are means of discovering hitherto unknown truth.

Humboldt, 1905, p. 27

For thought is a bird of space, that in a cage of words may indeed unfold its wings but cannot fly.

Kahlil Gibran, 1960

Language disguises the thought; so that from the external form of the clothes one cannot infer the form of the thought they clothe, because the external form of the clothes is constructed with quite another object than to let the form of the body be recognized.

Wittgenstein, 1933, p. 63

Language was given us to enable us to conceal our thoughts.

Russell, 1940, p. 27

If one asks me, I know; but if I want to explain to someone who asks me, I do not know.

St. Augustine

A country may be overrun by an armed host but it is only conquered by the establishment of fortresses. Words are the fortresses of thought. They enable us to realize our dominion over what we have already overrun in thought; to make every intellectual conquest the base of operations for others.

Sir William Hamilton, 1788–1856

. . . We see this complex process of the inter-action of language and thought actually taking place under our eyes. The instrument makes possible the product, the product refines the instrument.

Sapir, 1921, p. 17

These noted philosophers, writers, and linguists think that there is an intimate relation between language and thought. They do not all agree on what the relationship is. In this chapter we shall examine various relations between language and thought. When does language facilitate thinking, allowing it to be more complex, efficient, and accurate? When does it inhibit or misguide thinking? In the first two sections we ask these questions in terms of speakers of one language—first with children and then with speakers in general. In the third section, we ask whether those who speak different languages think differently, as they should if thought processes are influenced by language.

LANGUAGE AND SPEECH IN COGNITIVE DEVELOPMENT

Does language determine, guide, or reflect cognitive development? In Chapter 6 we suggested that cognitive development underlies children's acquisition of language. Now we ask: what roles do language and speech play in the cognitive development of normal children? To understand this question better, we have to contrast the development of normal children with that of deaf children who have little language. We must also consider animals with no language of the human kind.

First we discuss categorizing and labeling, fundamental aspects of language. In confronting the world any living organism must categorize. Otherwise the world events impinging on its sense organs would merely create the "blooming, buzzing confusion" that William James (1890) thought was the perceptual world of the newborn child. Certain categories come already built into the organism or are very quickly learned. Infants as young as 1–4 months can discriminate better across than within phoneme boundaries (Eimas et al., 1971). Of course, human children acquire thousands of categories as they grow up, and many of these categories are labeled by their language.

Speech in problem-solving

How do language and speech influence a child's cognitive activities? Here are several experiments that attempt to answer this question. More specifically, researchers in Switzerland, in the United States, and in the Soviet Union try to answer the questions: How does labeling and verbalizing influence the solution of Piaget's "conservation problems" (see Figure 6–1) and of other perceptual-cognitive problems? Recall that solution of conservation problems involves the "operational" level of thinking—two or more relationships must be varied simultaneously. The principle of conservation holds for concepts of number, quantity, space, and time.

The Geneva School The associates of Piaget, Inhelder, and co-workers (1966) in Switzerland point out that there are differences in the speech used by conservers (children who solve conservation problems) and nonconservers. For example, to describe one doll made of more clay than another doll, the conservers used relational terms—"One has more than the other," while the nonconservers simply stated that one has got a big bit, the other has a small bit. The conservers used more highly differentiated language. To describe pencils of different length and thickness they used pairs of opposites such as long/short or fat/thin. Nonconservers used one term to refer successively to two different dimensions (big/small; then large/ small). But nonconservers could obey the examiner's instructions that employed the linguistic structures found in the conservers' utterances. In other words, the nonconservers' comprehension of instructions was as good as that of the conservers, even though their produced utterances were not as advanced.

Inhelder and co-workers found that specific linguistic training on the use of relational terms made children express their arguments more clearly. For example, instead of saying there was more to drink in one glass, the children now explained that liquid goes up higher in a narrow glass. But verbal training did not by itself bring about solutions to the problems.

The Harvard Project A study by Sonstroem (1966) at Harvard shows that verbalizing can influence the learning of conservation problems. Her subjects were 81 first-graders whose median age was 7. She used three experimental conditions in different combinations. We discuss only the conditions where manipulation and labeling were combined.

Her experimental procedures were, in her own words, as follows.

After S had made a pencil (out of a clay ball), he was asked "which one is the longest?" If he indicated that the pencil was the longer, E then said, "Now tell me which one is the fattest?" If the child indicated the ball, E said, "O.K., the pencil is the longest, but the ball is the fattest; now tell me, does one of them have more clay than the other or do they have the same?" After the child had given his judgment, E said, "O.K., you told me the pencil is the longest and the ball is the fattest. Now I want you to take this long pencil and make it just as fat as the ball for me." As the child rolled the pencil back into a ball (which he usually did to make it just as fat), E asked him several times, "Is it as fat yet?" and "Is it still longer?" When the child asserted that it was just as fat, he was asked to judge the relative amounts of the two pieces again. In the second half of these trials, when S made a pencil from the other ball, he was asked to "make the fat ball just as long as the pencil," instead of the other way around as in the first half. (p. 217)

Manipulation and labeling were highly successful in inducing conservation; but each of these worked only when the other was present. By offering the child manipulation, the experimenter was encouraging "enactive" (action-dependent or centered) representation; and by offering verbal labels for compensating attributes the experimenter was encouraging symbolic representation. In short, the child was made to cognize the clay physically and verbally, instead of only perceptually.

The Russian studies   To Russian investigators such as Luria (1961), speech is an important factor that influences the perception and behavior of children from an early age. Moreover, speech affects children differently at different ages. The Russian investigators use problems other than conservation as perceptual-cognitive tasks for children. In one experiment, two kinds of visual stimulus are given to a young child. One is a red circle on a gray background, as shown in Figure 8–1A. The other is a green circle on a yellow background, as in Figure 8–1B. The child is asked to squeeze a balloon with the right hand if A appears, and with the left hand if B appears. A child older than some age between 3 and 5 will form the correct response habit after a while.

In a control experiment, a third stimulus—a red circle on a yellow ground (Figure 8–1C)—and a fourth, D—a green circle on a gray ground—are given to the child. The child will squeeze with the right hand for the red circle, C, and the left for the green D, regardless of their backgrounds. In short, the stronger element in the visual compound is shown to be the circle.

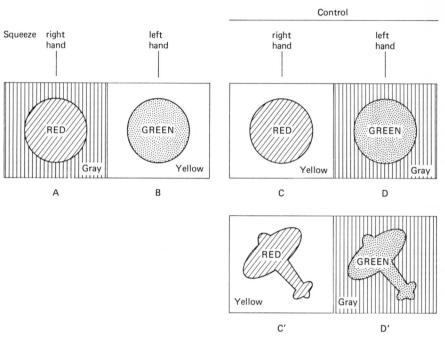

FIGURE 8–1   Visual stimuli with various figure (circle or plane)–ground (square) relationships. (After Luria, 1961.)

Now, by means of speech, Luria's associate alters the relative natural strength of the two elements, circle and ground. The experimenter draws attention to the grounds on which the circles are set, and asks the child to squeeze the balloon with the right hand for the gray *ground* and with the left for the yellow. Children of different ages respond differently to this verbal command. Children aged 3–4 show no stable adaptation of their total responses, and still react to the circle, the stronger element in the visual compound. Performance of children aged 4–5 is also comparatively unstable. Children aged 5–7 begin reacting to the background color, which verbal command has made the stronger element in the compound.

With more "meaningful" verbal instructions, the effect of speech in modifying the relative strength of the visual element appears at earlier ages. In another experiment, the circles are replaced by colored airplanes on the same gray or yellow grounds (refer back to Figure 8–1C', D'). The child is asked to squeeze the balloon with the right hand for a red airplane on a yellow ground (because "the plane can fly when the sun is shining and the sky is yellow"), and with the left hand for a green airplane on a gray ground (because "when it's rainy the plane can't fly and has to be stopped").

These meaningful verbal instructions elevate the otherwise weaker background element to the stronger role in the visual compound, and even 3–4-year-old children begin reacting to the backgrounds.

The child may need to replace the regulatory action of the external signal by a *self*-generated verbal command. The child aged 3–4 says "Go!" in response to each flash of light and simultaneously presses the bulb. This self-generated verbal command eliminates the diffuseness of the motor processes, strictly coordinates the movements with the signals, and imparts to them a distinct and organized character.

Vygotsky, another Russian psychologist, points out the usefulness of "egocentric" speech (talking to oneself) in children's mental development. Although his book *Thought and Language* was published in English only in 1962, his work was done in the early part of this century. Vygotsky and his associates could observe that young children would talk to themselves more than usual when confronted with frustrating situations. For instance, a child getting ready to draw would suddenly find that there was no paper, or no pencil of the color needed. The child would try to grasp and to remedy the situation by saying: "Where's the pencil? I need a blue pencil. Never mind, I'll draw with the red one and wet it with water; it will become dark and look like blue." Thus egocentric speech, besides being a means of expression and of release of tension, soon becomes an instrument of thought in the proper sense—in seeking and planning the solution of a problem.

An illuminating accident occurred during one of their experiments: A boy of 5½ was drawing a streetcar when the point of his pencil broke. He tried, nevertheless, to finish the circle of a wheel, pressing down the pencil very hard, but nothing showed on the paper except a deep colorless line. The boy muttered to himself, "It's broken," put aside the pencil, took watercolors instead, and began drawing a *broken* streetcar, continuing to talk to himself from time to time about the change in his picture. Vygotsky points out the similarity between what happened above and the well-known developmental sequence in the naming of drawings. A small child draws first, then decides what it is that has been drawn; at a slightly older age, the drawing is named when it is half done; and finally the child decides beforehand what to draw.

American studies on discrimination problems   Blank (1974) contends that language may not be called upon for dealing with concepts based on the familiar world of things, but it is called upon in dealing with concepts whose identity derives from the less tangible world of time. Blank and her associates found that preschool-age children can easily distinguish between one and two circles (or any other similarly organized stimuli), regardless of whether or not they apply language to the situation. These same children, however, cannot differentiate between one and two flashes of light if they do not apply the relevant verbal labels. The child's task is to discriminate between lights (1 sec in duration) that are flashed once or twice; there is an interval of 0.5 sec between the two successive flashes. The child is told to "pick the one that goes like this [pointing to the one flash] and not the one that goes like this [pointing to the two flashes]."

The children's performance on this task is quite remarkable. If they do not apply the appropriate verbal labels, they cannot perceive the difference between the stimuli. If they are taught to apply a differentiating label ("one" to the first light, "two" to the second, and so on), they can solve it.

Distinctiveness is lacking in the above stimuli. That is, each flash is identical, whether the total sum of flashes is one, two, or three. A differentiating label such as a number allows the children to retain information that enables them to distinguish temporally between the perceptions.

We have seen four approaches to the relation between speech and cognition. The Geneva School, spearheaded by Piaget, considers language as a part of a child's general symbolic functioning. Language may develop in parallel with cognition, and aids cognition in some cases but is not one of its constituent elements. A study at Harvard shows that labeling, plus the child's own manipulation of the test material, can induce solutions to conservation problems. The Russian investigators consider that speech, either given by an examiner or self-generated, can alter the child's perceptual field profoundly, and may then regulate the child's behavior. One American study also shows that labeling is important in a time-discrimination task. The Russian School, and Blank in the United States, seem to attribute a more active role to speech as a shaper of perception and behavior than does the Geneva School. The effects of language on thought probably depend on the circumstances.

Thinking without language

Deaf children How do deaf children without verbal language develop their cognitive skills? This question is very relevant to the question whether language determines cognitive development. If deaf children develop cognitive skills normally, then language cannot determine cognitive development.

Furth, in the United States, investigated this relationship extensively. In one of his studies (1961) he investigated how deaf children grasped the concepts of "sameness," "symmetry," and "opposition." To investigate "opposition acquisition," the experimenter selects four from a set of eight graduated wooden discs (hidden from the subject's view) and displays them on the table in front of the subject. If the experimenter next picks the largest of the four, the subject's task is to discover that the approved response is to pick the smallest. A subject who succeeds in this task is given "opposition transfer" to volume, length, and so on. Furth tested a large number of hearing and deaf children aged 7–12. Most deaf children in America do not learn English—written or spoken—until rather late in life, and in most cases English is never adequately acquired.

The deaf children performed as well as the hearing children on the first two concepts, "sameness" and "symmetry," but performed more poorly than the hearing children at all age levels on "opposition." Furth thinks that verbal language gives the hearing children an advantage over the deaf by the constant use of opposites. The concept of opposite may be a pseudoconcept (Vygotsky, 1962): behavior, mostly verbal, that gives the impression of mastery of a certain concept, but that under close scrutiny turns out to be mainly determined by frequent linguistic associations. Thus, a child may use the word "sufficient" in many correct contexts but, when urged to distinguish "full" and "sufficient," may reveal a relative ignorance of the mature concept.

The deaf were markedly inferior to the hearing children in other tasks. For example, Oléron and Herren (1961) in France tested deaf children's performance on conservation problems. The authors devised a series of pictures to serve as equivalents of the verbal responses "heavier," "same," "lighter," for the conservation of weight, and "more" or "less" for the conservation of volume. After training with these pictures, the age at which 50 percent of the hearing subjects succeeded on the weight problem was 8.5, and with the quantity-of-liquid problem, 10.5. The corresponding age levels of success for the deaf subjects were about 6 years later. The retardation of 6 years is serious enough to prompt Oléron to comment that Piaget's theory does not emphasize sufficiently the role of language in the emergence of logical behavior, particularly in the subordination of perceptual to conceptual conditions.

Furth (1964a) made a qualitative investigation of the deaf children's failure to solve conservation problems. Many more 8-year-old deaf children than 6-year-old hearing children made hesitant and inconsistant responses. Furth interpreted this as a possible clue that the older deaf children felt uncomfortable about the response and were really closer to the correct solution than a mere summary of failures or successes would indicate. He judged that experience with the physical world, rather than language or formal training, determines in part the age at which children pass from a perceptual to a logical judgment on many Piaget-type experiments. Deaf children rarely enjoy as much cognitive stimulation and social-emotional acceptance as do hearing children. They are usually neglected in some respects. Thus deaf children may perform poorly on some cognitive tasks because of sociological rather than linguistic deficiences.

After reviewing a number of studies on the cognitive development of deaf children who have not yet acquired language, Furth concludes that:

(a) Language does not influence intellectual development in any direct, general, or decisive way. (b) The influence of language may be indirect or specific, and language may accelerate intellectual development: by providing the opportunity for additional experience through giving information and exchange of ideas and by furnishing ready symbols (words) and linguistic habits in specific situations (p. 160, 1964b).

In short, he supports Piaget's position that language is not a constituent element of logical thinking (Furth, 1971).

The experiments Furth reviewed were all on deaf people's cognitive skill in handling observable, hence concrete, events. They have to be, because the cognitive tests must be the kind that can be communicated to the deaf without using linguistic means. I would ask this question: If we cannot even give verbal, abstract problems to deaf children, how can we say that they suffer no cognitive deficiences due to their lack of language? Can deaf children at ages 11–15 move on to the formal operations that allow hearing children to handle hypothesis-testing and other abstract thinking? A hearing child who can solve a relational problem with concrete objects may have difficulty with similar problems presented verbally: "If Allen is taller than John, and John is taller than Frank, who is the tallest of the three?" In verbal form, the problem becomes an abstract problem, hence more difficult. But such problems are often solved by reverting to imagery.

Piaget (1967) points out that a 12–24-months-old baby understands, in action, a sort of transitivity of relations that might be explained verbally as follows: "The watch was under the hat; the hat was under the blanket; therefore the watch is under the blanket." Put in a verbal form, only much older children can understand a sentence, such as this, that includes transitivity of serial relations or topological nestings. Piaget considers that language is a necessary but not a sufficient condition for the development of formal operations. This seems to imply that not all hearing children aged 11–15 may necessarily move on to formal operations, and that no child without language can do so. There are of course some deaf people like Helen Keller who have achieved a great deal in intellectual fields, but only after they have acquired some form of language.

Now that we have discussed cognitive functioning in deaf children, monolingual children, and bilingual children (Chapter 7), what can we conclude on relationships between languages and cognition? Low-level, concrete perceptual problems can be solved without a language. More abstract, formal problems may be better solved with than without a language. Problems requiring cognitive flexibility may be solved better with two than with one language. Solution of highly abstract and formal problems of physics and mathematics requires a specialized language.

Animals   Animals truly lack any human kind of language. Can they think? Let us define elementary thinking as some kind of symbolic activity, or simply as the internal representation of external events. We can picture in our minds' eyes what we are going to do and say in a particular situation.

Here are two kinds of "thinking" tasks that animals can perform. In the "delayed response" task, an animal watches as an experimenter places a food reward under one of two cups. However, the animal is not permitted to approach either of the cups until a predetermined delay has elapsed. When the animal is released, it can respond correctly only if it can somehow symbolically (visually?) represent to itself what the experimenter earlier did with the reward, because the reward is no longer in sight (or smell). Different animals tolerate different durations of delays; in one experiment, dogs could be delayed for 5 min while rats could wait only 10 sec (Hunter, 1912). For humans, the delay of a reward can be indefinitely long because one can store and rehearse the verbal description: "The treasure is in a chest, which is buried under the 9th tree. . . ."

In the double alternation problem, the animal is placed in a maze like the one shown in Figure 8–2. The animal has to learn to make turns at the choice point, and its turns depend upon its prior turns. Upon approaching the choice point for the first time the animal should turn left; when it arrives at the point for the second time it should turn left again. Having run around the left side of the maze, it should then shift and turn to the right on its next two choices. If it successfully executes the prescribed LLRRLLRR sequences, it receives a reward. To respond correctly to this problem the animal must keep record internally of its preceding turns, as there is no external cue for correct responses. While the lowly rat finds the problem impossible to solve, raccoons and cats do not. Human children cannot learn to perform the same alternation problem until they are about 3½ years old. By the age of 5, most normal children can both learn the test and verbalize the rule by which they perform it (Hunter and Bartlett, 1948).

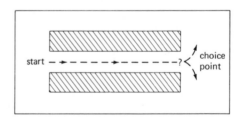

FIGURE 8–2   The double alternation problem for animals.

In short, nonprimates can solve some elementary problems of "thinking" (internal representations of external events). But without language, double alternation problems may be about the highest level of thinking problems raccoons and cats can solve. As discussed in Chapter 1, chimpanzees have abilities to learn some rudimentary aspects of human language, and might be able to solve somewhat more complex problems.

LANGUAGES AND WORLD VIEWS: WITHIN ONE LANGUAGE

How do verbal labels and grammatical features influence the way we perceive, think, and respond to reality? Again, we start our discussion with the simplest of language behavior, verbal labeling.

Labels

We can observe the power of labels in our daily life. How often do we buy things simply because they have the label "sale" attached to them? Compare the expressions, "It costs *only* $5" and "It costs *as much as* $5"; "He is expected *to die*" and "He is expected *not to live*." Why do stores in North America give their merchandise prices like $99.99? A label can change people's attitudes profoundly, either favorably or unfavorably. It is said that in India a (sacred) "cow" is sometimes called a "horse" so that people would not feel guilty in slaughtering and eating a "horse." Think of the introduction of the label "Ms." in order to change women's self-images.

A label can help us to focus our attention on certain critical features of an object. It, rather than the complexities of the object, can be stored in our memory. As long as two people agree on what class of objects the word "book" refers to, they can communicate about books in an economical way, even in the absence of any actual book. On the other hand, we can envisage situations where labeling may constrain or misguide our perception and cause misunderstanding between two speakers. Misunderstanding can occur when two people's categorizations of world events do not overlap. In behavioral science, the use of a label such as "obsessive-compulsive neurotic" may give us the illusion that a complex phenomenon has been explained.

Let us turn to experimental evidence that indicates the potent influence of labels on our behavior.

Beneficial effects   Carmichael, Hogan, and Walter (1932) conducted a classical experiment on the influence of labels on reproduction of schematic drawings. They briefly exposed to subjects stimuli such as the one shown in Figure 8–3, and later asked the subjects to reproduce the figures. The stimulus figures are somewhat ambiguous, so that the stimulus figure in

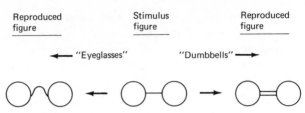

FIGURE 8–3   Effect of verbal labels on later reproductions of an ambiguous figure. (After Carmichael et al., 1932.)

Figure 8–3, for example, can pass either as eyeglasses or dumbbells. If it was labeled as eyeglasses by the experimenters at the time of the original exposure, it was reproduced as eyeglasses; if it was labeled as dumbbells, it was reproduced as dumbbells. In other words, the label tends to "channel" the stimulus figure in the direction of the concept represented by the label. Further experiment by Herman, Lawlers, and Marshall (1957) shows that it is principally the label that is remembered, rather than some direct representation of the figures. Indeed, even subjects who are not shown any verbal label will invent their own labels, and their later reproductions of the figures will often reveal the nature of these labels.

The names people learn may facilitate communication and enhance their ability to recognize and identify from memory particular sensory experiences, such as colors. Brown and Lenneberg (1954) demonstrated this in a well-known experiment. They established that colors differ in what they called "codability." Highly codable colors had short labels such as "red" or "blue," which were named promptly, with high agreement among subjects. Low-codable colors required more than one word to describe— "yellowish brown," for example.

The codability of a color was significantly related to how well the color could be recognized in a task such as the following: a subject was shown four colors simultaneously for 3 sec; then after 30 sec the subject had to find these colors in a large chart containing 120 colors systematically arranged. Codability had an even greater effect upon recognition when the delay was 3 min. Subjects reported that they named the colors to themselves while the colors were exposed, and then used the names they remembered in finding the colors on the large chart.

In such an experiment there is a possibility that both codability and recognition may result from a real perceptual primacy of the primary colors (red, blue, green, and yellow: see Bornstein, 1973). In that case, the experiment says nothing about labeling as such. French (1963) criticized Brown and Lenneberg's conclusion on another ground. There are unusual original color names that, in spite of their novelty, may be understood by the listener immediately. "Swiss cheese colored" is an unusual term of considerable phonemic length, thus a term of low codability, but it nevertheless conveys a uniform meaning to speakers of English. French here seems to be objecting to Brown and Lenneberg's definition of "codability" but recognizes the facilitatory effect of labeling in communication.

Lantz and Stefflre (1964) repeated the Brown and Lenneberg experiment with a different definition of codability. Codability is measured in three ways: communication accuracy, naming agreement, and brevity of description. One part of the experiment tested communication accuracy: one group of subjects (encoders) named each color in such a way that another group of subjects (decoders) would be able to pick the color out from a large set. The number of correct selections made by the decoders is the communication-accuracy score. The colors then were given to a new group of subjects in a recognition test. Recognition data were related to communication accuracy. That is, the colors that were communicated accurately between the encoders and the decoders were recognized well by subjects who had seen them earlier. In fact, communication accuracy was a better predictor of memory for colors than was either naming agreement or brevity of description. There might even be some causal relationship between communication accuracy and recognition. When Lantz (1963) taught encoders new names for previously poorly communicated color chips, the decoders' accuracy in recognizing the chips increased.

We have seen the advantage of verbal labels in various tasks. In the experiments described so far, the words are language items that the individual has already learned in the normal course of experience. What about nonsense syllables whose meanings are learned in the initial phase of the experiment? Shepard (1956) found that teaching a preschool child to call a series of red, reddish orange, orange, and yellow lights by the same nonsense-syllable names caused the subject to generalize a button-pushing response to all these lights, even though the original training was only to the red light. Here, not only do we see the effectiveness of nonsense syllables as labels but we also see another important property of labeling: If two "different" objects are assigned the same name, they are more likely to be responded to in the same way than if the objects are given different names. In other words, the common label makes the conceptualized objects more similar to each other than do the external stimuli alone and hence there is a tendency to treat them similarly.

Useless labels A label is not particularly useful when it does not readily refer to a well-learned class of experiences. For example, efforts by several experimenters to teach people to recognize novel visual patterns better by assigning nonsense syllables to them have not been successful (Carroll, 1964). Certain tasks can be better performed if figures rather than labels are stored in memory. Prentice (1954) kept his experiment entirely within the image mode. He showed subjects the same stimulus figures, along with the two sets of labels, as used by Carmichael and associates. The subjects' task was to recognize the 12 stimulus figures from among 60 presented to them visually. Their errors did not show that they chose a shape that fit the label used during learning. In other words, the use of labels during learning does not necessarily modify the original visual experience of figures or discriminatory memory, if a subject has to recognize stimulus figures among many similar figures.

Examine the novel, nonsense shapes with labels in Figure 8–4. Ranken (1963) had two experimental conditions. In the "Named" condition, he instructed subjects to think of these shapes in terms of assigned labels, which were names of animals that resembled the displayed shapes. In an "Unnamed" condition, he instructed subjects to visualize the shapes without using labels. The shapes were so constructed that the subjects had to use information from both top and bottom contours of each shape to respond successfully in a recognition task, a memory task, and a jigsaw-puzzle task. This was so in both the "Named" and "Unnamed" conditions. For the jigsaw puzzle, Ranken indicated the shape, randomly assigned, from which the puzzle was to start. The subject picked another shape that would fit under the first one—one whose top contour would match the bottom contour of the first shape. Then the subject picked a third shape that fitted under the second, and so on, until all eight shapes were fitted together.[1] The subjects did not see the shapes at any time during the problem solving.

Subjects in the "Named" condition made fewer errors in recalling the serial order of the shapes, but made more errors in solving the mental jigsaw puzzle and in drawing the shapes from memory, than did subjects in the "Unnamed" condition. For recalling a serial ordering of shapes, subjects in the "Named" condition merely have to store and retrieve the names in a serial order. For solving the jigsaw puzzle and in drawing the shapes from memory, the labels were not particularly helpful because labels do not relate to similarities of shapes, especially the bottom and top contours that were relevant for these tasks. Subjects who visualized the shapes would do better on the tasks that require recalling and manipulating figures, because they had all the necessary information on the shapes.

In sum, we categorize world events and assign labels to each class of events. Labels channel our attention to the critical features of a categorized event, aid us to store the perceived event in an efficient way, and facilitate communication. Labels are not useful if they do not relate to the critical features of objects, or when the solution of a problem requires mental manipulation of figures.

---

[1] Refer to Figure 8–4. If the experimenter indicates 7, the subject has to pick shapes 1, 5, 2, 6, 1, 3, and 8 (or 4, 2, 8, 3, 6, 1, and 5) in that order to solve the jigsaw puzzle.

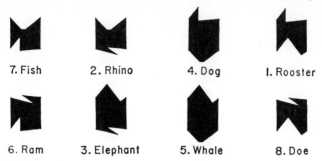

FIGURE 8–4   Stimulus shapes, with names, grouped vertically by bottom contour and horizontally by top contour. (From Ranken, 1963.)

Labels as traps: General Semantics

A label is an efficient and economical way of coding a bewildering amount of information. If we meet a stranger, a label such as "gardener" will tell us a lot about this person in one word. But this label at the same time makes us blind to any possibility of this particular gardener being an exception to our stereotyped image of a gardener. It may be Wittgenstein—the Philosopher of formidable intellect I have been quoting from. Wittgenstein in fact took various menial jobs, including those of a gardener and a hotel porter, after renouncing a vast fortune he inherited from his parents.

In this section we shall dwell upon a misguiding influence of labels in our daily life. We are going to see cases where the organization of reality done for us by labels can mislead us. An interesting example is given by Benjamin Whorf (Carroll, 1956),[2] a fire-insurance inspector who became an influential linguist. He observed that around a storage of "gasoline drums," people will exercise great care, while around a storage of *"empty* gasoline drums," their behavior will be careless, with little repression of smoking or of tossing cigarette stubs about. Yet the "empty" drums are perhaps the more dangerous since they contain explosive vapor. Here we are misled by the label "empty" which is synonymous with "null, void, negative, inert . . . not dangerous."

We apply many labels to people—"Negro," "Jew," "garbage collector," and so on. These labels can arouse our prejudices and activate stereotyped responses to the people thus labeled. Labels applied even to oneself can sometimes be harmful. For example, a label "I am only a woman" is an excuse for mediocrity in intellectual and physical pursuits. In all these cases, labels prevent us from having an open mind in dealing with each person or situation. General Semantics (GS) is a movement or a field of

---

[2] Carroll in 1956 published a collection of Whorf's papers from scattered sources, but Whorf wrote in the 1930s.

study that makes us aware of such traps of labels and gives specific hints on how to circumvent them. Korzybski (1933), a Polish-born American mathematician-engineer who developed General Semantics, holds that we can attain clear thinking and social progress through the reform of language. GS ultimately tries to change our attitude to language and therefore to reduce human conflicts.

GS is based on the following three principles. (1) The principle of nonidentity. The word is not the thing. Language and reality are related in the same way as a map is to the terrain to which it refers. (2) The principle of incompleteness. The representations in language are always less than complete representations of the world. The map inevitably ignores some details of the terrain. (3) The principle of self-reflex. Speech or language can refer not only to the real world but also to itself. A statement can be made about the real world, and another statement can be made about this statement, and so on.

All these principles can be considered to be features of the process of abstraction that is fundamental to all languages. Different levels of abstraction are involved when a statement (second level) is made about a statement (first level). High-level abstraction is often used by politicians and advertisers to confuse and befuddle people. Japan during World War II had the grand slogan "Greater East Asia Co-Prosperity Sphere" to disguise her invasion of Eastern Asian countries. Both word magic and demagogy aim to channelize the reactions of people to symbols so as to make responses automatic, uncritical, and immediate. Such reactions make possible gigantic sales, unrelated to the quality of the product, or make wars inevitable.

GS tries to educate us for "extensional orientation," that is, an orientation toward the concrete reality of the world. This stands in contrast to "intensional orientation," orientation toward words or verbal labels. The goal of extensional orientation can be achieved by a (seemingly simple) system using five extensional devices.

(1) *Index.* The index emphasizes that there are differences as well as similarities between things, even though they may both have the same label: $politician_1 \neq politician_2$ (nonidentity).

(2) *Dates.* Heraclitus said that you cannot step into the same river twice. The world and everything in it is in the process of change, although labels remain relatively static. $Red\ China_{1960} \neq Red\ China_{1973}$.

(3) *Etc.* No statement can be complete; there is always more to be said, etc. (infinite complexity or incompleteness).

(4) *Quotation marks.* Terms are being used in a specialized or particular sense. Such terms as "mind," "race," "same," should be used in quotation marks as a reminder that they are not to be trusted.

(5) *Hyphen.* What may be separable verbally may not be separable

on a nonverbal level. The problem of "body and mind" is not the same as the problem of "body-mind"; the latter more clearly indicates that both body and mind are interrelated and in reality inseparable. Einstein revolutionized physics by considering space and time together as "space-time."

Language has many traps. Labels can be traps. GS alerts us to these traps and recommends specific devices to help us avoid them. If we follow the five extensional devices literally, our speech will no longer be smooth and natural. But we should at least think of these devices once in a while. Another useful device is to ask the speaker to be more specific. If someone says, "Wait here. I will be back in *a jiffy*," ask the speaker, "Exactly how long—a few seconds, minutes, hours?" This inquiry may well save you from uncertainty and the boredom of waiting for the duration of time that is "a jiffy" to your friend but "an eon" to you. It is doubtful that reforming language alone can reduce and solve human conflicts as GS claims, but it should eliminate many misunderstandings in communications.

Grammatical features

Another aspect of language that might influence our cognition is grammar. One grammatical feature that has been singled out by Whorf as a potent shaper of our cognition is the form-class or grammatical category of words. The traditional, notional definition of form-class says that a noun is a name of a thing, and a verb refers to action. According to Whorf, our language with its dichotomy of verb and noun gives us a bipolar division of nature—short-lasting events or actions versus long-lasting, stable forms or things, even though nature itself is not thus polarized. Whorf goes on to say that:

. . . an "event" to us means "what our language classes as a verb" or something analogized therefrom . . . And it will be found that it is not possible to define 'event, thing, object, relationship,' and so on, from nature, but that to define them always involves a circuitous return to the grammatical categories of the definer's language (p. 215).

Following majority rule, we therefore read action into every sentence, even into "I hold it." A moment's reflection will show that "hold" is no action but a state of relative positions. Yet we think of it and even see it as an action because language formulates it in the same way as it formulates more numerous expressions like "I strike it," which deal with movements and changes (p. 243).

Do we perceive more action in a word meaning simply because the word is a verb, and nonaction because it is a noun? To answer this specific question, I did a simple experiment (unpublished), using the following four types of word as test material.

$$\text{verbs} \begin{cases} \text{action verb (to leap, to run, to jump)} \\ \text{nonaction verb (die, possess, to sleep, to stay)} \end{cases}$$

$$\text{nouns} \begin{cases} \text{action noun (a run, a leap, sport)} \\ \text{nonaction (thought, death, silence)} \end{cases}$$

I asked a class of university students to rate 45 words of the above types on a 7-point scale for "degree of action these words suggest," from very active (point 1) to neutral (4) to inactive (7). The test words were of course randomized.

The mean scores given to the various types of words were:

$$\text{verb} \begin{cases} \text{action} & 1.87 \\ \text{nonaction} & 5.08 \end{cases} 3.42$$

$$\text{noun} \begin{cases} \text{action} & 2.07 \\ \text{nonaction} & 5.41 \end{cases} 3.74$$

The verbs were considered slightly more active than the nouns (3.42 against 3.74). But note that within the verb and within the noun classes, the difference between action and nonaction meaning is large. Regardless of form-class, words that refer to action were perceived as suggesting action. There were seven nonaction words that could be either verbs or nouns. Examples are: think/thought, possess/possession. For such words, nonaction nouns scored in total 644 and nonaction verbs, 636 points. In the case of the same action words either as verbs (to leap) or nouns (a leap), the contrast was 236 and 254 points for the verbs and the nouns respectively. In both cases, a verb was on average very slightly more active than a noun when their semantic contents were nearly equivalent. This modest experiment also shows that we do not dichotomize nature by verb and noun classification into short-lasting and long-lasting events. Although the test words were deliberately selected for their clear action-nonaction contrasts, there was a graded range of action to nonaction, as the seven words in Table 8–1 show.

Another grammatical feature that might influence our perception of word meaning is gender. Hofstätter (1963) asked German students to rate "die Sonne" (feminine; German "sun") and "der Mond" (masculine; German "moon") on a semantic differential scale. Italian students rated "sole" (masculine) and "luna" (feminine). "Sonne" and "sole," in spite of their opposite genders, received highly similar ratings ($r = 0.92$). This result is not unreasonable: gender can be rather arbitrary, as "das Mädchen" or "das Weib" (neuter, German "maiden" and "wife") show.

In short, how we perceive the meaning of a word is largely determined by intrinsic semantic content of a word, and very slightly by its form-class

TABLE 8–1   A Graded Range of Action Meaning

Test word	Semantic content and form-class	Mean action score
a fight	action noun	1.29
to climb	action verb	1.82
a wave	action noun	2.65
thought	nonaction noun	3.88
to house	nonaction verb	4.59
to stay	nonaction verb	5.71
silence	nonaction noun	6.71

A score of 1 suggests a high degree of action and 7, nonaction. From Taylor, unpublished data.

or gender. There are of course many other grammatical features we can test, but they can be better discussed in the third section of this chapter when we compare different languages.

LANGUAGES AND WORLD VIEWS

In the first and second sections of this chapter we have seen that language and speech, at least labeling and verbalizing, may influence cognition. The logical question to ask now is: do differences among languages influence speakers to think differently? The idea that the structure of one's language shapes one's thought structure, hence that thought is relative to the language in which it is conducted, is known as the principle of *linguistic relativity*. The German philosopher Humboldt asserted that:

The mental characteristics and the development of language of a nation are so intimately bound up with each other that if the one were known the other could be completely deduced from it. For intellect and language permit and develop only forms which are mutually compatible. Language can be said to be the outward manifestation of the mind of nations. Their language is their mind, and their mind their language. One must imagine them as completely identical (p. 41, 1905).

At about the same time, and apparently independently of the German current, an American version of linguistic relativity was appearing. The American linguist-anthropologists Boas, Sapir, and Whorf, in the course of their studies of American Indian languages in the early twentieth century, opened the eyes of Western scholars to vast differences among languages.

It was Whorf who vigorously defended the principle of linguistic relativity, so much so that the principle is sometimes known as the *Whorfian Hypothesis.* Whorf claims that:

The background linguistic system (in other words, the grammar) of each language is not merely a reproducing instrument for voicing ideas but rather is itself *the shaper of ideas* [emphasis added], the program and guide for the individual's mental activity, for his analysis of impressions, for his synthesis of his mental stock in trade. Formulation of ideas is not an independent process, strictly rational in the old sense, but is part of a particular grammar and differs, from slightly to greatly, as between different grammars. We dissect nature along lines laid down by our native languages. . . . We cut nature up, organize it into concepts, and ascribe significances as we do, largely because we are parties to an agreement to organize it in this way—an agreement that holds throughout our speech community and is codified in the patterns of our language. . . . We cannot talk at all except by subscribing to the organization and classification of data which the agreement decrees (Carroll, 1956, pp. 212–214).

The statements by Humboldt and Whorf are provocative, but very general. We have to examine their assertions in more concrete terms. Specifically, we have to examine how languages differ in categorizing, labeling, and grammatical features. What aspects of sociocultural differences do these linguistic differences reflect? Do they in turn influence speakers' cognition and behavior?

Differences in categorizing and labeling

Instances of differences   Anyone who has studied foreign languages will notice that different languages categorize world events somewhat differently, hence "translation equivalents" do not have exactly the same referents. As mentioned in Chapter 3, English "green" and "blue" refer to light wavelengths of around 520 mμ and 470 mμ respectively, while Japanese "ao" would refer to both wave lengths. In the realm of food, English "hot" refers both to temperature and to the spicy flavor of chili pepper. Korean would have at least one distinct word for each of these.

There are instances where one language has a category and a name for it, while another language has only the category but not the name. A case in point is "gloating over another person's misfortune," which we definitely feel, though feel ashamed to admit. Lacking a label but experiencing the feeling, the English language can either borrow a word from other languages (such as German *Schadenfreude*, literally "shame-joy,"), or resort to the above circumlocution. Numerous examples of loan words—"chic," "touché," "nirvana," and so on—attest to the fact that the English language lacks labels for some categorized events. Other loan words have been introduced along with new objects and events—kayak, parka, spaghetti, and so on.

There are also cases where speakers of one language do not recognize an event readily and do not have a word for it. The English language lacks a word for a particular taste-flavor that comes from roasted ground sesame seeds (or pumpkin seeds), and English-speakers do not seem to be aware of this flavor as a distinct one until it is pointed out to them. Koreans treasure this flavor, and also have a distinct word for it. Then there are cases where a language lacks a superordinate name for certain events. The Wolof language, which we shall discuss shortly, does not have a word "color" but has names for individual colors such as red. Figure 8–5 shows graphically the ways in which two languages can differ in categorizing and labeling.

We can now ask a few interesting questions. First, how did such apparent differences in languages originate? Secondly, how do such differences in categorizing and labeling influence perception and behavior? We can only conjecture answers to the first question. In some cases, the apparent differences may be due to accident. Is there any good reason to think that Germans are more prone to "Schadenfreude" than English-speakers are? In other cases, we can easily see that events that are important in a culture are well categorized and labeled for convenience of communication. This is why Eskimos need several different terms for varieties of snow and seals,

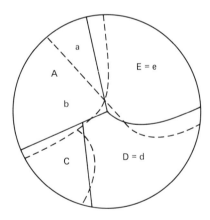

FIGURE 8–5   Differences in categorizing and labeling in two languages. The world event is divided into five categories, four of which are labeled as *a, b, d,* and *e* in Language 1 (dotted line). In L₂ (solid line), the reality is carved up into four categories, which are labeled as A, C, D, and E. Note that L₁ and L₂ overlap only for D=d and E=e. L has one category and one label, A, for which L₁ has two categories and labels, *a* and *b*. L₂ has a category and label C, for which L₁ has a category but no label. Note also that categorizations never exactly overlap in the two languages.

and nomadic Arabs many terms for different breeds of camels. The French language originally lacked words for various types of snow. But French Canadians felt a need for such words, and created new French words like "poudrerie" (drifting snow) from "poudre" (powder). Hindi has a distinct word "nirvana," because Buddhists value highly this state of being. In these cases we may conclude that differences in categorizing and labeling reflect sociocultural differences. If this reasoning is right, we have to suspect that English-speakers are relatively indifferent to the taste-flavor of food—the English language has far fewer terms than Korean in this area. Here we are inferring cultural data from linguistic data.

Another source of linguistic difference may come from differences in physiological processing. Bornstein (1973) points out that although *Homo sapiens* is relatively uniform, certain differences in visual processing exist. These differences in physiological processing account for his finding that 50 percent of a total sample of 150 societies have a single label for the two colors "green" and "blue."

Influence of labeling differences on behavior   The next question is: how do such differences in categorizing and labeling influence our perception and behavior? We shall consider this question as it applies to the domain of color coding, for differences in color coding among different languages are very obvious and easy to experiment on. Kopp and Lane (1968) compared English-speakers in America and speakers of Tzotzil (a Mayan language) for their identification of five English and four Tzotzil names, which partition the hue spectrum in different ways. In the first part of the experiment, subjects pressed a telegraph key to report all hue changes, however slight, in the patch of light on the screen (sweep discrimination procedure). In ABX discrimination triads, subjects pressed one of two buttons to indicate whether the third stimulus (X) was identical to the first (A) or the second (B).

As shown in Figure 8–6 for all speakers the identification response showed the wide plateaus and sharp drops characteristic of categorical responding. Discrimination was good at the category boundaries and at chance level within categories. The color discriminations for English- and Tzotzil-speakers were quite different, and these differences could be predicted from the way the color names are used in the two languages.

In another study on color-coding, Lenneberg and Roberts (1953) compared English-speakers and Zuni-speakers (an American Indian language spoken in New Mexico) for their color memory. Zuni codes colors somewhat differently from English—it has one word for orange and yellow, for example. Striking differences between English and Zuni appeared; colors that were highly codable in English were not always highly codable in Zuni, and vice versa. Furthermore, Zuni-speakers had more trouble in recognizing and remembering colors that were poorly coded in Zuni but well coded in English, and, conversely, English-speakers had more trouble for color ranges better coded in Zuni than in English. Interestingly, the performances of those Zuni who also spoke English fell between those of monolingual Zuni and monolingual English-speaking Americans.

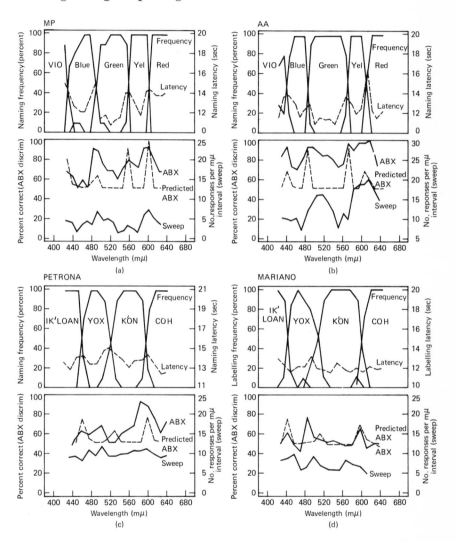

FIGURE 8–6 Identification probability, identification latency, sweep discrimination, and ABX discrimination measures as a function of wavelength for two speakers of English (MR and AA) and two of Tzotzil (Petrona and Mariano). Each point on the functions is the mean of 10, 10, 40, or 24 stimulus presentations, respectively. (From Kopp and Lane, 1968.)

Here labels may affect only sensory performance but not capacities. For example, with specific training, English-speakers have the capacity to discriminate and remember colors in Tzotzil or Zuni ways.

Next, the influence of categorizing and labeling on speakers' cognition is compared with the influence of schooling. Greenfield, Reich, and Olver (1966) studied children aged between 6 and 16 in Senegal, the westernmost tip of former French West Africa. The subjects were Wolofs, members of the country's dominant ethnic group. The children were composed of (1) bush unschooled; (2) bush schooled; (3) urban (Dakar) schooled. Schooled children learned French. Children were shown pictures of objects that can be grouped by color, form, or function, as shown in Figure 8–7. The subjects had to say which two objects were alike, and why. For example, the child might say the clock and the banana in Set 1 in Figure 8–7 are alike because they are both yellow (color), or the orange and the banana are alike because they are both for eating (function).

The Wolof language, in contrast to French, has neither the word "color" nor the word "shape." It has no word for "blue," and has one word for

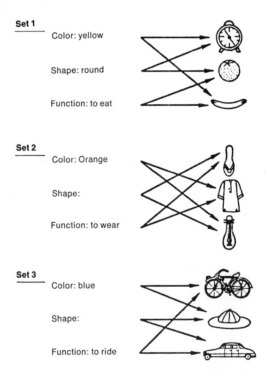

FIGURE 8–7   The three picture displays with their attributes. Set 1—clock, orange, banana; set 2—sandal, bubu (Wolof robe), guitar; set 3—bicycle, helmet, car. (From Greenfield et al., 1966.)

"orange" and "red." Yet Wolof-speakers showed a far greater tendency to group objects in terms of their color likeness than did French-speakers or even French-Wolof bilinguals. On the other hand, Wolof is not deficient in words refering to function, but Wolof speakers did not group objects by function. Furthermore, grouping by function increased with age in schooled children, but not in Wolof unschooled children.

Why Wolof-speakers tended to group objects by color is not clear. The authors' interpretation is that grouping objects by color is a more primitive form of classification than one based on form or function of the objects. Color can be indicated by pointing, hence is concrete. However, other studies (such as Brian and Goodnough, 1929; Riccuiti, 1965) show that young children, when given an opportunity to match stimuli for either form or color, consistently preferred form. One might assume that color is more important to the Wolof, not less, since the Wolof keep their color names segregated and not subsumed under "color." It is not important that an object is colored—it is important that the object is red.

At any rate, here the effect of schooling was greater than that of cultural and linguistic background, for the Wolof school child was much more akin to the American school child. Schooling forces the Wolof child to rely on more abstract linguistic encoding as a way of communicating.

Universal patterns

So far we have examined numerous differences across languages in categorizing and labeling. If we look for some universal pattern in these apparent differences, we may find what we look for. Berlin and Kay (1969) examined the color terms of 98 languages. First, they elicited basic color terms of the language in question from an informant. Second, each subject mapped both the focal point and the outer boundary of each of the basic color terms on the array of standard color stimuli (329 color chips of Munsell Color Co.) The investigators found that, although different languages encode in their vocabularies different numbers of basic color categories, a total universal inventory of exactly eleven basic color categories exists from which the eleven or fewer basic color terms of any given language are always drawn: white, black, red, green, yellow, blue, brown, purple, pink, orange, and gray. If a language encodes fewer than eleven basic color categories then there are strict limitations on which categories it may encode. The distributional restrictions of color terms across languages are:

1. All languages contain terms for white and black.
2. If a language contains three terms, then it contains a term for red.
3. If a language contains four terms, then it contains a term for either green or yellow (but not both).
4. If a language contains five terms, then it contains terms for both green and yellow (and so on and so forth).

As briefly mentioned earlier, such differences in color-naming may have a physiological basis. Bornstein's (1973) survey of 150 societies shows that with increasing proximity of societies to the equator, the color names applied to short wavelengths (green and blue) become more frequently the same and, under extreme conditions, blue plus green are identified with black. Exposure to ultraviolet radiation increases the density of yellow pigmentation in the eyes. This yellow pigment selectively absorbs short wavelength radiation that enters the eyes. The result is a decreased sensitivity to short wavelengths. In short, people near the equator have color vision that is insensitive to blue and green, hence may have one term to refer to the two colors.

Berlin and Kay further argued that each basic color has a *focal point*. Their informants of diverse languages tended to choose the same areas of the color space in choosing the best examples of their language's basic color terms from an array of Munsell chips. These clusters of best examples of color terms are focal points.

E.R. Heider (1971, 1972) provided evidence that the focal points of basic color terms represent areas of the color space that possess a particular perceptual-cognitive salience "prior to naming." "Prior to naming" can be taken in two senses: in the first sense, developmentally, 3-year-old American children oriented toward focal colors in preference to nonfocal colors, and 4-year-old American children matched focal colors more accurately than nonfocal colors.

In the second sense, cross-culturally focal colors enjoy perceptual primacy. The Dani of New Guinea lack all of the basic chromatic color terms (K.G. Heider, 1970); they possess two terms that divide the color space on the basis of brightness rather than hue. This color system is equivalent to the first and the simplest stage in Berlin and Kay's evolutionary ordering of colors. E.R. Heider demonstrated that even the Dani remembered focal colors more accurately than nonfocal colors—both in a short-term recognition task similar to that used by Brown and Lenneberg (1954) and in a long-term memory test. Rosch (1973) reports that learning was also more rapid for such focal colors.

According to Rosch, in general, categories are composed of a *core meaning* that consists of the clearest cases (best examples) of the category, surrounded by other category members of decreasing similarity to that core meaning. The core meaning of categories is not arbitrary but is "given" by the human perceptual system; thus both the basic content and structure of such categories are universal across languages. Such clear-set examples can be found in color, shape, and in other perceptual domains.

With regard to semantic dimensions, Osgood (1964) found that various languages of the world operate with the same basic three semantic dimensions (Evaluation, Potency, and Activity; see Chapter 3), however much they may disagree on the scaling of individual concepts like "Communism" and "Capitalism." As early as 1958, when only Japanese data were compared with American data, Roger Brown had already concluded that the fact that Japanese and Americans share the same basic semantic dimensions is a major disconfirmation of Whorf's linguistic relativity.

Granting that categorizing-labeling differences may be only skin deep, and that under such differences may lurk universal patterns, we need not hastily dismiss linguistic relativity. Let us see where linguistic relativity is important and where it is not. From the above discussion, we might say that behaviors closely tied to human basic perceptual-cognitive capacities are not too strongly influenced by linguistic relativity. The more abstract and removed from direct perception is the domain of discourse, the more opportunity there might be for linguistic relativity to be important.

Finally, being aware of differences among cultures and languages has a practical use. We realize that humans live basically in the same way everywhere. That is, a human everywhere tries to have a few meals a day; sleeps about one-third of the day; mates; has children; and dies. All humans have the same basic emotions: happiness, sadness, anger, fear, surprise, and disgust (Ekman, 1971). Humans also have the same basic aspirations in life—wealth, good health, and good offspring. All the same, when we visit a foreign country we often experience a "culture shock." It may be a comfort to know that all humans share the universal living modes, emotions, aspirations, and linguistic universals. But it is the knowledge about how and why a particular culture and language can differ from ours that helps us to cope with culture shock.

We see that there are still a number of interesting questions to be asked on the relations between language differences and behavior.

Differences in grammatical features

In Chapter 1 we examined some differences in grammatical features among Chinese, Korean, and Japanese, as well as between these three languages and some Indo-European languages. We can go on enumerating such linguistic differences, especially if we sample languages from widely different parts of the world with different cultures. In spite of these differences, we can safely assume that each language is sufficient unto itself—that is, each language is a perfectly adequate instrument for expressing the needs and interests of its speakers. This is so because each language must have evolved to meet the needs of its speakers.

How do these differences come about? As in labeling differences, some of them may have come about accidentally. For example, Indo-European languages have prepositions while Korean and Japanese have postpositions. A choice between pre- and post-positions has to be considered in relation to other linguistic features. At any rate, the adoption of one or the other feature may not have too great a cultural significance. But other linguistic differences may reflect sociocultural differences, as we shall see.

However they may have originated, languages contain grammatical features that appear different on the surface. Do they, in turn, influence our cognition? Chinese-speakers can express an idea in a sentence economically without employing all manner of linguistic paraphernalia that does not add too much to their information content—gender, number, case, article, tense, and so on. Are Chinese-speakers efficient thinkers to have evolved their language in that way? Alternately, are they crude thinkers to do away with subtleties of language that these grammatical features allow us to express? These questions are interesting and relevant to our discussion of the relation between thinking and language, but are beyond my ability to answer. But the next question is possible to test: if one thinks in Chinese does one think more efficiently than in, say, English? Of course one can think in any language; only relative efficiency might differ in the two languages. Even though this question is central to the Whorfian Hypothesis, there has not been any experimental test of it. After all, abstract physics or mathematics can only be efficiently discussed in special language and only clumsily in ordinary languages.

Now here is an experiment on an isolated grammatical feature of the Navaho language. Navaho has the interesting grammatical feature that certain verbs of handling—"to pick up, to drop, to hold in the hand," and so on—require special forms depending on what kind of thing is being handled. There are eleven different forms, one for round spherical objects, one for round thin things, one for long flexible objects, and so forth, and the Navaho child has to learn these in order to speak his language grammatically.

Casagrande (Carroll and Casagrande, 1958) determined first that very young Navaho-speaking children did in fact know and use these forms correctly. He then compared the Navaho- and English-speaking children, all Navahos on the reservation, matched for age, with respect to how often they used shape, form, or material as basis for sorting objects, rather than color. The experimenter used sorting tasks that are usually performed by very young children on the basis of color.

The Navaho-speaking children had a tendency to perform the sorting task on the basis of form at distinctly younger ages than the English-speaking children. Apparently, the fact that Navaho grammar requires children to pay attention to the shapes, forms, and materials of things makes them more likely to guide their behavior on the basis of this aspect of their environment. Language, however, is not the only influence that can produce this result: middle-class English-speaking children in metropolitan Boston performed the sorting task in about the same manner as the Navaho-speaking children, probably because of their abundant experience with shapes and forms in the toys they had played with.

A speaker of a language that lacks definite and indefinite articles seldom masters the correct use of articles in another language. The difficulty is not purely linguistic but is partly perceptual. If their native language lacks the articles "the" and "a," speakers do not learn to perceive linguistic and perceptual events in terms of the "specified" or "definite" and "unspecified," because there are no such concepts embedded in their native language. The "a"s and "the"s in this book have mostly been put there by English-speaking readers of the various drafts.

So far we have discussed some interesting grammatical features of different languages. We do not know for sure what aspects of sociocultural structures these features reflect. We can, however, sometimes test how these differences in grammatical features influence the cognitive function of speakers.

Linguist-anthropologists have observed the following two parallels between linguistic features and cultural practices. This time, we are not too sure what aspects of these observations we can put to a test. The way languages handle such important concepts as time, movement, social status, and so on might be considered as revealing some mental characteristics of the speakers. With regard to linguistic expression of time, Whorf observed that:

Among the peculiar properties of Hopi time are that it varies with each observer, does not permit of simultaneity, and has zero dimension; i.e., it cannot be given a number greater than one. The Hopi do not say, "I stayed five days," but "I left on the fifth day." A word referring to this kind of time, like the word "day," can have no plural (p. 216). "Ten days is greater than nine days" becomes "The tenth day is later than the ninth" (p. 140).

A linguistic honorific system may be another instance where we see a good parallel between linguistic and cultural data. Elaborate honorific systems in Korean and in Japanese reflect rigid social structures where class distinction by age, sex, status, and so on is maintained. With the influence of Western democracy and Chinese Communism, such rigid class distinction may give way eventually. In that case, linguistic honorific systems may also become simpler, if they do not fade away altogether.

The "weak" version of linguistic relativity

The current consensus among psychologists (such as Fishman, 1970) regarding the principle of linguistic relativity is that: (1) Languages reflect, rather than determine, cognition. (2) Languages may be different in their superficial features, but are similar in deeper ways—in basic requirements and organizations.

Some psychologists (such as Slobin, 1971) distinguish between "weak" and "strong" versions of the Whorfian Hypothesis.

The strong form—often espoused by Whorf himself—holds that the language determines thought and behavior patterns; that the language is a sort of *mold* for thought and philosophy. The weak form—usually held today in one way or another—merely asserts that certain aspects of language can *predispose* people to think or act in one way rather than another, but that there is no rigid determinism: One is not fully a prisoner of one's language; it is just a guide to thought and other sorts of behavior (p. 122).

Still other psychologists (such as Bourne, Ekstrand, and Dominowski, 1971) point out that there is a circularity in the arguments for linguistic relativity: "The language determined the outlook which determined verbal behavior—thus the circularity of evidence" (p. 298).

In my view, the fact that languages categorize and label reality in different ways and emphasize different aspects of the reality in grammatical features itself represents different world views. Whether these linguistic differences are superficial or deep seems to be a secondary point, which may be relevant to the question of how profoundly different these world views are. Relations between linguistic data and sociocultural data may be varied—sometimes parallels are obvious; sometimes they are conjectured; and other times they may be attributed to accident. In the first two cases, it is more reasonable to think that linguistic data reflect the sociocultural structures, than the other way around. Whatever relation might hold, there remains the fact that linguistic data are different in different sociocultural communities, representing different world views. Furthermore, we can safely assume that such different world views are preserved and perpetuated from generation to generation via linguistic data. The problems so far described are the kinds of problem philosophers can speculate about in armchairs, and anthropologist-linguists can study in the field.

Psychologists, on the other hand, find out through experiments in what specific ways and to what degrees any specific linguistic data influence our perception, thought, and behavior. We have seen that certain perceptual and cognitive performances are influenced by linguistic data to a degree. But language is not the only influence; schooling, for example, is more potent. There are further limits to the influence of language on cognition: (1) Reality exists outside of language. (2) The reality referred to in different ways in diverse languages is still the same, single reality. (3) The basic human perceptual-cognitive capacities are also outside the influence of languages, although perceptual-cognitive performances are often influenced by languages. Because of these three limitations, as well as the one mentioned earlier, namely that language is not the sole or most potent influence, we may say that the influence of language on our cognition is not very profound. Thus we may have to conclude that the principle of linguistic relativity is valid, but in a weak or shallow version. There is more opportunity for linguistic relativity to be important as the domain of discourse becomes more abstract and removed from direct perception.

As for the question of circularity in the argument of linguistic relativity, it seems to apply to cases such as Navaho verbs for handling objects. Navaho perhaps evolved its peculiar and complex verb forms because objects had to be distinguished for their various shapes in Navaho culture. We then turn around and test how the verb forms influence Navaho-speakers' mode of handling objects. But note that Casagrande's experiment compared the object-sorting performance of Navaho-speakers to that of English-speakers. Further, he compared the influence of this grammatical feature to the influence of early experience with objects.

Finally, note that the present conclusion that language influences performance but not basic capacity is in harmony with the conclusion of the preceding chapter: a bilingual person may change his outlook on life but not his basic personality in switching languages.

SUMMARY AND CONCLUSIONS

We categorize events and assign labels to each class of events. How do labeling and verbalizing influence the cognitive development of children? Studies from Piaget's Geneva School show that productive speech and cognition develop in parallel but that speech training cannot induce solution of conservation problems. One study from Harvard does show that labeling appropriate aspects of the conservation problems, plus manipulation, can induce solution. In Russian studies, speech, either given by the experimenter or self-generated, can alter the child's perceptual field, and thus regulate its behavior. One American study shows the importance of labeling in a time-discrimination task.

Deaf children can solve some cognitive problems that may include relations and other sophisticated concepts, as long as they are observable and concrete. Their performance is not up to the level of hearing children's performance. It is not certain how well deaf children can handle formal, abstract thinking. Animals without language can solve "thinking" problems, but only at a very elementary level.

How are the general speakers of a language influenced by labels? Labels channel our attention to the critical features of the categorized events and help us to store the perceived events in an efficient way. Labels also facilitate communication. Labels may be useless when they are not appropriate to the labeled objects, and when tasks require handling visual figures directly. Labels can also misguide our cognition. As General Semantics points out, we tend to identify a label with a thing, which leads to all sorts of misunderstandings. GS gives us specific methods to orient ourselves to the reality that lies beyond labels.

As for grammatical features, Whorf contended that our language with its dichotomy of verb-noun gives us a bipolar division of nature. My test did not support this claim. Intrinsic meaning of a word is very little colored by its form-class or gender.

In the third section, we examined the principle of linguistic relativity: that every language embodies a definite world view, because a language is a shaper of our thinking. Languages differ in categorizing and labeling perceptual events such as color. However, we may find that universal patterns underlie such superficial linguistic differences. Superficial as they may be, linguistic differences influence our cognitive and perceptual performances, if not capacities. Schooling also has a great influence on performance, perhaps more than does language.

Differences in grammatical features are numerous, but hard to put to test. One feature tested was Navaho verbs of handling, which influenced Navaho children to sort objects in a way different from English-speaking children. Children's experience with objects also influences their sorting performance.

After surveying the views of psycholinguists on the principle of linguistic relativity, and after summarizing our discussion on the topic, we concluded that linguistic differences represent, preserve, and perpetuate different world views. The principle of linguistic relativity is weak, however, since there are at least four limits to the influence of language on cognition.

9

Universal (?) Phonetic Symbolism

If you have a large ball and a small ball and know that [tipi] refers to one and [gargar][1] to the other, which would be which? Do you feel that the words "huge," "enormous," "large," and "vast" seem appropriate for designating something large? Do words such as "tiny" or "wee" seem appropriate for designating something small? According to Orr (1944), distance has appropriate sounds; the vowel [i] is appropriate in words denoting closeness, and more rearward vowels such as [a] or [u] in those denoting remoteness. Examples are: French "ici" and "la"; English "this" and "that"; German "hier" and "da"; Malay "ili" or "ika" (a little removed) or "kiku" (farther away).

The noted Danish linguist Jespersen (1922) observed that the back vowel /ʌ/ in "dull" or "dump" is used in English for symbolic expression of dislike or disgust. He goes on to cite many examples: "blunder, bungle, bung, clumsy, humdrum, humbug, strum, slush, slubber, sloven, muck, mud, mug, scug, juggins, numbskull, dunderhead, gull." It is fun to think of such words, so I may add, "dung, dullard, drudgery, glut, smut, smudge, slut, grumble," "ugh!" and so on.

---

[1] The brackets [ ] are used for enclosing speech sounds unless the sounds in questions are clearly phonemes of certain languages. Phonemes are enclosed in / /. I do not make a distinction between "phonetic/phonemic" symbolism, because the content of this chapter may apply to both.

The examples suggest that a sound or a sound configuration expresses a certain meaning directly and intrinsically. This phenomenon is called phonetic symbolism. Thus, even a nonsense syllable or a foreign word containing [ʌ] should sound unpleasant to English listeners. If [ʌ] directly and intrinsically suggests or expresses unpleasantness for "natural" reasons, it should have the same feeling to speakers of any language. It would be an example of universal phonetic symbolism (UPS).

Why should [i] and [e] suggest or express smallness (nearness) while [o] and [u] carry the impression of bigness (farness)? Various authors have suggested reasons such as: (1) The acoustic quality inherent in speech sounds; [i] and [e] are high-pitched sounds, [o] and [u] low-pitched sounds. (2) Small objects (piccolo, mouse) emit high sounds; large objects (bassoon, lion), low sounds. (3) When we produce sounds, [i] and [e] require small mouth openings while [o] and [a] require large openings. Similar rationales have been proposed for other effects of phonetic symbolism. For example, trilled [r] involves vibration of the tongue, and hence is appropriate for words such as "roll" or "rouler" (French). Phonetic symbolism could be universal because these suggestions all depend on intrinsic physical properties of speech sounds, objects, or mechanisms of articulation. Note, however, that they refer to size and distance, and perhaps to movement. No ready rationale suggests itself for other dimensions of meaning, such as pleasantness or warmth. For example, it is not clear why [ʌ] by itself should sound unpleasant.

How can we demonstrate whether phonetic symbolism really exists or whether it is universal? Enumeration of examples in various languages, even by famous linguists, is not good enough evidence of UPS. The camp that believes in UPS will search out examples that support its existence, while the camp that does not believe in UPS will look for counterexamples.

EXPERIMENTAL EVIDENCE

We have to resort to experiments to settle the issue. Unfortunately, experiments seldom provide unequivocal evidence for or against UPS, but they are the best evidence we have. Let us survey some of the representative experiments that have been carried out in the past fifty years or so in different parts of the world. In the end, we shall have to use our own judgment in interpreting the experimental results.

We should be clear at the outset that there are many different ways phonetic symbolism can manifest itself. First, there is the question asked of an individual: "Do you feel that the sound /ʌ/ makes words tend to be appropriate for unpleasant things?" Then the same question can be asked of English-speakers in general, of speakers of other Indo-European languages, and finally of anybody in the world—"Does everybody, regardless of their native language, feel that /ʌ/ is appropriate in words for unpleasant things?" A second set of questions concerns the usage of sounds within languages: "Does /ʌ/ occur disproportionately often in English words with unpleasant connotations?" This question also can be posed with regard to all Indo-European languages and to all languages. Both the questions of individual feeling and language occurrence have been used in the literature to define phonetic symbolism, and they are frequently mixed in experimental studies. The resulting confusion has been discussed by Taylor and Taylor (1965).

We shall distinguish four different approaches to the experimental investigation of UPS, which explore different questions. Let us begin with the first question.

What labels are appropriate for what objects?

We see in Figure 9–1 two nonsense figures, figures that do not represent any identifiable objects. If one is called ULOOMU, the other TAKETE, which name would you choose for (A) and which for (B)? Davis (1961) reports that African children in the Lake Tanganyika region, as well as English school children, consistently and overwhelmingly chose TAKETE for (A), and ULOOMU for (B). We naturally feel that (A), an angular, jagged shape, is properly labeled with a name that consists of the sharp sounds [t, k] plus [a, e], while (B), a roundish one, is best described with a name made up of the softer [l, m] and [u, oo]. Voiceless stop consonants plus high-pitched vowels seem appropriate for a jagged shaped, while low and "mellow" sounds seem appropriate for a roundish figure.

Obviously we need more analytic experiments to discover what sounds are perceived as appropriate for what qualities of figures. Also, we need more than two figures and two names, if we want to make a more general statement. Just such an experiment was done by Tsien-Lee (1969). The

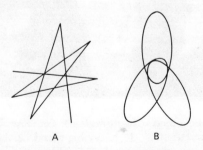

A   B

FIGURE 9–1   Which label—ULOOMU or TAKETE—goes with which figure?

test material consisted of eight three-dimensional objects, permitting the use of all combinations of the big/small, heavy/light, and pointed/round differentials, as in Figure 9–2. A large number of Chinese adults and children had to devise names for the nonsense objects, either by freely choosing sounds that suited the qualities of the objects or by choosing suitable sounds from a list of Chinese phonetic auxiliary symbols. The subjects were asked to hold the objects in hand while observing and naming them. For each object they could choose as many sounds as they wished, and the same sound could be chosen as often as they wished. In a control experiment, subjects chose from the nonsense words that Czurda (1953) used earlier with German subjects, so that responses of Chinese and German subjects could be compared. Some of the nonsense words used were: FAPP, SACKTA, NAHL, FAUGNUM, TEIKEI, BÖJÖN.

Table 9–1 shows the vowels and consonants subjects preferred for different qualities of the test objects.

It lists four different studies involving speakers of different languages: Czurda (1953), German-speakers; Czagan (1957), Italian-speakers; Fleiss (1965), Japanese-speakers; and Tsien-Lee (1969), Chinese-speakers. Tsien-Lee's study is further subdivided into a control experiment (C) and a main experiment (M).

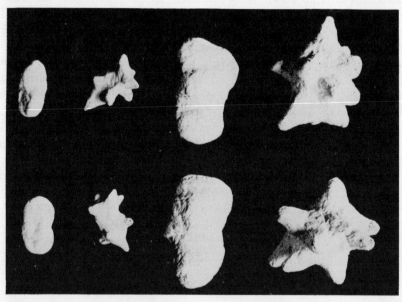

FIGURE 9–2 Nonsense objects. Identification: Top row, 2—4—1—3; bottom row, 6—8—5—7. Characteristics: 1: heavy-big-round, 2: heavy-small-round, 3: heavy-big-pointed, 4: heavy-small-pointed, 5: light-big-round, 6: light-small-round, 7: light-big-pointed, 8: light-small-pointed. (From Tsien-Lee, 1969.)

Tsien-Lee's experiment showed that adults gave more consistent responses than children. As noted earlier, results were more consistent in the choice of vowels than of consonants. All adults used longer names for heavy and big objects than for light and small ones. The greatest inconsistency was found in the names given to round and pointed objects.

To briefly describe one more study with the same approach, Tarte and Barritt (1971) used eight figures varying in size, four elliptical and four triangular. American English-speakers had to choose a CVC syllable from a prescribed set of nine CVCs (as, [kus]) that best described each figure. Subjects tended to give [a] to the larger of the pair and [i] to the smaller. To describe triangles, subjects preferred [i], then [a], and then [u]. For ellipses, the order was reversed. The three consonants used in constructing CVCs—[w, d, k]—were not consistently related to the figures. In this study the experimenters used only three consonants, which might have been low-symbolic consonants.

Speakers of different languages tend to associate certain speech sounds with certain qualities of figures or objects. In general, [a], [u], and [o] go with big, round, and heavy figures or objects, while [i] and [e] fit small, pointed, and light objects. Consonants in general do not show a neat and consistent pattern, but [t] might fit pointed objects, and [g] and [k] big objects. This approach is useful in establishing rationals for UPS.

What meanings do individual sounds suggest?

Now let us concentrate on speech sounds independently of visual figures and objects. The American linguist Sapir is the pioneer in investigating UPS along this approach. Sapir (1929), and a little later Newman (1933), had English-speaking subjects judge nonsense syllables for their size or brightness in a paired-comparison task. These nonsense syllables differed only in a single vowel: subjects compared for size MAL with MEL, or MEL with MIL, and so on. Both Sapir and Newman found the expected 'results; subjects judged [i] to be small and bright, and [a] to be large and dull.

The main shortcoming of these two studies is that they both involved only English-speakers. Even though Sapir used seven Chinese-speakers, they were residing in the United States and knew English. Still, on the contrast MAL-MIL, Chinese subjects showed less agreement than English subjects. Later Black and Brown (Brown, 1958) used the same pair with 19 Chinese subjects who knew little English. On the cited pair where English-speakers almost universally match MAL with large, the Chinese subjects responded at the chance level. In all of these analytical experiments, the investigators used only one or two dimensions of meaning, namely size and/or brightness. According to traditional rationales, these dimensions

TABLE 9–1 Sounds Chosen to Describe Different Qualities of Objects

Quality	Exp'ter	Vowels		Consonants			
				Stops		Continuant	
		Front	Back	Voiced	Voiceless	Voiced	Voiceless
heavy	Czurda		o au u	g			
	Czagan		o				
	Fleiss						
	Tsien-Lee (C)	ie	o au u ong	d	k	z	
	(M)		o ou u ong	d	k t		ʃ
round	C-d		o au u				
	C-g	e	o u			m	
	F	e	o au	b	p		f
	T-L (C)		o au / ou ü ong	d b		n l	
	(M)		o au / au ong	d	t p	m h r	f
big	C-d		o au u	g d	k		
	C-g	e	o u	g	k	n	
	F	e a / eu	ŏ au			m	s
	T-L (C)	a	o au u / ang	d		z r	
	(M)		a o u / ong	g d	k	m	chi

312

light	C-d	i																
	C-g																	
	F																	
	T-L (C)	i	ei	e					g							l		
	(M)	i		e		en an											s chi	
pointed	C-d	i									k	t						
	C-g	i										t				r		
	F	i		e	a					b		t					ts sch	
	T-L (C)	i		e				ü u	g			t		z	h			f
	(M)	i	ei ie	e	a			u	g		k						s	
small	C-d	i								b								f
	C-g	i																
	F	i														l r	sch tsch	
	T-L (C)	i		e									p					
	(M)	i		e		ai er	au											

Rearrangement of Tsien-Lee's Table 7, 1969.

of meaning might be expected to be closely related to the tonal properties of speech sounds.

What results do we obtain on other dimensions of meaning? Bentley and Varon (1933) had English-speakers judge the meanings of CVC nonsense syllables. In one experiment, the investigators did not supply any meaning dimensions to judge the CVCs on. In another experiment, they supplied five or ten differential scales: big/small, heavy/light, and so on. In these two experimental conditions, there was no clear-cut relation between certain CVCs and certain meaning contrasts. The smaller the number of meaning dimensions given to the subjects, the more positive the results tended to be. In a further experiment, the investigators prescribed only three meaning contrasts: angular, large, and hard, with their opposites. Subjects had to judge 36 nonsense syllables in pairs (for example, FAM, JAF, and MAF were, respectively, paired with FIM, JIF, and MIF). The [a] sounds were judged larger than the [i] sounds approximately in the ratio of 4:1; rounder than [i] at 3:1; and softer than [i] at 2:1. Here, with only three dimensions of meaning, again we have positive results. Further, the experiment shows that the size dimension gives the largest positive effect.

Taylor and Taylor (1962) included four dimensions of meaning—size, movement, pleasantness, and warmth. While these by no means exhaust the possible dimensions of meaning, they seemed to include several orthogonal or unrelated dimensions of meaning. The subjects were speakers of four unrelated languages (English, Japanese, Korean, and Tamil spoken in southern India and Ceylon) and were tested in their home countries. The sounds chosen for constructing CVC nonsense syllables were 12 legitimate consonantal phonemes "common" to all the four languages; they were expressed in the native alphabets or syllabaries. The phonemes are common in the sense that the underlying contrasts in articulation can be roughly equated. We combined these 12 consonants with 6 vowels in such a way that every consonant appeared with each vowel in an equal number of syllables. The subjects judged written nonsense syllables on a five-point scale on one of the four meaning dimensions. An example below illustrates the procedure.

(pleasant)   (unpleasant)

TEG   X

— — — — —

TEG in this example received a score of 4 (rather unpleasant).

People do associate certain sounds with certain meanings, but the same sound is associated with different meanings in different languages. English-speaking subjects show a high degree of agreement in ranking the initial consonants on the size dimension, with /g/ and /k/ as big sounds and /t/ and /n/ as small sounds. However, Korean-speaking subjects, though they too show a high degree of agreement among themselves in ranking the initial consonants for size, consider /t/ and /p/ to be the big sounds and /j/ and /n/, the small sounds. The vowels and final consonants show similar patterns of results. What is big in one language may be small or neutral in another language.

Concluding tentatively that phonetic or phonemic symbolism exists, but that the actual relations between sounds and meanings depend on the language, let us proceed to a third question.

Can we guess the meanings of foreign words?

With the third approach, we want to see whether people can match words of the same meaning from different unknown languages. With this question, we ask both "Do we feel something about this sound?" and "Does the foreign language in question use this sound symbolically?" This approach has generated by far the largest number of experiments, with confusing results. Let us see why.

To run a word-matching experiment, investigators typically prepare lists of frequently used English antonym pairs. These words are then translated into one or a few foreign languages. English-speakers try to match the foreign words to corresponding English words. Table 9–2 gives a few sample test words. Try to see which of the Chinese words "màn" and "k'uài" goes with "fast" and "slow," the first word pair. There are usually 20 to 30 antonym pairs in a list. Successful matches by the majority of sub-

---

TABLE 9–2   A Sample of Test Words in a Typical Word-matching Experiment

	English antonyms	Chinese
(1)	fast	k'uài
	slow	màn
(2)	warm	nŭan
	cool	liáng
(3)	hard	kāng
•	soft	joú
•		
•		
(20)		

Marks over the Chinese words indicate four tones: $\bar{a}$, level contour of pitch; $\acute{a}$ rising tone; $\ddot{a}$, falling and then rising; $\grave{a}$, falling tone.

jects on many of the test words are interpreted as evidence of UPS. Each word pair has a 50 percent chance to be either correctly or incorrectly matched. In 42 test results reported in various studies involving a number of different languages, the percentage correct ranged from 46.8 (Brackbill and Little, 1957) to 72.0 (Kunihira, 1972). The average of all the 42 tests was 52.7 percent correct matching.

Does this mean that the existence of UPS has been proven? Before making any hasty conclusion, we must examine the experimental procedures and test words carefully, even minutely. The first thing to note about the correct match percentage is that it is very little different from the chance level of 50 percent. Even though the difference is highly significant statistically because of the large number of matches involved, such a small deviation from chance could readily result from many possible subtle factors. In many papers on "experimental bias" Rosenthal (1966) discusses the influences of unintended factors on the outcome of experiments. Experimenter bias may influence the outcome of an experiment whenever the investigator, even unknowingly and unintentionally, communicates to his subjects the results he expects to obtain or the responses he expects them to make. Innocent scoring mistakes also occur more often in the favored direction.

In the case of UPS, a variety of possible cues may contribute to the tiny degree of UPS suggested by these experiments. We shall take some word pairs that produced better-than-chance correct matching in different experiments, and find out what possible cues might have aided English-speaking subjects in correct matching. We arrive at a possible cue by a process of elimination. For example, if two words are matched when they do not have similar sounds but have a similar word length, then we may attribute correct matching to the latter. Pay particular attention to the underlined letters in the test words.

Language relatedness as a cue

English antonyms	Czech	English	Hindi
<u>n</u>ew	<u>n</u>ový	down	niche
old	starý	<u>up</u>	<u>up</u>ar

These word pairs were in the original list used by Brown, Black, and Horowitz (1955), and many of the subsequent word-matching experiments used the same word list. Note that "new" and "nový" share the same initial consonant /n/, perhaps because English and Czech are related, both being members of the Indo-European Language Family. Words meaning "new" from many other languages from this family start with /n/:

nouveau (French)
nuevo (Spanish)
nou (Rumanian)
neu (German)
ny (Swedish, Danish, Norwegian)
nóvy (Russian), and so on.

As for "up" and "upar," is it surprising that English-speakers matched these two words? Again, English and Hindi belong to the Indo-European Language Family.

Word-matching among related languages is no proof of UPS. It merely confirms that two languages come from the same origin and have a degree of vocabulary correspondence, especially among the high-frequency words that are usually used in this type of experiment. All experiments that used related languages, but only some of the experiments that used unrelated languages, showed positive results.

Translation bias

	Japanese		Chinese
<u>o</u>ld	<u>o</u>ita	mature	laŭ
young	wakai	youthful	nyan chīng
(Tsuru and Fries, 1933)		(Klank et al., 1971)	

In the above Japanese example, the translator rendering English into Japanese, whether or not he was aware of the purpose of the experiment, chose "oita" rather than the more apt translation "toshitotta," perhaps because of the clang-association of the initial sound. In clang-association, people respond to sounds rather than to meanings of words.

In the Chinese translation, *laŭ* literally means "old." Had the experimenters used the more appropriate translation "chéng shu" (mature), a two-syllable word like "nyan chīng," would matching have been so successful?

Kunihira (1972) took up Taylor's (1963) warning on this translation bias and investigated it as an independent variable:

awa<u>k</u>e	o<u>k</u>iru (Japanese)	<u>s</u>ameru (alternate translation)
<u>s</u>leep	neru	nemuru

The first translation yielded 72 percent correct matching; the alternate translation, only 43 percent. In general, Kunihira could distinguish two lists of Japanese translations, one list containing one type of translations, and producing over-all positive results, and the other list containing alternate translations and producing negative or chance results.

Expressive voice   There are three different modes of presenting test words to subjects; auditory, visual, and audio-visual. The auditory mode can be further subdivided between uttering the test words in an expressive voice or in a monotonic voice or by computer-generated voice. The test words of word-matching experiments are usually of sensory or size meanings—"sharp blunt, hard soft"—that lend themselves easily to vocal expressions.

happy	ureshi (Japanese: Kunihira, 1971)
sad	kanashi

When "ureshi" and "kanashi" were spoken in a monotonic voice, matching was 39 percent correct, but in an expressive voice, 58 percent, and in printed forms, 47 percent.

Visual similarity

sit	suwaru (Japanese: Kunihira, 1971)
stand	tatsu

In the same study, this word pair produced the highest percentage of correct matching (64 percent) in the printed form. Presented auditorily, it produced 54 percent in a monotonic voice, and 53 percent in an expressive voice. Why? "Sit" and "stand" are not the kinds of meaning that can be expressed by voice. "Sit" and "suwaru" start with the same letter when printed; when pronounced, /s/ in "suwaru" (sit) becomes closer to /s/ in "stand."

In visual presentation of the test words, there is no guarantee that subjects are matching words on the basis of phonetic symbolism rather than on visual similarity of printed words. Greene (1965) actually asked his subjects to match English and Japanese words for their "similarity of appearance." Subjects so instructed matched just as well as those who were instructed in the usual manner to match words for their meaning. "Visual similarity" contains many components—the length of words, letters, letter combinations, a particular letter at a particular position, syllable structure, and so on. Greene partially separated out some of these components in an anagram experiment. In the anagrams, the letters in the Japanese words were scrambled so that the letter content and word length remained the same, but the letter configurations and syllable structures were changed, and the words now became meaningless. Subjects performed equally well with anagrams!

Klank, Huang, and Johnson (1971) point out that the same test words produced negative or positive results in different experimental conditions in their own experiment. If so, the positive results could not have been due to translation bias or to visual length. The conditions where the positive results were obtained used antonyms (condition 1); nonantonyms but pair members from opposite ends of the same semantic dimension (2 and 5); and nonantonym pairs with pair members from different semantic dimensions (3). Note that the word pairs have clear meaning contrasts in these conditions. The condition where they obtained only chance level matching is (4), where the word pairs did not have clear meaning contrasts, as each pair member was drawn from the same end of the same meaning dimension. Perhaps in such an unfavorable experimental .condition the non-UPS as well as any possible UPS cues we are discussing may have been rendered useless. As we have seen and shall see, the contrast in the meaning and sounds aids subjects in using cues in all types of phonetic symbolism experiments.

Onomatopoeia

twitch   massage
    piku-piku ugoku   dossato ochiru (Japanese; Weiss, 1966)
grind   thud

Note that "piku-piku ugoku" is somewhat onomatopoeic in that it reduplicates "piku" to describe the motion of twitching. As for "dossato ochiru," it literally means "falls with a thud." Even in direct imitation of sounds produced by a heavy object falling on the ground, the two languages use somewhat different-sounding words. Thus, the onomatopoetic nature of "dossato ochiru" escaped the experimenter, but not some alert subjects, who must look for any clue.

Inappropriate cues

frosty (adjective)
    shimo-no-orita (Japanese, literally "frost-of-covered"; Weiss, 1966)
gasp (verb)

What is expressed in one word must be translated into a compound of a few words in another language. In this case, a large part of the compound word, "of-covered," can be attached to other words of entirely different meanings. Also, as Barik (1969) points out, all Japanese adjectives end in *-a* or *-i*, while verbs end in *-u*. Subjects can perform matching on the basis of grammatical form in the last two examples.

The basis of matching is unidentifiable

| blunt | tu̱n (Chinese; as in "bo̱ok") | gothil (Hindi) |
| sharp | kʼuài | tez |

(Brown et al., 1955, and other experiments)

What cues could have helped subjects in matching the test words in this case?

Possible UPS

English	Chinese	Japanese	Korean	Czech	French
hard	kāng	katai	taktak	tvrdý	dur
soft	joú	yawai	mallang	mĕkký	mou
		or			
		yawarakai			

(Brown et al.; Kunihira; Klank et al.)

Korean and French pairs are added although they have not been reported in any experiment. "Hard" and "soft" have the same word length, eliminating visual length as a possible cue. The English antonym pair themselves do not seem to show much phonetic symbolism, but the words meaning "hard" from five foreign languages seem to. At least, four of them share [k] or [t] sounds, which are voiceless stops and suggest the tonal qualities of hardness. A hard rather than soft object may produce such sounds. The fact that not just one language but four languages contain these consonants strengthens the idea that such sounds could be used symbolically in words expressing this particular meaning. The tonal qualities of these sounds seem especially "hard" when they are contrasted to their antonyms that start with [m]. The only hitch in this neat reasoning is that English-speaking subjects matched Chinese "kāng (hard) to "soft"! (Weiss, 1963)

Even if "hard" and the corresponding word from the four remaining languages are matched on the basis of UPS, the nature of the symbolism is very ambiguous. Considering consonants, is [k] or [t] alone sufficient, or do [k] and [t] together enhance symbolism? Between [k] and [t], which plays the more important role? Do these consonants at any position in a word suggest symbolism? Do vowel contrasts such as [i] : [a] also contribute to symbolism?

So far we examined one possible UPS cue as well as several cues other than bona fide UPS that might aid subjects in word-matching. Since each word pair has its own peculiar characteristics, if we examined other word pairs from other languages we might find other possible cues. In the above scrutiny, I have had to limit myself mostly to word pairs that have been reported in published papers.

Whether subjects can take advantage of these possible cues is worth considering. The overwhelming majority of word-matching experiments used English-speakers in the United States, more specifically university students, as subjects. This is commonplace in psychological experiments, because these students are readily available in large numbers to professor-experimenters. I question the validity of choosing this type of subjects in word-matching experiments because the only two studies that did not use them produced negative results. Atzet and Gerard (1965) used Navaho-speakers, and Black and Brown (Brown, 1958), Chinese-speakers in Boston. Black and Brown note that their Chinese subjects who were recent immigrants (uneducated laborers, presumably) matched the test words in significantly different patterns from their English-speaking university subjects. Furthermore, Taylor and Taylor (1962) found English to be slightly correlated with all other languages tested. If this is a true language effect, English-speaking subjects should be expected to show slightly above-chance word matching with foreign languages, even with the most stringent controls.

What is so special about university students? Perhaps they are sophisticated about languages, having been exposed to diverse languages in their school and university environment. This kind of background is useful not only in recognizing cognates from related languages, but also in noting other possible cues that we have just discussed. Slobin (1968b) notes that in his study, American university student-subjects with foreign language experience matched test words better than those without such experience. Further, the diversity of foreign language contact and the duration of such contact were significantly related to success in word-matching. Such foreign language experience need not be with the test languages themselves. Slobin used three exotic foreign languages (Thai, Kanarese, and Yaruba) with which his subjects were not likely to have had direct contact. If speech sounds inherently express certain meanings across the words of world languages, why does one need university education to detect universal phonetic symbolism?

Many possible cues other than UPS can aid linguistically sophisticated subjects in word-matching. Correct matching reported is on the average around 52–53 percent, very slightly better than chance. How much of this slight deviation from chance can be attributed to non-UPS and how much to UPS cues, respectively?

Do words contain sounds appropriate for their meanings?

The analytical approach has shown that certain sounds express certain meanings to speakers of a particular language. The vowel /i/ expressing smallness, and /a/, bigness, in English are the best examples. The fourth approach is to examine the words of other natural languages and see whether words of, say, "small" meaning contain the small vowel /i/. In principle, successful word-matching is attributed to the same sounds being used for the same reasons in words of the same meaning in different languages. However, as we have seen, we do not have a clear answer on this question from word-matching experiments.

In words of natural languages   Some unsystematic observations of words, mostly in Indo-European languages, purport to demonstrate the existence of UPS. Some such examples were listed at the beginning of this chapter. Here let us examine more systematic observations. Newman (1933) found all the words in Roget's *Thesaurus* under the headings "greatness, smallness, size, littleness," and struck out the repetitions, derivatives, and phrases. Eleven judges then assessed the 500 words remaining, and a majority decision was taken as to whether each word belonged in either list and, if so, in which list it belonged. He wanted to see whether words denoting smallness contained /i/, and words denoting bigness, /a/ or /o/. He did not find a clear trend.

Taylor (1963) re-examined Newman's list, and found that "small" words tended to start with /t/ or /n/, the two consonants with the smallest size scores, and "big" words with /g/ and /k/, the two with the largest size scores obtained in Taylor and Taylor (1962). I also considered the initial vowel in Newman's size words, using the vowel scores from Taylor and Taylor's study. According to these scores, /ɪ/ in "is" and /ɛ/ in "ten" are the small vowels, /u/ and /o/ the large vowels. Of the words in Newman's list having small vowels as their first, 78 are "small" and 37 "large." Of the words having large vowels as their first, 9 are "small" and 18 are "large." The difference in ratio is even more marked than that for the initial consonants.

I listed the first three translation groups given in a Japanese dictionary for each of six English size-words—"small, little, minute," and "large, big, great." These are the first three adjectives given in Roget's *College Thesaurus* for the rubrics "littleness" and "size," respectively. In Japanese each translation group in turn has two to five synonyms or near synonyms. After striking out a few repetitions and compound words, 22 "small" words and 23 "big" words in Japanese remained.

In Japanese adjectives, the last vowel or syllable usually carries no semantic content but indicates grammatical function (for example, chisa*i*, chisa*na*); such variants were not counted. There were no clear differences between "big" and "small" words in their vowel compositions, except that /ʊ/ (as in "book") occurred about twice more often in "small" (9 occurrences) than in "big" (5) words. According to the data of Taylor and Taylor, /ʊ/ is the "smallest" vowel in Japanese phonetic symbolism, although it is a "large" vowel for English-speakers. The consonant /d/, the "biggest" consonant in Japanese, occurred six times in "big" words, and only once in "small" words. On the other hand, the "smallest" consonant in Japanese, /s/, occurred twice in "big" words, but ten times in "small" words.

All in all, this crude examination shows that sound occurrences in Japanese size-words tend to agree with Taylor–Taylor's size scores, at least for sounds having the most extreme scores.

Now we consider words referring to distance, in particular the locatives "here" and "there." We shall consider mainly the vowels. There may be some correspondence between large size and large distance on one hand, and small distance and small size on the other. If so, words signifying "here" should contain the high front vowel /i/; words signifying "there" should contain vowels that are longer or further back, such as /a/. Conveniently, in a number of languages the words for "there" and "here" are identical except for the vowels so that we have a more or less invariant basic word frame, with only the vowels varying. Table 9–3 lists words meaning "here" and "there" from 42 languages, some of them related, as collected by Tanz (1971).

The word "here" and "there" are two basic words in any language. There are not many synonyms for "here" and "there," and consequently we should not have too much difficulty in finding more or less unequivocal single translation equivalents for these two words from different languages. I leave you to detect a trend in the words of Table 9–3.

In subject-produced words   In another type of experiment, speakers of different languages produce words of size or of other meanings. The sounds occurring in these subject-produced words are then examined for any regular pattern. In the latest and largest experiment of this kind, Klank and others (1971) asked subjects to produce words related to "large–small," "fast–slow," and "good–bad." The subjects were Chinese-speakers in Taiwan and English-speakers in the United States. Initial vowels seemed to convey size, while initial consonants conveyed the "slow–fast" meaning. There was no trend in words related to "good–bad" either in English or in Chinese. The authors compared the two languages in terms of ratios of occurrence of different sounds. For example, the high vowel occurs preferentially in small words in a ratio of 1.282:1 in English, and 1.160:1 in Chinese (a parallel trend in the two languages). A central vowel occurs more often by 1.585:1 in English but less by 0.615:1 in Chinese (an opposite trend). Since the two languages show, on the whole, more parallel than opposite trends in their ratios, Klank and colleagues concluded that the two unrelated languages show the same phonetic symbolism, and hence that UPS exists.

Let us plot the ratios in a scatter graph (Figure 9–3): 1.282 (English) against 1.160 (Chinese) for the high vowel; 1.585 against 0.615 for the central vowel, and so on. If the two languages share the same phonetic symbollism, the dots from the two languages should fall on a more or less straight diagonal line (the dashed line Figure 9–3). As you can see, the

TABLE 9–3 Terms for "Here" and "There" from 42 Languages

Language Family	Language	here	there
Indo-European	Albanian	/kətú/	/atú/
"	Bengali	/ekhane/	/sekhane/
"	English	here	there
"	French	ici	la
"	German	hier	da
"	Hindi	/yəhã/	/vəhã/
"	Lithuanian	che	tan
"	Latin	hic	ibi
"	Norwegian	her	der
"	Polish	tu	tam
"	Rumanian	/aič/	/akólo/
"	Urdu	yahen	wahan
Indo-Aryan	Konkani	/haŋasər/	/thəinsər/
Indo-Iranian	Sinhala	mehe	ehe
Dravidian	Kanada	illi	alli
"	Koya	igge	agge
"	Tamil	inge	ange
"	Tulu	/mulpə/	/alpə/
Finno-Ugric	Hungarian	/itʰ/	/otʰ/
Ural-Altaic	Khalkha	/či/	/tani/
"	Kushan	iẏ	ôh́
"	Turkish	/burasí/	/buradá/
Semitic	Amhari	izzih	izzya
"	Arabic	/huna/	/hunaka/
"	Hebrew	poh/hine	sham
Macro-Sudanic Nilotic	Luo	-ni	-cha
Malayan	Malay	sini	sana
"	Tagalog	dito	do'on
Malayo-Polynesian	Woleolan	iga	igəlá
"	Indonesian	disini	disitu
Sino-Tibetan	Chinese		
	Mandarin	juh lee	nah lee
	Cantonese	li	nga
Maya	Yucatec	/-a'/	/-o'/
"	Tseltal	/ni dɛvŋ/	/ga dɛvŋ/
Uto-Aztecan	Aztec	/nika-n/	/onka-n/
"	Papago	/'ímɨ/	/'á-mɨ/
Australian	Djirbal	/bayḓ-i/	/bayḓ-a/
Eskimo	Eskimo	maani	taika
Korean	Korean	/i/-	/cə/-
Japanese	Japanese	koko/soko	asoko
Philippines	Cebuano	dinhi	didto
"	Ilocano	ditoy	idiay

From Tanz, 1971.

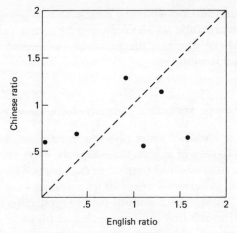

English ratio

FIGURE 9–3   Comparing Chinese and English ratios for initial vowels in small/ large words. (Based on data from Klank et al., 1971.)

dots are widely scattered, indicating that the two languages are not very similar in assigning vowels to small and big words. The correlation between rankings of ratios in the two languages is only .10. The data of Klank and others do not support their conclusion.

Unfortunately, the Klank study grouped consonants by their manner of articulation—stops, affricates, and the like. The category of stops is so inclusive that about one-third of the consonants that are common to the two languages belong to this category. Such gross classification could obscure possible differences of consonant symbolism in the two languages. For example, the two may have similar symbolism on bilabial stops /p,b/, but different symbolism on alveolar stops /t,d/, or on velar stops /g,k/. Voiced stops might be different from voiceless stops, and so on. Shriberg (1970) in fact found that four voiceless fricatives within one language, English, differed in their ratings on three dimensions of meaning. For example, /s/ rates highest on activity, /θ/ on potency.

In sum, this approach, too, indicates language-specific phonetic symbolism, and perhaps UPS in a very limited areas of meaning—size-related meanings. Again, vowels seem to show more consistent phonetic symbolism patterns.

THEORETICAL CONSIDERATIONS

Each approach to the investigation of UPS, in spite of flaws in its procedures and interpretations, has suggested certain trends. Here we consider results from all four approaches to arrive at a certain consensus on

UPS. Let us consider two possibilities. First, there is pervasive language-specific phonetic symbolism: we shall discuss its nature and implications. Secondly, we would not discount the possibility of limited UPS, and shall discuss its scope and limitations.

Language-specific phonetic symbolism (language-habit theory)

Languages and their speakers show phonetic symbolism, but the patterns of symbolism, seem to vary in at least three aspects. First, one language may be more susceptible to symbolism than other languages. Second, correlations of symbolism among different dimensions of meaning may vary from language to language. Third, speech sounds may suggest different meanings in diverse languages, thus refuting the universality of phonetic symbolism. We examined closely some of the studies that seem to show the existence of UPS and found that they are often inadequate in procedure and interpretation. We consider some remaining questions that lead to a theory of phonetic symbolism.

Why is there phonetic symbolism, differing from language to language? If we look only at the English results (upon which the old rationale was based) the traditional rationale works. The vowels /ɪ/ and /ɛ/ with their high pitch and small oral openings are given the smallest size scores, while /o/ and /u/ are given the biggest size scores. However, how do we explain with this rationale the finding that /ɪ/ was given the second largest, and /u/ the third smallest size score in Tamil, unless small objects emit low sounds in South India and Ceylon? Is there any good rationale why initial /g/ should suggest bigness to English speakers or smallness to Korean speakers?

Some factors that differ among unrelated languages must be the chief variables for phonetic symbolism. Among such factors we can consider different language habits. For example, people speaking English may develop the habit of associating initial /g/ with bigness, because of English words like "grand, great, grow, gain, gargantuan." On the other hand, initial /t/ is associated with smallness, probably because in English some frequently used "small" words start with /t/: "tiny, teeny, tip, trifle, tinge." Now, in Korean, /t/ is associated with bigness, perhaps because /t/ occurs in the Korean word "tae" meaning great or big. /J/, which received the smallest size score in Korean data, starts the Korean word "jaggeun," which means small. In Japanese, such big words as "debu" (fat), "dekkai" (huge), or "daikibo" (on a grand scale) start with /d/, which received the largest size score in Japanese. Staats and Staats (1957; see Chapter 3) demonstrated in a laboratory how neutral nonsense syllables can acquire specific meanings. They paired YOF with such pleasant words as "beauty," and XEH with unpleasant words like "thief." Eventually, YOF acquired a pleasant meaning and XEH, an unpleasant meaning. Now we can explain with the language-habit theory why Brown (1958) felt that "God," especially "Jehovah," suggests a very great magnitude, and why Jespersen felt that /ʌ/ in "dump" sounded unpleasant.

Not only linguists but philosophers from early times have been interested in UPS, hoping that it might explain the origin of human language. Speculating on the origin of language is a risky exercise, but it is interesting to sample some of the observations of philosophers. The German philosopher Humboldt in the early nineteenth century observed that in words such as "Wehen" (wave), "Wind," "Wolke" (cloud), "wirren" (mix up), "the vacillating, wavering motion with its confused impression on the senses is expressed through /v/ [German pronunciation of letter w] (quoted in Jespersen, 1922, p. 396). As soon as we venture out of the German language into other unrelated languages, we realize that Humboldt's observation too was a product of his German language habit. Just look at the word meaning "wind" in the following non-European languages: "baram" (Korean); "kaje" (Japanese); "szél" (Hungarian); "tuuli" (Finnish); "rüzgur" (Turkish); "angin" (Indonesian). To speakers of many languages other than German, it is not at all clear why /v/ expresses "vacillating, wavering motion with its confused impression on the senses." Some English words starting with /w/ are cognates of German words starting with /v/. The above (der) "Wind" is an example. How such sound shifts between related languages influence phonetic symbolism patterns will be interesting to investigate.

As language habits get solidified with increased age, one of the products of these habits, phonetic symbolism, has to become more consistent. Newman (1933) found such an age effect (up to the age of 11).

Once a certain sound or sound cluster has thus become associated with a certain meaning, then within that language a group of words of similar meaning may arise employing similar sounds. Some such examples from English are words meaning rapid movement and having "fli-"; "flick, flip, flit, flitter, flicker, fling." Some examples of words meaning "gentle" (in slope) or "slow" in Japanese and having similar sounds are: "yuru-yuru, yukkuri, yuttari, yururi, yuruyaka, yurui."

Using language-specific phonetic symbolism We are interested in UPS because of curiosity about the nature of language. But our findings have some utility. The extent and patterns of phonetic symbolism in different languages can be exploited in advertisements or in poetry. For instance, a name of a new cool beverage product can be coined by combining C-, -V-, and -C with the respective "cool" scores. "Coca-Cola" in fact is a very cool word in English, for it consists of consonants and vowels that received cool scores in the Taylor and Taylor study. According to those data, "Coke" is almost the coolest CVC that can be made for English-speakers. It is obvious why /k/ and /o/ received cool scores in English if we think of the words "cool" and "cold."

Another possible use of language-specific phonetic symbolism is in determining objectively and quantitatively the degree of relatedness between any pair of languages. Any two languages, if they are related, may share similar-sounding words for the same meaning, like German and English, which share initial /g/ for "big" words—"gross," "grossartig," "Gott," in German. For the medial vowel, we can quote Jespersen's (1922, p. 402) numerous words referring to something small in various Indo-European languages:

Foreign	English[a]
petit (French)	tip
piccolo (Italian)	pin
piccino	chink
Kind (German) /kint/	slit
pilt (Danish)	kid
chico (Spanish)	chit
mica (Latin)	little
quisquilioe	midge
mikros (Greek)	piddling
.	.
.	.
.	.

[a] The English words are not translations of the foreign words.

Phonetic symbolism patterns should be more similar among related than among unrelated languages. The closer the degree of language relation, the more similar the phonetic symbolism should be. As noted above, one has to be wary of the sound shift in making detailed comparisons, but over-all correlations should indicate the degree of relatedness of languages.

Limited UPS

Word-matching experiments hint at the possibility that *some* words in *some* languages may show UPS. "UPS" in that case may be a misnomer, but we shall still use this label. Studies with nonsense objects suggest that phonetic symbolism may relate to nonphonetic objects. If so, some aspects of phonetic symbolism may be universal. Taylor and Taylor's cross-language study failed to detect this limited scope of UPS, perhaps because the four dimensions of meaning were too gross or limited to reveal UPS that might exist only in a particular type of word.

Our main purpose here is to define the possible scope of UPS. UPS may be limited to speech sounds that have unambiguous, agreed-upon tonal qualities or articulatory features. For example, [i] is a high-pitched vowel with a small mouth opening, especially when contrasted with [a]. Speakers of many languages are expected to agree about such qualities of [i] and [a]. Speakers may also agree that small objects tend to emit higher-pitched sounds than big objects. We may therefore be justified in looking for [i] in "small" words and [a] in "big" words in many languages. The reason we did not always find clear UPS in size-words could be that the large number and variety of size-words in each language may have blurred the relation between sound and meaning. This seems not to be the case with the two locatives "here" and "there." Incidentally, what trend have you found in Table 9–3 on "here-there" pairs? There seem to be more word pairs that show the vowel contrast in the predicted than in the other direction.

Hard, angular, heavy, and their opposites, are other qualities that speech sounds might be able to express, because objects with such qualities emit characteristic sounds, on which speakers of many languages can agree. However, even the words expressing such qualities do not show phonetic symbolism in every language. As we have seen, English "hard" and "soft" seem less symbolic than Korean "taktak" and "mallang." We expect that English-speakers might match this Korean pair with their corresponding English words, but Korean speakers may not succeed too well in the reverse direction.

Where onomatopoeia ends and UPS starts is hard to define. Onomatopoeic words patently imitate the sounds objects or animals produce, and the sound structures of such words are naturally very similar in different languages. Examine the following list of the sounds attributed to roosters in different languages, and note the common patterns: /k/ is predominent, and /kok/ or /kek/ reduplicates in a word.

kokkux (Greek)　　　　　cock-a-doodle-doo (English)
coquelico (French)　　　　kykeliky (Danish)
kikeriki (German)　　　　kukeliku (Swedish)

Especially interesting are the two examples from non-Indo-European languages:

kokyo (Korean)　　　　　kokekokkyo (Japanese)

Some onomatopoeic words also imitate the sounds animals produce but do not show a neat pattern. A dog barks:

bowwow (English)
wangwang (Japanese)
mongmong (Korean, pronounced as /mɔŋ/)

Here we already see that the initial consonants as well as the medial vowels are not the same or even similar. The words still tend to contain reduplicated syllables. Consider again Korean "taktak" (hard): it also imitates the sound produced by a hard object, and contains reduplicated syllables. Should it be considered as an onomatopoeic word or a UPS word?

Beyond this handful of speech sounds, a majority of speech sounds cannot be assigned tonal qualities, at least in a way on which speakers of many languages would agree. For example, [ʌ] in "dung" is lower in pitch than [i], but would speakers of different languages consider low vowels unpleasant? Do unpleasant objects in many cultures tend to produce low- rather than high-pitched sounds? How can we relate the meaning of "sit" or "stand," or what-have-you, with tonal qualities of sounds?

The difficulty of finding plausible rationales for a relation between sound and meaning applies to most speech sounds and to the great majority of our words. Hence UPS should not be pervasive. In any particular language there might be a handful of onomatopoeic words and an equally small number of phonetically symbolic words (if we can always clearly distinguish the two types). Of this small number, an even smaller number might show a similar pattern of phonetic symbolism in a number of different languages. Does UPS of such a minute scope deserve so much effort over so long a period (since ancient Greek days)? Should we not redirect our effort from proving whether UPS exists to finding more about language-specific phonetic symbolism patterns?

SUMMARY AND CONCLUSIONS

Phonetic symbolism means that a sound or a sound configuration directly and intrinsically suggests or expresses a certain meaning. Good examples are [i] suggesting smallness and [a], bigness to English-speakers. If the same sound-meaning correspondences were found in many languages we would have universal phonetic symbolism (UPS).

Four experimental approaches to UPS have been discussed. Following the first approach, we find that speakers of different languages tend to use the contrast between [i] and [a] for describing small or large; angular or round; and light or heavy objects.

Using the second approach, experimenters asked English-speakers to judge nonsense syllables as to their size or brightness. Again, [i] is judged to be small and bright, and [a] to be large and dull. Bentley and Varon showed that to obtain consistent results there have to be prescribed dimensions of meaning on which to judge nonsense syllables, and the number of dimensions has to be less than five for positive results to occur.

Taylor and Taylor expanded this approach to speakers of languages other than English. Tamil, Korean, Japanese, and English speakers show different patterns of phonetic symbolism—for example, [i] expresses smallness to English-speakers, but not to Tamil-speakers. Both consonants and vowels in CVC syllables show such language-specific phonetic symbolism.

In the third approach, English-speaking university students tried to match English antonym pairs with foreign translation equivalents. This type of word-matching experiment typically yields 53 percent correct matching, slightly above the 50 percent chance level. Several non-UPS cues such as translation bias, visual similarity, or expressive voice may be just as potent as possible UPS in aiding subjects to match words correctly.

Following the fourth approach, words from natural languages are examined to see whether they contain appropriate sounds. In English and in Japanese, "small" and "big" words seem to contain appropriate vowels and consonants. The locatives "here" and "there" from a large number of languages seem to contain [i] and [a] for "near" and "far," respectively.

When findings from all the four approaches are considered together, there seems to be pervasive phonetic symbolism, but it is langnage-specific. A language-habit theory was proposed to account for this language-specific phonetic symbolism. A few possible uses of phonetic symbolism were suggested.

UPS, if it exists at all, is limited to speech sounds that have specific tonal qualities on which speakers of different languages can agree, and to a handful of words that might contain these sounds to express the appropriate meanings.

10

Speech Disorders

*Stuttering starts not in the child's mouth but
in the parent's ears.*

Wendell Johnson

Normal speakers are not always perfectly fluent—they mispronounce, they
hesitate, and they produce incomplete or ungrammatical utterances. Such
minor imperfections are not considered to be speech disorders. A speech
disorder is a deviation from the normal pattern extreme and consistent
enough to interfere with communication. Speech deviations may involve
articulation, rhythm, voice, and language usage.

All workers in speech disorder report more disorders by a ratio of
about 1.8:1 among males than among females at all age levels, and more
speech disorders in the first three grades of school than earlier or later. A
study of various disorders in 87,288 children and some adults in New England found 7.8 percent to be handicapped in speech or hearing (Pronovost,
1951). Table 10–1 shows the distribution of the types of disorder among
this 7.8 percent in decreasing order of incidence. Note that hearing difficulties often lead to problems with speech.

We have from time to time referred to deafness, and have also mentioned a variety of "abnormal" speech types such as the speech of the
mentally retarded, of anarthrics, and of other people with physical defects.
In this chapter we shall discuss voice disorders very briefly and the relation of deafness to speech a little further. We shall discuss articulation
disorders and stuttering in some depth because they are more psychological
than physiological in origin, and because these are two of the most common
speech disorders. They reveal speech difficulty patterns that interest psyco-

TABLE 10-1   Distribution of Types of Speech Handicaps among the 7.8% of Individuals Found to have Some Kind of Speech Difficulty

Types of disorder	Relative incidence, %
Articulation	50
Hard of hearing	15.4
Stuttering	10.9
Deaf	8.4
Voice	6.6
Delayed speech	4.4
Miscellaneous	1.6
Cleft palate	1.2
Cerebral palsy	1.2
Aphasia	0.5

Rearranged from W. Pronovost, 1951.

linguists. Aphasia, a language disorder caused by brain damage, is one of our important sources of information on the relation between language and brain mechanisms, and is discussed in the following chapter.

Deafness

Deafness is common. It causes a serious speech problem when it is congenital and profound. Congenital deafness is correctly referred to as deaf-mutism, since without special education lack of speech is an inevitable sequel of profound hearing loss. According to a report of the World Health Organization (1953), the prevalence of deaf-mutism ranges from 0.3 to 3 per thousand population. In all countries males are more frequently deaf than females. About 80 percent of the children in the United States identified as deaf by age 6 are thought to have been born deaf (Gentile, 1972).

Deafness does not have a single cause; it can be due to a congenital malformation, the effect of disease, or the result of physical damage to the hearing organs or to the brain. It can also result as a part of the aging process. K. S. Brown (1973) cites several common observations that suggest that human deafness has some hereditary basis. For example, deafness affects the relatives of deaf people more commonly than it does the general population; identical twins more often than fraternal twins are both deaf or both have good hearing.

Psycholinguists are interested in the speech development of congenitally deaf people. Without exposure to sound, how do they develop language? We have discussed babbling and the sentence structures of profoundly deaf people in Chapter 6. We also discussed in Chapter 8 how they develop cognitive faculties. In all cases, we have found that deaf people do not behave exactly like hearing children and adults.

A deaf person's difficulties in mastering speech are due to delay in exposure to speech. Nowadays researchers in the field believe that even congenitally deaf children have some residue of hearing, and this small hearing ability should be amplified and put to use as early as possible so that the deaf children can be exposed to speech. In the Nuffield Hearing and Speech Center in England,

. . . no child has been found in whom it was impossible to develop responses to sound. The impression that a child cannot hear at all is often the result of unsuitable methods of testing and of faulty observation. It has been found, further, that no matter how small the amount of hearing the child has initially, this hearing can be used in the development of speech and will in fact show every evidence of increasing in amount with teaching. As a result, the clinic has produced many instances of children with very severe hearing losses (70, 80, 90 dB over the whole audible range in the better ear) who have developed excellent speech, sometimes indistinguishable from normal, and who have consequently been educated successfully among normally hearing children in an ordinary school (Fry, 1966, p. 200).

Here we shall discuss briefly the phonetic deficiencies of the deaf who have not received the Nuffield treatments. Deaf children often cannot master a natural tone of voice or intonation, even with special training. Their intonation is frequently "flat" and monotonous; their rhythm is either lacking or incorrect. Lack of rhythm occurs when all syllables are equally stressed, incorrect rhythm when the stress patterns are wrong. Hudgins and Numbers (1942), who studied 192 deaf children, found that errors of rhythm contributed as much to loss of intelligibility as did errors of consonant articulation. In addition, deaf children have to pause for breath more frequently and speak more slowly than do hearing children. Their average pitch tends to be high. Many deaf children put undue effort into producing speech. This tendency leads to a pattern known as *overfortis* that is characterized by excessive breath pressure, overemphasis in articulation, and sometimes fluctuating pitch.

Deaf children may make errors in articulating both consonants and vowels. They may omit one of the consonants constituting a cluster. They may confuse voiceless consonants with voiced consonants, perhaps because these cannot be discriminated visually—externally /p/ and /b/ are articulated in the same way. Difficulties with vowels involve errors in timing and nasalizing. The deaf may use the neutral /ə/ as a general-purpose vowel, or may make vowels into diphthongs.

There have been some recent attempts (such as Nickerson and Stevens, 1973) to develop a computer-based system of speech-training aids for the deaf. Various characteristics of speech can be visually displayed; amplitude, frequency, timing, nasalization, and so forth have been tried. A deaf person learns to approximate his speech characteristics to those of his trainer.

Voice disorder

Voice problems are traditionally grouped into three categories. (1) Pitch problems: A person's habitual pitch level may be either too high or too low for the age and sex. During the period of voice change a boy's voice drops approximately an octave and a girl's voice three or four semitones. A husky 17-year-old football player with a high voice might feel embarassment. (2) Loudness problem: A child may habitually talk too loud (about 86 dB) or too soft (46 dB). (3) Voice quality problems: They include voices that are harsh, breathy, hoarse, or excessively nasal. Such voice qualities are unpleasant for listeners. Hypernasality has some virtue in enabling the speaker to get his message across in the presence of masking noise, for it carries piercingly. Auctioneers and barkers at carnival sideshows find it useful, if not ornamental.

Often voice disorders are due to organic-physiological factors such as absence, underdevelopment, malfunction, or deformities of speech organs —larynx, vocal folds, nasal passages, and so on. As we have seen, deafness also can cause an "unnatural" voice quality. Some organic factors are congenital, and others are due to vocal abuse such as excessive shouting. Such abuse may cause fatigue, dehydration, or swelling in any part of vocal mechanisms. Singers are very conscious of the possible consequences of overusing their voices.

Voice disorders are functional when there is nothing wrong with the vocal mechanisms. Overaggressiveness or having deaf parents may cause a habitually loud voice. Hoarseness may be related to emotional disturbances or psychic trauma. A loss of voice (aphonia) can be psychosomatic. It is also possible for a child to have a voice problem as a result of imitating others with voice problems in his environment, the cleft-palate speech of a brother, for example.

Surgery may correct some organically caused voice problems. Functional disorders may disappear with therapy that teaches children how to use the vocal organs correctly, or that removes underlying emotional problems. (Partly based on Wilson, 1972.)

FUNCTIONAL DISORDERS OF ARTICULATION

Problems of articulation are the most common speech disorders in children. A child may say /baf/ instead of "bath," or /wito/ for "little." Fortunately, children usually outgrow this problem. Three boys have this problem for every two girls. Its incidence is high at the kindergarten level, but declines with the advance of age and grade.

Etiology

Certain organic defects, particularly cleft palate, cerebral palsy, and deafness are frequently associated with articulation disorders. Other abnormalities or variations in articulatory organs, such as malformation of the teeth, different sizes and shapes of the tongue, differences in length or height of the palate or the size of the lips, do not seem to be major factors in articulation disorders. According to Van Riper (1963), adults with no teeth, or with no tongue or only half of a tongue, can speak with fair intelligibility.

Other physiological factors that researchers have looked into are: handedness; kinesthetic sensibility (muscular sensitivity to position, movement, and tension); development and physical health (the acquisition time of certain physical and motor skills, the presence or absence of a history of certain childhood diseases); general motor ability. Winitz's (1969) extensive survey of the literature on these factors found that there is no conclusive evidence of their relation to articulation disorders.

In addition to sex and age, other factors that seem to be related to articulation defects are (based on Winitz):

Intelligence   Intelligence shows a low relation in a population of children within the normal range of intelligence and who, in addition, are without psychological and organic involvements. The proportion of articulatory errors is greater for children with IQ below 70 than for children with IQ above 70.

Socioeconomic status   More misarticulating children and more articulatory errors are found in the lower than in the upper socioeconomic groups. The relation is weak, however.

Sibling status   There is a significant difference for ordinal position (in favor of the first-born children) and intersibling age differences (articulation improves as the age spacing increases). The factors of sibling status and socioeconomic status suggest that first-born children in well-to-do homes have better opportunities to listen to, and practice, well-articulated speech sounds.

Auditory memory span   The ability to store and recall recently given auditory verbal stimuli may be involved. There is some evidence that misarticulating children have poor recall of consonants, but perhaps not of vowels or digits.

Auditory discrimination   The evidence is strong that misarticulating children discriminate poorly. Substitution errors described below suggest that faulty auditory discrimination could be at least partly responsible for faulty articulation. The fact that deaf children often have articulation problems also implicates difficulties in auditory discrimination.

Symptoms of misarticulation

There are many different types of misarticulation—continuance of infantile speech patterns, lisping, sound omission, substitutions, distortions, and additions. We first look at sound substitutions; here we can find a pattern that ties in with other psycholinguistic data. Some of the common substitution errors are shown in columns 2 and 3 in Table 10–2.

TABLE 10–2   Common Sound Substitution and Sounds with Few or Many Errors

"Difficult" sounds		"Easy" sounds	
From 100 to 1,067 errors	Correct sounds	Substituting sounds	From 1 to 91 errors
l or r ———	l or r ———————————▶	w ———————	w
	f ————————————▶	p ———————	p
	g ————————————▶	d ———————	d
ð ———	ð ———		
dʒ ———	dʒ ———		
θ ———	θ ————————————▶	f, t —————	f
	k ————————————▶	t ———————	t
ʃ ———	ʃ ————————————▶	s	
tʃ ———	tʃ ————————————▶	s, ʃ	
ŋ			n
j			m
s			b
v			h
z	•		k
			y
			g

An "easy" sound /w/ substitutes for a "difficult" sound /l/ or /r/; /d/ substitutes for /g/, /ð/, and /dʒ/, and so on.

Columns 1 and 4 are from Snow, 1963; "Errors of first-grade children"; columns 2 and 3 are from various sources: Messer, 1967; Menyuk, 1968; Compton, 1970.

Columns 1 and 4 show the sounds on which first-grade children make many or few errors respectively. Notice that some of the "easy" sounds in column 4 replace some of the "difficult" sounds in column 1.

Let us examine some individual substitution errors more closely. The consonants [k] and [g] are produced at the back of the mouth, and children may have difficulty in learning how they are produced. The sounds commonly substituted for [k] and [g] are produced at the front of the mouth in the same manner as those they replace. In other words, substituting sounds are easier to learn to produce and still sound similar to the substituted sounds. The voiceless stop [k] is replaced by another voiceless stop [t]; and the voiced stop [g], by another voiced stop [d]. In Chapter 2 we discussed an experiment on auditory confusion among English consonants. Confusion was prevalent among consonants articulated at different places but in a similar manner, such as between [k] and [t] and between [g] and [d].

Compton (1970) also noted that sound substitution errors are highly consistent and systematic. For example, one child's initial consonants showed a pattern in which [tʃ] was replaced by [s]; and [s], in turn, by [t]. [dʒ] was replaced by [d]; and [d] by [g]. The regularity underlying the substitutions shown in this pattern is to "trade" or replace one place of articulation for another, with the restriction that the voice/voiceless feature of the displaced or substituted sounds remains invariant.

Children's articulatory difficulties often persist until the age of 7 or 8, at least with certain sounds. A survey of literature by Palermo and Molfese (1972) shows that children aged between 5 and 8 have difficulties in producing: (1) sounds that occur in the medial or final position of a word; (2) consonant sounds that involve the features of continuancy and stridency (as, /θ/, /f/); and (3) consonant clusters such as -lfth in "twelfth."

Medial and final sounds may be misarticulated because these sounds tend to be less stressed in the English language. Such difficulties might again be due to acoustic discrimination difficulties. But usually it is the initial consonant that causes difficulty to younger children, aphasics, and stutterers. Here we may have to invoke the articulatory difficulty of producing a consonant without a preparatory vowel. Consonant clusters are difficult to articulate; they involve a rapid series of complicated articulatory movements unrelieved by vowels, which can give speakers time to readjust their articulators in readiness for the next consonant. This may be why one of the common ways to cope with consonant clusters is to insert a vowel between two adjacent consonants, as do Japanese adults speaking English and some aphasics. We can also suspect that the acoustic discrimination of consonant clusters is not easy—a child hearing "twelfth" may not hear distinctly all the component consonants in /-lfθ/. The sound not heard clearly may be dropped in articulation.

The difficulties involved in articulating consonants with +continuancy and +stridency have already been discussed in Chapter 5. Here we note the fact that analyzing misarticulation in terms of distinctive features is profitable. The degree of intelligibility of the misarticulated sound may be accounted for by which features are missed as well as by how many features are missed, for some features carry high information. To correct some misarticulations involving a feature that may be absent from children's repertoires, training them to produce a phoneme with this feature may help them to produce other phonemes with the same feature. For example, McReynolds and Bennett (1972) trained in /f/ a child who lacked +stridency. Another sound with +stridency, /θ/, served as a control—it was used to determine that only the feature being trained was changing during the training. The feature of +stridency generalized to other phonemes with this feature, namely /s, z, tʃ, v/.

To sum up, mild articulation errors are common in early childhood. They show certain patterns, often analyzable in distinctive features, that are of interest to psycholinguists. Some consonants and consonant clusters require more complex articulation and fine auditory discrimination, and are mastered late by children. As prevention and cure, we can provide a good speech environment and hope that the child will outgrow articulation errors. What happens when parents become unduly concerned with such errors and try too hard to correct them can be seen in the following discussion of stuttering.

STUTTERING

We can recognize a severe stutterer easily. Stuttering is a disturbance of rhythm and fluency of speech by intermittent blocking, convulsive repetition, or prolongation of sounds, syllables, words, or phrases. Stuttering more than any other speech disorder arouses our curiosity.

Incidence

Who stutters? Almost all cultures from ancient times seem to have had stutterers. If it is any comfort to stutterers, Demothenes, Aesop, Aristotle, George VI, Churchill, Charles I, and Darwin have been among the well-known stutterers. Some of these people overcame their speech handicaps, as we know. A quick way to find out whether a certain culture has many stutterers is to see whether it has a specific word for stuttering. Japanese "domori"; Korean "dodum"; Chinese "nanawei"; German "stottern"; Fiji Island "kaka"; and Salish (an American Indian tribe) "sutsuts" mean "stutter," and all these groups have stutterers among their speakers. The words for stuttering in different cultures are often onomatopoeic, sometimes repeating consonants as in "stutter," "kaka," or "dodum." Some tribes, such as the Bannock and Shoshone Indians in North America, do not have a word for stuttering, and seem to be among the rare groups without stutterers (Snidecor, 1947).

The incidence of stuttering in the general population, as surveyed in many parts of the world over many years, is about 1 percent. For example, it was 1.02 percent in a sample of 231,468 people in Hungary as studied in 1901 by Sarbo, and 1.2 percent among 7,358 people in Newcastle upon Tyne in England as studied by Andrews and Harris (1964).

Stuttering may begin at any age during childhood. Many children apparently begin to stutter with their first attempts to say sentences. But new cases continue to appear in considerable numbers up to about 9 years of age, and some arise later.

About five times as many boys as girls stutter. Further, girls tend to begin stuttering later, to stutter less severely, and to recover faster than boys. Some workers (such as West, 1958) regard this phenomenon as evidence that there is a sex-linked genetic predisposition to stuttering. There is more infant mortality, more birth injury, and greater susceptibility to most childhood diseases among boys than among girls. A broad congenital vulnerability of the male constitution may be responsible for all of the handicaps men suffer.

Other workers explain the sex ratio on environmental grounds. Goldman (1967) has reported some evidence that the sex ratio is related to greater environmental pressures on the male. In a sample of 694 stutterers identified in a statewide survey of school-age children in Tennessee, the sex ratio was only 2:1 among the black children, as opposed to 5:1 among white children. He attributed this to the fact that the lower socioeconomic segment of southern Afro-American society possesses distinct matriarchal features and imposes less responsibility on the male than on the female. Both genetic and environmental factors may be relevant to stuttering, as we shall see.

Etiology

The most interesting question is how stuttering starts and develops. If we know the etiology we are in a better position to prevent and perhaps cure stuttering. Let us examine the origin of stuttering from an organic-physiological and from a psychological-environmental viewpoint.

Organic-physiological There is a tendency for stuttering to appear in successive generations of the same family, suggesting a genetic basis. West, Nelson, and Berry (1939) separated out stuttering that resulted from association with another stutterer and that which seemed to be genetically determined, as shown in Table 10–3. They asked stutterers and fluent speakers to identify stutterers in the family. A danger of misinterpreting

TABLE 10-3   Stutterers in the Family

	Stutterers	Controls
Number of families studied (matched in age and sex)	204	204
Number of family members (parents, siblings, relatives . . .)	6,600	6,266
Number of stutterers in the family	210	37
Number of stuttering parents or grandparents	54	4
Number who had no association with other stutterers	129	144
Number who associated with other stutterers	75	60

Based on data from West, Nelson, and Berry, 1939.

this kind of survey arises from the probability that stutterers may search for stutterers in the family tree more carefully than do nonstuttering controls. According to Table 10-3, having a stutterer in the family is more important than being exposed to stutterers in the family. Stuttering frequently appears in children of stuttering parents with whom the children have had little if any contact.

Another way to estimate the genetic influence in stuttering is to compare the incidence of stuttering among identical and fraternal twins. Among 200 twin pairs, Nelson, Hunter, and Walter (1945) found 30 fraternal pairs and 10 identical pairs in which at least one member stuttered. In 9 of the 10 pairs of identical twins, both twins stuttered, while among 30 fraternal pairs, in only 2 did both twins stutter.

Those two pieces of evidence seem to suggest that some hereditary factor may be operating in the development of stuttering, but the method of transmission is unknown, as is the degree to which it can be modified by environmental factors. We may argue that a predisposing factor rather than faulty speech itself may be inherited. Automatic reactivity, conditionability, and the acquisition of anxiety responses (all possible ingredients of stuttering) are interrelated and in part constitutionally determined. Speakers who have inherited such a predisposition may stutter or show other speech disorders in adverse environments.

Researchers have so far failed to identify any organic defects, even in the articulatory organs, as causes of stuttering. When differences between stutterers and nonstutterers are viewed in all sorts of ways, comparing articulatory organs, audition, diabetes, handedness, motor coordination, perseveration, allergy . . . (you name it, researchers have searched everywhere), the early studies commonly showed some differences. However, the more recent the studies (and presumably the better the control procedures) the smaller become the differences between the two groups. Stutterers do not seem to differ from nonstutterers in handedness. The long-standing contention that enforced change of handedness may cause stuttering has never been borne out in a satisfactory way by scientific research.

In some cases stutterers and nonstutterers may differ in the functioning of the central nervous system, if not in their peripheral organs. The sample of handwriting by a stutterer given in Figure 10–1 shows that he has a tendency for prolongation even in writing. This is suggestive of a general motor predisposition for the kind of problem manifest in stuttering.

Sayles (1971) found abnormal brain wave patterns in 30–40 percent of stutterers. The brain wave patterns of stutterers as a group occupied a region somewhere between those of normal controls and those of epileptics. There was great variability among the stutterers, however. Curry and Gregory (1969) showed that stutterers and nonstutterers, all right-handed, differed in ability on *dichotic word tests*. When different verbal materials are simultaneously presented to the left and the right ear, normal listeners hear better with their right ears (reflecting perhaps the fact that the left hemisphere controls verbal processing). In this experiment 75 percent of the normal listeners obtained higher right-ear scores, while 55 percent of the

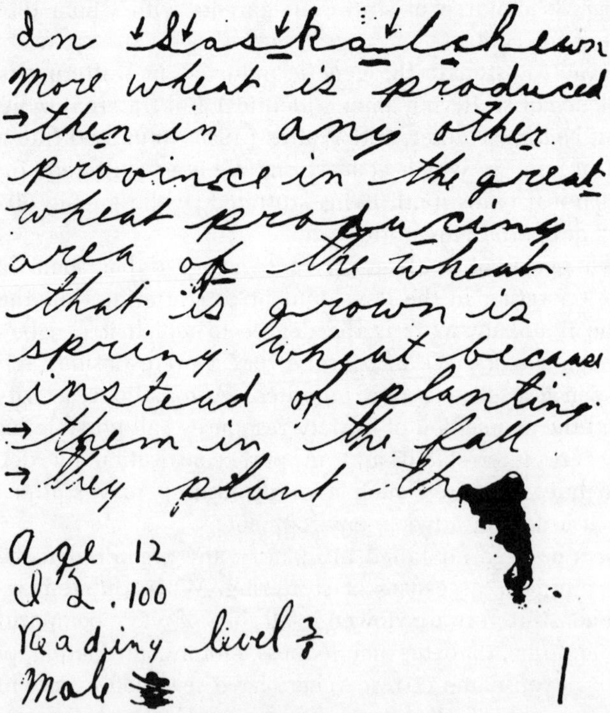

FIGURE 10–1 Stutterer, male, age 12, IQ 100. Poor motor coordination manifested in writing. Note overstretched initial and connecting strokes, indicating drawling in the attempt to maintain continuity and flow. (From Roman, 1968.)

stutterers had higher *left*-ear scores. The two groups did not differ in non-verbal dichotic tasks or the monotic word memory test. The results suggest that cerebral hemispheric organization with regard to processing verbal material may be slightly different in stutterers and nonstutterers.

Environmental factors   Wendell Johnson, who has studied stuttering for many years and whose influence has been very potent in modern speech therapy, advocates a functional (diagnosogenic) theory of stuttering (see, for example, Johnson, 1955). He points out that (1) whether a child is regarded as a stutterer depends upon the opinion of a lay person—a parent; (2) the symptoms that give rise to a diagnosis of stuttering are similar to disfluencies[1] found in every young child; (3) "true" stuttering develops *after* the diagnosis.

Let us examine some of the evidence supporting Johnson's position. Davis (1939, 1940) found that repetitions ranged from 6.2 to 43.9 percent in one-hour verbatim records of 62 children aged 2 to 5 in free play. She concluded that a child who repeats approximately ¼ of his speech either in part or in whole in a word or a phrase is talking "normally." She thought that syllable repetition perhaps has more relevance to the genesis of stuttering, because it had a skewed distribution, with 16 of the 62 children showing no syllable repetition. Discrepancy between thought and speech tempos might be the cause for such numerous repetitions—young children cannot formulate their thoughts fast enough. Paucity of vocabulary and other means of expressing thoughts might be another cause of frequent repetitions.

Other studies show that children who are regarded as "normal" speakers may be judged to stutter by persons instructed to listen for abnormalities in the tape-recorded speech of children. Parents of stuttering children are more likely to diagnose stuttering from recorded speech than are parents of nonstuttering children (Bloodstein, Jaeger, and Tureen, 1952).

However, a study by Johnson and associates (1959) showed distinct differences in the descriptions offered by the parents of controls and of stutterers. The earliest disfluencies were characterized by phrase repetitions, pauses, and interjections, far more often than were the earliest remembered

---

[1] *Disfluency* (occasionally spelled *dysfluency*) refers to repetitions, prolongations, interjections, and pauses that can be considered "normal," not stuttering. In an experiment by MacDonald and R. Martin (1973) judges could reliably and unambiguously identify disfluency and stuttering as two separate response classes. Most stuttering occurred on words while most disfluency in intervals bounding words. Other investigators (for example, Davis, 1939, 1949; Johnson and associates, 1959) say that syllable repetitions, sound prolongations, and "tensed" articulation tend to be judged as stutterings, while repetitions of words or pauses and interjections between words tend to be judged as "normal."

stutterings. The earliest stutterings, on the other hand, were more often described as syllable repetitions and sound prolongations. They were more frequently accompanied by unusual force, effort, or muscular tension in "getting words out" than were the earliest disfluencies. Here one wonders: could this not be because laymen regard only this sort of thing as stuttering and hence take note of it when they are worried that the child might stutter?

In the light of the above findings Johnson modified slightly his diagnosogenic theory to an "interaction hypothesis," which says that the onset of stuttering may be a joint product of the parents' high standards of fluency, the child's unusual kind or degree of disfluency, and the child's proneness to react to either or both of these. A number of observations and experiments support this hypothesis. Bloodstein and West (1969, p. 225) cite a mother of a 3-year-old boy who was sufficiently disturbed by the boy's inability to say the /l/ and /g/ sounds that she undertook her own program of remedial speech training. Not only did she persistently correct the boy's pronunciation of words beginning with /l/ and /g/, but she attempted to do so by showing him how she put her mouth when she said them. The boy had barely learned how to produce these sounds when he began to stutter. The earliest sympton recalled by the mother was the repetition of initial /l/ and /g/.

I once knew a Japanese girl aged about 20 who had trouble pronouncing /θ/ correctly. As noted earlier, this is a difficult sound for a foreigner whose native language lacks it. She was constantly corrected by her English-speaking friends whenever she mispronounced it. Eventually, she became tense and started to stutter whenever she had to say a word with initial /θ/.

The child-rearing attitudes and practices of stutterers' parents are of paramount interest in explaining how stuttering develops. Johnson portrays stutterers' parents as largely anxious, perfectionistic, and demanding, particularly in regard to the child's speech. Among many experiments testing this contention, let us examine one with an interesting approach and with results that are comparable to other studies.

Goldman and Shames (1964a, 1964b) found that parents of stutterers did not appear to set higher goals for themselves in a motor task than did the parents of controls. However, the fathers of stutterers set unrealistic goals when asked to predict the child's scores and also the number of words on which the child would have difficulty in telling a story. Further, when confronted with their children's failures on both the motor and speech tasks, the fathers of the stutterers tended to persist in relatively high estimates of their children's success to a greater extent than did the fathers of the nonstutterers. The two groups of mothers did not differ, although the mothers of the stutterers tended to make higher initial estimates of their children's success.

Although researchers agree that stuttering runs in the family, they do not agree as to why. We discussed earlier the possibility of genetic transmission of stuttering. Johnson has another explanation: stuttering frequently occurs in the same family because of the handing down of a "climate of anxiety" about the hesitant speech of children.

Gray's (1940) investigation of a "stuttering family" in Iowa seems to support this viewpoint. Although there had been stutterers in this family for the last five generations, it appeared that in a fairly large branch of the family living in Kansas there was very little stuttering, as shown in the detailed geneology in Figure 10–2. About 40 percent of the Iowa branch (the descendants of IIIA) were, or had been, stutterers, but of the 17 living members of the Kansas branch (descendants of the siblings of IIIA) only one was a stutterer. Gray interpreted that the stuttering in the Iowa branch arose largely out of attitudes that were conducive to the diagnosis of normal speech as stuttering.

The following events strengthen this interpretation. At the time that Gray did her study of this family, various members of the Iowa branch received advice and information about stuttering in the context of a diagnosogenic orientation toward the problems. Twenty years later Johnson (1961) reported that of 44 people in the sixth generation, only one has ever been considered a stutterer.

Child-rearing practices seem to differ between cultures where no stutterers are found and cultures having a high incidence of stuttering.

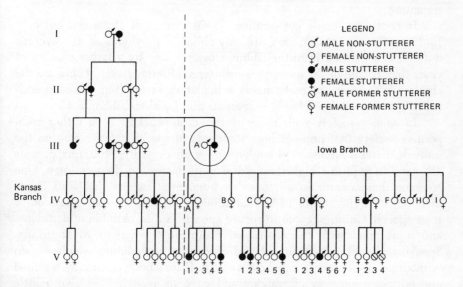

FIGURE 10–2   Five generations of a stuttering family. IIIA is in a circle. A dashed line separates the "Kansas Branch" (right) and the "Iowa Branch" (left). (The circle and the dashed line added to Gray's figure, 1940.)

No stuttering was found in the Bannock and Shoshone Indians whom Snidecor studied. He personally interviewed 800 persons and obtained information on 1,000 more, and failed to find "one pure-blooded Indian who stuttered." In these cultures, the investigator noted, the children were allowed a relatively large measure of freedom, and little was expected of them in the way of adherence to culturally approved standards of behavior until adolescence. Correspondingly, children were likely to receive little criticism of the way in which they spoke. Even for adults there was rarely the feeling of necessity to speak under pressure. It was not obligatory to talk merely to keep a conversation going. In a tribal council an opinion could be expressed by a simple "yes" or "no."

Two cultures with a high incidence of stuttering, studied by Morgenstern (1953), are the Idoma and Ibo people of West Africa. Of the Idoma an American anthropologist reported to Morgenstern, "Stammering is practically a mass phenomenon here." Among the Ibo, 2.67 percent of a group of school children were reported to stutter. In these cultures the ability to speak well in public is vastly admired, and people make speeches on the slightest pretext.

Herbert (in Beech and Fransella, 1968) says that in South Africa the incidence of stuttering was much greater among children of East Indian parents than among those of African or white parents. A further inquiry revealed that cultural differences were strongly implicated—severe punishment for disfluencies was far more common among the East Indian community.

In regard to family composition, 18–20 percent of stutterers, but only 10–12 percent of nonstutterers, are only children. Furthermore, the average stutterer is separated from the sibling closest in age by a larger number of years than is true of the average nonstutterer (Rotter, 1939). These are the children who may not make many articulatory errors, but whose speech is likely to be watched closely by parents and by older siblings.

In sum, a society with many stutterers appears to be a rather competitive society that imposes high standards of speech achievement on the individual and is intolerant of inadequacy or abnormality. Stutterers' parents also tend to impose a high standard of performance on their children. One common denominator in all these environmental factors that lead to, or increase, stuttering seems to be that children are made to pay attention to their speech. Children come to regard speech as a formidable undertaking, and to respond with the tense and fragmented reactions of stuttering. Speaking should be as natural and automatic as walking, which we do without much awareness as to how we do it. If somebody constantly watched and criticized our way of walking and gave such advice as "give a little more pressure on the right foot"; "swing the left arm a few inches higher"; "the right leg a little less bent," and so on and so forth, what would happen to our walking? Even though there may be a constitutional basis that pre-disposes some children to stuttering, environmental factors seem to play a far more important role in the actual development of stuttering.

Psychological characteristics of stutterers

What are stutterers like, apart from their speech handicaps? People often have a stereotype of stutterers in their minds. Let us turn to research findings on this topic. First of all, are stutterers as a group brighter or duller than nonstutterers? Schindler (1955) and Andrews and Harris (1964) drew samples of stuttering school children from a large population representing a broad range of socioeconomic backgrounds and compared their intelligence with that of similarly selected nonstuttering children. The results in both studies were an average IQ of only about 95 for the stutterers as against about 100 for the nonstutterers. In both instances the difference was statistically significant.

In special classes for mentally retarded children in the schools, the incidence of stuttering appears to be at least 3 percent (Louttit and Halls, 1936), while among the institutionalized mentally deficient the estimates are much higher, most of them ranging from 10 to 20 percent (Schlanger and Gottsleben, 1957). Stuttering—apparently of all degrees of severity and complexity—would seem to occur more frequently in this population than in any other single identifiable group of people. On the other hand, Terman and Oden (1947, 1959) report that among the "gifted" children whom they studied longitudinally over many years, stuttering was less frequent than in the general population. Physical handicaps, such as blindness, may also have relevance to stuttering; a Japanese survey shows 3.7 percent stuttering among children in schools for the blind as compared to 0.99 in normal school children (Okada, 1969).

In personality characteristics, male stutterers are "nervous or fearful" and "shy and insecure," at least in speech therapists' eyes, according to Woods and Williams (1971). Is such a stereotype justified? Various pencil-and-paper personality tests have rarely, if ever, revealed well-defined psy-choneurotic categories such as anxiety, depression, obsessive-compulsiveness, or the like among stutterers. On the other hand, both the conventional adjustment inventories and various projective and expressive techniques very frequently reveal signs of mild social maladjustment within the normal range, as might be expected to result from the problems associated with stuttering.

How do stutterers view themselves? Wallen (1960) used the Q-technique—100 self-referent statements made by stutterers were sorted into six personality trait areas: self-acceptance, independence, self-rejection, dependence, lack of emotional control, and withdrawal. Stutterers were significantly lower on self-acceptance and independence, and significantly higher on self-rejection and lack of emotional control.

When their level of aspiration was studied, stutterers showed a significantly lower discrepancy between their goals and their accomplishments. If we interpret this result favorably, such a close correspondence between the goal and achievement may mean that stutterers have a realistic estimation of their performance level. If we interpret it unfavorably, it means that they have an exaggerated defense against failure (Sheehan and Zelen, 1955).

To sum up, stutterers as a group emerge as being slightly less intelligent and less well adjusted emotionally and socially than nonstutterers. But we must not forget that there are individual differences among stutterers as among other people. Whether people of a certain intelligence level or personality are more likely to develop into stutterers, or stutterers develop such characteristics due to their speech handicap, cannot be determined.

STUTTERING BEHAVIOR

We shift our attention now from stutterers to their stuttering behavior, and examine some of its common characteristics.

Consistency and anticipation

Stutterers tend to stutter on the same words when reading the same passage several times. Johnson and Knott (1937) reported that about 60–70 percent of stutterings occurred on the same words on rereading, and no findings have been reported since then that unequivocally contradict this. Moreover, stutterers can anticipate the words on which they are likely to stutter consistently. Adult stutterers can indicate, during silent reading, each word on which they consider they would experience difficulty if they were to read aloud. In one study 94–96 percent of the anticipated words were stuttered on as opposed to only 0.4–3 percent of those not anticipated (Knott, Johnson and Webster, 1937). When the anticipated "difficult" words were deleted, 98 percent of the stuttering was eliminated. The remaining blocks tended to occur on words adjacent to words that had been blotted out. The blotting-out appeared to have served as a cue for further stuttering (Johnson and Millsapps, 1937). Similarly, Peters and Simonson (1960) increased the frequency of stuttering on rarely stuttered words by pairing each of these words repeatedly with a word that had been stuttered.

The results of the studies of anticipation, consistency, and the role of cues led Johnson and his associates to formulate the following sequence of events in stuttering:

Cue (from past difficulty) → Anticipation → Avoidance (effort to avoid stuttering, an effort which *is* stuttering).

They claim that it is the stutterer's attitude to the difficulty of a sound, rather than any inherent difficulty of the sound itself, that makes stuttering on it likely. This raises the question: how does such an attitude start, and why does a bad attitude develop only to some sounds (and words), and not to other sounds (and words)?

The following discussion of the properties of stuttered sounds and words convinces us that some sounds or words are indeed inherently "difficult" to stutterers, and these are the sounds and words on which stutterings are likely to occur and to be anticipated. Within a word, 90 percent of stutterings occur on the initial sound, and within a phrase or sentence, words with particular characteristics discussed below are likely to cause stuttering.

What words are stuttered?

To study the kinds of word or sound consistently stuttered, one marks where stuttering occurs while stutterers read running texts, and examines characteristics of the stuttered words and sounds. In analyzing the results, one has to guard against the possibility that each of the characteristics may interact with the others in affecting stuttering. Suppose that words like "in, on, at" tend to be stuttered infrequently. These words are prepositions (function words); are short; start with vowels; and are not likely to occupy the initial position of a sentence. Which of the above characteristics is most related to stuttering? To avoid this kind of problem Taylor (1966a) used a technique of analysis that could separate out the effects of each factor, and at the same time determine its relative contribution. Here are the results of analysis of performance in reading a simple text.

The initial sounds of words   Many studies (such as Hahn, 1942; Quarrington, Conway, and Siegel, 1962) that attempted to rank consonants in order of difficulty failed because of large intersubject variability. Thus I examined only the consonant-vowel difference, and found that 14.5 percent of the initial consonants but only 2.7 percent of the initial vowels were stuttered. When the sounds were ranked, there was no overlapping between consonants and vowels. A number of Japanese studies (such as Yamamoto, 1958) agree that consonants are stuttered more often than vowels.

The position of words in a sentence   The probability of the initial stuttering event gradually goes down as the stutterer progresses toward the end of a phrase or a sentence, as shown in Figure 10–3. Here, stuttering

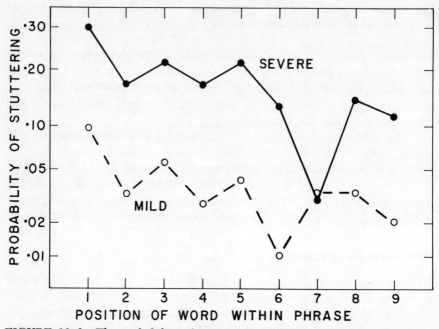

FIGURE 10–3   The probability of stuttering at nth word of a phrase with no prior stuttering in the same phrase. Normal transformation used for ordinate. (From Taylor, 1966b.)

probability—the probability that the nth word of a phrase will be stuttered if no prior word in the phrase was stuttered—is shown for each of the first nine word positions in the phrase. Severe as well as mild stutterers show the position effect.

Grammatical class of words   Some studies (such as S.F. Brown, 1937; Quarrington et al., 1962) show that adverbs, nouns, verbs, and adjectives (content words) are stuttered more than pronouns, prepositions, articles, and conjunctions (function words), but the order of grammatical classes within content words and within function words seems to vary from study to study. Thus I set out to see whether content words as a group were stuttered more than function words. I had to examine the content-function difference by itself, because there were not enough long function words to permit the simultaneous inclusion of word length and the content-function dichotomy in the original analysis (again showing how length and grammatical class are interrelated). Content words were indeed stuttered more than function words. However, the content-function correlations computed separately for words starting with consonants and for those starting with vowels were essentially zero, indicating that the apparent effect of grammatical class may be due to the tendency of function words to start with vowels more often than do content words.

There is one point to be made about the difference between content and function words. When listening to stutterers I often get the impression that stutterings on function words seem to be in anticipation of the difficult content words to come. This is akin to normal speakers repeating "the" in an effort to search for a right content word, especially when a content word is on the tip of the tongue. An example might be: "We had dinner and talked to the, . . . the maitre de . . . d'hôtel of the restaurant." If my impression is correct, we must determine when stutterings occur on function words because of problems related to those words themselves, and when they are in anticipation of coming content words.

Word length When the word list was dichotomized into words with five or less letters and those with six or more, long words were stuttered more than short words. The length effect with this simple text was smaller than either the sound or the position effect. We may expect that in a text with more long words, the length effect would probably be more pronounced. Longer words tend to be infrequent words, as we discussed in Chapter 5. When Soderberg (1966) compared the relative influence of length and frequency, he found the length to be a more potent influence.

Two further results of the analysis were: the consonant-vowel difference was about twice as important as position within the phrase, and about seven times more important than length effects. The four factors seemed to account for most of the dependence of stuttering on word characteristics.

Why are these three or four factors associated with stuttering? First, stuttering may occur at places that require thoughts about the next word. Stuttering is similar to hesitation pauses of normal speakers in this respect. According to Goldman-Eisler (1968), hesitation pauses are one manifestation of a general blocking activity that occurs when organisms are confronted with a situation of uncertainty, when the selection of the next step requires an act of choice. Hesitation pauses in spontaneous speech tend to occur before long words, before content words, and before words of high information value. These are the kinds of words that are hard to guess when deleted in a context. Silverman and Williams (1967) investigated directly the loci of disfluencies in the oral reading of normal speakers. They found all of the above four characteristics of words to be operating except that of position in the sentence (they considered only the first three words of a sentence).

We can also confirm directly that stutterings occur on high-information words. Schlesinger, Forte, Fried, and Melkman (1965) found that most stutterings occurred on such words. When high- and low-information words were equated in frequency, high-information words were still stuttered more.

We end here the analogy between stutterings and hesitation pauses of normal speakers. The consonant-vowel differences in stuttering is far greater than the effects of any other factors we have considered, and requires an additional explanation. Consonants are articulated with various articulatory organs in the mouth and larynx coordinating in subtle ways to interfere with the air stream coming from the windpipe. In words of many languages consonants and vowels tend to alternate, perhaps because vowels give articulators time to get ready for the next consonant, rather than the other way around. Some languages avoid consonant clusters altogether. Articulatory problems may make initial consonants points of particular anxiety in a tense speaker trying to talk correctly.

For stutterers, any speech act is a difficult task, to be approached with tension. Such tension may be particularly great at the beginning of a speech act, be it a sentence or a word. Only about 10 percent of stutterings occur at noninitial positions within words, but we do not know whether the probability of stuttering decreases from the beginning to the end of words, as it does within sentences.

Stuttering decreases with repeated speaking or reading of the same material on several occasions under relatively constant environmental conditions. The time interval between readings has to be short—in the order of zero to a few minutes—for adaptation to occur. In the typical situation there is a reduction of about 50 percent in the number of stuttering events over five successive readings of the same passage. However, when the material differs from trial to trial, the reduction in stuttering is less than 20 percent. We may therefore attribute roughly 30 percent to adaptation to the reading material, and 20 percent to adaptation to the reading situation. When stutterers become accustomed to the speech situations and feel less tense, and to reading material that has become predictable, there should be a decrease in stuttering.

Experimental manipulation of stuttering rates

Experimenters can reduce or increase stuttering rates in laboratory conditions. Stutterers may sometimes be able to carry over their reduced stuttering rates to situations outside the laboratory. What conditions reduce stuttering?

Reduced hearing   When hearing is reduced 50 dB or more by deafness, hearing loss, or auditory masking, the frequency and severity of stuttering apparently decrease considerably. The less a stutterer can hear himself speak, the less he stutters. For example, Maraist and Hutton (1957) report a sizeable decrease in severity of stuttering with 50 dB of masking, and close-to-normal reading with 90 dB masking. Stuttering may be totally inhibited if the voice is masked by high-intensity white noise. Low-frequency masking is more effective than high-frequency masking (Cherry and Sayers, 1956). In one condition air-conducted sound was eliminated by blocking the ears of subjects, while in another condition both air- and bone-conducted sounds were masked by relaying a very loud noise through earphones. Only the second condition eliminated stuttering completely. We expect that deaf children should stutter infrequently because of their reduced hearing. Backus (1938) surveyed 13,691 deaf children and found only 0.04 percent (compared to over 1 percent in normal children) to be stutterers.

Cherry and Sayers also showed that if a stutterer reads along with a nonstutterer from the same text (shadowing), stuttering is reduced. Even when the nonstutterer switches to a text different from that being read by the stutterer, the stutterer maintains his fluency. The actual physical sounds made by the normal speaker, rather than the specific words read, must effect the modification of stuttering. Thus, switching to gibberish that has a similar phonetic structure to that of the language employed is equally useful. The normal speaker's sounds presumably are the best possible masker for the stutterer's speech.

Delayed auditory feedback (DAF) Normally, we have immediate auditory feedback when we speak. We may not be always aware of such feedback, but it enables us to monitor what we say so that we can continually adjust our articulation during our speech. What happens when auditory feedback is delayed by a fraction of a second? In a nonstutterer, there will be considerable disruption of speech behavior over which the speaker has very little control; blocking, prolongation, hesitation—"stuttering-like speech"—occurs to a marked degree. The optimal time delay for obtaining such disrupted speech is 50 to 300 msec, depending upon the individual. However, listeners had little difficulty in distinguishing the DAF speech of normal speakers from the speech of stutterers not influenced by DAF (Neelley, 1961). Severe stutterers tend to improve under DAF, while milder stutterers tend to increase stuttering, much as do normal speakers.

How does DAF reduce the frequency of stuttering? Soderberg (1968) proposed three explanations of the beneficial effects, two of which are indirect. The first possible explanation is that DAF causes stutterers to raise their vocal pitch. If the phase differential between bone-tissue and air-conducted feedback is greater near the fundamental frequency of the stutterer's voice, then DAF might achieve the same effect on fluency as does masking, by altering or filtering the lower frequencies in the return signal. A second possible explanation is that slowing of speech under DAF may coerce the stutterer into speaking in a manner that may be more appropriate for him. Some stutterers have to speak slowly to achieve a degree of stability in their speech-auditory feedback loops. Soderberg's third explanation is that if the bone-tissue feedback of stutterers is out of phase with that of air-conducted feedback, DAF may restore a more suitable phase relationship between these two pathways for stutterers. However, the time relation seems wrong for this explanation. Five msec (half a cycle at the fundamental frequency of speech) should be the largest delay for which this explanation of Soderberg could be tenable. As mentioned earlier, the optimal time delay to obtain the DAF effect is between 50 and 300 msec. We suspect that DAF may also reduce stuttering because it acts as a distractor.

Operant conditioning   Experimenters can alter the stuttering rate by manipulating the consequences of stuttering, as is the case with other ongoing operant behaviors such as crying or speaking. If we reward stuttering, it will increase; if we punish stuttering, it will decrease. One of the first experiments to apply operant conditioning to stuttering was that of Flanagan, Goldiamond, and Azrin (1958). They asked stutterer-subjects to read aloud. After 30 min, during which the baseline stuttering rate had been established, they introduced a punishment schedule: they gave a noxious stimulus (very loud white noise) to subjects immediately following a nonfluency. Such punishment was extremely effective in controlling nonfluencies. One subject had almost entirely stopped stuttering by the end of a 30-min punishment period, even a few minutes after punishment ceased. Such temporary suppression of the punished act is consistent with the effect of punishment on other kinds of behavior. Other investigators have often reported that stuttering frequency *increases* under conditions of aversive stimulation. We must note that the aversive stimulus has to be contingent upon emission of a stuttering for it to reduce stuttering.

In a second condition, Flanagan and co-workers used an escape schedule: each stuttering event switched off the noise, and thus brought about an escape from the noxious stimulus, noise. The stuttering rate increased under this condition, as predicted. In another study (1959), Flanagan used normal speakers as subjects and electric shock as a noxious stimulus, and obtained similar effects.

Biggs and Sheehan (1969) replicated Flanagan and others' experiment with an increase of the number of subjects from three to six and the addition of a noncontingent control condition, in which the tone was randomly presented independent of the subjects' stutterings. Stuttering decreased in all conditions; they attributed the improvement to distraction effects of hearing tones. Their subjects rated the noise (a tone of 4,000 Hz, 108 dB) not as punishing but as distracting.

In an experiment that lasted nine months with one subject, Goldiamond (1965) obtained a slow, prolonged pattern of speech using an escape schedule with DAF as a "noxious" stimulus. If a stutterer's speech is prolonged, it is free from stutterings because DAF is not disruptive. Prolongation is one of the several novel patterns of speech that emerge under DAF and lends itself readily to shaping. Goldiamond first produced in a stutterer a slow but fluent speech under DAF, and then gradually attenuated DAF. After that he gradually restored a normal rate of speech by machine control of successive displays of reading material at faster rates. He reported marked success with this method, including carry-over to situations outside the laboratory.

R. Martin (1968) notes that stuttering frequency can be brought under discriminative stimulus control; a stimulus light that had been illuminated during a period of shock (delivered contingent on stuttering) served to depress the stuttering rate when later presented alone. Therapists observe that stutterers often experience a decrease in stuttering frequency while in a particular therapy environment, but fail in their attempts to maintain this relatively low stuttering level in "outside" situations. Carefully programmed discrimination training might extend such reduced frequency into other environments.

Rhythm Speaking in rhythm to a regular beat has been one of the oldest and most effective therapies in the reduction or elimination of stuttering. The effect usually ceased when the external rhythm stopped. Is rhythm effective because it is distracting? To answer this question, Fransella and Beech (1965) had 18 male stutterers speak under three experimental conditions: rhythmic metronome; arrhythmic metronome; and no metronome. Further, each rhythmic condition was presented either at the usual rate of speech or more slowly. Their findings are shown in Figure 10–4.

Note that there is not much difference between no metronome and arrhythmic conditions, whereas the rhythmic metronome had a large effect in reducing speech errors. Thus, the rhythmic effect is not due to distraction in a simple and obvious sense, especially as the instructions in the arrhythmic condition required subjects to pay careful attention to the beats in order to detect any patterning. Subjects made slightly fewer errors in the arrhythmic than in the no-metronome condition. Here we may invoke the effect of distraction alone, but the effect was much smaller than the effect of rhythm. The slower rate produced fewer speech errors under all conditions, and this effect was independent of the rhythmic effect.

To isolate the rhythm effect from the distraction effect even more convincingly, Fransella (1967) compared reading with the rhythmic metronome against reading while writing down a continuous series of numbers relayed by a tape recorder. There were 5.17 stuttering events for the metronome and 13.56 for writing numbers. Thus, writing numbers, which should

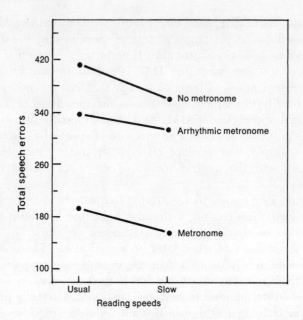

FIGURE 10–4   Total speech errors elicited at "usual" and "slow" speeds by the three metronome conditions in a group rhythm experiment. (From Fransella and Beech, 1965.)

have been highly distracting, did not reduce stuttering as much as did rhythm.

Could it be that stutterers lack a sense of rhythm, and when rhythm is provided externally they can speak fluently? One old study by Ingerbregsten (1936) showed that more than 40 percent of his sample of stutterers were unable to reproduce a melody and seemed to have little sense of rhythm.

Drugs   Since anxiety-provoking situations aggravate stuttering, tranquilizers that reduce anxiety seem to be logical drugs to try with stutterers. Although tranquilizers do induce changes in the behavior of stutterers, there is no clear evidence that these changes result in a significant reduction in stuttering. This is so whether the drugs are used alone or as adjuncts to speech therapy (Kent, 1963).

To sum up, the various conditions that reduce or eliminate stuttering seem to share one common denominator, distraction. Distract stutterers' attention from their own speech acts by making them unable to hear themselves speak, or by drawing attention to tasks other than speech, and they stutter less. One of the main factors that lead to, or increase, stuttering is forcing stutterers to pay attention to their speech acts. It makes sense that distraction should reduce or eliminate stuttering as long as the conditions remain distracting.

Distraction is not the only device that reduces stuttering. Punishing stuttering events in operant conditioning also reduces stuttering. So does externally provided rhythm. Forcing stutterers to speak slowly by DAF or by instruction also seems to be effective.

Recovery and treatment

In Roman times stutterers were viewed as being possessed by evil spirits, and various types of exorcism were employed. In the Middle Ages, the tongue was viewed as the seat of the trouble, and hot irons, spices, and noxious substances were applied to that organ to drive away the evil. Francis Bacon, noting that the tongue seemed to be stiff and frozen in the act of stuttering, recommended that the tongue be thawed with hot wine, a procedure which undoubtedly produced more fluency!

Fortunately for stutterers, 80 percent recover spontaneously, according to Sheehan, an authority on stuttering. Sheehan and Martyn (1970) surveyed 5,138 University of California students, and compared characteristics of recovered and active stutterers. Recovery is a gradual process and tends to occur in adolescence and early adulthood. Severe stutterers are less likely to recover (50 percent recovery rate) than moderate (75 percent) or mild stutterers (87 percent). None attributed their improvement to public school therapy (perhaps speech therapy at that time was inadequate). Those who recovered had initially shown syllabic repetitions, whereas those whose stuttering was still active had begun with blockings. Recovery is attributed to role acceptance as a stutterer; growing self-esteem (Sheehan, 1965); development of adequacy and self-confidence; relaxation and greater understanding of the problem (Shearer and Williams, 1965).

What should we expect to be the best strategy for preventing and curing stuttering? Having examined various causes for stuttering, conditions that reduce or modify stuttering rates, and characteristics of stutterers and stuttering behavior, the following ideas emerge.

1. The possible inheritance of a disposition to faulty speech, including stuttering, is beyond our control.

2. Parents can provide a pressure-free home atmosphere while children are acquiring language. Especially they should not overreact to the minor articulatory disorders prevalent in early childhood.

3. Once stuttering has developed, the stutterer and other family members should face it with as little anxiety as they can: accept it with equanimity.

4. If therapy is desired, stutterer and therapist should choose the

method most suitable for a particular stutterer from among various scientifically tested methods that can modify stuttering rates.

5. Finally, stutterers can hope that they are among those four out of five stutterers who recover spontaneously.

SUMMARY AND CONCLUSIONS

A speech disorder is defined as a deviation from the normal speech pattern extreme enough to interfere with communication. More boys than girls, and more younger than older children, suffer from speech disorders. Among several types of disorders, deafness and voice disorder are selected for brief discussion, and articulation disorder and stuttering for in-depth discussion. Deafness can cause voice disorder and articulatory errors. Many normally hearing children show articulatory errors, which they outgrow by age 8. Misarticulation is related not to defects in articulatory organs but rather to faulty acoustic discrimination. Usually consonant clusters and consonants with +strident and +continuant features cause most difficulty.

Another important functional speech disorder is stuttering, which occurs in about 1 percent of the population in many cultures. There may be an unspecified inherited basis for stuttering. Stutterers and nonstutterers are not noticeably different in organic or physiological factors.

Environmental factors play an important role in the development of stuttering. The factors examined—cultural practices, parental attitudes, the child's status in the family—all point to the conclusion that stutterers are made to pay attention to their own speech until they regard speaking as a formidable task and dread it.

Stutterers as a group are slightly less intelligent and less well adjusted emotionally than nonstutterers.

Stutterers can anticipate the words they will stutter, and different stutterers tend to stutter on the same kinds of word. Such words typically start with consonants, are long, are at initial positions of a sentence, and possibly are content words. Words of high information value seem to be stuttered, just as in normal speech they are preceded by pauses. In addition, stutterers have difficulty in articulating complex consonants and in initiating speech acts at syllable, word, and sentence levels. With repeated reading of the same material adaptation occurs, and stutterings decrease.

Rates of stuttering as well as disfluencies of normal speakers can be manipulated with operant conditioning. Punish stuttering, and it decreases; reward it, and it increases. Stuttering rates can be manipulated also with masking noise, delayed feedback, and externally provided rhythm. These conditions reduce stuttering rates not merely because they are distracting; we considered other possible explanations.

Some stutterers recover spontaneously after developing positive attitudes toward themselves and their speech problems. With our deepening understanding of how stuttering develops and how stuttering rates can be manipulated experimentally, someday we may be able to prevent and treat stuttering effectively.

11

Aphasia and Neural Mechanisms of Speech

"Ah . . . little boy . . . cookies, pass . . . a . . . little boy . . . Tip, up . . . fall. Wipe dishes . . . ah, dishes, wipe . . . Water spill off." A brain-damaged patient of Goodglass (1962) thus described a picture of a child stealing a cookie. In this chapter, we learn about aphasia, a disturbance of language and speech caused by brain damage. The French surgeon Broca (1861), a pioneer in the study of aphasia, described another brain-damaged patient, an 84-year-old man who could not tell his age orally but could do so with his fingers. Aphasia literally means the lack of speech (a = lack of, *phasia* = speech). In spite of the name, there is almost always some residual language if the brain damage occurs after natural language has been acquired.

Aphasia is a valuable source of information on the brain mechanisms of speech. As usual, we learn best how a machine works by seeing how it goes wrong. Our normal speech processes are smoothly coordinated; but when different parts are selectively impaired, we may learn something about their nature and interrelationships.

NEUROLOGICAL INVESTIGATION OF APHASIA AND SPEECH

Localization of brain functions in aphasia

The fact that damage of the brain can cause loss or disturbance of speech has been known since ancient times. In Egypt around 3000 B.C., the author of the famous Edwin Smith papyrus gave a number of eloquent descriptions of the effects of wounds of the skull: ". . . one having a wound in his temple, perforating his temporal bone; while he discharges blood from his nostrils, . . . and he is *speechless*. An ailment not to be treated!" (from Critchley, 1970, p. 55). So a wound through the skull is correctly related to the symptom of speechlessness. But where in the brain should wounds be for this symptom to appear? Are specific loci of lesions in the brain associated with specific types of language disturbance?

Broca's aphasia   Because of limited space, our history of aphasia is hurried, and we make a giant leap from 3000 B.C. to the nineteenth century A.D. In 1861 Broca published the protocols of two patients with language disorders caused by brain damage. They had lost almost all speech before they died. After autopsies, Broca could link the patients' aphasia to specific lesions, predominantly in the frontal or anterior portion of the brain (see *Broca's area* in Figure 11–1). Broca noted that the damaged anterior portion was in the left hemisphere. Damage to Broca's area is thought to cause Broca's type of aphasia, sometimes called *motor aphasia, expressive aphasia,* or *nonfluent aphasia.*

Such an aphasic characteristically produces little speech; such speech as is produced is emitted slowly, with great effort, and with poor, crude articulation. The small function words and the inflectional endings of words are

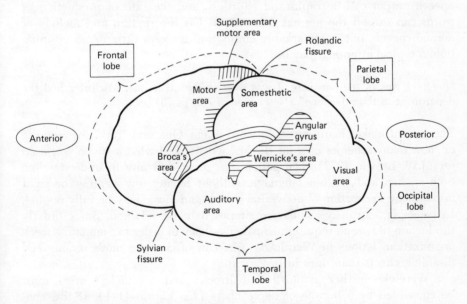

FIGURE 11–1   Speech areas (shaded) in the left hemisphere of the human brain (side view). The figure also shows sensory and motor areas; four lobes; and two fissures.

omitted to produce "telegraphic speech." An example of telegraphic speech is given at the beginning of this chapter. Japanese aphasics may drop honorifics and postpositions (Pance and Shimoyama, 1973), both of which are dispensable items. The patient may comprehend spoken and written language normally or nearly normally. Writing is often impaired. Because Broca's area lies so close to the motor cortex, that region is often damaged simultaneously, so that these patients frequently suffer from paralysis of the right side of the body. However, aphasia is not the result of paralysis of the muscles involved in speech production. As evidence for this, Geschwind (1972) notes that the patient who can utter at most only one or two slurred words may be able to sing a melody rapidly, correctly, and even with elegance. Usually the patient is aware of the language deficit. Presumably other language functions and general intelligence are more or less intact if the damage is limited to Broca's area.

Wernicke's aphasia   About a decade after Broca, the German neurologist Wernicke (1874) noted a type of linguistic difficulty different from Broca's aphasia. Wernicke's aphasia (also called *receptive aphasia, sensory aphasia,* or *fluent aphasia*), is produced by damage in a broad region outside Broca's area, specifically in the *temporal lobe* (see Figure 11–1) of the left hemisphere. There is no paralysis of the opposite side of the body. Speech output can be rapid and effortless, and the rate of production of words can exceed the normal. The output has the rhythm and melody of normal speech, but is remarkably empty and conveys little or no information. A typical utterance may be:

"Before I was in the one here, I was over in the other one. My sister had the department in the other one" (Geschwind, 1972, p. 78).

The patient makes many errors in word usage. One said "fork" for "spoon," or "how many schemes on your throat," when asked what a spoon was used for (J.W. Brown, 1972). The patient has great difficulty in understanding both spoken and written language, without having any hearing or sight impairment. Perception of nonverbal sounds and music may be fully normal. In principle, expressive skills are supposed to be retained. Since orderly production of speech requires acoustic feedback in order to maintain speech organization, lesions in Wernicke's area can often have more serious and disabling effects than ones in Broca's area.

Wernicke further assumed that Broca's and Wernicke's areas must be connected by a bundle of nerve fibers (see Figure 11–1). If this connection is interrupted by lesions, *conduction aphasia* results. The main difficulty of the patient with conduction aphasia is in repeating spoken material. Table 11–1 lists five types of aphasia. The table is a very rough

TABLE 11-1 Five Types of Aphasia

Type of aphasia	Site of lesion	Speech production	Articulation	Compre-hension	Repetition	Grammar	Naming
Broca's (motor; expressive) aphasia	anterior; frontal	nonfluent	impaired	mildly impaired?	limited (omission)	simplified syntax	limited
Wernicke's (sensory; receptive) aphasia	posterior; temporal	fluent	normal	impaired	impaired; (substitution; paraphrase)	complex syntax with errors	impaired; neologism, jargon
conduction aphasia	connection be-tween Broca's & Wernicke's areas	fluent	some incorrect sounds	intact	impaired	occasionally simplified	impaired
anomic (amnesic) aphasia	angular gyrus	fluent	normal	intact	intact	normal	impaired
global aphasia	Broca's & Wernicke's areas	like Broca's aphasia		like Wernicke's aphasia			

summary of the sites of some lesions and their associated linguistic disturbances.

The conclusions of Broca and Wernicke were based on studies of only a few aphasics, most of them aged patients who had suffered strokes. Major vascular lesions such as strokes or hemorrhages have a widespread effect upon the brain and thus cloud the picture of the relationship between specific brain areas and behavior. The patients were not tested with a series of carefully constructed linguistic tests, and their brains were rarely dissected after death.

Penfield and Roberts (1959) stimulated the exposed cortex in patients undergoing surgery for epilepsy. The patients were conscious and could describe their experiences. Electric stimulation either caused speech disturbance or evoked vocalization. Stimulation in Broca's and Wernicke's areas and *supplementary motor areas* (see Figure 11–1) caused speech disturbances that involved complete arrest of speech, hesitation, slurring, and repetition of words or syllables. Stimulation of the motor areas (Rolandic and supplementary) of either hemisphere evoked vocalizations: the patient continued to cry "ah . . ." until the electrode was withdrawn or until he had to take a breath.

This technique interferes with ongoing neural activities of the brain, and can examine only certain accessible structures. Lenneberg (1973) points out that there is not much symmetry between stimulation and destruction; behavior elicited by stimulation of a given spot is not necessarily abolished by the destruction of that same place. Yet it also shows that some areas of the brain are more involved in speech than other areas.

Fuzzy dichotomy   In 1935 Weisenburg and McBride examined 60 American patients who were all under 60 years of age, and who had suffered brain damage of varied kinds. As controls they examined people with brain damage in the right hemisphere and no aphasia, as well as normal people. They used standardized measurements of linguistic performance, averaging 19 hours of examination on each patient. They concluded that both receptive and expressive skills were always disturbed in aphasia, and did not find isolated disturbances of a single skill. Consequently they classified patients into "predominantly expressive," "predominantly receptive," *amnesic* (having difficulty in finding words; see Table 11–1), and "expressive-receptive."

The Soviet neurologist Luria (1970) studied an even larger number of cases; World War II provided him with 394 patients with gunbullet injury in the left hemisphere, of whom 61 percent showed signs of speech impairment soon after the injury. The speech disorders took various forms. Most often, during the first days or even weeks their speech was totally disrupted. Even during this time, however, Luria often observed that a given aspect of the patients' speech might be severely disturbed while other aspects remained relatively intact. After two or three months, noticeable signs of aphasic disturbances remained in only 43 percent of the patients. Luria also noted that the relative frequency of various speech disorders depended upon the site of the lesions. As Figure 11–2 shows, the occurrence of speech disturbance is not an all-or-none phenomenon—rather, it is statistical in nature. Certain sites close to Broca's and Wernicke's areas are more likely than others to be associated with aphasia; for more distant sites the likelihood of aphasia seems to be lower.

A pure case? On extremely rare occasions, a specific speech disorder may be precisely linked to a lesion in a specific area in the brain. Geschwind (1972) cites Dejerine's (1892) description of such a case. In a pure case one is able to predict the type of linguistic disorder from the brain damage,

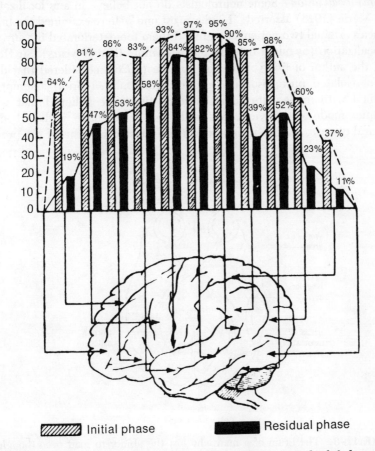

FIGURE 11–2   Distribution of aphasias following injury to the left hemisphere. (From Luria, 1970.)

and vice versa. Dejerine's patient could visually perceive written material but could not understand the content. The patient could speak, comprehend spoken language, and write—even copy written material correctly. Autopsy of the man's brain showed that the left visual cortex and a portion of the *corpus callosum* (the mass of nerve that connects the two hemispheres) had been destroyed by blockage of the left posterior cerebral artery (see Figure 11–3). The left visual cortex serves the right visual fields of both eyes while the right cortex serves the left visual fields. Thus, with one intact visual cortex Dejerine's patient could see words properly. But the words received by the right visual cortex could not cross over to the language areas in the left hemisphere because of the damaged portion of the corpus callosum.

Anti-localization   Some neurologists do not believe in any localization. Pierre Marie (1926) asserted: "L'aphasie est une." He re-examined the brains of Broca's original two patients and found them too deteriorated for any precise localization (as might be expected after more than 60 years). Sir Henry Head, the author of two volumes on aphasia (1926), considered that diagnosis of isolated pure disorders resulted from false a priori assumptions combined with inadequate clinical examinations. He believed that when a complex mode of behavior, such as the use of language, is disturbed by structural disease, the loss of functions is manifested in terms of the process

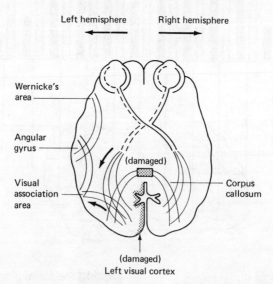

FIGURE 11–3   The brain of a man who lost the ability to read even though he had normal visual acuity and could copy written words. (After Geschwind, 1972.)

itself, and does not reveal the elements out of which it has been built up. Lenneberg (1967) asserted that the brain functions as a single unit such that except for the visual cortex there are no identifiable neuro-anatomical correlates of specific behavioral function, including language. His assertion seems to be based on the lack of evidence about different neuroanatomic features for different language areas.

Recently, Luria (1974) has said that the acquisition and performance of language have to be understood as complex "functional systems" that may not be localized in separate zones, but rather distributed in widespread cortical constellations. According to Luria, the brain can be divided into three basic functional parts. The first part (upper brain stem and the *limbic system*—a set of interconnected structures in the center of the brain) provides the adequate tone of the cortex and is responsible for vigilance or alertness. The second part (the posterior parts of the brain hemispheres) is responsible for reception, elaboration, and storage of received information— in short, for basic cerebral mechanisms of cognition. The third part (anterior parts of the hemispheres) is for programming, regulating, and controlling human actions.

According to Luria, no form of human behavior is a property of only one of these functional parts, but all behavior requires the coordination of all three functional units, each of them playing its own highly specific role in the organization of behavioral processes. Only if such coordination is preserved can the acquisition and performance of linguistic structures take place.

Even the speech areas may be dispensable sometimes. In rare cases a patient with destroyed Wernicke's area was in full command of both understanding and speaking although he could not repeat utterances (Benson et al., 1973). Penfield's excision of Broca's area led at most to nothing more than transient aphasia (Penfield and Roberts, 1959). Burklund (1970) also says that removal of Broca's area has always resulted in only a temporary loss of expressive speech. Following recovery, the only discernible dysfunction is at most a mild, insignificant impairment in vocal musculature, affecting both linguistic and nonlinguistic vocalizations. Recently Mohr (1973) published three well-documented cases of right-handed patients who could speak despite complete destruction of Broca's area.

On balance, however much some aphasiologists would like to forget the localization theory (derogatorily called "map-drawing") because of inconsistency in specific locations, rough localization still seems to serve a useful function in predicting the types and levels of aphasia and in treating aphasia. Even Luria's functional parts are "localized" in the three parts of the brain. Granting that most of evidence for localization is statistical in nature, some areas are more important, if not indispensable, to language than other areas.

In the end, Wernicke's and Broca's areas in the left hemisphere emerge as the important speech areas. Of the two, Wernicke's area seems to be the more important. The supplementary motor areas may become important if other areas of speech are destroyed, according to Penfield and Roberts.

Cerebral dominance

We have seen that lesions in the left hemisphere cause aphasia, because the left hemisphere plays the dominant role in language and speech. This cerebral dominance is one of the most remarkable features of humans. M. Dax, an obscure French physician, seems to be the first person to have noted this phenomenon after examining more than 40 cases of brain damage in the years after 1800; his observation was not published until 1865. There are strong but largely independent tendencies for humans to be right-handed and to develop speech organization or dominance in the left hemisphere. The relation between handedness and left-hemisphere dominance for speech is not a causal dependency. For one thing, handedness is established around age 2, while cerebral organization for speech continues to develop until the early teens. Further, almost all right-handers but about half of the left-handers have left-hemisphere speech dominance. Left-handed people tend to suffer milder aphasia and have better prognoses than right-handers, perhaps because left-handed and ambidextrous people tend to be less clear in hemispheric dominance. A family history of left-handedness is also a factor that influences the severity and prognosis of aphasia. In a nutshell, most of us (over 90 percent; Rife, 1951) are right-handed, and nearly all of us (about 97 percent; Penfield and Roberts, 1959) have left-hemisphere dominance. There is ample physiological, behavioral, and anatomical evidence for cerebral dominance, almost from birth.

Physiological and behavioral evidence   The most obvious evidence for cerebral dominance in older children is the fact that aphasia usually develops from lesions in the left hemisphere. Out of 100 people with permanent language disorder caused by brain lesions approximately 97 will have damage on the left side (Geschwind, 1972). The most dramatic evidence is the fact that in the adult the nondominant hemisphere may be surgically removed with virtually no permanent aphasia (Whitaker, 1969).

The *Wada test* determines the dominant hemisphere for language: sodium amytal (a rapid-acting nerve depressant) is injected into one *carotid artery* at a time (the right and left carotid arteries are the principal vessels in the neck carrying blood to the respective hemispheres). Since the right hemisphere controls the left side of the body, and the left hemisphere, the right side, the injection produces an immediate contralateral effect; the arm and leg are paralyzed on the affected side, but the other side stays normal. The effect lasts five to ten minutes. If the injection affects the dominant hemisphere, speech will be disturbed and the affected person makes errors in naming, talks nonsense, and shows other peculiarities of speech.

With normal subjects, Carmon and Gombos (1970) showed that the systolic (contracting), and to a lesser degree, the diastolic blood pressures in the ophthalmic artery were higher on the right side of most right-handed subjects; higher on the left side of most left-handed subjects; and equal on both sides in most ambidextrous subjects. As the ophthalmic artery pressure is an accepted indicator of the pressure in the carotid artery, the differences in the blood supplies of the two cerebral hemispheres seem to be related to cerebral dominance and interhemispheric behavioral differences.

Behaviorally, if an infant is placed on its back it will turn its head to one side. Gesell and Ames (1947) point out that a majority of babies will turn their heads most of the time to the right. The direction of head-turning correlates well with the later development of handedness.

Dichotic listening tasks demonstrate hemispheric dominance for speech in normal subjects. An experimenter presents acoustic stimuli to both of the subject's ears simultaneously. If the stimulus is verbal material, the right ear will hear it better than the left ear, but with nonverbal material such as music or environmental noise, the reverse is true (Kimura, 1961, 1964). Left-handers, especially left-handers with a family history of left-handedness, show less left–right ear asymmetry in this test. A right ear superiority was found on a dichotic listening task as early as age 3 (Ingram, 1975).

Some of the acoustic nerve fibers cross over in the brain so that a majority of the verbal signals originating in the right ear will project ultimately in the left-hemisphere. Anatomical evidence indicates that more fibers cross over than remain on the same side (see, for example, Rosenzweig, 1951).

Relation between the two hemispheres Traditionally, the two hemispheres were thought to be equal at birth. According to this model, the development of dominance of one hemisphere takes place while the higher mental functions are being developed. After one hemisphere has gained dominance, all new functions of a particular type are relegated to the dominant hemisphere so that the difference between the two hemispheres becomes increasingly larger.

Landsdell's (1969) study supports this model. He studied 18 subjects with speech controlled by the right hemisphere. Most were slightly below average in general intelligence (IQ about 90) as a result of early brain damage. The main finding was that the earlier the brain damage, the better was their verbal development.

However, recent research indicates that cerebral dominance may exist even in infancy. Molfese (1972, 1973) recorded auditorily evoked responses to speech syllables, words, music, and mechanical noise from the temporal-parietal (see Figure 11–1) language-processing area in the left hemisphere and from the corresponding area in the right hemisphere. He compared responses of three groups of subjects—infants (average age 5.8 months), children (mean age 6 years), and adults (mean age 25.6 years). Verbal stimuli elicited greater responses from the left hemisphere, while the mechanical stimuli elicited the largest responses from the right hemisphere in *all* subjects.

Dennis and Kohn (in press) have been studying nine subjects (aged 8–29 years) who have had one hemisphere removed soon after birth due to cerebral disease. Five lost the left (LH) and four, the right hemisphere (RH). These groups were matched on relevant medical and educational data. IQs of both groups ranged from 78 to 95. Neither group showed signs of aphasia on conventional tests. However, the RH group performed more poorly than LH in visuospatial tasks (such as maze-tracing), but better than LH on a verbal comprehension task. In the verbal task subjects matched pictures to sentences of varying syntactic complexity. According to traditional thought, there ought to have been ample opportunity for the one remaining hemisphere to develop functions for both hemispheres. Yet early left-hemisphere removal seems to cause long-lasting, subtle linguistic deficiencies, which can be revealed perhaps only in sensitive tests.

How much does the right hemisphere contribute to language? The differences between the two hemispheres are always quantitative rather than qualitative, and vary according to the task. The relatively small contribution of the right hemisphere to speech functions is often increased when an aphasic patient recovers from his speech loss after left hemisphere lesions. Smith and Burklund (1966) removed the left hemisphere of a right-handed adult, and noted a continuing recovery of his ability to speak, read, write, and understand during the first year after operation.

With patients whose two hemispheres are surgically divided, neurologists can independently test the two on the same task and determine directly each hemisphere's contribution to various skills. Early reports on such patients did not find any evidence that the minor (right) hemisphere contributed to expressive language (Gazzaniga and Sperry, 1967). However, Butler and Norrsell (1968) reported that one of their patients could say short words such as "cup," identifying pictures seen in his left visual field (controlled by the *right* hemisphere; see Figure 11–3). Two conditions are needed for such results: (a) sufficient time is allowed for the test, and (b) the number of stimuli is limited and their identity is known to the patients ahead of time.

In the last century (1887) Gowers noted even more eloquent evidence that the right hemisphere participates in speech recovery. He observed patients who recovered from speech loss caused by permanent destruction of the speech region in the left hemisphere. Their recovery must have involved the corresponding part of the right hemisphere, because in some of these patients speech was again lost when a fresh lesion occurred there.

Anatomical difference   Neurologists agree that there are quantitative, if not qualitative, functional differences between the left and right hemisphere. Is there a corresponding anatomical difference? Once some neurologists claimed that there was. In the past few decades, neurologists have tended to assume that the left and right hemispheres are symmetrical. They thought that cerebral dominance is based on undetected subtle physiological differences not reflected in gross structures. The pendulum is now swinging back to the original claim. Geschwind and Levitsky (1968) looked again into the possibility that the human brain is anatomically asymmetrical. They studied 100 normal human brains, and were surprised to find that striking asymmetries were readily visible. The area they studied was the upper surface of the temporal lobe, an extension of Wernicke's area; it was larger on the left side of the brain in 65 percent of the specimens, equal in 24 percent, and larger on the right side in 11 percent. The larger left extension of Wernicke's area was nearly a centimeter longer on the average than its fellow on the opposite side in absolute terms, and one-third longer than the right in relative terms. It is odd that the right and left percentages do not coincide with the split of right- and left-hemisphere dominance in the general population. The authors do not indicate the dominance in life of the brains with larger Wernicke's area on the left side. Geschwind (1972) reports that Wada studied brains from infants who died soon after birth and found that such asymmetry was present. If this is the case, some of the asymmetries of the brain may be genetically determined.

Witelson and Pallie (1973) also report that the size of the left-right difference of Wernicke's area in 14 neonates was proportionately at least as large as that in an adult sample. Further, they noted a possible sex difference in left-right asymmetry in neonates: the anatomical difference was not as marked for males as for females.

Origin of lateralization   When and why did lateralization (handedness and cerebral dominance) originate? Many animals prefer one paw or hand, but *Homo sapiens* is the only predominantly right-handed species. Monkeys and apes also show some rudimentary dominance, but in these species it is neither generalized to as many situations nor to as many functions as in humans. We seem to have acquired language and become right-handed at about the same time in evolution. Even though handedness and cerebral dominance are not causally related, they may have a common cause. The cause may be efficiency of neural organization, as we shall discuss shortly.

What interests us at this moment is whether we can trace the origin of handedness. If we can, this information might shed some light on the origin of cerebral dominance, hence indirectly of language. The oldest evidence of handedness is Peking Man's (now classed together with Pithecanthropus) stone artifacts, which seem to be better suited for use in the right hand than in the left. Also in Pithecanthropus the left frontal area of the brain was larger than the right. This evidence sets the origin of right-handedness at least 350,000 years B.P. (before present), if not earlier. Neanderthal man (35,000–70,000 years B.P.) apparently had the left hemisphere more massive than the right, suggesting cerebral dominance. More recently, cave paintings of the Cro-Magnon period done between 25,000–10,000 B.P. at El Castillo in Europe show silhouettes of hands on the wall; 28 out of 35 of these silhouettes are left hands. The painting would have been done by the right hand, using the left as a stencil. These interesting odd bits of information are mentioned by Critchley (1970).

In pondering why lateralization has evolved, it is instructive to consider the chaffinch. Marler (1970) reports that the song-box of a chaffinch is symmetrical, with nerves coming to it from both sides of the brain. However, the effects of severing these nerves on the right and left side are strikingly different. With the left-sided operation, the majority of the elements of the song may be lost. Once lost, the capacity for normal singing is not regained. If this operation is done on a young male who has not yet come into full song, the bird can develop a complete pattern of song. It can develop song quite normally as long as one or the other side is intact. The song-box is organized much like the larynx; both are structures in the midline, and have to make the subtle and complex movements involved in vocalization. Such a task may be difficult to accomplish with symmetrical nerves from two sides of the brain, each vying for control. It may well be more efficient for the dominance of one side to be foreordained to control sound production, while the other side takes a subordinate role in this task. Similarly, when bilateral structures must co-operate closely in generating new and complex motor outputs, as with our hands, lateral dominance may be favored. It may also help, in humans, to have all the language functions close together in one hemisphere for quick and coordinated functioning.

Why we prefer the right and not the left hand, and why the left hemisphere is ordinarily dominant and not the right, are interesting questions, but we do not have any ready answer.

Neural organization of speech

Now that we have gained some knowledge of the neural organization of the brain for language, we can ask what happens in the normal brain during speech processing. Geschwind (1972) suggests the following specific model.

1. A word is heard in the primary auditory area and then is sent to Wernicke's area.

2. If a word is to be spoken, the neural pattern is transmitted from Wernicke's area to Broca's area. In Broca's area, the articulatory form is aroused and passed on to the motor area that controls the movement of the muscles of speech.

3. If the spoken word is to be spelled, the auditory pattern is passed to the *angular gyrus* (see Figure 11–1), where it elicits a visual pattern. The angular gyrus, which lies at the juncture of the visual, auditory, and somesthetic association areas, is ideally suited for the establishment of such association between sensory stimuli.

4. When a word is read, the pattern in the visual areas passes to the angular gyrus, which in turn arouses the corresponding auditory form of the word in Wernicke's area.

The model predicts specific speech disorders:

1. If Wernicke's area is damaged, the person should have difficulty comprehending both spoken and written speech, but so long as Broca's area is intact, speaking should be fluent and well articulated.

2. If only Broca's area is damaged, articulation is disrupted. Speech should be slow and labored but comprehension should remain intact.

3. If Wernicke's area and Broca's area are both intact, but dissociated by a lesion, speech should be fluent but abnormal. Repetition of spoken language should be grossly impaired, but comprehension of spoken and written speech should be intact. This syndrome is conduction aphasia.

The cortex has sensory (visual, auditory, and somesthetic) and motor areas (Figure 11–1). These areas receive signals directly from the environment: the visual area receives visual signals, the auditory area receives auditory signals, and so on. In the rat and other low-order mammals, the cortex is almost completely occupied by sensory and motor areas, but in higher animals much of the frontal, temporal, and parietal cortex does not respond directly to sensory input. These "silent" regions are *association areas* in which signals arriving in the sensory and motor areas mingle and become associated with one another. Geschwind's model assumes that horizontal or transcortical connections have to be made in the association areas to connect areas of vision, audition, somesthesis, and motion.

Is the model sound? It does not tie in with an earlier observation by Penfield and Roberts (1959) that there is no one site where the motor engrams (memory traces) of speech are stored. For example, excision of Broca's area or damage to that area does not always cause severe linguistic disturbance. Further, Penfield and Roberts could not find any localized center in the angular gyrus for the recognition of letters, numbers, and words.

Pribram (1971) asks: How can a sector of the cortex associate the effects of inputs to other more primary parts of the brain when its disruption from those parts has no effect? Association between different modalities (vision, audition, and so on) are more disrupted by lesions of the sensory and motor areas than by lesions of the so-called association areas.

Penfield and Roberts, Pribram, and other neurologists suggest an alternate way to connect sensory and motor functions. Functional connection between any two sensory, or between a sensory and the motor area is made vertically through subcortical structures such as the *thalamus* at the base of the brain, where incoming and outgoing nerve impulses of different areas of the cortex are integrated. Schaltenbrand and co-workers (1971) have observed patients uttering words and whole phrases upon stimulation of the thalamus. The entire issue of *Brain and Language*, 1975, 2, is devoted to discussion on the role of the thalamus in language. Small thalamic lesions seem to cause language deficits in some but by no means all patients. Moreover, language-related functions are most often associated with the left side of the thalamus. However J. W. Brown (1972) (after evaluating several cases of thalamus removal) believes that given an intellectually normal subject and an uncomplicated operation the removal of the thalamus in the speech-dominant hemisphere does not produce a distinct impairment in speech.

In an experiment that directly compared vertical with horizontal connections, Doty (1961) attached electrodes to the skulls of cats so that the electrical contacts rested either in one of the outer layers of the cortex or on its surface. At least one electrode was placed in the visual area, and a second in the motor area of the cortex. Doty then employed a classical conditioning procedure: when the motor area of the cortex was electrically stimulated (the unconditioned stimulation) a discrete movement of one of the limbs (the unconditioned response) occurred. By repeatedly pairing electrical stimulation of the visual area (the conditioned stimulus) with stimulation of the motor area, Doty eventually produced a limb movement in response to stimulation of the visual area alone (the conditioned response). He then operated on the visual area in two ways, severing either its horizontal (transcortical) connections with the motor area or its vertical (subcortical) connections. The cats with the severed vertical connections did not show the conditioned response while the cats with the severed horizontal connections did. It thus appears that the vertical connections are the more important ones.

Geschwind (1967) points out the possibility that the animal normally uses the transcortical connections and starts to use the direct subcortical connections only when the normal pathway is no longer available. He believes that humans are more dependent on the transcortical connection in the sense that they compensate less readily than monkeys for damage to these areas.

In this part we have raised several questions on neurological mechanisms of speech without being able to supply definite answers. Are there speech areas in the brain? If so, how many are there, and what are they?

How does cerebral dominance develop in an individual—does it exist from birth? Does it increase or decrease with age? How are two or more sensory and motor areas connected—through transcortical or subcortical connections? Neurological investigation of the human brain is developing rapidly, with increasing sophistication in techniques and equipment. These questions may eventually be answered in definite terms.

PSYCHOLINGUISTIC INVESTIGATION OF APHASIA

Psycholinguists try to explain aphasia within a framework of normal language and speech processes, often independently of the neurological aspects. We can examine aphasia at the phonetic, lexical, morphological, and syntactic levels. On the phonetic level, aphasics may show the loss of certain phonemes, or confusion of phonemes. On the lexical level, patients cannot find words, misname things, or use circumlocutions to replace difficult words. Their vocabulary may be restricted to frequent words. On the syntactic level, function words may be lost, and word order may be jumbled. In one aphasic's utterance, disorders at all four levels may manifest: ". . . and till in the as a poison plesident, now he is a /fərsən/ should be" (Whitaker, 1969, p. 96). The patient had been shown a picture of Harry S. Truman. The nature of the brain damage was not checked, but the speech disorder was diagnosed as Wernicke's aphasia.

A number of psycholinguistic experiments have investigated how linguistic aspects are lost or disordered in aphasia. Let us review some of these experiments on the several levels of language. In the process, we examine Jakobson's proposal (1941) that speech disintegration in aphasics mirrors the developmental sequence of speech in children.

Phonetic disintegration

Shankweiler and Harris (1966) studied the articulation problems of five aphasics of Broca's type. In general, the patients made more errors on consonants than on vowels; more on initial than on final consonants; more on consonant clusters than on single consonants; more on fricatives and affricatives than on any other type of consonants. This pattern of error is remarkably reminiscent of the errors in stuttering or of young children. Table 11–2 lists some of the consonants and consonant clusters with high error rates.

We recognize that /θ, v, z/ are the three phonemes children acquire late. Shankweiler and Harris point out that the particular difficulty with the fricatives and clusters, the frequent occurrence of errors of voicing and nasalization, and the integrity of the vowels all point to a disturbance of coordinated sequencing of several articulators.

TABLE 11-2   Speech Sounds with Highest Error Rates[a] Among a Group of Broca's Aphasics

Initial position		Final position	
v	63	ʃ	58
z	65	ð	58
θ	75	θ	62
tʃ	55	lk	47
dʒ	55	ps	65
sm	65		
kl	73		
pl	82		

[a] As percentage of total opportunity for error.
From Shankweiler and Harris, 1966: rearranged in order of increasing error rates.

The patients found difficult some of the same sounds young children find difficult, but there is little reason to assume that the difficulty has the same basis. For one thing, children and adults with articulatory defects make predictable substitutions, whereas variability is one of the striking features of the speech of the aphasics. A relatively small proportion of the errors—substitution of stop consonants for fricatives (for example, [p] for [f]—represents phonetic simplifications typical of young children. The patterns of aphasics' errors that differed from those of children were: (1) Aphasics tended to break up consonant clusters by insertion of a vowel between the normally linked pair of consonants. (2) There was no significant tendency for front consonants such as [p] to be better produced than middle or back consonants such as [t] or [k]. (3) Aphasics might replace unvoiced sounds by voiced ones. From clinical experience, Critchley (1970) also observed inconsistency in some aphasic patients' phonetic difficulties. A patient may emit a given consonant correctly, but a moment later may fail entirely on the same consonant. When the aphasics substitutes an easy sound for a difficult one, there are many alternative substitutions and none is adhered to consistently.

Word usage

What kind of words cause difficulty to aphasics? First of all, infrequent words are difficult. Newcomb, Oldfield, and Wingfield (1965) studied the object-naming performance of five groups of subjects. The experimental group consisted of 102 aphasics with penetrating gunshot wounds, aged between 37 and 61. This group was compared to university students and a hospital control group, as well as two other groups, which we shall ignore. The experimenters presented to each subject 26 cards bearing pictures of objects, and observed subjects' time to name each of the objects. The less frequently a word appears in general usage, the longer the subject took to use it as a name. The correlation between mean latency and the logarithm of word frequency was high—r was up to $-.87$. There was also a high correlation between accuracy and frequency—frequently used words were more accurately applied as names. Performance of aphasics was poorer than that of either the hospital control group or the university students on the two measures. The less frequently a word is used, the greater were the differences among the groups of subjects. In other words, aphasics' performance was similar to the other groups' for very frequent words but much poorer than the other groups' for infrequent words.

Schuell and Jenkins (1961) studied the kinds of error aphasics make in word usage. The experimenters asked an unselected sample of 117 aphasics to choose the response to a test word from multiple-choice pictures. For example, one of the pictures had the object referred to by the experimenters ("chair"); one an object with a name that rhymed with "chair" ("stair"); one an object closely associated with the test object ("table"); and one an unrelated object ("apple"). Given the test word "chair," aphasic subjects could, in principle, erroneously choose any one of the three wrong pictures.

The subjects' actual errors were predominantly associative. Errors of the rhyming type were much less frequent, and choices of the unrelated picture were extremely rare. Most random errors were made by severely impaired patients and most associative errors by the least impaired subjects. The patients seemed to know the meaning of the words they intended to say. Only at severe levels of vocabulary deficit do the associative processes themselves begin to break down. The same kinds of errors tended to appear whether patients were asked to point to objects named by the experimenter, to name objects, to match words to pictures, to match spoken to printed words, or to write words to dictation.

Are the difficulties of aphasics in word usage similar to those of other types of speakers? Rochford and Williams (1962, 1963) investigated the breakdown of the use of names by aphasics and by adults under stress, and the acquisition sequence by children ranging in ages from 2 to 12. The 32 aphasic subjects varied in the degree and nature of their language impairment. The subjects' task was to name three objects ("comb," "watch," and "basket") and four of their parts ("handle," "hands," "teeth," and "buckle") from pictures.

In terms of proportion correct and number of cues required, the order of difficulty of these seven names was as given. That is, "comb" was the easiest and "buckle" was the most difficult item for all groups. There was a close parallel between the degree of aphasics' difficulty in naming and children's age of acquisition of these names. For example, "comb" was acquired at age 2, "handle" at age 6, and "buckle" at age 11. Normal speakers under stress, distraction, or confusion after electroconvulsive treatment showed the same pattern. Reacquisition of names by aphasics tended to follow the same rule. A further experiment with different words showed that there was some relationship between frequency of word usage and ease of naming. In the authors' view, the normal correct naming response is the end-product of a complicated preconscious selection process. What is observed in aphasia is an exaggeration of tendencies to error that are successfully inhibited in normal speech.

The experiments on word usage described so far do not emphasize possible differences among different types of aphasia. We explore such differences in the experiments on syntax to be described later.

Morphology, the use of inflectional endings

English-speaking children master 14 morphemes in an invariant order, as shown in Table 6–2. Do aphasics show the same order of difficulty? J. de Villiers (1974) analyzed speech transcripts from eight nonfluent aphasics (Broca's aphasics) and five normal controls for the presence of or absence of the 14 morphemes in their obligatory contexts. Despite the size of the transcripts, for the aphasics obligatory contexts occurred with reasonable frequency (10 or more times per transcript) for only 8 of the 14 morphemes. Hence, comparisons between the aphasics and children are made on these 8 morphemes.

A stable ordering of difficulty was found for the aphasics that differed from the invariant order of acquisition of these morphemes established for children. The major differences between the orderings are that the copula morphemes ("is," "am," "are," and so on) are intact in aphasia but relatively late to develop for children, whereas the past irregular ("came," "fell") is acquired early by children but poorly used in aphasia. The third-person regular (-s) is the most difficult morpheme, while progressive (-ing) and plural (-s) are the two easiest morphemes for the two groups.

The investigator concludes that each of such variables as grammatical and semantic complexity, redundancy, stress, and frequency, may account for a portion of the ordering shown by the aphasics.

Goodglass and Berko (1960) studied the productive use of inflections, including ten endings to make their study comparable to Berko's study (1958) on children's use of endings. Aphasic subjects found complex possessives the most difficult, the comparative and two forms of plural the easiest, and others in between. Unlike children, the aphasics showed no progressive difference between the two forms of the plural, (-s) in "books" and (-es) in "houses," or of the past tense, (-d) and (-ed). In fact, they omitted more (-s) than (-es). (-ks) in "books" is a cluster of consonants and perhaps becomes phonetically difficult for Broca's type of aphasic. Three aphasics failed all of the possessive endings in the simple (-s), while 4-year-old children could consistently supply a simple possessive. In addition, the study showed that there was a degree of independence between morphology and syntax; some subjects with syntactic difficulty (see next section) did not do so badly in the use of inflections.

Syntactic difficulty

What aspects of syntax cause most difficulty to the various types of aphasics? Shewan and Canter (1971) tested three groups of adult aphasics— Broca's type, Wernicke's type, and amnesic—as well as normal controls for auditory comprehension of speech. Aphasics differed from the normal controls quantitatively but not qualitatively. Similarly, the three types of aphasia differed quantitatively, Wernicke's type scoring the lowest on comprehension. Of the three types of material tested—vocabulary, syntax, and sentence length—syntax complexity proved to be most difficult for all subjects. Syntax varied in its transformational complexity: the least complex was the simple active declarative sentence, the next most complex syntax was either the negative or the passive sentence, and the most complex involved both negative and passive transformations.

Parisi and Pizzamiglio (1970) in Italy found similar results. Patients had to select the picture depicting the correct choice between two sentences that displayed a syntactic contrast. There were 20 syntactic and semantic contrasts, ranging from an easy contrast, such as near/far, to such contrasts as subject/object ("The train bumps the car" or "The car bumps the train"). Other contrasts included singular/plural, affirmative/negative, and so on. Wernicke's and Broca's types gave different quantitative, but not qualitative, results, the Wernicke and mixed aphasics being more severely impaired than the Broca's or amnesic patients. The dissolution of syntactic comprehension in the aphasics was highly correlated with the order of acquisition of the same rules in children.

Now here is an experiment that is similar in procedures to the preceding two but reaches contradicting conclusions. Goodglass, Gleason, and Hyde (1970) investigated the auditory comprehension of speech by aphasics of five types—anomic, Broca's type, Wernicke's type, global (see Table 11–1), and conduction—as well as normal adults and children aged 4–9. The test items included vocabulary, two kinds of prepositions, and sequential pointing span (the experimenter gives words in series; the subject points to the corresponding pictures in the same order as the given words).

Three of the five types of aphasics showed different patterns of scores:

anomics did poorly on the vocabulary test; Broca's type on the pointing-span test; and Wernicke's type on recognition of correct grammatical usage of prepositions. Table 11–3 summarizes some of the basic findings.

TABLE 11–3   Mean Correct Scores of Eight Groups of Subjects on Four Types of Linguistic Tests

Test subjects	Vocabulary		Directional preposition		Preposition preference		Pointing span		Summed rank
	score	rank	score	rank	score	rank	score	rank	
3–4 yr old	54.1	8	17.6	7	4.4	8	6.2	6	29
9–10 yr	68.9	6	23.4	2	10.5	3	18.1	2	13
Normal adults	120.7	2	23.9	1	10.8	1	21.8	1	5
Conduction	121.14	1	20.0	5	10.7	2	7.17	4	12
Broca	107.1	3	20.82	4	9.39	5	2.36	8	20
Anomic	100.82	4	22.3	3	10.2	4	9.17	3	14
Wernicke	93.8	5	17.37	6	6.4	6	6.60	5	22
Global	68.2	7	13.7	8	5.35	7	2.50	7	29

"Rank" refers to the rank ordering of scores among the eight groups of subjects. The groups can be ordered in terms of performance on all tests (or summed ranks) as follows from the worst to the best performance: 3–4-year-old children and global aphasics; Wernicke; Broca; anomic; 9–10-year-old; conduction; normal adults.
Table 1 of Goodglass et al., 1970: the ranks added.

In no case could the performance pattern of an aphasic be mistaken for that of a child. For example, on vocabulary, the global aphasics' mean score was at the level of an 8-year-old, but even anomics (with their word-finding difficulty) scored higher than children. On prepositions, the global aphasics were near random level, while the children performed perfectly. On pointing span, the mean score of the best aphasic group, anomics, was below the 6-year-old level. The group who did most poorly on pointing span, Broca's type, could not reliably point to two objects, something that even the youngest children could do. Pointing span perhaps entails some form of production; in order to point subjects may have to reproduce, inwardly, the words just heard.

The authors further concluded that comprehension ability is not always related to production ability. For example, Broca's type patients who omit prepositions in production do well on the test of preposition comprehension. On the other hand, anomics, who are defined as aphasics with name-finding difficulty, also show noun-comprehension difficulty.

Can we resolve the conflicting conclusions from the three studies? Whether one finds qualitative or quantitative differences among various types of aphasics as well as between aphasics and children depends partly on experimental procedures. We assume that the different groups of aphasics in the three experiments were selected on a similar basis. But all three experiments tested only one type of skill, comprehension, as opposed to production. Goodglass and co-workers found qualitative differences among various groups of subjects, perhaps because their test materials were more heterogeneous than the ones used in the two other experiments. Further, Goodglass and co-workers suspect that pointing span may entail some form of production. They also tested vocabulary in isolation, while Shewan and Canter tested it in sentences.

Finally, the investigators can emphasize different aspects of their results. My scrutiny of Parisi and Pizzamiglio's results reveals that even on one homogeneous type of test the different aphasic groups and children showed different patterns of scores on a few items. For example, the contrast from/ to ranked as the most difficult (rank 1) among the 20 test items for children, but was a relatively easy item (14) for the Wernicke's aphasics, and intermediate (9.5) for Broca's aphasics. Relative sentences were the most difficult for the Wernicke's aphasics but were easy for Broca's aphasics, and so on.

On the other hand, Goodglass and co-workers seem to have emphasized qualitative differences among groups of subjects at the expense of quantitative differences. A cursory look at Table 11–3 indicates that any group of subjects that is poor on one type of test is similarly poor on the other three types of test. In other words, rank orders among the nine groups of subjects for each of the four types of test are similar enough. In that sense, group differences seem not to be as qualitative as the authors assert.

THEORETICAL ISSUES

Aphasics and children

To the extent that linguistic materials can be ordered in difficulty, speech disintegration in aphasics mirrors the developmental sequence in children. However, psycholinguistic experiments show that the difficulties of aphasics are similar but not always identical to those of children. There are further dissimilarities. Most aphasics have some residual language and speech and do not learn language from scratch but relearn the language they had before the brain damage. As evidence for this, when aphasics recover speech through therapy, they may recover their old accents even when their speech therapists speak with different accents. This is not the case with children—they are ready to take on any accent to which they are exposed. Moreover, unlike a child, who is usually sure of the correctness of an utterance, a classic Broca's aphasic whom Goodglass, Gleason, Bernholz, and Hyde (1972) tested was constantly dissatisfied with his speech. The aphasic's grammatical performance seems to be influenced by a residual memory of what sounds correct in standard English.

Aphasics are also more variable than children. Aphasics may show varied linguistic impairment depending on a variety of factors, such as site and severity of lesion, educational background, or age. With normal children, we talk about a uniform sequence (if not rate) of development: every child goes through predictable and distinguishable stages of development (see Chapter 6). An individual patient's performance on the same item in successive trials can be also variable. We mentioned experimental and clinical observations on this question with regard to phonetic difficulties. In grammatical performance, Goodglass and co-workers (1972) point out that the patient's successive attempts on each trial usually improve the grammaticality of the output.

In short, aphasia reveals many interesting data on speech mechanisms of normal speech. But it is limited as a clue to understanding speech of normal children and adults.

Are there different types of aphasia?

From the purely linguistic point of view, there can be two types of aphasia, according to Jakobson (1956). As mentioned in Chapter 3, normal linguistic processes involve paradigmatic and syntagmatic processes. The paradigmatic process refers to the selection of appropriate linguistic units in any given context, and therefore to the substitution of one alternative for another in the same context. The syntagmatic process determines the sequencing of the linguistic units, hence the building of larger units from smaller ones. These two processes are smoothly coordinated in normal speech processes but may be selectively disturbed in aphasia.

Similarity and continguity disorders   When the paradigmatic process is disturbed, the patient has difficulty in spontaneous selection or substitution of words. In extreme cases, speech is reduced to a form of jargon in which the structure of the language is preserved but the substance is meaningless. The syntagmatic process is relatively undamaged. Jakobson called this type of linguistic disorder a "similarity disorder." A "contiguity disorder" results when the syntagmatic process alone is affected. The patient experiences severe difficulty in combining words into more complex constructions, in transforming sentences grammatically, and in rhythmic and sequential performance generally. Function words and inflectional endings are most susceptible to this type of disorder, the patient in extreme cases being reduced to "telegraphic speech."

The question arises how Jakobson's similarity and contiguity disorders relate to the classic expressive and receptive typing of aphasia.

Jakobson himself (1964) seems to equate the contiguity disorder with the expressive type and the similarity disorder with the receptive type. Is this equation justified? Experiments and clinical observations that we have reviewed so far and review below seem to indicate otherwise.

Here we examine in some detail two more experiments that test the combination skills of both expressive and receptive aphasics. Von Stockert (1972) tested two subjects, one classical expressive and one receptive aphasic, using a sentence-order test. The subjects had to put three constituents (the girl—from Boston—is pretty) in their correct order. The Wernicke's aphasic, who could not understand the meaning of very simple written commands and questions, was able to order the three constituents at a level far better than chance. However, his performance on more complex sentence forms—embedded, question, and imperative—was not significantly better than chance; it was inferior to the Broca's aphasic on all of these sentence forms. His performance was better than the Broca's aphasic only on declarative sentence, and was equal to the Broca's aphasic on declarative-nonconstituent and question-nonconstituent groupings. In a nonconstituent test, the subjects had to order such nonconstituents as "the—girl from—Boston is pretty" in a proper order.

In short, both Broca's and Wernicke's types have disordered combination skills, which may become more apparent as the sentences become more complex. One interesting implication of von Stockert's experiment is that on a certain level structure and sentence meaning may be processed separately. The Wernicke's aphasic did not understand the sentence meaning, yet could order the constituents and nonconstituents correctly in simple declarative sentences.

Zurif, Caramazza, and Myerson (1972) found that Broca's aphasics group words in a somewhat deviant manner in a word-sorting task. As in production, expressive aphasics seem to exclude anything nonessential to the intrinsic meaning of a sentence. Figure 11–4 shows how typical aphasics' word-sorting differs from that of controls. Assuming that word-sorting tasks tap receptive combination skills, the authors concluded that expressive aphasia is only one aspect of an impairment involving all language modalities. Contrary to the authors' assumption, the tasks may be considered to tap expressive skills as well. In short, the two experiments seem to show that both expressive and receptive types of aphasics have some disorders in combination skills (the syntagmatic process). At the same time, disorders in either an expressive or a receptive skill cannot be always distinguished clearly. The paradigmatic process may be disordered independently of the syntagmatic process, at least in anomic patients. We only question Jakobson's equation of the similarity disorder (disorder in paradigmatic process) with the receptive disorder.

Later Jakobson (1964) expanded his classification system into three dichotomies: the first dichotomy is between disorders of encoding (com-

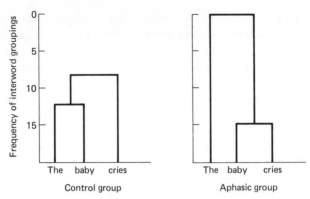

FIGURE 11–4 Phrase markers for control and aphasic groups. The controls group "the" and "baby" closely, as they should because "the baby" is a noun phrase. The aphasics, on the other hand, group "baby" and "cries" closely leaving "the" by itself.

bination, contiguity) and of decoding (selection, similarity); the second between limitation and disintegration; and the third between sequence and concurrence. Jakobson's contribution here is to make the already confusing field even more confusing.

Unidimensionality This confusion in classifying aphasics raises the question whether there are indeed different types of aphasia distinguishable either in skills or in processes. Aphasia may vary only in amount of deficit, and not in kind, modalities, tasks, or processes.

Schuell and Jenkins (1959) asserted more vigorously than others this position that aphasia is unidimensional. They could arrange certain items of the Minnesota Test for Differential Diagnosis of Aphasia in a hierarchical order to provide a unidimensional scale of aphasic disturbance. The test items tapping different linguistic skills and processes were arranged according to their difficulty levels, as determined by the percentage of aphasic subjects passing. The easiest test was "Reading: word to picture," which 84 percent of subjects passed; for "Speech: serial responses," 50 percent passed; the most difficult test was "Auditory: long paragraph," which only 14 percent passed, and so on. Smith (1971) gave the Minnesota Test to 78 stroke aphasics, with results supporting the theory of unidimensionality.

Osgood and Miron (1963) criticized Schuell and Jenkins's analysis on the ground that their selection procedures eliminated approximately one-third of the original test items on the basis of low *phi* coefficients.[1] In their subject population, more than half were over 50 years old, and more than

---

[1] A good *phi* coefficient means that a particular test is highly successful in measuring the target of the battery of which it is a part.

half were classified as having cerebrovascular etiology; the injuries characteristic of both the age and the etiology are known to be diffuse in nature. This criticism should apply equally to the more recent findings by Smith mentioned above. When patients were minimally screened, Jones and Wepman (1961) and Osgood and Miron identified group factors representing independent dimensions, which Osgood and Miron called "stimulus interpretation" and "response elicitation" (similar to receptive and productive skills, respectively).

A final conclusion is hard to draw on this confusing topic, but let us try. In both neurological and psycholinguistic investigations, we seem to encounter again and again the two main types—*predominantly* expressive and *predominantly* receptive disorders. I emphasize that the dichotomy is not clear-cut but fuzzy. Each of these two types may show deficiencies in either syntagmatic or paradigmatic processes or both. The inevitable next question is how many types of aphasia we should distinguish. Apparently it is up to each aphasiologist's personal inclination. Some aphasiologists no doubt can easily list more than a dozen types. But in Table 11–1 I have listed the five types that are most commonly used in psycholinguistic research, and have been mentioned in this chapter.

Competence or performance disorder?   Finally, a debate is going on as to whether aphasia is a disorder in competence or performance. Whitaker (1969) equates competence with central, and performance with peripheral, language systems. If a patient cannot read prepositions but uses them correctly when speaking and comprehends them normally, he has a performance deficit. Although a competence disorder may be manifested accidentally in one modality, it is capable of being manifested in all peripheral systems. Whitaker cites a patient who could not read, speak, write, or understand personal pronouns. Whitaker thus believes that brain damage can affect both competence and performance.

Lenneberg (1967) considers aphasia a disruption of the timing of events in the central nervous system, hence more a performance deficit. Weigl and Bierwisch (1973) also claim that aphasic syndromes are disturbances of components or subcomponents of the system of performance, while the underlying competence remains intact. To support their claim, Weigl and Bierwisch cite the fact that one or several components of speech performance are disturbed, while others are not. Even within one and the same component, there is a high fluctuation of performance (for example, an object that can be named one day cannot be named next day). Then there is the "deblocking" phenomenon: a transference of a still intact component of performance to a disturbed one. For example, a patient with intact repetition capability but with disturbed naming is able to name "ball" after repeating the word.

On the other hand, Zurif and colleagues (1972) assert that expressive aphasics' telegraphic speech is only one aspect of an impairment involving all language modalities.

Do we know whether aphasia is due to loss of stored information, difficulties of access to this information, or both? The debate on whether the deficit is in competence or performance seems to be fruitless. On one hand, we do not know enough about neural mechanisms to settle the issue, and on the other hand, even if we did settle it, the settlement would not lead to new insights or research.

Aphasia in multilingualism

A multilingual possesses a particularly extended vocabulary and has two or more competing systems of language. When a multilingual person suffers brain damage, does it cause disorders in all of his languages, or only in selected languages? In the latter case, which languages are likely to suffer? Aphasia in multilinguals might shed some light on how two or more languages are organized in a multilingual's brain. Three "rules" have been proposed on the question of which of a multilingual's many languages will be most resistant to aphasic damage. Ribot's (1883) "primacy rule" says that linguistic habits acquired early, as in early childhood, are more resistant to aphasic damage than those acquired subsequently. Pitres's "habit rule" (1895) states that the languages most used before the onset of aphasia will be the first to recover. Minkowski (1928) thinks that an emotional factor related to the use of one language might account for the survival of that language.

If we do not already have diverse enough views, let us listen to anecdotal accounts of experts who gathered at a symposium on aphasia (de Reuck and O'Conner, 1964, pp. 118–121). My own comments on each of the anecdotes are in parentheses.

Stengel reports cases of non-Italian tourists who became aphasic while on holiday in Italy and whose residual language was Italian (most recent or most needed language preserved). Jakobson recalls that after a motor accident he was aphasic for a couple of hours. Without any need he automatically translated each of several sentences into four or five languages. (Is he equally competent and emotionally involved in these languages? Or are the neural mechanisms that normally inhibit unnecessary languages impaired?) In New York hospitals old Jews who for decades had spoken only English were observed to speak only Yiddish (their childhood language) for many days after a motor accident (Jakobson's report; the first learned [emotional, but not lately practiced] language preserved). Aphasic Puerto Ricans in New York City who had learned English late had to identify a series of pictures in any language. Most of them identified the pictures in Spanish but all of them identified some pictures in English, especially the pictures that were related to the American culture (Eisenson's report; selective to culture-specific words).

Penfield and the French neurologist Hécaen express views opposed to the concept that aphasia is a language-selective disorder. Penfield (Penfield and Roberts, 1959) had occasion to study bilingual aphasics in Montreal, Canada, and concludes:

The mechanism that is developed in the brain is the same whether one, two, or more languages are learned. French is not subserved by one area of the brain and English and Chinese by others, in spite of the fact that cases have been published of adults who lost one language and preserved another as the result of stroke or other injury to the brain. Our conclusion is that these patients must have been inadequately studied, or else there were psychological reasons why one language was preferred in the recovery period. After 30 years of experience in the bilingual community of Montreal, I have never seen such an example. (p. 253)

Similarly, Hécaen (1965), speaking of aphasics who spoke English, Russian, and German, states:

. . . la destruction des diverses langues s'est révélée similaire, tant dans la phase initiale que dans la progression ou la récupération du trouble, et aussi bien dans l'intensité que dans les caractères spécifiques des perturbations (p. 93).

I leave the quotation in French, as this passage is an excellent example of my assertion that educated English speakers can read French easily if they use its many cognates (see Chapter 7 on bilingualism).

If any conclusion is possible at all on this question, it is that there is no single "rule" on how aphasia develops in a multilingual patient. Multilingual backgrounds as well as the severity and type of aphasia are so heterogeneous that we must approach each multilingual case without a preconceived "rule." The language retained could be the language that is learned first, or most needed, or most practiced, or most emotional, or most recently used, or any other reason one can think of. Alternately, a multilingual's many languages may not be selectively impaired at all.

SUMMARY AND CONCLUSIONS

The fact that brain damage can cause speech disorder has been known since ancient times. Only in the late nineteenth century did specific areas in the brain begin to be linked to specific types of disorder. Broca asserted that damage in the frontal area of the left hemisphere caused expressive disorder. Broca's aphasics have difficulty in producing speech, without much impairment in the ability to comprehend. Wernicke later claimed that injury to a posterior part of the temporal lobe in the left hemisphere causes receptive disorder. Wernicke's aphasics can speak fluently but have trouble in comprehension. Localization of brain functions is still a controversial issue, but some areas in the left hemisphere, including the above two, seem to be important speech areas.

There is a functional asymmetry between the two hemispheres, and in most people speech areas are located in the left hemisphere. This can be demonstrated in several ways, such as by dichotic listening tasks. The brain seems to be specialized from birth to process speech and nonspeech sounds differently, but functional organization of the brain for speech may continue throughout childhood. There also seem to be anatomical differences between the two hemispheres in adults as well as in neonates.

Stone artifacts show that Pithecanthropus already may have been left-hemisphere-dominant. Did this creature also possess language? In both human and chaffinch, lateralization appears efficient in that one side of the brain takes a leading role in sound production, which involves complex motor outputs.

Geschwind proposed a specific model of speech processing based on transcortical connections among sensory and motor areas. He predicted specific speech disorders according to which connection was damaged. Other neurologists emphasize vertical connections between cortical areas and the thalamus. The neurological mechanisms of speech are still in the stage of exploration, and their investigation is full of controversies.

Psycholonguists examine aphasic speech at the phonetic, lexical, morphological, and syntactic levels. Broca's aphasics make a variety of phonetic errors, especially on fricatives and consonant clusters. Their errors are less predictable than those of children. Infrequent words cause difficulty to aphasics. The aphasics' errors in choosing a word are not random, but related in meaning to the word they intend to say. Words that are acquired at later ages by children are more difficult for aphasics to produce in naming things.

Nonfluent aphasics show a stable ordering of eight English morphemes. The ordering is not the same as that shown by children. Of two forms of plural and past tense morphemes, aphasics find the simpler one more difficult; aphasics differ from children here too.

Wernicke's and global aphasics perform most poorly in comprehension of syntactic features. Broca's aphasics perform better than Wernicke's aphasics, but not as well as normal adults. With more heterogeneous test material, some qualitative differences among different types of aphasics, and between children and aphasics, emerge.

On the whole, the disintegration of speech in aphasics does not always mirror the developmental sequence of speech in children. Aphasics' performance shows variability and is influenced by whatever residual language the patients may have.

Jakobson says that a deficiency in the paradigmatic process is a similarity disorder, while an impairment in the syntagmatic process is a contiguity disorder. Both expressive and receptive aphasics might be disordered in either one or both of the two linguistic processes.

Some aphasiologists assert that aphasia may vary only in amount of deficit, and not in kind. However, a rough distinction between predominantly expressive and receptive types seems to be useful. Aphasia may involve the central language system, but be manifested in varying degrees in different modalities.

Which of multilinguals' languages will be more resistant to disintegration in aphasia? Experts' anecdotal accounts of multilingual aphasics convince us that there is no single rule such as "primacy" that can describe the behavior of all multilingual aphasics of heterogeneous backgrounds.

Epilogue

In eleven chapters we have discussed eleven main topics. We had to cover at least these eleven varied topics in order to gain even a working knowledge of the processes of language and speech. The relative lengths of the chapters roughly reflect their relative importances. The two longest chapters discuss the two most important topics, "grammar and speech" and "language acquisition." Numerous cross-references among the chapters reflect the fact that the eleven topics are interrelated.

Now I would like to summarize and comment briefly and informally on each chapter. What are my "excuses" for having each of the eleven chapters?

1. Language: An Informal Look. Is human language unique? In the process of answering this question, we learned some characteristics of animal communication and human languages. I preferred to use this approach, since it seemed to be a better way of illuminating the nature of human language than giving a cryptic one-sentence definition of language, as most other books on psycholinguistics do.

Human language is unique, but also diverse: an impressive number of widely different languages exist in the world. How do they differ? One current fashion or passion in linguistics is to find language universals. We can identify universals only after first learning about other languages, especially those very different from our own. Another reason for finding out about a variety of languages is that differences arouse some people's curiosity more than similarities do.

2. *Linguistic Units and Speech Behavior.* A language has a structure made from units. The linguistic units called "phoneme" and "distinctive feature" sound abstract when they are discussed by themselves. They become real when they are shown to influence our speech behavior in psycholinguistic experiments.

3. *Words—Psychological Investigation.* Besides being familiar and useful linguistic units, words have many interesting characteristics. Above all, words have meanings. But the essence of word meaning has eluded us once again!

4. *Grammar and Speech.* By presenting a developmental history of grammar, I wanted to prepare the reader for the eventual presentation of the rather abstract and forbidding Transformational Generative Grammar (TGG). Whether I wanted to or not, I had to describe TGG, because it has inspired many psycholinguistic experiments. Some psychologists (such as Greene, 1972) even go so far as to use the term "psycholinguistics" in such a narrow sense as to cover only the relation between TGG and TGG-inspired experiments.

Although TGG at one time looked promising as a model for speech, it no longer seems so. In this chapter, I pointed out that the real psycholinguistic question is: How do we produce and comprehend utterances to communicate semantic messages in varied contexts? Current research efforts and grammars may perhaps be on the right track at last.

5. *The Statistical Structure of Language.* Despite the academic title, this chapter is intended to show the reader that the statistical structure of language influences our speech all the time. The statistical structure arises from basic principles of human nature—such as the principle of maximum communication with least effort.

6. *Language Acquisition.* Currently this is a very fashionable topic in psycholinguistics, partly inspired by new models of grammar such as TGG and Case Grammar. This inspiration from grammars has its desirable as well as undesirable effects. One of the desirable effects is that many experiments are carried out in diverse languages, and one of the undesirable effects is that syntax acquisition tends to be overemphasized at the expense of the more fundamental semantic development, especially semantic development in relation to cognitive development. Even syntactic development should be studied in relation to cognitive development. But this imbalance seems to be being corrected.

Many cross-language comparisons are made in an effort to find universals. This is a worthy effort, except that when speech similarities are found they often are interpreted to fit the experimenters' own preconceived theoretical positions. As in Chapter 4, we should, at our present state of understanding, be more concerned with studying speech than with fitting a particular grammar to speech.

7. Bilingualism. The phenomenon is not usually given as prominent a place as it is in this book. I chose to emphasize bilingualism not only because it is interesting in its own right, but also because the questions raised are relevant to the more traditional topics of psycholinguistics. Studying how a young child acquires two languages may shed light on how one normally acquires one language; bilingual cognitive functioning helps us understand cognitive operations in general; bilingual storage and retrieval of words is related to the same processes in monolinguals; and bilingual sentence processing may deepen our understanding of monolingual sentence processing. In each case, bilingual errors are illuminating.

8. Language and Understanding the World. Language and speech play an important, though not indispensable, role in children's cognitive development and in adults' understanding of the world. The principle of linguistic relativity is not as fashionable a topic as it used to be some years ago. Instead of dismissing it altogether, I chose to explore the questions of when it is relevant and when it is not.

9. Universal (?) Phonetic Symbolism. This topic has been kept alive sporadically since the ancient Greek days among philosophers, linguists, and psychologists without becoming a major issue in psycholinguistics. The question is essentially whether the same speech sounds express the same meanings in all languages. Our short chapter on this topic forces us to conclude that UPS is limited to a small group of speech sounds that have specific tonal qualities on which speakers of different languages agree. On the other hand, language-specific phonetic symbolism seems to be prevalent.

10. Speech Disorders. What kinds of linguistic elements and rules tend to be disordered, and why? Speech disorders not only arouse our curiosity, but also help us to understand normal speech processes more fully. I hope I may have suggested ways to prevent and cope with speech disorders, especially such functional disorders as stuttering and articulatory disorders in childhood.

11. Aphasia and Neural Mechanisms of Speech. A better understanding of the neurological mechanisms of speech and language ultimately may lead to a better understanding of speech and language. I have discussed many issues of aphasia and neurology, wading through jargon, controversies, conflicting experimental findings, and theories. A confused rather than coherent picture may have emerged in this chapter, but we learned at least a few well-established facts such as lateralization, and posed many psychoneurological questions.

Final comment

What over-all picture emerges from the book as a whole? The raison d'être of language and speech is to communicate ideas, which are products of human perceptual and cognitive activities. These ideas have to be put in conventional structures and speech sounds for effective communication. The linguistic structures and speech sounds are constrained by human cognitive and physical capacities, but they are relatively "fixed" or overlearned forms through which ever-varying contents have to be expressed. Thus, once acquired, they are perhaps less subject to active cognitive planning than are the semantic contents of speech.

We can expect that human languages and speech everywhere will share certain fundamental characteristics because of the constraints imposed by human physical and cognitive capacities. We should always keep our ears open for such shared aspects or linguistic universals. On the other hand, there is great diversity among the ways in which the basic requirements are expressed by different individuals of one speech community or by speakers of different languages. We examined some of these diversities—their characteristics, functions, and reasons. All this is in the hope of better understanding our fellows, be they babies, foreigners, the speech-handicapped, or even "normal" speakers (whoever they may be).

Conventional Symbols and Abbreviations Used in Psycholinguistics

A	Active or affirmative sentence	IPA	International Phonetic Alphabet (e.g., θ for "*th*in")
BE	Black English		
C	Constant* Consonant*	IQ	Intelligence quotient
CV	Consonant-vowel	L_1L_2	Language 1, language 2
D	Declarative sentence Determiner (the, my . . .)	m	Meaningfulness (of words)
		MLAT	Modern Language Aptitude Test
D_4	Polarity score in SD	MLU	Mean length of utterance
DAF	Delayed auditory feedback	$m\mu$	Millimicron (1 meter × 10^{-9})—unit of light wavelength
dB	Decibel—unit of loudness		
DSK	Dvorak Simplified Keyboard		
		msec	Millisecond
E	Experimenter Exclamatory sentence	N	Noun Negative sentence
EVS	Eye-voice-span	NI	Negative-imperative sentence
f	Frequency of occurrence		
F_1F_2	First formant, second formant	NP	Noun phrase
		NPC	Noun phrase complement
GS	General Semantics	O	Object of sentence
Hz	Hertz (cycles per second), unit of sound frequency	P	Passive sentence
		PN	Passive-negative sentence
I	Imperative sentence	PNQ	Passive-negative-question

PQ	Passive-Question		TTR	Type-token ratio
PS-rules	Phrase structure rules		UPS	(Universal) phonetic
Q	Question sentence			symbolism
r	Correlation coefficient		V	Verb
r	Rank		VC	Vowel-consonant
RT	Reaction time		VOT	Voice-onset time
S	Subject for experiments		VP	Verb phrase
	Sentence		WAT	Word association test
	Subject of sentence		[p]	Speech sound p
	Stimulus		/p/	Phoneme p
SAAD	Simple, active, affirmative,		*	Ungrammatical
	declarative sentence		á	Primary stress
SD	Semantic differential		û	Secondary stress
SE	Standard English		à	Tertiary stress
S/N	Signal-to-noise ratio		ă	Weak stress
SVO	Subject-verb-object		mā	Level tone (in Chinese)
TAT	Thematic Apperception		má	Rising tone
	Test		mǎ	Falling and then rising
TGG	Transformational generative		mà	Falling tone
	grammar			

* Contexts will resolve whether *C* stands for "constant" or "consonant."

References

ABORN, M., RUBINSTEIN, H., and STERLING, T. D. Sources of contextual constraint upon words in sentences. *J. exp. Psychol.*, 1959, 57. 171–180.

AKMAJIAN, A. On deriving cleft sentences from pseudocleft sentences. Unpublished manuscript, Massachusetts Institute of Technology, 1969.

ALLEN, G. D. The location of rhythmic stress beats in stress English: An experimental study. *Language and Speech*, 1972, *15*, 72–100.

ALLPORT, F. H. *Social psychology*. Boston: Houghton Mifflin, 1924.

ALTMANN, S. A. *Social communication among primates*. Chicago: University of Chicago Press, 1967.

ANDERSON, J. R. Verbatim and propositional representation of sentences in immediate and long-term memory. *J. verb. Learn. verb. Behav.*, 1974a, *13*, 149–162.

ANDERSON, J. R. Retrieval of propositional information from long-term memory. *Cognitive Psychol.*, 1974b, *6*, 451–474.

ANDERSON, J. R., and REDER, L. M. Negative judgments in and about semantic memory. *J. verb. Learn. verb. Behav.*, 1974, *13*, 664-681.

ANDERSON, S. W., and BEH, W. The organization of verbal memory in childhood. *J. verb. Learn. verb. Behav.*, 1968, 7, 1049–1053.

ANDREWS, G., and HARRIS M. *The syndrome of stuttering*. London: Spastic Society Medical Education and Information Unit, 1964.

ANGLIN, J. M. *The growth of word meaning*. Cambridge, Mass.: MIT Press, 1970.

ANISFELD, M., BARLOW, J., and FRAIL, C. M. Distinctive features in the pluralization rules of English speakers. *Language and Speech*, 1968, *11*, 31–37.

ASCH, S. E., and NERLOVE, H. The development of double function terms in children: an exploratory investigation. In B. Kaplan and S. Wapner (Eds.) *Perspectives in psychological theory: Essays in honor of Heinz Werner.* New York: International Universities, 1960.

ATTNEAVE, F. Psychological probability as a function of experienced frequency. *J. exp. Psychol.,* 1953, *46,* 81–86.

ATZET, J., and GERARD, H. B. A study of phonetic symbolism among native Navajo speakers. *J. Person. soc. Psychol.,* 1965, *1,* 524–528.

BACKUS, O. Incidence of stuttering among the deaf. *Ann. Otol. Rhinol. Laryngol.,* 1938, *47,* 632–635.

BAIN, B. Toward an integration of Piaget and Vigotsky: Bilingual considerations. Paper presented at the 18th International Congress of Applied Psychology, Montreal, 1974.

BAKER, S. J. The pattern of language. *J. gen. Psychol.,* 1950, *42,* 25–66.

BAR-HILLEL, Y. A quasiarithmetical notation for syntactic description. *Language,* 1953, *29,* 47–58.

BARIK, H. Some critical comments on visual presentation in word matching studies of phonetic symbolism. *Language and Speech,* 1969, *12,* 175–179.

BEECH, H. R., and FRANSELLA, F. *Research and experiment in stuttering.* London: Pergamon, 1968.

BELLUGI, U. The emergence of inflections and negation system in the speech of two children. Paper presented to New England Psychological Assn., 1964.

BENSON, D. F., SHEREMATA, W. A., BONCHARD, R., SEGARRA, J. M., PRICE, D., and GESCHWIND, N. Conduction aphasia: A clinicopathological study. *Arch. Neurol.,* 1973, *28,* 339–346.

BENTLEY, M., and VARON, E. An accessory study of "phonetic symbolism." *Amer. J. Psychol.,* 1933, *45,* 76–86.

BERKO, J. The child's learning of English morphology. *Word,* 1958, *14,* 150–186.

BERLIN, B., and KAY, P. *Basic color terms: Their universality and evolution.* Berkeley, Calif.: University of California Press, 1969.

BEVER, T. G. The cognitive basis for linguistic structures. In J. R. Hayes (Ed.) *Cognition and development of language.* New York: Wiley, 1970.

BEVER, T. G., LACKNER, J., and KIRK, R. The underlying structures of sentences are the primary units of immediate speech processing. *Perception and Psychophysics,* 1969, *5,* 225–234.

BIGGS, B. E., and SHEEHAN, J. G. Punishment or distraction? Operant stuttering revisited. *J. abnorm. Psychol.,* 1969, *74,* 256–262.

BLANK, M. Cognitive functions of language in the preschool years. *Develop. Psychol.,* 1974, *10,* 229–245.

BLICKENSTAFF, C. B. Musical talents and foreign language learning ability. *Modern Lang. J.,* 1963, *47,* 359–363.

BLOODSTEIN, O., JAEGER, W., and TUREEN, J. A study of the diagnosis of stuttering by parents of stutterers and non-stutterers. *J. speech hearing Disorders,* 1952, *17,* 308–315.

BLOODSTEIN, O., and WEST, R. *A handbook on stuttering.* Chicago: National Easter Seal Society for Crippled Children and Adults, 1969.

BLOOM, L. *Language development: Form and function in emerging grammar.* Cambridge, Mass.: MIT Press, 1970.

BLOOM, L. *One word at a time: The use of single word utterances before syntax.* The Hague: Mouton, 1973.

BLOOM, L., HOOD, L., and LIGHTBOWN, P. Imitation in language development: If, when, and why. *Cog. Psychol.,* 1974, *6,* 380–420.

BLUMENTHAL, A. L. Prompted recall of sentences. *J. verb. Learn. verb. Behav.,* 1967, *6,* 203–206.

BOLINGER, D. The atomization of meaning. *Language,* 1965, *41,* 555–573.

BORNSTEIN, M. H. Color vision and color naming: A psychophysiological hypothesis of cultural difference. *Psychol. Bull.,* 1973, *80,* 257–285.

BOURNE, L. E. JR., EKSTRAND, B. R., and DOMINOWSKI, R. *The psychology of thinking.* Englewood Cliffs, N.J.: Prentice-Hall, 1971.

BOUSFIELD, W. A. The problem of meaning in verbal learning. In C. N. Cofer (Ed.) *Verbal learning and verbal behavior.* New York: McGraw-Hill, 1961.

BRACKBILL, Y., and LITTLE, K. B. Factors determining the guessing of meanings of foreign words. *J. abnorm. soc. Psychol.,* 1957, *54,* 312–318.

BRAINE, M. D. S. On learning the grammatical order of words. *Psychol. Rev.,* 1963, *70,* 323–348.

BRAINE, M. D. S. Length constraints, reduction rules, and holophrastic processes in children's word combinations. *J. verb. Learn. verb. Behav.,* 1974, *13,* 448–456.

BRANSFORD, J. D., BARCLAY, J. R., and FRANKS, J. J. Sentence memory: A constructive versus interpretive approach. *Cognitive Psychol.,* 1972, *3,* 193–209.

BRANSFORD, J. D., and FRANKS, J. J. The abstraction of linguistic ideas. *Cognitive Psychol.,* 1971, *2,* 331–350.

BRIAN, C. R., and GOODNOUGH, F. L. The relative potency of color and form perception at various ages. *J. exp. Psychol.,* 1929, *12,* 197–213.

BROCA, P. Remarques sur le siège de la faculté du langage articulé, suives d'une observation d'aphémie. *Bull. Soc. Anatomique,* 1861, 330–357.

BROWN, J. W., *Aphasia, apraxia and agnosia.* Springfield, Ill.: Thomas, 1972.

BROWN, K. S. Genetic features of deafness. *J. acoust. Soc. Amer.,* 1973, *54,* 569–575.

BROWN, R. *Words and things.* Glencoe, Ill.: Free Press, 1958.

BROWN, R. *A first language: The early stages.* Cambridge, Mass.: Harvard University Press, 1973.

BROWN, R., and BELLUGI, U. Three processes in the child's acquisition of syntax. *Harvard Education Review,* 1964, *34,* 133–151.

BROWN, R., and BERKO, J. Psycholinguistic research methods. In P. H. Musson (Ed.) *Handbook of research methods in child development.* New York: Wiley, 1960, pp. 517–557.

BROWN, R., BLACK, A. H., and HOROWITZ, A. E. Phonetic symbolism in natural languages. *J. abnorm. soc. Psychol.,* 1955, *50,* 388–393.

BROWN, R., CAZDEN, C. B., and BELLUGI, U. The child's grammar from I to III. Paper read at 1967 Minnesota Symposium on Child Psychology, Minneapolis, 1967.

BROWN, R., and HANLON, C. Derivational complexity and the order of acquisition in child speech. In J. R. Hayes (Ed.) *Cognition and development of language.* New York: Wiley, 1970, pp. 11–54.

BROWN, R., and LENNEBERG, E. A study in language and cognition. *J. abnorm. soc. Psychol.,* 1954, *49,* 454–462.

BROWN, S. F. The influence of grammatical function on the incidence of stuttering *J. speech Disorders,* 1937, *2,* 207–215.

BRUCK, M., LAMBERT, W. E., and TUCKER, G. R. Cognitive and attitudinal consequences of bilingual schooling: The St. Lambert project through grade six. *International J. Psycholinguistics* (in press).

BÜHLER, K. Tatsachen und Probleme zu einer Psychologie der Denkvorgänge. *Archiv für die gesamte Psychologie,* 1908, *12,* 92.

BURKLUND, C. W. Cerebral hemisphere function in the human: Fact and tradition. Paper presented at the Second Annual Cerebral Function Symposium, Denver, 1970.

BURLING, R. Language development of a Garo- and English-speaking child. *Word,* 1959, *15,* 45–68.

BURTON, N. G., and LICKLIDER, J. C. R. Long-range constraints in the statistical structure of printed English. *Amer. J. Psychol.,* 1955, *68,* 650–653.

BURTT, H. E. An experimental study of early childhood memory. *J. genet. Psychol.,* 1941, *58,* 435–439.

BUTLER, S., and NORRSELL, U. Vocalization possibly initiated by the minor hemisphere. *Nature,* 1968, *220,* 793–794.

CARMICHAEL, L., HOGAN, H. P., and WALTER, A. A. An experimental study of the effect of language on the reproduction of visually perceived forms. *J. exp. Psychol.,* 1932, *15,* 73–86.

CARMON, A., and GOMBOS, G. M. A physiological vascular correlate of hand preference: Possible implications with respect to hemispheric cerebral dominance. *Neuropsychologia,* 1970, *8,* 119–128.

CARRINGTON, J. F. The talking drums of Africa. *Scientific American,* 1971, Dec., 90–94.

CARROLL, J. B. (Ed.) *Language, thought, and reality: selected writings of Benjamin Lee Whorf.* New York: Wiley, 1956.

CARROLL, J. B. Review of Osgood, Suci, and Tannenbaum's "The measurement of meaning." *Language,* 1959, *35,* 58–77.

CARROLL, J. B. *Language and thought.* Englewood Cliffs, N.J.: Prentice-Hall, 1964.

CARROLL, J. B. The contributions of psychological theory and educational research to the teaching of foreign languages. In A. Valdman (Ed.) *Trends in language teaching,* New York: McGraw-Hill, 1966.

CARROLL, J. B., and CASAGRANDE, J. B. The function of language classification. In E. E. Maccoby et al. (Eds.) *Readings in social psychology.* New York: Holt, Rinehart and Winston, 1958, pp. 18–31.

CARROLL, J. B., and SAPON, S. M. *Modern language aptitude test, Form A.* New York: The Psychological Corporation, 1959.

CHAO, Y.-R. *Language and symbolic systems.* London: Cambridge University Press, 1963.

CHAO, Y.-R. *A primer of spoken Chinese*. Chicago: University of Chicago Press, 1968.

CHERRY, C., and SAYERS, B. Experiments upon the total inhibition of stammering by external control and some clinical results. *J. psychosomat. Res.*, 1956, *1*, 233–246.

CHOMSKY, C. *The acquisition of syntax in children from 5 to 10*. Cambridge, Mass.: MIT Press, 1969.

CHOMSKY, N. *Syntactic structures*. The Hague: Mouton, 1957.

CHOMSKY, N. *Aspects of the theory of syntax*. Cambridge, Mass.: MIT Press, 1965.

CHOMSKY, N. *Language and mind*. New York: Harcourt Brace Jovanovitch, 1968.

CHOMSKY, N. Remarks on nominalization. In R. A. Jacobs and P. S. Rosenbaum (Eds.) *Readings in English transformational grammar*. Boston: Ginn & Co., 1970.

CHOMSKY, N. Deep structure, surface structure, and semantic interpretation. In D. D. Steinberg and L. A. Jokobovits (Eds.) *Semantics: An interdisciplinary reader in philosophy, linguistics, and psychology*. London: Cambridge University Press, 1971, pp. 183–216.

CHOMSKY, N., and HALLE, M. *The sound pattern of English*. New York: Harper and Row, 1968.

CHOTLOS, J. W. Studies in language behavior: IV. A statistical and comparative analysis of individual written language samples. *Psychol. Monogr.*, 1944, *56*, 75–111.

CLARK, E. What's in a word? On the child's acquisition of semantics in his first language. In T. Moore (Ed.) *Cognitive development and the acquistion of language*. New York: Academic Press, 1973.

CLARK, H. H. Semantics and comprehension. In T. A. Sebock (Ed.) *Current trends in linguistics*. Vol. 12: *Linguistics and adjacent arts and sciences*. The Hague, Mouton, 1973.

CLARK, H. H., and LUCY, P. Understanding what is meant from what is said: A study in conversationally conveyed requests. *J. verb. Learn. verb. Behav.*, 1975, *14*, 56–72.

COHEN, A. D. The Culver City Spanish Immersion Program: The first two years. *Modern Lang. J.*, 1974, *58*, 95–103.

COLE, R., and SCOTT, B. Toward a theory of speech perception. *Psychol. Rev.*, 1974, *81*, 348–374.

COLEMAN, E. B. Approximations to English: Some comments on the method. *Amer. J. Psychol.*, 1963, *76*, 239–247.

COLEMAN, E. B. On understanding prose: Some determiners of the complexity. Washington, D.C.: National Science Foundation (NSF final report, GB–2604), 1965.

COLLINS, A. M., and QUILLIAN, M. R. Retrieval time from semantic memory. *J. verb. Learn. verb. Behav.*, 1969, *8*, 240–247.

COMPTON, A. J. Generative studies of children's phonological disorders. *J. speech hearing Disorders*, 1970, *35*, 315–339.

CONDON, W. S., and SANDER, L. W. Neonate movement is synchronized with adult speech: interactional participation and language acquisition. *Science*, 1974, *183*, 99–101.

CONRAD, C. Cognitive economy in semantic memory. *J. exp. Psychol.*, 1972, 92, 149–154.

COWAN, G. M. Mazateco whistled speech. In D. Hymes (Ed.) *Language in culture and society: A reader in linguistics and anthropology.* New York: Harper & Row, 1964.

CRAMER, P. *Word association.* New York: Academic, 1968.

CRITCHLEY, M. *Aphasiology and other aspects of language.* London: Edward Arnold, 1970.

CROMER, R. F. "Children are nice to understand": Surface structure clues for the recovery of a deep structure. *Brit. J. Psychol.*, 1970, 61, 397–408.

CUMMINS, J. P., and GULUTSAN, M. Some effects of bilingualism on cognitive functioning. In S. Carey (Ed.) *Bilingualism, biculturalism and education.* Proceedings from the conference at College Universitaire Saint-Jean, The University of Alberta, 1974.

CURRY, F. K. W., and GREGORY, H. H. The performance of stutterers on dichotic listening tasks thought to reflect cerebral dominance. *J. speech hearing Research*, 1969, 12, 73–82.

CZAGAN, F. Die Verwending lautlicher Ausdruckmittel zur Wiedergabe von Körpereigenschaften. *Zschr. f. angew. Psychol.*, 1957 (6).

CZURDA, M. Beziehungen zwischen Lautcharacter und Sinneseindrücken. *Wr. Arch. f. Psychol., Psychiatr., Neurol.*, 1953 (3).

DALE, P. S. *Language development: Structure and function.* Hinsdale, Ill.: Dryden, 1972.

DAVIS, D. M. The relation of repetitions in the speech of young children to certain measures of language maturity and situational factors: Part I. *J. speech Disorders*, 1939, 4, 303–318.

DAVIS, D. M. The relation of repetitions in the speech of young children to certain measures of language mastery and situational factors: Parts II and III. *J. speech Disorders*, 1940, 5, 235–246.

DAVIS, R. The fitness of names to drawings: A cross-cultural study in Tanganyika. *Brit. J. Psychol.*, 1961, 52, 259–268.

DAX, M. Lésions de la moitié gauche de l'encéphale coincident avec l'oubli des signes de la pensée. *Gaz. Hebdom.*, 1865, S2, 11:259–260.

DE CAMP, D. Linguistics and teaching foreign language. In A. A. Hill (Ed.) *Linguistics today.* New York: Basic, 1969.

DEESE, J. On the structure of associative meaning. *Psychol. Rev.*, 1962, 69, 161–175.

DEESE, J. *Principles of psychology.* Rockleigh, N.J.; Allyn & Bacon, 1964.

DEESE, J. *The structure of associations in language and thought.* Baltimore: Johns Hopkins University Press, 1965.

DEJERINE, J. Contribution à l'étude anatomo-pathologique et clinique des différentes varietés de cécité verbale. *Mém. Soc. Biol.*, Fév. 27. Abstract in *Brain*, 1893, 16, 318–320.

DE LAGUNA, G. *Speech: Its function and development.* New Haven: Yale University Press, 1927.

DENES, P. B. On the statistics of spoken English. *J. acoust. Soc. Amer.*, 1963, 35, 892–904.

DENNIS, M., and KOHN, B. Comprehension of syntax in infantile hemiplegics after cerebral hemidecortication: Left hemisphere superiority. *Brain and Language*, in press.

DE REUCK, A. V. S., and O'CONNER, M. (Eds.) *Disorders of language—Ciba Foundation symposium.* London: J. & A. Churchill, Ltd., 1964.

DERWING, B. L. *Transformational grammar as a theory of language acquisition.* London: Cambridge University Press, 1973.

DE SAUSSURE, R. *Cours de linguistique générale.* Paris: Payot, 1916.

DE VILLIERS, J. Quantitative aspects of agrammatism in aphasia. *Cortex*, 1974, *10*, 36–54.

DE VILLIERS, J. G., and DE VILLIERS, P. A. Development of the use of word order in comprehension. *J. psycholing. Res.*, 1973, *2*, 331–341.

DE VILLIERS, P. A., and DE VILLIERS, J. G. Early judgments of semantic and syntactic acceptability by children. *J. psycholing. Res.*, 1972, *1*, 299–310.

DEWEY, G. *Relative frequency of English speech sounds.* Cambridge, Mass.: Harvard University Press, 1923.

DILLARD, J. L. *Black English.* New York: Random House, 1972.

DI VESTA, F. J. A developmental study of the semantic structure of children. *J. verb. Learn. verb. Behav.*, 1966, *5*, 249–259.

DOTY, R. W. Conditioned reflexes formed and evoked by brain stimulation. In D. E. Steer (Ed.) *Electrical stimulation of the brain.* Austin: University of Texas Press, 1961.

EATON, H. S. *An English-French-German-Spanish word frequency dictionary.* New York: Dover, 1961.

EIMAS, P., SIQUELAND, E., JUSCZYK, P., and VIGORITO, J. Speech perception in early infancy. *Science*, 1971, *171*, 303–306.

EISENBERG, R. Auditory behavior in the human neonate: Methodological problems and the logical design of research procedures. *J. auditory Res.*, 1965, *5*, 159–177.

EKMAN, P. Universals and cultural differences in facial expression of emotion. In J. K. Cole (Ed.) *Nebraska symposium on motivation.* Lincoln: University of Nebraska Press, 1971.

ENTWISLE, D. *Word associations of young children.* Baltimore: Johns Hopkins University Press, 1966.

ERDMANN, B. *Umrisse zur Psychologie des Denkens* (ed. 2). 2 Mohr., 1908.

ERDMANN, B., and DODGE, R. *Psychologische Untersuchungen über das Lesen auf experimenteller Grundlage.* Halle (Saale): Voss, 1898.

ERVIN, S. M. Correlates of associative frequency. *J. verb. Learn. verb. Behav.*, 1963, *1*, 422–431.

ERVIN, S. M. Language and TAT content in bilinguals. *J. abnorm. soc. Psychol.*, 1964, *68*, 500–507.

ERVIN-TRIPP, S. M. An analysis of the interaction of language, topic, and listener. In J. A. Fishman (Ed.) *Readings in the sociology of language.* The Hague: Mouton, 1968.

ERVIN-TRIPP, S. M. *Language acquiistion and communicative choice.* Stanford, Calif.: Stanford University Press, 1973.

ERVIN, S. M., and MILLER, W. R. Language development. In *Child Psychol.*, 62nd Yearbook, National Society for the Study of Education, Chicago: University of Chicago Press, 1963, pp. 108–143.

ERVIN, S. M., and OSGOOD, C. E. Second language learning and bilingualism. *J. abnorm. soc. Psychol., suppl.*, 1954, *49*, 139–146.

FARWELL, B. *Burton.* New York: Holt, Rinehart and Winston, 1963.

FELDMAN, C. F., and RODGON, M. The effects of various types of adult responses in the syntactic acquisition of two- to three-year-olds. Unpublished paper, Department of Psychology, University of Chicago, 1970.

FERGUSON, C. A. Diglossia. *Word*, 1959, *15*, 325–340.

FILLMORE, C. J. The case for case. In E. Bach and R. T. Harms (Eds.) *Universals in linguistic theory.* New York: Holt, Rinehart and Winston, 1968, pp. 1–87.

FISHMAN, J. A. *Sociolinguistics.* Rowley, Mass.: Newbury House, 1970.

FLANAGAN, B. Instatement of stuttering in normally fluent individuals through operant procedures. *Science*, 1959, *130*, 979–981.

FLANAGAN, B., GOLDIAMOND, I., and AZRIN, N. Operant stuttering: The control of stuttering behavior through response-contingent consequences. *J. exptl. Analysis Behavior*, 1958, *1*, 173–177.

FLAVELL, J. H. *The developmental psychology of Jean Piaget.* Princeton, N.J.: Van Nostrand, 1963.

FLEISS, I. Experimentelle Untersuchungen über inhärente Laut-Sinn-Beziehungen in der Japanischen Sprache. *Phil.-Diss.*, Wien, 1965.

FLESCH, R. *The art of plain talk.* New York: Harper and Brothers, 1946.

FLESCH, R. *The art of readable writing.* New York: Collier Books, 1962.

FODOR, J. A., and BEVER, T. G. The psychological reality of linguistic segments. *J. verb. Learn. verb. Behav.*, 1965, *4*, 414–420.

FODOR, J. A., and GARRETT, M. Some syntactic determinants of sentential complexity. *Perception and Psychophysics*, 1967, *2*, 289–296.

FOSS, D. J., and SWINNEY, D. A. On the psychological reality of the phoneme: Perception, identification, and consciousness. *J. verb. Learn. verb. Behav.*, 1973, *12*, 246–257.

FRANKS, J. J., and BRANSFORD, J. D. The acquisition of abstract ideas. *J. verb. Learn. verb. Behav.*, 1972, *11*, 311–315.

FRANKS, J. J., and BRANSFORD, J. D. Memory for syntactic form as a function of semantic context. *J. exp. Psychol.*, 1974, *103*, 1037–1039.

FRANSELLA, F. Rhythm as a distractor in the modification of stuttering. *Behav. Res. Ther.*, 1967, *5*, 253–255.

FRANSELLA, F., and BEECH, H. R. An experimental analysis of the effect of rhythm on the speech of stutterers. *Behav. Res. Ther.*, 1965, *3*, 195–201.

FRENCH, D. The relationship of anthropology to studies in perception and cognition. In S. Koch (Ed.) *Psychology. A study of a science.* Vol. VI. New York: McGraw-Hill, 1963, pp. 388–428.

FRENCH, N. R., CARTER, C. W., and KOENIG, W. The words and sounds of telephone conversations. *Bell Syst. Tech. J.*, 1930, *9*, 290–324.

FRICK, F. C., and SUMBY, W. H. Control tower language. *J. acoust. Soc. Amer.*, 1952, *24*, 595–596.

FRIES, C. C. *The structure of English.* New York: Harcourt, Brace & World, 1952.

FROMKIN, V. A. Slips of the tongue. *Scientific American*, 1973, Dec., *229*, 110–116.

FROMKIN, V., KRASHEN, S., CURTISS, S., RIGLER, D., and RIGLER M.

The development of language in Genie: A case of language acquisition beyond the "critical period." *Brain and Language*, 1974, *1*, 81–107.

FROMKIN, V., and RODMAN, R. *An introduction to language.* New York: Holt, Rinehart and Winston, 1974.

FRY, D. B. The development of the phonological system in the normal and the deaf child. In F. Smith and G. A. Miller (Eds.) *The genesis of language: A psycholinguistic approach.* Cambridge, Mass.: MIT Press, 1966.

FURTH, H. G. Visual paired-associates task with deaf and hearing children. *J. speech hearing Research*, 1961, *4*, 172–177.

FURTH, H. G. Conservation of weight in deaf and hearing children. *Child Developm.*, 1964a, *34*, 143–150.

FURTH, H. G. Research with the deaf: Implications for language and cognition. *Psychol. Bull.*, 1964b, *62*, 145–164.

FURTH, H. G. Linguistic deficiency and thinking: research with deaf subjects 1964–1969. *Psychol. Bull.*, 1971, *76*, 58–72.

GALTON, F. Psychometric experiments. *Brain*, 1879–1880, *2*, 149–162.

GAADER, A. B. The first seventy-six bilingual education projects. In J. E. Alatis (Ed.) *21st annual round table: Bilingualism and language contact: Anthropological, linguistic, psychological, and sociological aspects.* Washington: Georgetown University, School of Language and Linguistics, Monograph Series on Language and Linguistics, 1970, No. 23.

GARDNER, B. T., and GARDNER, R. A. Two-way communication with an infant chimpanzee. In A. M. Schrier and F. Stollnitz (Ed.) *Behavior of nonhuman primates.* Vol. 4. New York: Academic, 1971, pp. 117–184.

GARDNER, R. A., and GARDNER, B. T. Teaching sign language to a chimpanzee. *Science*, 1969, *165*, 664–672.

GARNER, W. *Uncertainty and structures as psychological concepts.* New York: Wiley, 1962.

GARRETT, M., BEVER, T. G., and FODOR, J. A. The active use of grammar in speech perception. *Perception and Psychophysics*, 1966, *1*, 30–32.

GAZZANIGA, M. S., and SPERRY, R. W. Language after section of the cerebral commisures. *Brain*, 1967, *90*, 131–148.

GENTILE, A. Characteristics of hearing impaired students under six years of age. *Annual survey of hearing-impaired children and youth.* Series D, No. 7, Gallaudet College, Washington, D.C., 1972.

GESCHWIND, N. Brain mechanisms suggested by studies of hemispheric connections. In C. C. Darley (Ed.) *Brain mechanisms underlying speech and language: Proceedings.* New York: Grune and Stratton, 1967.

GESCHWIND, N. Language and brain. *Scientific American*, 1972, Apr., 76–83.

GESCHWIND, N., and LEVITSKY, W. Left-right asymmetries in temporal speech region. *Science*, 1968, *161*, 186–187.

GESELL, A., and AMES, L. B. Development of handedness. *J. genet. Psychol.*, 1947, *70*, 155–175.

GIBRAN, KAHLIL. *The Prophet.* New York: Knopf, 1960.

GLEASON, J. B. Code switching in children's language. In T. Moore (Ed.) *Cognitive development and the acquisition of language.* New York: Academic, 1973.

GLUCKSBERG, S., and COHEN, J. A. Acquisition of form-class membership by syntactic position. *Psychonomic Science*, 1965, *2*, 313–314.

GLUCKSBERG, S., TRABASSO, T., and WALD, J. Linguistic structures and mental operations. *Cognitive Psychol.*, 1973, *5*, 338–370.

GOLDIAMOND, I. Stuttering and fluency as manipulable operant response classes. In L. Krasner and L. P. Ullman (Eds.) *Research in behavior modification: New developments and their clinical applications.* New York: Holt, Rinehart and Winston, 1965.

GOLDMAN, R. Cultural influences on the sex ratio in the incidence of stuttering. *Amer. Anthropologist*, 1967, *69*, 78–81.

GOLDMAN, R., and SHAMES, G. M. Comparisons of the goals that parents of stutterers and parents of nonstutterers set for their children. *J. speech hearing Disorders*, 1964a, *29*, 381–389.

GOLDMAN, R., and SHAMES, G. H. A study of goal-setting behavior of parents of stutterers and parents of nonstutterers. *J. speech hearing Disorders*, 1964b, *29*, 192–194.

GOLDMAN-EISLER, F. *Psycholinguistics: Experiments in spontaneous speech.* New York: Academic, 1968.

GOLDMAN-EISLER, F., and COHEN, M. Is N, P, and NP difficulty a valid criterion of transformational operations? *J. verb. Learn. verb. Behav.*, 1970, *9*, 161–166.

GOODGLASS, H. Redefining the concept of agrammatism in aphasia. Proceedings of XII International Speech and Voice Therapy Conference, Padua, 1962, pp. 108–116.

GOODGLASS, H., and BERKO, J. Agrammatism and English inflection. *J. speech hearing Research*, 1960, *3*, 257–267.

GOODGLASS, H., GLEASON, J. B., BERNHOLZ, N. A., and HYDE, M. R. Some linguistic structures in the speech of a Broca's aphasic. *Cortex*, 1972, *8*, 191–212.

GOODGLASS, H., GLEASON, J. B., and HYDE, M. R. Some dimensions of auditory language comprehension in aphasia. *J. speech hearing Research*, 1970, *13*, 595–606.

GORMAN, A. M. Recognition memory for nouns as a function of abstractness and frequency. *J. exp. Psychol.*, 1961, *61*, 23–29.

GOULD, L. N. Auditory hallucinations and sub-vocal speech: Objective study in a case of schizophrenia. *J. nerv. ment. Dis.*, 1949, *109*, 418–427.

GOWERS, W. R. *Lectures on the diagnosis of diseases of brain.* Philadelphia: P. Blakiston, 1887.

GRAHAM, V. T. The intelligence of Italian and Jewish children in the Habit Clinic of the Massachusetts Division of Mental Hygiene. *J. abnorm. soc. Psychol.*, 1925, *20*, 371–376.

GRAY, M. The X family: A clinical and laboratory study of a "stuttering" family. *J. speech Disorders*, 1940, *5*, 343–348.

GREEN, J. An experiment in English. *Harper's Mag.*, 1941, *183*, 397–405.

GREENBERG, J. H. Some universals of grammar with particular reference to the order of meaningful elements. In J. H. Greenberg (Ed.) *Universals of language.* Cambridge, Mass.: MIT Press, 1963.

GREENBERG, J. H., and JENKINS, J. J. Studies in the psychological correlates to the sound system of American English. *Word*, 1964 *20*, 157–177.

GREENE, J. Phonetic symbolism: A doubtful phenomenon. Paper read at Midwestern Psychol. Assn. convention, Chicago, May, 1965.

GREENE, J. *Psycholinguistics*. Baltimore: Penguin, 1972.

GREENFIELD, P. M. Who is "DADA"? Unpublished paper. Syracuse University, 1967 (or see McNeill, D., 1970).

GREENFIELD, P. M., REICH, L. C., and OLVER, R. On culture and equivalent valence: II. In J. S. Bruner et al. (eds.) *Studies in cognitive growth*. New York: Wiley, 1966.

GRIGGS, R. A. The recall of linguistic ideas. *J. exp. Psychol.*, 1974, *103*, 807–809.

GUILLAUME, P. Les debuts de la phrase dans le langage de l'enfant. *Journal de Psychologie*, 1927, *24*, 1–25.

GUIORA, A. Z. *The role of personality variables in second language behavior*. Washington, D.C.: Army Defense Language Institute, 1971.

HAHN, E. F. A study of the relationships between stuttering occurrence and grammatical factors in oral reading. *J. speech Disorders*, 1942, 7, 329–335.

HALL, R. A. JR. *Pidgin and Creole languages*. Ithaca, N.Y.: Cornell University Press, 1966.

HALLE, M. On the bases of phonology. In J. A. Fodor and J. J. Katz (Eds.) *The structure of language*. Englewood Cliffs, N.J.: Prentice-Hall, 1964.

HALLE, M., and STEVENS, K. N. Analysis by synthesis. In W. Wathen-Dunn (Ed.) *Proceedings of the seminar on speech compression and processing*. Vol. 2, paper D-7, technical report 59-198. Cambridge, Mass.: Air Force Cambridge Research Center, 1959.

HALLIDAY, M. A. K. Notes on transitive and theme in English: Part 2. *J. Linguistics*, 1967, *3*, 177–244.

HALWES, T. Effects of dichotic fusion on the perception of speech. Unpublished doctoral dissertation, University of Minnesota. Reproduced as supplement to Haskins Laboratory Status Report on Speech Research, 1969.

HARRIOT, P. The comprehension of active and passive sentences as a function of pragmatic expectations. *J. verb. Learn. verb. Behav.*, 1969, 8, 116–169.

HARTLEY, R. V. L. Transmission of information. *Bell System Tech. J.*, 1928, 7, 535.

HATTORI, S. The sound and meaning of language. *Found. Lang.*, 1965, *1*, 95–111.

HAYES, C. *The ape in our house*. New York: Harper, 1951.

HAYHURST, H. Some errors of young children in producing passive sentences. *J. verb. Learn. verb. Behav.*, 1967, 6, 634–639.

HEAD, H. *Aphasia and kindred disorders of speech*. London: Cambridge University Press, 1926 (2 volumes).

HEBB, D. O., LAMBERT, W. E., and TUCKER, G. R. Language, thought and experience. *Modern Language J.*, 1971, 55, 212–222.

HÉCAEN, H., and ANGELERGUES, R. *Pathologie du langage l'aphasie*. Paris: Larousse, 1965.

HEIDER, E. R. "Focal" color areas and the development of color names. *Developmental Psychol.*, 1971, 4, 447–455.

HEIDER, E. R. Universals in color naming and memory. *J. exp. Psychol.*, 1972, 93, 10–21.

HEIDER, K. G. *The Dugum Dani: A Papuan culture in the highlands of West New Guinea.* Chicago: Aldine, 1970.

HERBERT, M. Personal communication to Beech, H. R., and Fransella, F. *Research and experiment in stuttering.* London: Pergamon Press, 1968.

HERMAN, D. T., LAWLERS, R. H., and MARSHALL, R. W. Variables in the effect of language on the reproduction of visually perceived forms. *Percep. mot. Skills Monogr.* Suppl., 1957, 2, 171–186.

HERMAN, S. Exploration in the social psychology of language choice. *Human Relations*, 1961, 14, 149–164.

HIRSCH, I. J. General discussion. In F. Smith and G. A. Miller (Eds.) *The genesis of language: A psycholinguistic approach.* Cambridge, Mass.: MIT Press, 1966.

HOCKETT, C. F. *A course in modern linguistics.* New York: Macmillan, 1958.

HOFSTÄTTER, P. R. Farbsymbolik und Ambivalenz. *Psychol. Beitr.*, 1955, 2, 526–540.

HOFSTÄTTER, P. R. Uber sprachliche Bestimmungleistungen: Das Problem des grammatischen Geschlechts von Sonne und Mond. *Z. exper. angew. Psychol.*, 1963, 10, 91–108.

HOGBEN, L. *The mother tongue.* London: Secker and Warburg, 1964.

HOLLIEN, H. Peculiar case of "voiceprints." *J. acoust. Soc. Amer.*, 1974, 56, 210–213.

HÖRMANN, H. *Psycholinguistics: An introduction to research and theory.* New York: Springer-Verlag, 1971.

HORNBY, P. A. Surface structure and presupposition. *J. verb. Learn. verb. Behav.*, 1974, 13, 530–538.

HOWES, D. An approach to the quantitative analysis of word blindness. In J. Money (Ed.) *Reading disability.* Baltimore: Johns Hopkins University Press, 1961.

HOWES, D. A word count of spoken English. *J. verb. Learn. verb. Behav.*, 1966, 5, 572–606.

HOWES, D., and SOLOMON, R. L. Visual duration threshold as a function of word-probability. *J. exp. Psychol.*, 1951, 41, 401–410.

HUDGINS, C. V., and NUMBERS, F. C. An investigation of the intelligibility of the speech of the deaf. *Genetic Psychology Monogr.*, 1942, 25, 280–392.

HUMBOLDT, W. v. *Über das vergleichende Sprachstudium in Beziehung auf die verschiedenen Epochen der Sprachentwicklung: Gesammelte Schriften.* Vol. 4. Berlin: Königlich-Preussische Akademie der Wissenschaften, 1905.

HUNTER, W. S. The delayed reaction in animals and children. *Animal Behavior Monogr.*, 1912, 2, (1), 274–295.

HUNTER, W. S., and BARTLETT, S. C. Double alternation behavior in young children. *J. exp. Psychol.*, 1948, 38, 558–567.

IANCO-WORRALL, A. Bilingualism and cognitive development. *Child Developm.*, 1972, 43, 1390–1400.

INGERBREGSTEN, E. Some experimental contributions to the psychology and psychopathology of stuttering. *Amer. J. Orthopsychiat.*, 1936, 6, 630–651.

INGRAM, D. Cerebral speech lateralization in young children. *Neuropsychologia,* 1975, *13,* 103–105.

INHELDER, B., BOVET, M., SINCLAIR, H., and SMOCK, C. D. On cognitive development. *Amer. Psychologist,* 1966, *21,* 160–164.

JAKOBSON, R. *Kindersprache, Aphasie, und allgemeine Lautgesetz.* Uppsala: Almqvist and Wiksell, 1941. English translation by A. Keiler, *Child language, aphasia, and general sound laws.* The Hague: Mouton, 1968.

JAKOBSON, R. Two aspects of language and two types of aphasic disturbances. In R. Jakobson and M. Halle (Eds.) *Fundamentals of language.* The Hague: Mouton, 1956, pp. 55–71.

JAKOBSON, R. Why "mama" and "papa"? In *Roman Jakobson: Selected writings.* Vol. I. The Hague: Mouton, 1971.

JAKOBSON, R. Towards a linguistic typology of aphasic impairments. In A. V. S. de Reuck and M. O'Conner (Eds.) *Disorders of language—Ciba Foundation Symposium.* Boston: Little, Brown & Co., 1964, pp. 21–46.

JAKOBSON, R., FANT, C. C. M., and HALLE, M. *Preliminaries to speech analysis: The distinctive features and their correlates.* Cambridge, Mass.: MIT Press, 1963.

JAKOBSON, R., and HALLE, M. Phonology and phonetics. In *Roman Jakobson: Selected writings.* Vol. I. The Hague: Mouton, 1971, pp. 464–504.

JAMES, C. T., THOMPSON, J. G., and BALDWIN, M. J. The reconstructive process in sentence memory. *J. verb. Learn. verb. Behav.,* 1973, *12,* 51–63.

JAMES, W. *Principles of psychology.* New York: Holt, 1890.

JENKINS, J. J. Degree of polarization and scores on the principal factors for concepts in the semantic atlas. *Amer. J. Psychol.,* 1960, *73,* 274–279.

JENKINS, J. J., and PALERMO, D. S. Mediation processes and the acquisition of linguistic structure. In U. Bellugi and R. Brown (Eds.) *The acquisition of language.* Monographs of the Society for Research in Child Development, 1964, *29,* No. 1, 141–169.

JENKINS, J. J., and RUSSELL, W. A. Associative clustering during recall. *J. abnorm. soc. Psychol.,* 1952, *47,* 818–821.

JENKINS, J. J., RUSSELL, W. A., and SUCI, G. J. An atlas of semantic profiles for 360 words. *Amer. J. Psychol.,* 1958, *71,* 688–699.

JESPERSEN, O. *Language, its nature, development, and origin.* London: Allen and Unwin, 1922.

JESPERSEN, O. *The philosophy of grammar.* London: Allen and Unwin, 1924.

JOHNSON, M. K., BRANSFORD, J. D., and SOLOMON, S. K. Memory for tacit implications of sentences. *J. exp. Psychol.,* 1973, *98,* 203–205.

JOHNSON, R. L., MILLER, M. D., and WALL, D. D. Content analysis and semantic classification. Mimeo (1965), contract No. DA 49–193–MD 2490.

JOHNSON, W. (Ed.) *Stuttering in children and adults.* Minneapolis: University of Minnesota Press, 1955.

JOHNSON, W. *Stuttering and what you can do about it.* Minneapolis: University of Minnesota Press, 1961.

JOHNSON, W. et al. *The onset of stuttering: Research findings and implications.* Minneapolis: University of Minnesota Press, 1959.

JOHNSON, W., and KNOTT, J. R. Studies in the psychology of stuttering: The distribution of moments of stuttering in successive readings of the same material. *J. speech Disorders*, 1937, *2*, 17–19.

JOHNSON, W., and MILLSAPPS, L. S. Studies in the psychology of stuttering: VI. The role of cues representative of stuttering moments during oral reading. *J. speech Disorders*, 1937, *2*, 101–104.

JOHNSON-LAIRD, P. N., and STEVENSON, R. V. Memory for syntax. *Nature*, 1970, *227*, 412.

JONES, L. V., and WEPMAN, J. M. Dimensions of language performance in aphasia. *J. speech hearing Research*, 1961, *26*, 220–232.

JUNG, C. G. *Studies in word-association*. London: W. Heinemann, 1918.

KAEDING, F. W. *Häufigkeitswörterbuch der deutschen Sprache*. Berlin: Selbstverlag des Herausgebers Mittler Sohn, 1897.

KAHANE, H., KAHANE, R., and SAPORTA, S. Development of verbal categories in child language. *International J. Amer. Linguistics*, 1958, *24*, 34–37.

KATZ, J. J., and FODOR, J. A. The structure of a semantic theory. *Language*, 1963, *39*, 170–210.

KENT, H. G., and ROSANOFF, A. J. A study of association in insanity. *Amer. J. Insanity*, 1910, *67*, 37–96 and 317–390.

KENT, I. R. The use of tranquilizers in the treatment of stuttering: Reserpine, chlopromazine, meprobamate, Atarax. *J. speech hearing Disorders*, 1963, *28*, 288–294.

KIECKERS, E. *Die Sprachstämme der Erde*. Heidelberg: Carl Winters Universitätsbuch-handlung, 1931.

KIMBLE, G. A., and GARMEZY, N. *Principles of general psychology*. New York: Ronald, 1968.

KIMURA, D. Cerebral dominance and the perception of verbal stimuli. *Canad. J. Psychol.*, 1961, *15*, 166–171.

KIMURA, D. Left-right differences in the perception of melodies. *Quart. J. exp. Psychol.*, 1964, *14*, 355–358.

KINCAID, J. P., and DELIONBACH, L. J. Validation of the automated readability index: A follow-up. *Human Factors*, 1973, *15*, 17–20.

KINTSCH, W. Recognition memory in bilingual Ss. *J. verb. Learn. verb. Behav.*, 1970, *9*, 405–409.

KINTSCH, W., and KEENAN, J. Reading rate and retention as a function of the number of propositions in base structure of sentences. *Cog. Psychol.*, 1973, *5*, 257–274.

KINTSCH, W., and KINTSCH, E. Interlingual interference and memory processes. *J. verb. Learn. verb. Behav.*, 1969, *8*, 16–19.

KLANK, L. J., HUANG, Y.-H., and JOHNSON, R. C. Determinants of success in matching word pairs in tests of phonetic symbolism. *J. verb. Learn. verb. Behav.*, 1971, *10*, 140–148.

KLEE, H., and EYSENCK, M. W. Comprehension of abstract and concrete sentences. *J. verb. Learn. verb. Behav.*, 1973, *12*, 522–529.

KLIMA, E. S., and BELLUGI, U. Syntactic regularities in the speech of children. In J. Lyons and R. J. Wales (Eds.) *Psycholinguistic papers*. Edinburgh University Press, 1966, pp. 183–208.

KNOTT, J. R., JOHNSON, W., and WEBSTER, M. J. Studies in the psychology of stuttering: II. A quantitative evaluation of expectation of stuttering in relation to the occurrence of stuttering. *J. speech Disorders*, 1937, *2*, 20–22.

KOLERS, P. A. Interlingual word associations. *J. verb. Learn. verb. Behav.*, 1963, *2*, 291–300.

KOLERS, P. A. Reading and talking bilingually. *Amer. J. Psychol.*, 1966a, *79*, 357–376.

KOLERS, P. A. Interlingual facilitation of short-term memory. *Amer. J. Psychol.*, 1966b, *79*, 314–319.

KOPP, J., and LANE, H. L. Hue discrimination related to linguistic habits. *Psychonomic Science*, 1968, *11*, 61–62.

KORZYBSKI, A. *Science and sanity*. Lancaster, Pa.: Science Press, 1933.

KUHL, P. K., and MILLER, J. D. Speech perception by the chinchilla: The voiced-voiceless distinction in alveolar plosive consonants. *Science* (in press).

KUHL, P. K., and MILLER, J. D. Speech perception by the chinchilla: phonetic boundaries for synthetic VOT stimuli. Program of the 89th Meeting, J. acoust. Soc. Amer., Austin, Texas, 1975.

KUNIHIRA, S. Effects of the expressive voice on phonetic symbolism. *J. verb. Learn. verb. Behav.*, 1971, *10*, 427–429.

KUNIHIRA, S. Effects of phonetic symbolism on verbal learning. Abstract guide of XXth International Congress of Psychology, Tokyo, 1972, p. 387. (In English)

LAMBERT, W. E., HAVELKA, J., and CROSBY, C. The influence of language acquisition contexts on bilingualism. *J. abnorm. soc. Psychol.*, 1958, *56*, 239–244.

LAMBERT, W. E., HODGSON, R. C., GARDNER, R. C., and FILLENBAUM, S. Evaluational reactions to spoken languages. *J. abnorm. soc. Psychol.*, 1960, *60*, 44–51.

LAMBERT, W. E., and RAWLINGS, C. Bilingual processing of mixed-language associative networks. *J. verb. Learn. verb. Behav.*, 1969, *8*, 604–609.

LANCE, D. *A brief study of Spanish-English bilingualism*. Final report. Research project Orr–Liberal Arts–15504. College Station, Texas: Texas A and M, 1969.

LANDSDELL, H. Verbal and nonverbal factors in right-hemisphere speech: Relation to early neurological history. *J. comp. physiol. Psychol.*, 1969, *69*, 734–738.

LANE, H. The motor theory of speech perception: A critical review. *Psychol. Rev.*, 1965, *72*, 275–309.

LANTZ, D. L. Color naming and color recognition: Study in the psychology of language. Unpublished doctoral dissertation, Harvard University, 1963.

LANTZ, D. L., and STEFFLRE, V. Language and cognition revisited. *J. abnorm. soc. Psychol.*, 1964, *69*, 472–481.

LEEPER, R. N. A study of a neglected portion of the field of learning: The development of sensory organization. *J. genet. Psychol.*, 1935, *46*, 41–75.

LENNEBERG, E. H. Understanding language without ability to speak: A case report. *J. abnorm. soc. Psychol.*, 1962, *65*, 419–425.

LENNEBERG, E. H. The natural history of language. In F. Smith and G. A. Miller

(Eds.) *The genesis of language: A psycholinguistic approach.* Cambridge, Mass.: MIT Press, 1966.

LENNEBERG, E. H. *Biological foundations of language.* New York: Wiley, 1967.

LENNEBERG, E. H. The neurology of language. *Daedalus,* 1973, summer, pp. 115–133.

LENNEBERG, E. H., and ROBERTS, J. M. The denotata of color terms. Paper read to Linguistic Society of America, Bloomington, Indiana, 1953.

LEOPOLD, W. F. *Speech development of a bilingual child: A linguistic record.* Evanston, Ill.: Northwestern University Press, 1939–1949 (4 volumes).

LEOPOLD, W. F. Patterning in children's language learning. In A. Bar-Adon and W. F. Leopold (Eds.) *Child language: A book of readings.* Englewood Cliffs, N.J.: Prentice-Hall, 1971.

LEVELT, W. J. M. A scaling approach to the study of syntactic relations. In G. B. Flores d'Arcais and W. J. M. Levelt (Eds.) *Advances in psycholinguistics.* Amsterdam: North-Holland Publishing Co., 1970, pp. 109–121.

LEVIN, H., and KAPLAN, E. Eye-voice span (EVS) within active and passive sentences. *Language and Speech,* 1968, 2, 251–258.

LEWIS, D. G. Bilingualism and non-verbal intelligence: A further study of test results. *Brit. J. educ. Psychol.,* 1959, 29, 17–22.

LEWIS, M. M. *How children learn to talk.* New York: Basic, 1959.

LEWIS, M. M. *Language, thought and personality.* New York: Basic, 1963.

LIBERMAN, A. M. Some results of research on speech perception. *J. acoust. Soc. Amer.,* 1957, 29, 117–123.

LIBERMAN, A. M., COOPER, F. S., SHANKWEILER, D. P., and STUDDERT-KENNEDY, M. Perception of the speech code. In E. E. David Jr. and P. B. Denes (Eds.) *Human communication: A unified view.* New York: McGraw-Hill, 1972.

LIBERMAN, A. M., DELATTRE, P., and COOPER, F. S. The role of selected stimulus variables in the perception of the unvoiced stop consonants. *Amer. J. Psychol.,* 1952, 65, 497–516.

LIBERMAN, A. M., HARRIS, K. S., HOFFMAN, H. S., and GRIFFITH, B. C. The discrimination of speech sounds within and across phoneme boundaries. *J. exp. Psychol.,* 1957, 54, 358–368.

LIBERMAN, A. M., MATTINGLY, I. G., and TURVEY, M. Language code and memory codes. In A. W. Melton and E. Martin (Eds.) *Coding processes in human memory.* Washington, D.C.: Winston and Sons, 1972.

LIEBERMAN, P. Some effects of semantic and grammatical context on the production and perception of speech. *Language and Speech,* 1963, 6, 172–187.

LIEBERMAN, P. On the acoustic basis of the perception of intonation by linguists. *Word,* 1965, 21, 40–54.

LIEBERMAN, P. Primate vocalizations and human linguistic ability. Unpublished paper, Linguistic Department, University of Connecticut, Storrs, Conn., 1968.

LINDSAY, P., and NORMAN, D. A. *Human information processing: An introduction to psychology.* New York: Academic, 1972.

LINDSLEY, J. R. Producing simple utterances: How far ahead do we plan? *Cognitive Psychol.,* 1975, 7, 1–19.

LIN YUTANG. *The wisdom of Confucius.* New York: Random House, 1938.

LOBAN, W. D. *Problems in oral English.* Research report No. 5. Champaign, Ill.: National Council of Teachers of English, 1966.

LOUTTIT, C. M., and HALLS, E. C. Survey of speech defects among public school children of Indiana. *J. speech Disorders,* 1936, *1,* 73–80.

LURIA, A. R. *The role of speech in the regulation of normal and abnormal behavior.* New York: Liveright, 1961.

LURIA, A. R. *Traumatic aphasia: Its syndromes, psychology and treatment.* The Hague: Mouton, 1970.

LURIA, A. R. Language and brain. *Brain and Language,* 1974, *1,* 1–13.

LYONS, J. *Introduction to theoretical linguistics.* London: Cambridge University Press, 1968.

MacDONALD, J. D., and MARTIN, R. Stuttering and disfluency as two reliable and unambiguous response classes. *J. speech hearing Research,* 1973, *16,* 691–699.

MACLAY, H., and OSGOOD, C. E. Hesitation phenomena in spontaneous English speech. *Word,* 1959, *15,* 19–44.

MACLAY, H., and WARE, E. E. Cross-cultural use of the semantic differential. *Behav. Sci.,* 1961, *6,* 185–190.

MACNAMARA, J. The effect of anticipation on the language switching speeds of bilinguals. St. Patrick's College, Dublin, 1966 (mimeo).

MACNAMARA, J., and KUSHNIR, S. L. Linguistic independence of bilinguals: the input switch. *J. verb. Learn. verb. Behav.,* 1971, *10,* 480–487.

MALHERBE, E. G. Comments on Dr. R. M. Jones's paper, "How and when do persons become bilingual." In Kelly, L. G. (Ed.) *Description and measurement of bilingualism.* Toronto: University of Toronto Press, 1969.

MANDELBROT, B. An informational theory of the structure of language based upon the theory of the statistical matching of messages and coding. *Proceedings of a symposium on applications of communication theory,* London, 1952. Published by Butterworth Scientific Publications, London, 1953.

MARAIST, J. A., and HUTTON, C. Effects of auditory masking upon the speech of stutterers. *J. speech hearing Disorders,* 1957, *22,* 385–389.

MARIE, P. *Travaux et mémoires.* Paris: Masson et Cie., 1926.

MARLER, P. Birdsong and speech development: Could there be parallels? *Amer. Scientist,* 1970, *58,* 673.

MARTIN, E. Toward an analysis of subjective phrase structure. *Psychol. Bull.,* 1970, *74,* 153–166.

MARTIN, J. Hesitations in the speaker's production and listener's reproduction of utterances. *J. verb. Learn. verb. Behav.,* 1967, *6,* 903–909.

MARTIN, R. The experimental manipulation of stuttering behaviors. In H. N. Sloane and B. D. MacAulay (Eds.) *Operant procedures in remedial speech and language training.* Boston: Houghton Mifflin, 1968.

MAYZNER, M. S., and TRESSELT, M. E. Anagram solution times: A function of letter order and word frequency. *J. exp. Psychol.,* 1958, *56,* 376–379.

McCAWLEY, J. D. The role of semantics in a grammar. In E. Bach and R. T. Harms (Eds.) *Universal in linguistic theory.* New York: Holt, Rinehart and Winston, 1968.

McGUIGAN, F. J. Covert oral behavior and auditory hallucinations. *Psychophysiology*, 1966, *3*, 73–80.

McNEILL, D. A study of association. *J. verb. Learn. verb. Behav.*, 1966a, *5*, 548–557.

McNEILL, D. Developmental psycholinguistics. In F. Smith and G. A. Miller (Eds.) *The genesis of language: A psycholinguistic approach.* Cambridge, Mass.: MIT Press, 1966b.

McNEILL, D. *The acquisition of language.* New York: Harper and Row, 1970.

McNEILL, D., and LINDIG, K. The perceptual reality of phonemes, syllables, words and sentences. *J. verb. Learn. verb. Behav.*, 1973, *12*, 419–430.

McREYNOLDS, L. V., and BENNETT, S. Distinctive feature generalization in articulation training. *J. speech hearing Disorders*, 1972, *37*, 463–470.

MEAD, M. Group intelligence and linguistic disability among Italian children. *School and Society*, 1927, *25*, 465–468.

MEHLER, J. Some effects of grammatical transformations on the recall of English sentences. *J. verb. Learn. verb. Behav.*, 1963, *2*, 346–351.

MENYUK, P. Syntactic rules used by children from preschool through first grade. *Child Developm.*, 1964, *35*, 533–546.

MENYUK, P. The role of distinctive features in children's acquisition of phonology. *J. speech hearing Research*, 1968, *11*, 138–146.

MENYUK, P. *The acquisition and development of language.* Englewood Cliffs, N.J.: Prentice-Hall, 1971.

MENYUK, P., and BERNHOLTZ, N. Prosodic features and children's language production. *Research Laboratory of Electronics Quarterly Progress Report* No. 93, 1969. (Or see Menyuk, 1971.)

MESSER, S. Implicit phonology in children. *J. verb. Learn. verb. Behav.*, 1967, *6*, 609–613.

MILLER, E. E. Context in the perception of sentences. *Amer. J. Psychol.*, 1956, *69*, 653–654.

MILLER, G. A. *Language and communication.* New York: McGraw-Hill, 1951.

MILER, G. A. Decision units in the perception of speech. *I.R.E. Transactions on Information Theory*, 1962a, 81–83.

MILLER, G. A. Some psychological studies of grammar. *Amer. Psychologist*, 1962b, *17*, 748–762.

MILLER, G. A., BRUNNER, J. S., and POSTMAN, L. Familiarity of letter sequences and tachistoscopic identification. *J. gen. Psychol.*, 1954, *50*, 129–139.

MILLER, G. A., HEISE, G. A., and LICHTEN, W. The intelligibility of speech as a function of the context of the test materials. *J. exp. Psychol.*, 1951, *41*, 329–335.

MILLER, G. A., NEWMAN, E. B., and FRIEDMAN, E. A. Length-frequency statistics for written English. *Inform. Control*, 1958, *1*, 370–389.

MILLER, G. A., and NICELY, P. E. An analysis of perceptual confusion among some English consonants. *J. acoust. Soc. Amer.*, 1955, *27*, 338–352.

MILLER, G. A., and SELFRIDGE, J. A. Verbal context and the recall of meaningful material. *Amer. J. Psychol.*, 1950, *63*, 176–185.

MILLER, W. R., and ERVIN, S. M. The development of grammar in child language. In U. Bellugi and R. Brown (Eds.) *The acquisition of language.* Monographs of the Society for Research in Child Development, 1964, *29,* 9–33.

MINKOWSKI, M. Sur un cas d'aphasie chez un polyglotte. *Rev. Neurol.,* 1928, *1,* 362–366.

MOHR, J. P. Rapid amelioration of motor aphasia. *Arch. Neurol.,* 1973, *28,* 77–82.

MOLFESE, D. L. Cerebral asymmetry in infants, children, and adults: Auditory evoked responses to speech and music stimuli. Abstract, 84th meeting of the Acoustical Society of America, 1972.

MOLFESE, D. L. Cerebral asymmetry: The development of speech perception in the human brain. Paper presented at Midwestern Psychol. Assn., Chicago, Ill., 1973.

MORGENSTERN, J. J. Psychological and social factors in children's stammering. Ph.D. dissertation, University of Edinburgh, 1953.

MORRISON, J. R. Bilingualism: Some psychological aspects. *Advanc. Sci.,* 1958, *56,* 287–290.

MURDOCK, G. P. World ethnographic sample. *Amer. Anthropologist,* 1957, *59,* 664–687.

NAKAZIMA, S. A comparative study of the speech developments of Japanese and American English in childhood. *Studia Phonologica,* 1962, *2,* 27–39.

NEELLEY, J. N. A study of the speech behavior of stutterers and non-stutterers under normal and delayed auditory feedback. *J. speech hearing Disorders,* 1961, *7,* 63–82.

NEISSER, U. *Cognitive psychology.* New York: Appleton-Century-Crofts, 1967.

NELSON, S. E., HUNTER, N., and WALTER, M. Stuttering in twin types. *J. speech Disorders,* 1945, *10,* 335–343.

NEWCOMB, F. B., OLDFIELD, R. C., and WINGFIELD, A. Object-naming by dysphasic patients. *Nature,* 1965, *207,* 1217–1218.

NEWMAN, S. S. Further experiments in phonetic symbolism. *Amer. J. Psychol.,* 1933, *45,* 53–75.

NICKERSON, R. S., and STEVENS, K. N. Teaching speech to the deaf: Can a computer help? *IEEE Transactions on Audio and Electroacoustics,* 1973, *21,* No. 5.

NOBLE, C. E. An analysis of meaning. *Psychol. Rev.,* 1952, *59,* 421–430.

NOBLE, C. E. The meaning-familiarity relationship. *Psychol. Rev.,* 1953, *60,* 89–98.

NOBLE, C. E. Measurements of association value (a), rated associations (a'), and scaled meaningfulness (m') for the 2100 CVC combinations of the English alphabet. *Psychol. Rep.,* 1961, *8,* 487–521.

NOBLE, C. E., and PARKER, G. V. C. The Montana Scale of meaningfulness (m). *Phychol. Rep.,* 1960, *7,* 325–331.

OBLER, L. K., ALBERT, M. L., and GORDON, H. W. Asymmetrical cerebral dominance for language in fluent bilinguals. Paper read at Academy of Aphasia, Victoria, September, 1975.

O'CONNER, J. *Born that way.* Baltimore: Williams-Wilkins Co., 1928.

OETTINGER, A. G. The distribution of word length in technical Russian. *Mechanical Translation,* 1954, *1,* 38–40.

OGDEN, C. K. *The system of basic English.* New York: Harcourt Brace, 1934.

OGDEN, C. K., and RICHARDS, I. A. *The meaning of meaning.* New York: Harcourt, Brace and World, 1923.

ÖHMAN, S. E. G. Coarticulation in VCV utterances: Spectrographic measurements. *J. acoust. Soc. Amer.*, 1966, *39*, 151–168.

OKADA, A. *Psychology of language education.* Tokyo: Sinkokaku shoten, 1969 (in Japanese).

OLÉRON, P., and HERREN, H. L'acquisition des conservations et le langue: Etude comparative sur des enfants sourds et entendants. *Enfance*, 1961, *14*, 203–219.

OLSON, D. R. Language and thought: Aspects of cognitive theory of semantics. *Psychol. Rev.*, 1970, 77, 257–273.

OLSON, D. R., and FILBY, N. On the comprehension of active and passive sentences. *Cognitive Psychol.*, 1972, *3*, 361–381.

OMAR, M. K. The acquisition of Egyptian Arabic as a native language. Unpublished doctoral dissertation, Georgetown University, 1970 (or see Slobin, D. I., 1973).

O'NEILL, B. Defineability as an index of word meaning. *J. Psycholing. Research,* 1972, *1*, 287–298.

ONO, S. et al. *Thoughts on the Japanese language.* Tokyo: Yomiuri Shinbunsha, 1967 (in Japanese).

ORR, J. On some sound values in English. *Brit. J. Psychol.*, 1944, *35*, 1–8.

OSGOOD, C. E. Semantic differential technique in the comparative study of cultures. *Amer. Anthropologist,* 1964, *56*, 171–200.

OSGOOD, C. E. Toward a wedding of insufficiencies. In T. R. Dixon and D. L. Horton (Eds.) *Verbal behavior and general behavior theory.* Englewood Cliffs, N.J.: Prentice-Hall, 1968.

OSGOOD, C. E. Where do sentences come from? In D. D. Steinberg and L. A. Jakobovits (Eds.) *Semantics.* London: Cambridge University Press, 1971.

OSGOOD, C. E., and MIRON, M. S. *Approaches to the study of aphasia: A report of an interdisciplinary conference on aphasia.* Urbana: University of Illinois Press, 1963.

OSGOOD, C. E., SUCI, G. J., and TANNENBAUM, P. H. *The measurement of meaning.* Urbana: University of Illinois Press, 1957.

OSSER, H., and PENG, F. A cross cultural study of speech rate. *Language and Speech,* 1964, 7, 120–125.

PAIVIO, A. On the functional significance of imagery. *Psychol. Bull.*, 1970, 73, 385–392.

PAIVIO, A., YUILLE, J. C., and MADIGAN, S. Concreteness, imagery, and meaningfulness values for 925 nouns. *J. exp. Psychol.*, 1968, *76*, Monograph suppl. (1, Pt. 2).

PALERMO, D. S., and JENKINS, J. J. Sex differences in word associations. *J. gen. Psychol.*, 1965, *72*, 77–84.

PALERMO, D. S., and MOLFESE, D. L. Language acquisition from age five onward. *Psychol. Bull.*, 1972, 78, 409–428.

PANCE, F., and SHIMOYAMA, T. On the effects of aphasic disturbance in Japanese: Agrammatism paragrammatism. In H. Goodglass and S. Blumstein

(Eds.) *Psycholinguistics and aphasia.* Baltimore: Johns Hopkins University Press, 1973.

PARISI, D., and PIZZAMIGLIO, L. Syntactic comprehension in aphasia. *Cortex,* 1970, *6,* 204–215.

PARK, T.-Z. Language acquisition in a Korean child. Unpublished paper. University of Bern, Switzerland, 1970a.

PARK, T.-Z. The acquisition of German syntax. Unpublished paper. University of Bern, Switzerland, 1970b.

PEAL, E., and LAMBERT, W. E. The relation of bilingualism to intelligence. *Psychological Monographs: General and Applied,* 1962, *76,* No. 546.

PENFIELD, W., and ROBERTS, L. *Speech and brain mechanisms.* Princeton, N.J.: Princeton University Press, 1959.

PETERS, R. W., and SIMONSON, W. E. Generalization of stuttering behavior through associative learning. *J. speech hearing Research,* 1960, *3,* 9–14.

PIAGET, J. *The origin of intelligence.* New York: International Universities, 1952.

PIAGET, J. Language and thought from the genetic point of view. In D. Elkind (Ed.) *Psychological studies.* New York: Random House, 1967.

PICK, A. *Die agrammatischen Sprachstörungen: Studien zur psychologischen Grundlegung der Aphasielehre.* Berlin: Julius Springer, 1913.

PIMSLEUR, P. Language aptitude testing. In A. Davies (Ed.) *Language testing symposium: A psycholinguistic approach.* Oxford University Press, 1968.

PITRES, A. Etude sur l'aphasie chez polyglottes. *Rev. Medic.,* 1895, *15,* 873–899.

POOLE, I. Genetic development of articulation of consonant sounds in speech. *Elementary English Review,* 1934, *2,* 159–161.

POSTAL, P. M. *Aspects of phonological theory.* New York: Harper & Row, 1968.

PREMACK, D. The education of Sarah. *Psychol. Today,* 1970, Apr., 54–58.

PREMACK, D. Language in a chimpanzee? *Science,* 1971, *172,* 808–822.

PRENTICE, W. C. H. Visual recognition of verbally labelled figures. *Amer. J. Psychol.,* 1954, *67,* 315–320.

PRIBRAM, K. H. *Languages of the brain.* Englewood Cliffs, N.J.: Prentice-Hall, 1971.

PRONOVOST, W. A survey of services for speech and hearing handicapped in New England. *J. speech Disorders,* 1951, *16,* 148–156.

QUANTZ, J. O. Problems in the psychology of reading. *Psychol. Rev.* 1897, *2,* Monograph suppl., No. 1.

QUARRINGTON, B., CONWAY, J., and SIEGEL, N. An experimental study of some properties of stuttered words. *J. speech hearing Research,* 1962, *5,* 389–394.

RANKEN, H. B. Language and thinking: Positive and negative effects of naming. *Science,* 1963, *141,* 48–50.

RAPAPORT, D., GILL, M., and SCHAFER, R. *Diagnostic psychological testing.* Vol. II. Chicago: Yearbook Publications, 1946.

REBER, A. S. Locating clicks in sentences: Left, center, and right. *Perception and Psychophyhics,* 1973, *1,* 133–138.

RIBOT, T. A. *Les maladies de la mémoire.* Paris: Libraire Germer Bailliere, 1883.

RICCUITI, H. N. Object grouping and selective ordering behavior in infants 12–24 months old. *Merrill Palmer Quarterly,* 1965, *11,* 129–148.

RICHARDSON, M. W. An evaluation of certain aspects of the academic achievement of elementary pupils in bilingual program: A project. Department of Education dissertation, University of Miami, 1968. (mimeo)

RIFE, D. C. Heredity and handedness. Sci. Mon., 1951, 73, 188–191.

RIPS, L. J., SHOBEN, E. J., and SMITH, E. Semantic distance and the verification of semantic relations. J. verb. Learn. verb. Behav., 1973, 12, 1–20.

ROCHESTER, S. R., and GILL, J. Production of complex sentences in monologues and dialogues. J. verb. Learn. verb. Behav., 1973, 12, 203–210.

ROCHFORD, G., and WILLIAMS, M. Studies in the development and breakdown of the use of names: I. The relationship between nominal dysphasia and the acquisition of vocabulary in childhood. J. Neurol. Neurosurg. Psychiat., 1962, 25, 222–233.

ROCHFORD, G., and WILLIAMS, M. Studies in the development and breakdown of the use of names: III. Recovery from nominal dysphasia. J. Neuro. Neurosurg. Psychiat., 1963, 26, 377–381.

ROMAN, K. Encyclopedia of the written word: A lexicon for graphology and other aspects of writing. New York: Frederick Ungar, 1968.

ROSCH, E. H. On the internal structure of perceptual and semantic categories. In T. Moore (Ed.) Cognitive development and the acquisition of language. New York: Academic, 1973.

ROSENTHAL, R. Experimenter effects in behavioral research. New York: Appleton-Century-Crofts, 1966.

ROSENZWEIG, M. R. Representations of the two ears at the auditory cortex. Amer. J. Physiol., 1951, 67, 147–158.

ROSENZWEIG, M. R. Études sur l'association des mots. Année Psychol., 1957, 57, 23–32.

ROSENZWEIG, M. R. Word associations of French workmen: Comparisons with associations of French students and American workmen and students. J. verb. Learn. verb. Behav., 1964, 3, 57–69.

ROTTER, J. B. Studies in the psychology of stuttering: XI. Stuttering in relation to position in the family. J. speech Disorders, 1939, 4, 143–148.

RUMBAUGH, D. M., GILL, T. V., and GLASERFELD, E. C. v. Reading and sentence completion by a chimpanzee (Pan). Science, 1973, 182, 731–733.

RUMELHART, D. E., LINDSAY, P. H., and NORMAN, D. A. A process model for long-term memory. In E. Tulving and W. Donaldson (Eds.) Organization of memory. New York: Academic, 1972.

RUSSELL, B. An inquiry into meaning and truth. London: Allen & Unwin, 1940.

RUSSELL, W. A., and JENKINS, J. J. The complete Minnesota norms for responses to 100 words from the Kent-Rosanoff association test. Minneapolis University of Minnesota, ONR Tech Report, No. 11, 1954.

RUSSELL, W. A., and MESECK, O. R. Der Einfluss der Assoziation auf das Erinnern von Worten in der deutschen, französischen und englischen Sprache. Z. exp. angew. Psychol., 1959, 6, 191–211.

SACHS, J. Recognition memory for syntactic and semantic aspects of connected discourse. Perception and Psychophysics, 1967, 2, 439–442.

SACIA, C. F., and BECK, C. J. The power of fundamental speech sounds. Bell Syst. Tech. J., 1926, 5, 393–403.

SAER, D. J. The effects of bilingualism on intelligence. *Brit. J. Psychol.*, 1923, *14*, 25–38.

SAPIR, E. *Language.* New York: Harcourt, Brace, 1921.

SAPIR, E. A study in phonetic symbolism. *J. exp. Psychol.*, 1929, *12*, 225–239.

SAVIN, H. B., and BEVER, T. G. The nonperceptual reality of the phoneme. *J. verb. Learn. verb. Behav.*, 1970, 9, 295–302.

SAVIN, H. B., and PERCHONOCK, E. Grammatical structure and immediate recall of sentences. *J. verb. Learn. verb. Behav.*, 1965, *4*, 348–353.

SAYLES, D. G. Cortical excitability, perseveration, and stuttering. *J. speech hearing Research*, 1971, *14*, 463–475.

SCHALTENBRAND, G., SPULER, H., WAHREN, W., RÜMMLER, B. Electroanatomy of the thalamic ventro-oral nucleus based on stereotactic stimulation in man. *Z. Neurol.*, 1971, *199*, 259–276.

SCHINDLER, M. D. A study of educational adjustments of stuttering and non-stuttering children. In W. Johnson (Ed.) *Stuttering in children and adults.* Minneapolis: University of Minnesota Press, 1955.

SCHLANGER, B. B., and GOTTSLEBEN, R. H. Analysis of speech defects among the institutionalized mentally retarded. *J. speech hearing Disorders*, 1957, *22*, 98–103.

SCHLESINGER, I. M. *Sentence structure and the reading process.* The Hague: Mouton, 1968.

SCHLESINGER, I. M. The grammar of sign language and the problems of language universals. In J. Morton (Ed.) *Biological and social factors in psycholinguistics.* London: Logos Press, 1971a.

SCHLESINGER, I. M. Production of utterances and language acquisition. In D. I. Slobin (Ed.) *The ontogenesis of grammar: A theoretical symposium.* New York: Academic Press, 1971b.

SCHLESINGER, I. M., FORTE, M., FRIED, B., and MELKMAN, R. Stuttering, information load, and response strength. *J. speech hearing Disorders*, 1965, *30*, 32–36.

SCHUELL, H. M., and JENKINS, J. J. The nature of language deficit in aphasia. *Psychol. Rev.*, 1959, *66*, 45–67.

SCHUELL, H. M., and JENKINS, J. J. Reduction of vocabulary in aphasia. *Brain*, 1961, *84*, 243–261.

SEGALOWITZ, N. Psychological perspectives on bilingual education. In B. Spolsky and R. L. Cooper (Eds.) *Current trends in bilingual education* (in press).

SHANK, R. C. Conceptual dependency: A theory of natural language understanding. *Cog. Psychol.*, 1972, *3*, 552–631.

SHANKWEILER, D., and HARRIS, K. S. An experimental approach to the problem of articulation in aphasia. *Cortex*, 1966, *2*, 277–292.

SHANNON, C. E. A mathematical theory of communication. *Bell Syst. Tech. J.*, 1948, *27*, 379–423.

SHANNON, C. E. Prediction and entropy of printed English. *Bell Syst. Tech. J.*, 1951, *30*, 50–64.

SHEARER, W. M., and WILLIAMS, J. D. Self-recovery from stuttering. *J. speech hearing Disorders*, 1965, *30*, 288–290.

SHEEHAN, J. G. Speech therapy and recovery from stuttering. *The Voice*, 1965, *15*, 3–6.

SHEEHAN, J. G., and MARTYN, M. Stuttering and its disappearance. *J. speech hearing Research*, 1970, *13*, 279–289.

SHEEHAN, J. G., and ZELEN, S. L. Level of aspiration in stutterers and non-stutterers. *J. abnorm. soc. Psychol.*, 1955, *51*, 83–86.

SHEPARD, W. O. The effect of verbal training on initial generalization tendencies. *Child Developm.*, 1956, *27*, 311–316.

SHEWAN, C., and CANTER, G. J. Effects of vocabulary, syntax, and sentence length, on auditory comprehension in aphasic patients. *Cortex*, 1971, *7*, 209–226.

SHRIBERG, L. D. Phonetic symbolism in four voiceless fricatives. *Percept. mot. Skills*, 1970, *30*, 295–299.

SILVERMAN, F. H., and WILLIAMS, D. E. Loci of disfluencies in the speech of nonstutterers during oral reading. *J. speech hearing Research*, 1967, *10*, 790–794.

SINCLAIR, H., and BRONCKART, J. P. S.V.O. a linguistic universal? A study in developmental psycholinguistics. *J. exp. Child Psychol.*, 1972, *14*, 329–348.

SINCLAIR-DE ZWART, H. Language acquisition and cognitive development. In T. Moore (Ed.) *Cognitive development and the acquisition of language*. New York: Academic, 1973.

SKINNER, B. F. *Verbal behavior*. New York: Appleton, 1957.

SLOBIN, D. I. Grammatical transformations and sentence comprehension in child-hood and adulthood. *J. verb. Learn. verb. Behav.*, 1966a, *5*, 219–227.

SLOBIN, D. I. The acquisition of Russian as a native language. In F. Smith and G. A. Miller (Eds.) *The genesis of language: A psycholinguistic approach*. Cambridge, Mass.: MIT Press, 1966b.

SLOBIN, D. I. Comments on "Developmental psycholinguistics." In F. Smith and G. A. Miller (Eds.) *The genesis of language*. Cambridge, Mass.: MIT Press, 1966c.

SLOBIN, D. I. Recall of full and truncated passive sentences in connected discourse. *J. verb. Learn. verb. Behav.*, 1968a, *7*, 876–881.

SLOBIN, D. I. Antonymic phonetic symbolism in three natural languages. *J. Pers. soc. Psychol.*, 1968b, *10*, 301–305.

SLOBIN, D. I. *Psycholinguistics*. Glenview, Ill.: Scott, Foresman, 1971.

SLOBIN, D. I. Cognitive prerequisites for the development of grammar. In C. A. Ferguson and D. I. Slobin (Eds.) *Studies of child language development*. New York: Holt, Rinehart and Winston, 1973, pp. 175–208.

SMITH, A. Objective indices of severity in chronic aphasia in stroke patients. *J. speech hearing Disorders*, 1971, *36*, 167–207.

SMITH, A., and BURKLUND, C. W. Dominant hemispherectomy. *Science*, 1966, *153*, 1280–1282.

SMITH, C. S. An experimental approach to children's linguistic competence. In J. R. Hayes (Ed.) *Cognition and the development of language*. New York: Wiley, 1970.

SNIDECOR, J. C. Why the Indian does not stutter. *Quart. J. Speech*, 1947, *33*, 493–495.

SNOW, K. A detailed analysis of the articulation responses of normal first grade children. *J. speech hearing Research*, 1963, *6*, 277–290.

SODERBERG, G. A. The relations of stuttering to word length and word frequency. *J. speech hearing Research*, 1966, *9*, 584–589.

SODERBERG, G. A. Delayed auditory feedback and stuttering. *J. speech hearing Disorders*, 1968, *33*, 260–267.

SONSTROEM, A. M. On the conservation of solids. In J. S. Brunner et al. *Studies in cognitive growth*. New York: Wiley, 1966.

SPREEN, O., and SCHULZ, R. Parameters of abstraction, meaningfulness, and pronunciability for 329 nouns. *J. verb. Learn. verb. Behav.*, 1966, *5*, 459–468.

STAATS, A. W. *Learning, language, and cognition*. New York: Holt, Rinehart and Winston, 1968.

STAATS, C. K., and STAATS, A. W. Meaning established by classical conditioning. *J. exp. Psychol.*, 1957, *54*, 74–80.

STEIN, GERTRUDE. *Selected writings*. C. v. Vechten (Ed.). New York: Random House, 1962.

STEVENS, K. N., and HOUSE, A. S. Speech perception. In J. Tobias (Ed.) *Foundations of modern auditory theory*. Vol. 2. New York: Academic, 1970.

STREETER, L. A. The effects of linguistic experience on phonetic perception. Unpublished doctoral dissertation, Columbia University, 1974, (or see Kuhl and Miller, in press).

STREETER, L. A., and LANDAUER, T. K. Effects of learning English as a second language on the acquisition of a new phonemic contrast. Program of the 89th Meeting, *J. acoust. Soc. Amer.*, Austin, Texas, 1975.

STUDDERT-KENNEDY, M., LIBERMAN, A. M., HARRIS, K. S., and COOPER, F. S. Motor theory of speech perception: A reply to Lane's critical review. *Psychol. Rev.*, 1970, *77*, 234–249.

STUDDERT-KENNEDY, M., and SHANKWEILER, D. Hemispheric specialization for speech perception. *J. acoust. Soc. Amer.*, 1970, *48*, 579–594.

SUMBY, W. H., and POLLACK, I. Short-term processing of information. *HFORL Report Tr.*, 1954, 54–56.

TANZ, C. Sound symbolism in words relating to proximity and distance. *Language and Speech*, 1971, *14*, 266–276.

TARTE, R. D., and BARRITT, L. Phonetic symbolism in adult native speakers of English: Three studies. *Language and Speech*, 1971, *14*, 158–168.

TAYLOR, I. Phonetic symbolism re-examined. *Psychol. Bull.*, 1963, *60*, 200–229.

TAYLOR, I. The properties of stuttered words. *J. verb. Learn. verb. Behav.*, 1966a, *5*, 112–118.

TAYLOR, I. What words are stuttered? *Psychol. Bull.*, 1966b, *65*, 233–242.

TAYLOR, I. Content and structure in sentence production. *J. verb. Learn. verb. Behav.*, 1969, *8*, 170–175.

TAYLOR, I. How are words from two languages organized in bilinguals' memory? *Canad. J. Psychol.*, 1971, *25*, 228–240.

TAYLOR, I. Similarity between French and English words—a factor to be considered in bilingual behavior? *J. psycholinguistic Res.* (in press).

TAYLOR, I., and TAYLOR, M. M. Phonetic symbolism in four unrelated languages. *Canad. J. Psychol.*, 1962, *16*, 344–356.

TAYLOR, I., and TAYLOR, M. M. Another look at phonetic symbolism. *Psychol. Bull.*, 1965, *64*, 413–427.

TAYLOR, L., CATFORD, J. C., GUIORA, Z., and LANE, H. Psychological variables and ability to pronounce a second language. *Language and Speech*, 1971, *14*, Part 2, 146–157.

TAYLOR, W. L. "Cloze" procedure: A new tool for measuring readability. *Journalism Quarterly*, 1953, *30*, 415–433.

TERMAN, L. M., and ODEN, M. *The gifted child grows up.* Stanford, Calif.: Stanford University Press, 1947.

TERMAN, L. M., and ODEN, M. *The gifted group at mid-life.* Stanford, Calif.: Stanford University Press, 1959.

THORNDIKE, E. L., and LORGE, I. *The teacher's word book of 30,000 words.* New York: Bureau of Publications, Teachers College, Columbia University, 1944.

THUMB, A., and MARBE, K. *Experimentalle Untersuchungen über die psychologischen Grundlagen der sprachlichen Analogiebildung.* Leipzig: Engelmann, 1901.

TITCHENER, E. B. *Lectures on the experimental psychology of the thought processes.* New York: MacMillan, 1909.

TOPPINO, T. C. The underlying structures are not primary units of speech processing. *Percept. Psychophy.*, 1974, *15*, 517–518.

TOSI, O., OYER, H., LASHBROOK, W., PEDREY, C., NICOL, J., and NASH, E. Experiments on voice identification. *J. acoust. Soc. Amer.*, 1972, *51*, 2030–2043.

TRAGER, G. L., and SMITH, H. L., JR. *An outline of English structure.* Studies in linguistics, occasional paper No. 3, Norman, Okla., 1951.

TRAVIS, L. E., JOHNSON, W., and SHOVER, J. The relation of bilingualism to stuttering. *J. speech Disorders*, 1937, *2*, 185–189.

TREHUB, S. E., and RABINOVITCH, M. S. Auditory-linguistic sensitivity in early infancy. *Developmental Psychol.*, 1972, *6*, 74–77.

TREHUB, S. E. Infants' sensitivity to vowel and tonal contrasts. *Develop. Psychol.*, 1973, *9*, 91–96.

TREHUB, S. E. Natural syllabic and polysyllabic sound discrimination abilities of young infants. Paper presented at meeting of the American Speech and Hearing Association, Las Vegas, 1974.

TSIEN-LEE, M. Sound and meaning in Chinese language: A study of phonetic symbolism. *Psychologia Belgica*, 1969, *IX-I*, 47–58.

TSUNODA, T. The difference of the cerebral dominance of vowel sounds among different languages. Paper given at 10th World Congress of Otorhinolaryngology, Venice, 1973.

TSURU, S., and FRIES, H. S. A problem in meaning. *J. gen. Psychol.*, 1933, *8*, 281–284.

TUCKER, G. R., and LAMBERT, W. E. White and Negro listeners' reactions to various American English dialects. *Social Forces*, 1969, *47*, 463–468.

UHR, L., and VOSSLER, C. Recognition of speech by a computer program that was written to simulate a model for human visual pattern recognition. *J. acoust. Soc. Amer.*, 1961, *33*, 1426.

VAN RIPER, C. *Speech correction.* Englewood Cliffs, N.J.: Prentice-Hall, 1963.

VON STOCKERT, T. R. Recognition of syntactic structure in aphasic patients. *Cortex,* 1972, 8, 323–334.

VYGOTSKY, L. S. *Thought and language.* Cambridge, Mass.: MIT Press, 1962.

WALLEN, V. A Q-technique study of the self-concepts of adolescent stutterers and nonstutterers. *Speech Monogr.,* 1960, 27, 257–258.

WARREN, R., and WARREN R. Auditory illusions and confusions. *Scientific American,* 1970, Dec., 30–36.

WASON, P. C. The contexts of plausible denial. *J. verb. Learn. verb. Behav.,* 1965, 4, 7–11.

WASON, P. C., and JOHNSON-LAIRD, P. N. *Psychology of reasoning.* London: B. T. Batsford, 1972.

WEIGL, E., and BIERWISCH, M. Neuropsychology and linguistics: Topics of common research. In H. Goodglass and S. Blumstein (Eds.) *Psycholinguistics and aphasia.* Baltimore: Johns Hopkins University Press, 1973.

WEINREICH, U. *Language in contact.* New York: Publications of Linguistic Circle, 1953.

WEINSTEIN, E. A., LYERLY, O. G., COLE, M., and OZER, M. N. Meaning of jargon aphasia. *Cortex,* 1966, 2, 165–187.

WEIR, R. H. *Language in the crib.* The Hague: Mouton, 1962.

WEIR, R. H. Some questions on the child's learning of phonology. In F. Smith and G. A. Miller (Eds.) *The genesis of language.* Cambridge, Mass.: MIT Press, 1966.

WEISENBURG, T., and McBRIDE, K. E. *Aphasia: A clinical and psychological study.* New York: The Commonwealth Fund, Brattleboro, Vt.: E. L. Hildren & Co., 1935.

WEISS, J. H. Role of "meaningfulness" versus meaning dimensions in guessing the meanings of foreign words. *J. abnorm. soc. Psychol.,* 1963, 66, 541–546.

WEISS, J. H. A study of the ability of English speakers to guess the meanings of nonantonym foreign words. *J. gen. Psychol.,* 1966, 74, 97–106.

WENNER, A. M. Sound communication in honey bees. *Scientific American,* 1964, Apr., 116–124.

WERNICKE, C. *Der aphasische Symptomencomplex.* Breslau: Max Cohn & Weigert, 1874.

WEST, R. An agnostic's speculations about stuttering. In J. Eisenson (Ed.) *Stuttering: A symposium.* New York: Harper & Row, 1958.

WEST, R., NELSON, S., and BERRY, M. F. The heredity of stuttering. *Quart. J. Speech,* 1939, 25, 23–30.

WHITAKER, H. *On representation of language in the human brain.* UCLA Working Papers in Phonetics. 1969, No. 12, Sept.

WIEGER, L. *Chinese characters, their origin, etymology, history, classification and signification.* New York: Dover, 1965.

WILKINS, M. C. Unpublished M.A. thesis, Columbia University, 1917. (Mentioned R. Woodworth, *Experimental Psychology.* New York: Holt, 1938.)

WILSON, D. K. *Voice problems of children.* Baltimore: Williams and Wilkins, 1972.

WINITZ, H. *Articulatory acquisition and behavior*. New York: Appleton-Century-Crofts, 1969.

WITELSON, S., and PALLIE, W. Left hemisphere specialization for language in the newborn. *Brain*, 1973, *96*, 641–646.

WITTGENSTEIN, L. *Tractatus Logico-philosophicus*. London: Kegan Paul, 1933.

WITTGENSTEIN, L. *Philosophical investigation*. Oxford: Basil, Blackwell & Mott, 1958.

WOODROW, H., and LOWELL, F. Children's association frequency tables. *Psychol. Monogr.*, 1916, *22*, No. 97.

WOODS, C. L., and WILLIAMS, D. E. Speech clinicians' conceptions of boys and men who stutter. *J. speech hearing Disorders*, 1971, *36*, 225–234.

WORLD HEALTH ORGANIZATION. The prevalence of blindness and deaf-mutism in various countries. Epidemilogical Vital Statistics Rep., 1953, *6*, 1–32.

YAMAMOTO, S. Principle and treatment of stuttering. In Tokyo University Stuttering Research Institute (Ed.) *Literature on stuttering*, 1958 (in Japanese).

YAVUZ, H. S., and BOUSFIELD, W. A. Recall of connotative meaning. *Psychol. Rep.*, 1959, *5*, 319–320.

YNGVE, V. H. A model and an hypothesis for language structure. *Proc. Amer. Phil. Soc.*, 1960, *104*, 444–466.

YNGVE, V. H. Computer programs for translation. *Scientific American*, 1962, Jun., *206*, 68–76.

ZIPF, G. K. *The psycho-biology of language*. Boston: Houghton Mifflin, 1935.

ZIPF, G. K. *Human behavior and the principle of least effort: An introduction to human ecology*. Cambridge, Mass.: Addison-Wesley, 1949.

ZURIF, E. B., CARAMAZZA, A., and MYERSON, R. Grammatical judgments of agrammatic aphasics. *Neuropsychologia*, 1972, *10*, 405–417.

Author Index

Subject Index